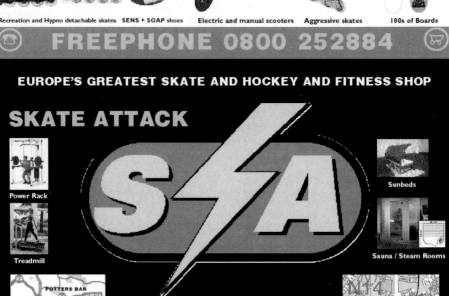

THE ICE HOCKEY ANNUAL

2002-03

EDITED AND COMPILED BY STEWART ROBERTS

First published in Great Britain by
Stewart Roberts
The Old Town Hall
142 Albion Street
Southwick
Brighton BN42 4AX

Cover Design by **Channel Graphic Communication**

Digital Artwork by **James Mansell**

British Library Cataloguing-in-Publication Data.
A catalogue record for this book is available from the British Library.

The Ice Hockey Annual 2002-03

ISBN 0-9536410-3-1

The Ice Hockey Annual's official website is at www.graphyle.com/IHA.
Past editions of *The Ice Hockey Annual* are archived in the Hockey Hall of Fame, London Life Resource Centre, Toronto, Canada.

Printed in Great Britain by **DAP (Sussex) Ltd**
Rowan House, Rowan Close, Portslade, Brighton BN41 2QQ

CONTENTS

COVER - *Clockwise from left*: **JEFF HOAD**, captain of Belfast Giants, the *Sekonda* Superleague winners, with the Monteith Bowl; **TONY HAND**, player-coach of Dundee Stars, the *Findus* British National League and cup champions; **SCOTTY BOWMAN**, coach of the NHL's Detroit Redwings, with the Stanley Cup; **INVICTA DYNAMOS**, winners of the English Premier League.

Photos: Michael Cooper, Mike Smith/Icepix, Bruce Jessop/Ice Hockey Archives, *Medway Today*.

ACKNOWLEDGEMENTS

Welcome to the 27th edition of The *Ice Hockey Annual*, the sport's longest running publication.

I hope the *Annual* can shed a little light on the sport and the strange times in which it finds itself. There are more wealthy club owners and a higher standard of play than ever before, but the absence of a well-promoted national league makes it hard for ice hockey to gain the recognition it deserves.

Enough of all that. This is the page where I take a moment to thank all the many people who have helped to make this book possible, supplying information on their specialist areas of the sport, whether it be their team or their league, their statistics or their photographs.

My especial gratitude goes, of course, to the advertisers for their invaluable financial backing.

Statistics are the lifeblood of all North American sports and though **Gordon Wade** is Hampshire born and bred, his work is right up there with the best of the Canadian stattos. Gordon is responsible for all the Superleague, Challenge Cup and Ahearne Cup details, the GB Team Register and much of the Roll of Honour.

Stan Wiltshire, the secretary of the *Findus* British National League, has compiled all the league's scoring info., and **Sue** and **Steve Tomalin** are the husband and wife team who provided the figures for the English Leagues.

Many others have helped in this area, notably the clubs who sent in scoresheets, **Val Wilkinson** and **Alan Moutrey** who filed junior reports and **Malcolm Preen** who compiled the Women's League stats.

The IIHF's comprehensive website, www.iihf.com, provided us with details of the Winter Olympics, the World Championships and the Continental Cup.

Thanks as well to all the club correspondents for their reports, and to the many good folk who supplied the all-important visual record of the season, the team photographs.

Greatly embellishing the visuals were the specialist photographers, **Mike Smith**, **Michael Cooper** from Belfast, **Tony Boot** in London, **Chris Valentine**, **Roger Cook** and Scotland's **Peter Jones**.

If I've omitted anyone, my apologies, but my thanks are just as warm.

Our advertisers have been as generous as ever and I do hope you will support them wherever possible.

Bauer-Nike Hockey need little introduction as the skate and equipment makers are a household name. We're pleased to have their distributors, **H D Sports**, on board again as we are to have **Airport & Road Equipment Ltd** who supply another household name, the **Zamboni** ice resurfacing machine.

The nationally known opticians' chain, **Specsavers**, are backers of the Cardiff Devils and **Stiga** are the makers of the world-famous Stanley Cup hockey game.

Talking of which, **The Hockey News** is the only newspaper dedicated to the NHL and the best way to subscribe to this Canadian weekly is through **Barkers Worldwide Publications**.

Britain's weekly hockey magazine is **Powerplay** while those who like reading about the 'good old days' will find details of two new books on page 155.

Igloo Trading Co Ltd supply a wide variety of hockey and skating equipment to your rink. **Ice'N' Easy** have skate shops in Basingstoke and their own inline rink in Rotherham.

For books, souvenirs and heaps more, go to **Armchair Sports**, and if you like to browse before you buy then you'll be in heaven in **Skate Attack**, retailers of everything hockey.

D&P Trophies provide cups, shields or other mementoes for every occasion. If you need skates, go to **Flying F Skates**; for sticks and other hockey kit, it must be **Miras Sports & Warehousing Ltd**, who have a wide range of brands to choose from.

If you prefer surfing the net for your requirements, *www.crazykennys.com* is the site for you. For your more exotic, overseas needs, try Transatlantic Sports at *www.TA-sports.net*.

The A-Z Encyclopaedia of Ice Hockey at *www.azhockey.com* is probably the world's best website for ice hockey facts. This is compiled by Phil Stamp of **Graphyle Consultants** who also look after the *Annual*'s own website at *www.graphyle.com/IHA* where you can complete your collection of *Annuals*.

Last but not least, my thanks go to the backroom boys - digital typesetter, *James Mansell*, cover designers, *Channel Graphic Communication*, and, of course, printers, **DAP (Sussex) Ltd**.

SR

FOREWORD

BRIAN STOREY

It gives me great pleasure to be asked to contribute to *The Ice Hockey Annual*. I know that it has always been treated as a great resource of information handed down over the years and probably has settled more bets than *Wisden*, the cricketers' almanach!

Every year, **Stewart Roberts** and his colleagues compile not only the hard statistics of the game at all levels in the UK, but also those amusing and informative anecdotes from coaches, players and grey-suited administrators like myself, that give a flavour to the background of this wonderful game we all love.

Of all the many challenges which constantly face the sport - not only here in the UK but throughout the world - perhaps the most crucial is the financing of the grass roots and the national teams. The sport has been treated quite harshly over the years by funding organisations for these two things.

Quite rightly, some of the blame for that must lie squarely with the sport's administrators, but it's also fair to say that it's always been a struggle to convince funding agencies of the value of the sport and its wider appeal to the public.

'WE ACTUALLY PLAY ICE HOCKEY QUITE WELL IN THE UK'

In saying that, it would be foolish not to acknowledge Sport England's commitment to buildings like the Nottingham Ice Centre, and Sport Scotland's backing for Dundee Ice Arena. Without facilities like these - and they are not cheap - there can be no ice hockey or other ice sports. What is also required, though, is a concerted effort by everyone to spread the word that not only do we play ice hockey in the UK, but also that we actually play it quite well.

OK, so Britain's senior men are still in Division 1 of the IIHF World Championship, but that has largely been because of the break-up of the Soviet Union 11 years ago and everyone is still feeling the draught.

But if Slovenia with such a small population and so few clubs can do it, why not Britain?

So where do we go from here? Certainly there are many paths to choose but the most obvious is to get more kids into the system in the first place. After the parents, the next most important person in a player's career is that first coach, who can make or break a player's enthusiasm, or discourage the parents with a wrong approach.

BRIAN STOREY
Superleague's Chief Admin. Officer

No one has to play hockey, after all. There are many other sports to pursue and in truth many younger players are equally adept at others, anyway.

Having got them into the system, we need to keep them there. We need to provide a pathway so that when they reach the age of discovery and need further education - work or girls! - they can progress to a higher level.

That pathway has to allow for the most dedicated to continue their involvement in the sport, give them the opportunity to consider a professional hockey-playing life and get GB into the Olympic finals or the actual World Championship event.

Again, this requires funding, plus the recognition by all concerned in the sport of what needs to be achieved.

All these are just words, of course, and can mean diddly squat. What we need is action and the money to do it. I know there is a concerted effort to remedy the situation but it will take a long time to bear fruit. There have been many false dawns in recent years but that doesn't mean that the plans drawn up and implemented or the enthusiasm shown was wrong, just that it's a hard slog. We must not give up!

All these words apply equally to officials, on and off the ice. They also need that support.

Finally, I would like to dedicate this Foreword to the two groups of people without whom the sport would die - the parents and the many unpaid helpers at club and association level up and down the country. Without them, the time they give voluntarily to the sport, the unearthly practice times and not least the expense they personally commit, we would all be lost.

HONOURS AND AWARDS

HONOURS ROLL CALL 2001-02

SUPERLEAGUE Playoff Championship
SHEFFIELD STEELERS
Sekonda Superleague
BELFAST GIANTS
The Challenge Cup
AYR SCOTTISH EAGLES

Findus **BRITISH NATIONAL LEAGUE** Playoffs
DUNDEE STARS
Findus British National League
DUNDEE STARS
Findus Challenge Cup
FIFE FLYERS

ENGLISH LEAGUES
National Premier Playoff Championship
INVICTA DYNAMOS
National Premier League
INVICTA DYNAMOS
Premier Cup
ROMFORD RAIDERS
National League North
WHITLEY WARRIORS
National League South
BASINGSTOKE BUFFALO
National League Playoffs
WHITLEY WARRIORS
English Cup
WHITLEY WARRIORS

SCOTTISH NATIONAL LEAGUE
EDINBURGH CAPITALS
Caledonia Cup
DUNDEE STARS

WOMEN'S LEAGUE
GUILDFORD LIGHTNING

Top League Points Scorers
Sekonda *Superleague*
KEVIN RIEHL, Belfast
Findus *British National League*
TONY HAND, Dundee
English National League
DUNCAN COOK, Solihull

Best Goaltending Percentages
Sekonda *Superleague*
MIKE BALES, Belfast
Findus *British National League*
SHAWN SILVER, Fife
English Premier League
CHRIS DOUGLAS, Romford/Haringey

BRITISH ICE HOCKEY WRITERS' ASSOCIATION AWARDS

ALL-STAR TEAMS

SEKONDA *SUPERLEAGUE*
First Team
Goal   MIKE BALES, Belfast
Defence   JOHAN SILFWERPLATZ, Ayr
          ROB STEWART, Belfast
Forwards KEVIN RIEHL, Belfast
          SEAN BERENS, Belfast
          JASON RUFF, Belfast
Second Team
Goal   JOAQUIN GAGE, Belfast
Defence   ALAN SCHULER, Ayr
          MAURIZIO MANSI, London
Forwards PC DROUIN, Nottingham
          ED COURTENAY, Ayr
          SCOTT ALLISON, Sheffield

FINDUS *BRITISH NATIONAL LEAGUE*
First Team
Goal   STEPHEN MURPHY, Dundee
Defence   SCOTT YOUNG, Dundee
          NEIL LIDDIARD, Basingstoke
Forwards TONY HAND, Dundee
          DOMENIC PARLATORE, Paisley
          TEEDER WYNNE, Dundee
Second Team
Goal   SHAWN SILVER, Fife
Defence   KARRY BIETTE, Fife
          JAN MIKEL, Dundee
Forwards JASON LAFRENIERE, Edinburgh
          CLAUDE DUMAS, Coventry
          RUSSELL MONTEITH, Fife

OTHER AWARDS

Top British Scorer (Ice Hockey Annual *Trophy*)
JONATHAN WEAVER, Ayr
Best British Defenceman (Alan Weeks Trophy)
NEIL LIDDIARD, Basingstoke
Best British Netminder (BIHWA Trophy)
STEPHEN MURPHY, Dundee

AWARDS TO OFFICIALS
Micky Curry Memorial Trophy - Most Improved
NIGEL BONIFACE
Keith Franklin Memorial Trophy - Most Dedicated
DAVE TOTTMAN

Above right: Eagles' **JOAQUIN GAGE**, *Sekonda* Player of the Year; *above left:* Sheffield's **RICK BREBANT**, the *Sekonda* runner-up; *below right:* Nottingham Panthers' All-Star **PC DROUIN**; *below left:* Eagles' **JONATHAN WEAVER**, Superleague's top British points scorer.

Photos: Mike Smith/Icepix, Chris Valentine.

BRITISH ICE HOCKEY WRITERS' ASSOCIATION AWARDS, contd.

PLAYERS OF THE YEAR

Superleague	KEVIN RIEHL, Belfast Giants
Findus *BNL*	TONY HAND, Dundee Stars

KEVIN RIEHL Belfast Giants

Superleague's top scorer, **KEVIN RIEHL**, was the pivot on Superleague's most potent line with **Jason Ruff** (left-wing) and **Sean Berens**.

The pint-sized centreman (he's 5ft, 7in) from Saskatchewan has been among the league's leading shooters since he joined Bracknell Bees in 1999-2000.

He headed Bees' scorers and finished fourth in the league behind Sheffield Steelers' top line of **Ed Courtenay-Teeder Wynne-Dale Junkin**. After joining Giants' for their first campaign, he ended runner-up in their scoring chart.

Kevin, a 1991 draft pick of the NHL's New Jersey Devils, has spent most of his career in the East Coast Hockey League, Italy and Germany.

Scotland's own **TONY HAND** has long been rated our finest homegrown player. Now he has added the quite different skill of coaching to his already formidable array of hockey talents.

In his first campaign in charge, he not only hand-picked his team, Dundee Stars, he also guided them to the top of the *Findus* BNL and the playoff championship in their rookie season.

Though he listed former Murrayfield hardman **Roger Hunt** and ex-Ayr and Fife forward **Colin Wilson** as his assistants, they were the first to insist that Hand was the boss.

His new duties did not distract him from his traditional role as his team's most feared playmaker. He finished as the league's leading scorer with 104 points, including an eye-popping 79 assists in 44 games.

This is the fourth time Tony has been honoured with the Writers' Player of the Year award, his first coming in 1988-89 with Murrayfield Racers.

COACHES OF THE YEAR

Superleague	DAVE WHISTLE, Belfast Giants
Findus *BNL*	TONY HAND, Dundee Stars

Former Canada West University All Star, **DAVE WHISTLE**, won the Writers' Coach of the Year award for the second time in three years after taking Belfast Giants to the top of Superleague in their first full season.

'Whis' carried off his first coaching title in 1999-2000 when he was behind the bench for Bracknell Bees' only Superleague crown to date.

He had Giants so far ahead of the pack that they had first place tied up by mid-January.

THE SEKONDA PLAYER OF THE YEAR

JOAQUIN GAGE, Ayr Scottish Eagles

For each month of the season, Superleague's sponsor, Sekonda, awarded a watch to the player nominated as giving the best performance during that period.

At the end of the season, one of those players was chosen as the Sekonda Player of the Year and received a £1,000 holiday voucher.

The monthly winners were:

September	ED COURTENAY, Ayr
October	MARK CADOTTE, Bracknell
November	COLIN WARD, Belfast
December	SCOTT ALLISON, Sheffield
January	MIKE BALES, Belfast
February	RICK BREBANT, Sheffield
March	JOAQUIN GAGE, Ayr

In his first season in Europe, Vancouver-born goalie **JOAQUIN GAGE** impressed fans and fellow players alike, helping Eagles to finish as Superleague runners-up and shutting out Belfast Giants as they captured the Challenge Cup.

His coach, **Paul Heavey**, said: "We stated when he came here that he had the ability to win games by himself and he has done just that. He enabled the team to play with more confidence. He's the ultimate professional."

Gage, 28, who enjoyed a second spell with the NHL's Edmonton Oilers in the season before he joined Ayr, is the second goalie to win the *Sekonda* award in four years. Manchester's **Frank Pietrangelo** was honoured in 1998-99.

EDITORIAL

Stewart Roberts

A new spirit of co-operation?

As the great man said, this is not the beginning of the end but it is, perhaps, the end of the beginning. (Churchillian is not a word one would normally use to describe the fine mess this sport has got itself into. Ah, Laurel and Hardy. Much closer to the mark.)

After six long years, the men at the top of two of our leagues are holding regular meetings. Better still, **Brian Storey**, Superleague's new point man, and **Gary Stefan**, his opposite number at the British National League (BNL), are known to be genuine hockey men.

Don't expect any sort of merger of these leagues, though. They have very different agendas. The Superleague clubs have invested millions in trying to make professional ice hockey work and while they continue to believe it can (only if it's run a lot better than it has been so far, it says here), they will not, as they see it, dilute their product.

You can read some of Brian's thinking in his *Foreword.* At his summer meeting with the fans in Sheffield, I could have written some of his reported words myself. "Hockey is a small sport and it won't go anywhere by being divided," he said. "We all need to pull together in ways that we haven't even begun to explore properly."

Brian's and Stef's influence should not be over-estimated, however, as they are both employees of the clubs who have the last word on where this game is going. No one has ever confused ice hockey with a forward-thinking sport. But at a time when there is so little to cheer about, it's good to know that the men at the top have the game's best interests at heart.

Four teams to watch

Four teams will be starting the new season in a league with a different style of play from the one their fans have become used to.

Cardiff Devils and Newcastle Vipers (previously Cobras, Riverkings and Jesters) are moving into the BNL from Superleague, while Milton Keynes Kings and Peterborough Phantoms (née Pirates) will be battling in the English Premier League after years in the BNL.

Many clubs would have you believe that this is a recipe for disaster as they spend hundreds of thousands of pounds trying to keep their fans happy with a team in a league higher than their gate receipts alone can justify.

If Vipers succeed in attracting good crowds to their 7,500-seater, and the Kings and Phantoms can persuade their fans that hockey is still good entertainment even in a league with a three-import limit (the *Annual's* ideal), it will prove that it's not so much the fans who are to blame for the over-spending but the owners' desire for glory.

But then you knew that already, didn't you?

One voice, please

This is the 20th anniversary of the creation of the British League in 1982-83. Sadly, it broke up on the formation of Superleague in 1996-97. Those 14 seasons were the longest ice hockey has managed to keep a national league together.

The increasing wealth of the clubs combined with the difficulty the governing body has in acquiring public funding have strengthened the teams at the expense of the sport as a whole.

Ice hockey must reunite before it can go forward. Government is threatening not to fund sports like ours at all until they have one body that genuinely represents the whole game. A truly national league will enable sponsors like *Findus* to promote the sport more widely than they can at present.

I hate to put pressure on the over-worked Gary Stefan and Brian Storey, but I can only see the sport coming together under their banner. By the time you read this there may be a new chairman of Ice Hockey UK. For the good of the game, I hope one of them has taken the job.

Enjoy your hockey and tell your friends.
Stewart Roberts
August 2002

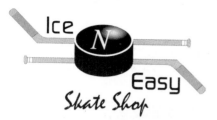

QUOTES OF THE YEAR

Super joke

"It's all become a bit of a joke, and the joke's on us." *Brian Storey, Superleague's secretary, on the troubles in Superleague that reduced the nine-team league to seven in the early part of season 2001-02 and led to many of its early games being postponed.*

Or look at it this way...

"...if the [Super]league could survive this past year, without TV money and with two teams dropping out, then we are in a very strong position. I think it shows how strong the sport is and that the league can survive anything." *Gary Cowan, Manchester Storm's co-owner.*

"We should be happy that we have seven strong teams with owners who I would be prepared to lend money to." *Bob Zeller, co-owner of Belfast Giants and Superleague's deputy chairman.*

"...I think that as a sport Superleague ice hockey is ready to explode!" *Bevan Thompson, on his appointment as Superleague's commercial manager in September 2001.*

More Eye wash

"Everyone at Fablon is fully behind the Jesters and all we ask is that the fans show similar commitment. We have pumped hundreds of thousands of pounds into this club in order to keep it afloat, and we are happy for that to continue as long as we can see that the region is keen to maintain an ice hockey club at the highest level. I feel **Paul [Smith]** hasn't had the credit he deserves." *Graham Gutteridge, chairman of Fablon, the parent company of the Eye Group, owners of Newcastle Jesters, on the September 2001 resignation of Paul Smith as club chairman.*

The Lion

"Brebant is in a mess right now. His knee is just huge. I don't know how he kept playing. He couldn't walk after the game. The doctor and the trainer told him not to play, but he walked straight past them and went out on the ice. That's just Rick." *Mike Blaisdell, Sheffield Steelers' coach, after his 37-year-old forward badly damaged his knee in a game at Nottingham.*

"I'm excited to have him with a Lion on his shirt as well as in his heart." *Chris McSorley, GB's head coach, confirming Brebant's selection.*

Expensive

"I've only ever met **Bill Morrison** twice and at £750 per meeting, he's an expensive man to whom I've only said `hello'." *Alex Whelan, Paisley's backer, on having to pay Pirates' ex-goalie £1,500 in wages owing before Mr Whelan joined the club.*

BNL have problems, too

"It's always tough being a new franchise. You bring in the best players you can and hope you're not going to finish in last place. If that had happened, the fans wouldn't have turned up, the sponsors wouldn't have shown up." *Tony Hand, player-coach of league and playoff winners, Dundee Stars.*

"This year's been worse than ever. The only teams really bringing on young British players have been the teams that have no alternative because of financial trouble, like Peterborough and Slough." *Steven King, Fife Flyers' All-Star defenceman.*

The wage cap

"We've made everybody comfortable. There's not a guy in this league who's worrying about his job right now." *Mike Blaisdell, coach of Sheffield Steelers, bemoaning Superleague's £400,000 wage cap. The cap was ten per cent below the old one and 'Blaiser' was concerned about being unable to bench poor performers because the lower limit left the club without the money to pay for more players.*

"...no one at league level gives a damn. Ask any coach who's got the balls to say it and he'll say the same thing - it's not doing anything for hockey." *Bob Leslie, coach of London Knights who, like most Superleague teams, had short benches due to the cap.*

"Either we have a wage cap so we can operate like a real pro league or we drop down to the BNL. You can't be a little bit pregnant." *Enio Sacilotto, coach of Bracknell Bees.*

At a post-game press conference in London Arena on Boxing Day, Leslie declined to add to his previous comment. "I've been told not to say anything more about the wage cap. Apparently, I don't know what I'm talking about."

TONY HAND
Britain's first 1,000-goal scorer

Scotsman **Tony Hand** scored his 1,000th goal in British league ice hockey on 19 January 2002 in typical style. While his Dundee Stars were short-handed, he collected a loose puck, soloed down the ice and beat former GB international, **Stephen Foster**, in the Hull Thunder net. His unassisted effort gave Stars a 2-0 lead at 16.20 of the *Findus* British National League contest in the new Dundee rink.

The player-coach completed his hat-trick with a goal in each of the other two periods (including a second short-handed) and was the driving force in his team's 5-3 mauling of Thunder. By the time the league ended he had fired in ten more goals for a total of 1,010 in 738 career league games. *(His complete league statistics are on the next page.)*

After adding in the other major competitions like playoffs and the Autumn Cup, Tony has a grand total of 1,380 goals in 1,043 games. His *Findus* BNL scoring title was his sixth league crown in the last ten seasons. Before he joined the league, he was the all-time leading points scorer in the professional, import-dominated Superleague.

Though he's filled the nets with pucks his scoring titles were earned by his true forté - playmaking. His goals tally pales in comparison to the number of assists he has accumulated - 1,584 in the league alone.

Don't even ask how many points he has in all recognised games. Oh, all right then. It's 3,476.

Even all that doesn't take into account his international record with Britain. Hand is the top scorer there, too, with 43 goals and 119 points in 59 games.

In this age of the import, it's pleasing that Tony was born in Britain, learned to play in Britain and, apart from a tiny handful of games in Canada (see later), he has played all his ice hockey in Britain. What's more, he has always competed at the top level of the game here, right up until last season when he added coaching duties to his playing role in the second tier *Findus* BNL.

And he looks like being as successful a coach as he is a player. He took Stars - most of whose players he recruited himself - to the top of the league in their first season.

A whistle-clean forward with excellent vision, he is a natural skater with the softest of hands who can lay on passes with an accuracy that many an NHL player would die for.

Coach **Alex Dampier**, his mentor at his first club, Murrayfield Racers, added: "He's very good defensively, though many people don't think so. He can adapt to any style, Russian or North American, and he can play tough, too."

Chris McSorley, his coach on the national team, was equally fulsome in his praise. "He can change his game dramatically for each opponent, and he is one of the few players who can truly impact the outcome of a game."

In 1986 Hand was drafted by the NHL's Edmonton Oilers, on the recommendation of **Garry Unger**, the NHL's former Iron Man who played in Britain during the Eighties. Only 18, he became homesick and returned after a few training camp games, a decision he now rather regrets.

Oilers' four-time Stanley Cup coach, **Glen Sather**, was a Hand fan. "He was the smartest guy at camp other than **Wayne [Gretzky]**," he said at the time.

FIRST GOAL AT 14

Tony broke into the senior game at the tender age of 14 in 1981 with Murrayfield, his home town club. He scored his first goal on 15 November that year in Durham against Racers' Northern League rivals, Wasps. At the end of the campaign, he had four goals and 11 points. A small step on the road to greatness.

His best season was his draft year of 1986-87 when he chalked up an incredible 105 goals and 111 assists in just 35 games in the old *Heineken* British League. As the standard of play improved, Hand simply stepped up his game.

He credits his partnerships with Sheffield Steelers' **Ken Priestlay** - a Stanley Cup winner with the Pittsburgh Penguins - and Ayr's **Ed Courtenay** - a former San Jose Shark - for his league-leading tally of 220 points (including 60 goals) in Superleague's first five seasons.

He dropped out of the league in 2001-02 when he was offered a two-year contract as player-coach with Dundee. Club director, **Mike Ward**, is an old friend and team-mate on the Murrayfield and GB teams.

His deep understanding of the game should ensure him a long career as coach but, with over 100 points last season, he has no intention of retiring from playing for a while. "There's guys in Superleague still going at 40-plus so I have another six years yet!" he said.

HOW TONY HAND SCORED 1,000 GOALS IN 21 SEASONS

TONY HAND in his Superleague days with Ayr Scottish Eagles, beaten - for once - by another Brit, Bracknell Bees' goalie, **JOE WATKINS**.

Forward. *Born:* Edinburgh, 15 August 1967. *Height:* 5ft 10in *Weight:* 13st 3lb (185 lbs).

Season	Club	League	GP	G	A	Pts	Pim	
1981-82	Murrayfield Racers	Northern & Scottish	19	4	7	11	12	
1982-83	Murrayfield Racers	British	22	18	21	39	23	
1983-84	Murrayfield Racers	*Heineken* Premier	30	52	43	95	28	
1984-85	Murrayfield Racers	*Heineken* Premier	36	72	92	164	36	*Assists leader*
1985-86	Murrayfield Racers	*Heineken* Premier	32	79	85	164	49	
1986-87	Murrayfield Racers	*Heineken* Premier	35	105	111	216	86	*Assists leader*
1987-88	Murrayfield Racers	*Heineken* Premier	36	81	111	192	54	
1988-89	Murrayfield Racers	*Heineken* Premier	35	86	126	212	57	*Assists leader*
1989-90	Murrayfield Racers	*Heineken* Premier	32	53	91	144	26	*Assists leader*
1990-91	Murrayfield Racers	*Heineken* Premier	34	60	96	156	46	
1991-92	Murrayfield Racers	*Heineken* Premier	36	60	80	140	46	
1992-93	Murrayfield Racers	*Heineken* Premier	35	66	119	185	100	*Points leader*
1993-94	Murrayfield Racers	British Premier	44	72	150	222	44	*Points leader*
1994-95	Murrayfield Racers	British Premier	42	71	136	207	28	*Points leader*
1995-96	Sheffield Steelers	British Premier	35	46	77	123	65	*Points leader*
1996-97	Sheffield Steelers	Superleague	41	13	32	45	26	
1997-98	Sheffield Steelers	Superleague	28	9	30	39	16	*Points leader*
1998-99	Sheffield Steelers	*Sekonda* Superleague	36	11	27	38	6	
1999-00	Ayr Scottish Eagles	*Sekonda* Superleague	40	8	35	43	52	
2000-01	Ayr Scottish Eagles	*Sekonda Superleague*	46	19	36	55	42	
2001-02	Dundee Stars	*Findus* British National	44	25	79	104	18	*Points leader*
	Career Totals		738	1010	1584	2594	860	
	***Superleague Totals**		191	60	160	220	142	

Edmonton Oilers' 12th choice (252nd overall) in 1986 NHL Entry Draft.
*Leading overall points scorer in first five years of Superleague

compiled by Gordon Wade

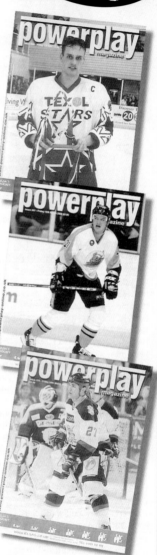

MORE QUOTES

GB just a flea

"The trouble in Britain is that the clubs believe the leagues are more important than their national team. That's the tail wagging the dog. But it's worse than that. They think the national team is the flea in the tail of the dog." *Chris McSorley, GB coach, citing one of the problems he faces in preparing his team for the World Championships.*

A real body checker

"I make so many checks. I never, ever sign a player on stats. I phone a player in his team or two coaches who had him or coached against him. I check, I check and then I check."

"Our road trips have played a big part in our success because we stay overnight every time. That's a good team builder."

"I've learned when to ease up on the players. When players are tired, that's when they get hurt. We've only had more than two guys out once and that was only for one game."

"We've got really, really strong personalities in the room but they all get along with each other." *Dave Whistle, coach of Belfast Giants, revealing some of the secrets of his team's success.*

Where it's going wrong

"The clubs with the money are buying all the best players and the gap between the big boys and the rest is getting bigger.

"I made my senior debut with Fife when I was 14 in the days of three imports and at 15 or 16 I got regular ice-time. That's where they've gone wrong. You never see a 16-year-old playing regularly these days but I know the kids are out there as good as I was at that age.

"Eight imports is too many for British ice hockey because too many teams can't afford it." *John Haig, who quit the BNL's Guildford Flames saying he was "disillusioned" after his fellow Scot and team-mate, David Smith, was released by the Flames.*

Rivals? No, we're just good friends

"The Giants have always had an excellent relationship with the Eagles. This is just another way of improving relations." *A Belfast Giants' spokesman in July 2002, denying rumours that Giants' Canadian owners, Albert Maasland and Bob Zeller, were to take a financial stake in Ayr Scottish Eagles.*

Did he mean this?

"I'll stay until it's impossible for Peterborough to qualify and then move." *Pasi Raitanen, on his loophole-in-the-rules move from Pirates to Edinburgh.*

What do we want?

'Belfast are an excellent team, but I certainly don't get any 'tingle' when we play against them. Even booing **Paxton**] **Schulte** has become passé now. Where are the [**Brad**] **Rubachuks**, the [**Tommy**] **Plommers**, even the **Andy Bezeaus**? The players who played the game with a smile and a snarl at the same time? We seem to have replaced them with faceless names and numbers.' *A fan's view expressed on the web*

"It was a great honour for us to play them. The Russians play the game with such speed and skill. That is entertainment - not the thuggery and cheap shots that sometimes occur in our league. It's what Superleague coaches should be aspiring to." *Enio Sacilotto, coach of Bracknell Bees, after playing Russian touring side, Ak Bars Kazan.*

"We [the coaches] don't bring guys in to bang, crash and have the odd scrap to end up penalising the fighter. We don't want to end up with a league where it's like watching paint dry.

"I go to Europe and watch Sweden play - it's very nice, but the best part of the night is the hot dog and the beer. The British are a people who don't mind getting their noses dirty and we have to play that way." *Alex Dampier, Nottingham Panthers' director of hockey and ex-GB coach.*

What a diff. a season makes

"We brought in **Chris Lipsett** to score goals, but he's had to use patched up and broken sticks for three weeks because the owner won't let us buy any more without getting three quotes." *Mike Blaisdell, coach of Sheffield Steelers, feeling the cold wind of financial reality from new club owner, Norton Lea.*

Wind up

"Right after the [last league] game I could hear this baby crying. But it was actually **Neil Black** all the way down in London." *Blaisdell again, this time teasing the owner of their great rivals, Nottingham Panthers, when Steelers finished higher up the league than Panthers.*

NEW RINKS NEWS

Talk's cheap, bricks cost money

BY THE EDITOR

First, a warning to new fans and Superleague - ice rink plans are two a penny, far more than ever get built or even receive planning permission. As a Brightonian who has seen a dozen or more since our rink was knocked down in 1965 and has yet to be replaced, I think I can speak with some authority!

Former Dundee Rockets' owner, **Tom Stewart**, is another who can testify that there are so many obstacles - money, land, planning permission, money, traffic regulations, local politics and, of course, money - that one just can't be too sceptical about this subject.

Nonetheless, we at the *Annual* remain incorrigibly optimistic and will pass on what we've heard, though we will try and guide you as to which ones are likely to be built. If you care to look at our back issues, you will see our strike rate. (On second thoughts, perhaps not!)

Plans for a £400 million Sports Village in the **CARDIFF BAY** redevelopment area were granted outline planning permission (for the second time) in July 2002. The plans, which were first drawn up five years ago, include a 10,000-seat arena but this has now been moved back into the second phase of building.

Meanwhile, Superleague have heard of plans to build an arena somewhere in their South West Wales franchise area but as we went to press they told us they were still waiting for the building to materialise. Oddly, they wouldn't tell the *Annual* or indeed anyone else where this arena might be - unless you fancy bidding for the league rights - but we've heard **PORT TALBOT**.

As described more fully in our *Review of the Year*, Superleague surprisingly awarded their **IRELAND** franchise to American real estate developer, **Burke McHugh**, in May 2002.

Mr McHugh from Colorado is trying to put together funding for an arena on the campus of Dublin City University in the Glasnevin area in north **DUBLIN**.

Meanwhile, the DIAL consortium, Dublin International Arena Ltd, is planning a 15,000-seat arena as part of the Irish government's plans for Sports Campus Ireland in the capital city. (See *The Ice Hockey Annual 2000-01*.)

Everything hinges on the government's announcement of their intentions, expected in autumn 2002.

Now for a real long shot. Everton, the Premiership football club, have plans for an 8,500-seat arena on the King's Waterfront in **LIVERPOOL** which the club say would be suitable for ice hockey.

Very sophisticated plans they are, too, according to their website, www.evertonfc.com. Estimated to cost £300 million, the main 55,000-seat football stadium would be transformed into an ice hockey arena in just four hours by sliding the playing surface out, closing the roof (20 minutes), and moving one entire end of the stadium in on tracks.

Can't see anything likely to go wrong at the last minute there, can you?

It may not be built before yours truly is called to a better world, but then again it sounds like it might just be worth my hanging on for.

The Anschutz Entertainment Group, owners of Superleague's **LONDON** Knights, are part of a consortium who took over the Millennium Dome in May 2002. They intend to convert the ill-fated building into a 20,000-seat European version of Madison Square Garden with Knights moving the short distance from London Arena by 2006. (*See Review of the Year*.)

MANCHESTER Storm owner, **Gary Cowan**, is talking to the Manchester City Council about building a 6,000-seat multi-purpose arena on land at 'Sports City', the home of the 2002 Commonwealth Games. The plans would call for Storm to move from the MEN Arena, which Mr Cowan admits is too large for their purposes.

The only rink actually under construction is in **SHEFFIELD**. Yes, I know the city already has two rinks but Steelers' home is not available for public skating and the one in Queens Road is over 25 years old. Still, lucky b's, aren't they?

The new place, which will have two international-size pads (lucky, lucky b's), will be almost next door to Sheffield Arena.

Superleague's old sparring partners, **Martin Jenkinson** and **Andy Cooke** (of CJS fame), have already talked putting a BNL team in the main rink which has 1,500 seats. The word on the street is they'll have to fight Steelers' owner, **Norton Lea**, for the rights to a team there.

Known as Ice Sheffield and with £13 million of lottery funding from Sport England, the building is scheduled to open in August 2003.

THEY SHALL NOT PASS Britain's veteran defender **SCOTT YOUNG** attempts to poke the puck away from Belfast Giant **Dave Matsos** in the challenge game at the Odyssey Arena.

Photo: Michael Cooper

AND MORE QUOTES

Cardiff pickets
"It's tough when you don't have the city or the fans behind you. It was strange at the first game which was the first picket line I've had to cross." *Import* **Mike Nicholishen**, *the newly appointed Cardiff Devils' captain, in September 2001.*

The McSaviour
'After the forum I was left with no doubts that this man is a shining example of how ice hockey should be run in this country.

'A man with a great long term vision, and a passion that combines both the sport of ice hockey and the development of the game in Britain'. *Cardiff fan overwhelmed by the visit of* **Chris McSorley** *and his ex-NHL brother,* **Marty**, *to try and save the club.*

"I'm cutting off my shirtsleeves when I meet the fans to show them I've got nothing up them!" *Chris McSorley, on preparing to meet the Devils' fans and explain his plan to take over the club.*

Our favourite headline
"Beast of Boston sups with the Devils." The Guardian, *less than ecstatic over the visit of* **Marty McSorley**, *the former NHL hard man. [Do we detect former ice hockey reporter* **Bob Pryce**'s *hand here?]*

Smiles all round in Cardiff
"**Bob Phillips**'s intentions were pure. He just wanted to see ice hockey back in the city." **Chris McSorley** *graciously giving credit to the former owner of Cardiff Devils in the protracted negotiations which ended in July 2002 with the GB coach taking over the reigns.*

"Being managing director of Cardiff Devils is the greatest honour anybody could possibly have. In football terms it's like being appointed manager of Liverpool." **Bill Buglass**, *a retired Caerphilly businessman and Devils' season ticket holder, on taking up his new job.*

Life imitates 'Slap Shot' imitates...
'London Knights will be hosting a fashion shoot at the London Arena on 15 January for department store, the *House of Fraser.*

'Knights' players **Mike Barrie, Ian McIntyre, Dave Trofimenkoff, Nate Leslie, Richie Bronilla** and **Dave Clarke** will be modelling a variety of top designer fashions, including *Armani, Kenzo, Paul Smith* and *Calvin Klein.*

'One of Europe's top photographers will be flying in from Spain especially for the shoot, which will be featured in the magazine, *Docklands.*
Knights' press release. Belfast Giants and Manchester Storm players were subjected to the same 'Slap Shot' treatment.

The Peterborough crisis
"It's not just the imports. It's the international transfer cards (ITCs), the accommodation, the car... A £200 a week wage bill will cost you twice that much with all the things that go with it."

"If we agree to have more native British players, I believe it will open the market by bringing in players who would otherwise hang up their skates at 21. Right now, there's an awful lot of those guys who pack up and leave the sport if they don't break into the BNL."

"The BNL is not run by an independent body. It's run by 12 guys each of whom have their own interests. The reason wage capping doesn't work is because these people don't want it to work." **Phil Wing**, *former director of the BNL's Peterborough Pirates who became a director of the new Peterborough Phantoms in the English Premier League.*

"My BNL proposal was sent to **Mike Petrouis** at Planet Ice and it basically said we needed to raise about £50,000 in sponsorship to put a very entertaining side on the ice." **Paul Macmillan**, *former Pirates' director. (He later joined the BNL's Cardiff Devils.)*

"I can see two sides to the situation. I would like to stay in the BNL and spend another season playing under **Glenn Mulvenna** who I believe is the nearest thing the club have had to **Rocky Saganiuk** as a coach in ten years.

"But on the other hand over those ten years there has hardly been a season gone by that [the club] have not struggled financially." **Jon Cotton**, *Pirates' veteran player.*

With grateful acknowledgements to **Ice Hockey News, Powerplay, Daily Telegraph, BBC Sport On-line, Daily Express, Daily Star, The Guardian, Northern Echo, Newcastle Evening Chronicle, South Wales Echo, Paisley Daily Express, Peterborough Evening Telegraph, Scottish Sun, Nottingham Evening Post, Face-Off magazine, Belfast Evening Telegraph** *and* **Sunday Life**, *and many club websites.*

RINK ATTENDANCES

OVERALL PICTURE	2001-02 TOTAL	ATTENDANCE GAMES	AVERAGE	2000-01 AVERAGE	AVE. DIFF. ON 2000-01
SUPERLEAGUE					
Sekonda league	603,791	168	3,594	3,579	No diff.
Challenge Cup Finals	20,961	5	4,192	4,765	(Diff. teams)
Playoffs	61,090	21	2,909	3,607	Down 19%
Playoff Finals	21,016	3	7,005	6,780	Up 3.3%
Ahearne Trophy	40,504	14	2,893	--	(New comp.)
TOTALS	**747,362**	**211**	**3,542**	**3,645**	**Down 2.8%**
FINDUS **BRITISH NATIONAL LEAGUE**					
League	269,226	264	1,020	1,024	No diff.
Playoffs	45,358	30	1,512	1,227	Up 23%
Challenge Cup, inc. finals	45,293	49	924	974	Down 5.1%
TOTALS	**359,877**	**343**	**1,049**	**1,042**	**No diff.**
TOTALS	**1,107,239**	**554**	**1,999**	**2,328**	**Down 14.1%**
ENGLISH NATIONAL LEAGUE					
Premier Division	41,764	97	430	485	Down 11%
Playoffs	7,107	14	508	745	Down 32%
TOTALS	**48,871**	**111**	**440**	**497**	**Down 1%**
GRAND TOTALS	**1,156,110**	**665**	**1,739**	**1,974**	**Down 11.9%**

THE TOP LEAGUE CROWD-PULLERS			2001-02 LEAGUE	ATTENDANCE Total Average+		2000-01 Average	Changes
1	(3)	Belfast Giants	Super	145,717	6,071	5,331	First full year
2	(4)	Nottingham Panthers	Super	104,969	4,374	4,128	Up 5.9%
3	(1)	Manchester Storm	Super	98,036	4,085	5,920	Down 31%
4	(2)	Sheffield Steelers	Super	96,900	4,038	5,750	New owner
5	(5)	London Knights	Super	75,583	3,149	3,284	Down 4.1%
6	(9)	Ayr Scottish Eagles	Super	43,885	1,828	1,773	Up 3.1%
7	(12)	Coventry Blaze	BNL	37,936	1,724	1,585	Up 8.8%
8	(11)	Fife Flyers	BNL	36,312	1,650	1,589	Up 3.8%
9	(8)	Bracknell Bees	Super	38,701	1,612	1,838	Down 12.3%
10	(-)	Dundee Stars	BNL	35,357	1,607	--	New club
11	(10)	Guildford Flames	BNL	34,284	1,558	1,632	Down 4.5%
12	(13)	Basingstoke Bison	BNL	24,863	1,130	1,163	Down 2.8%
13	(14)	Milton Keynes Kings	BNL	24,100	1,095	1,088	No diff.

List includes teams that averaged at least 1,000 fans to league games only (excluding playoffs).
Last season's position in brackets.
+ Superleague teams each played 24 home games; British National League (BNL) teams played 22 home games.
Figures are based on those shown on the leagues' media information releases.

The only way is up

STEWART ROBERTS

If there's any chance of being positive during these difficult times, the *Annual* intends to take it. Here the best I can say is that there's plenty of scope for attracting more crowds to games.

I promise not to mention that Superleague's lowest crowd ever was at Bracknell on Thursday 24 January. Blast! Oh well, since it's slipped out I'll whisper that only 801 fans turned up to watch Sheffield Steelers.

Returning hastily to the positive, the place with the greatest potential for growth would seem to be Ireland, judging from the packed houses watching Belfast Giants.

Managing director **Bob Zeller**'s big gamble paid off in spades as Superleague's newest team went to the top of the attendance list with over 6,000 fans a game in their first full season. In fact, Giants almost always played in front of capacity crowds.

And there's more. Belfast's success has shown the Irish not only what a great sport this is, (or great craic, as they say) but also that there's no 'history' to worry about. This has encouraged the creation of a new semi-pro team in Belfast's Dundonald rink as well as the planning of a big arena (or two) in Dublin, ready for a Superleague team in a couple of years. *See New Rink News.*

Elsewhere, it was good to see capacity crowds in the Nottingham Arena for the Superleague finals weekend which was probably the most successful climax to the season since the great Wembley days.

The new Ahearne Trophy drew respectable crowds, too, proving there is a market (though not a large one) for European competition. These crowds would undoubtedly have been bigger, however, had the tournament been arranged before the start of the season. Many fans stayed away as the games were not included on their season tickets.

BNL sponsors, *Findus*, will have been content with their investment as the league's attendances held up well. Coventry Blaze and Fife Flyers both outdrew one Superleague club. This league closed the gap with Superleague, too, as the total crowds watching the BNL increased by almost half (46.9 per cent) while those watching the pros fell off by 17 per cent.

Perhaps the most sobering fact revealed by our survey is how few teams attract more than a thousand fans a game. Only 13 last season, one fewer than ten years ago. The only way is up, folks.

• How are we doing compared to our continental neighbours?.... According to the world body, the IIHF, in October 2001 the average crowd in the elite leagues in Sweden, Finland, Switzerland and Germany was 5,133.

REVIEW OF THE YEAR

Season 2001-02 was not a good vintage. For the sixth straight year, there were three different league champions in **Belfast Giants** *(Superleague),* **Dundee Stars** *(Findus British National League) and* **Invicta Dynamos** *(English Premier League).*

A highly favoured British national team disappointed in the World Championships.

Television screened very little of the sport and other national media coverage was at its lowest for some 20 years. Superleague's failure to increase their crowds or attract a major sponsor forced them to reduce their wage cap again, making it difficult for many teams to carry sufficient players.

The success of the first full year of sponsorship of the British National League by Findus was marred at the end of the campaign when Paisley Pirates went out of business and three other teams dropped out of the league.

He's gone!

Ian Taylor, the chief executive of Ice Hockey Superleague Ltd, left the organisation 'by mutual agreement' on 30 April 2002. Taylor, a Olympic gold medal winner in field hockey, took over the post on 1 December 1997 during the league's second season.

The league were spending freely at that time with chairman **David Temme** boasting at the launch of London Knights a month later that the clubs had already spent £20 million.

The league were too shy to reveal the terms of his release from his contract, saying only that they were 'reasonable'. The remuneration for his position had originally been advertised in the national press as being 'a six-figure package.'

It hardly needs the *Annual* to point out that the league's ambitious business plan, which was based on having at least a dozen arenas by now, turned out to be seriously flawed.

The chief executive's reign coincided with a series of disasters which hit the league. A major part of Mr Taylor's brief was to market the sport but during his term of office the league lost the *Sky Sports* TV contract and, apart from *Sekonda*, failed to secure a major sponsor.

Taylor himself became universally unpopular. The media wearied of his constant promises of new franchises and there were regular personality clashes with the rival British National League. The damaging split between the top two leagues reached fever pitch during the disastrous summer of 2001 when they engaged in highly

publicised wrangles which ended with Newcastle without a team, Sheffield with dramatically fewer fans, and Cardiff in the BNL.

Ian Taylor will be sadly missed, however, by the readers of our *Quotes of the Year*.

• Superleague's Events Manager, **Hannah Tattersall** (née **Skinner**), and Commercial Manager, **Bevan Thompson**, both left the organisation at the end of season 2001-02. They were responsible for organising and acquiring sponsorship for the league's showpiece events - the All-Star Game, the Challenge Cup final, the Ahearne Trophy and the Playoff finals.

Hannah, who was appointed in 2000, took a similar role with Nottingham's National Ice Centre.

Super Storey

Most in the sport were pleased though surprised by the appointment of former Superleague secretary, **Brian Storey**, as the league's chief administration officer on 30 April 2002.

League chairman, **Martin Weddell**, spoke for many people both within and outside the league when he said: "During Brian's previous employment with the league, he built up a tremendous amount of respect with the Board, clubs and fans."

The appointment came as a surprise because Brian had resigned as secretary only five months earlier, citing travelling from his Manchester home to the league's office in Hugglescote, Leicester as the reason for his decision. His new job will enable him to work mainly from home.

Prior to joining Superleague, Storey, 54, was a detective inspector with the Greater Manchester Police. He has been a hockey fan for over 20 years, his favourite team being Altrincham Aces.

Despite the glowing references, the league couldn't quite bring themselves to make him chief executive, even though they confirmed he was taking over from **Ian Taylor**. The strictly administrative role was understood, however, to have more to do with the clubs' desire to keep a firm control over the league rather than any distrust of his capabilities.

From his first day, Brian made it clear that one of his main aims was to unite the warring factions in our game. "I will need the help of everyone connected with the sport....to meet and achieve our objectives," he said.

True to his word, one of his first acts on taking up his post at the end of May was to meet with the British National League's general manager,

Gary Stefan, and chairman, **Tom Muir**. In July, he met with the Sheffield Steelers' fans and frankly explained many of the league's problems.

Annual readers can read some of Brian Storey's thoughts on the game from the *Foreword* he kindly contributed.

• Helping the new chief admin. officer at Superleague's Hugglescote office are **Frank Dempster**, hockey manager; **Andy French**, officials' manager; **Alyson Pollard**, publicity; and **Jennifer Bayley**, secretary.

Sekonda clock off

The three-year, £1 million title sponsorship of Superleague's league and playoff games expired at the end of the 2000-01 season.

Owing to problems with the league's TV deal (see later), the contract was not renewed but the watch distributing company agreed to a one-season extension for the league only in 2001-02 when they also sponsored the monthly Face to Watch and Player of the Year awards.

The value of the extension was not disclosed.

THE SCOTTISH CRISIS 2002
The Battle to save the Eagles

Bill Barr OBE is not the sort of man to conduct his private business affairs in public. So we are unable to inform you exactly why it took his Ayr Scottish Eagles almost the entire summer, until 30 July 2002, to tell their fans where, or even if, they would be playing in 2002-03.

The four-month silence from the club's Centrum offices made a welcome contrast from the raucous and unedifying row over Sheffield Steelers, Newcastle Jesters and Cardiff Devils which so damaged the sport 12 months earlier.

But it did little for the support of professional ice hockey in Scotland. Eagles' loyal fans were livid at being given 'the mushroom treatment' - kept in the dark until it was time to heap fertiliser on them (this is a family publication - Ed.) - before being told their team would move 30 miles to a new arena in a Glasgow suburb.

The problems stemmed from Mr Barr's construction business which had been suffering heavy losses. Cutting costs was the order of the day, so he was determined to move his team away from Ayr's Centrum where he claimed a Superleague side did not make financial sense. The obvious alternative was the state-of-the-art, 4,000-seater at Braehead which opened in 1999 and was still without an ice hockey team.

But before this could happen there were some major hurdles to overcome - mostly financial ones, of course. The construction magnate had purchased Superleague's Scotland franchise for a reported £250,000 in 1998 and while we cannot

be certain that Mr Barr put it up for sale, if he did there were no takers.

So not only was he stuck with the Eagles, if he moved them to Braehead, he would also have to pay rent. According to one report, Spectacor Management General International (SMGI), who took over as the arena's operators in April 2002, were asking £300,000 for a year's rental.

SUPERLEAGUE'S RECORD OCTOBER

London Knights' forward **Kim Ahlroos** shot himself into the record books with a lightning fast double against the Belfast Giants on 14 October 2001.

Only 19 seconds separated Ahlroos' goals making them the fastest two short-handed goals ever in Superleague, beating both the individual and team records.

When Nottingham's **Greg Hadden** hit Panthers' third goal in their 3-3 draw at Ayr ten days later, it not only put Panthers on the 700-goal mark in Superleague, but also gave Hadden an unusual record. This was the fourth time he had scored a Panthers' century marker. He also tallied the 100th, the 500th and the 600th.

Dan Ceman's second goal for Bracknell Bees in their 5-2 home win over London Knights 24 hours later was Bees' 800th in Superleague. Bees are the league's highest scoring team.

There was no chance of SMGI taking over the team themselves. Though they operate the Superleague buildings in London, Manchester, Newcastle and Belfast it is their company policy not to run ice hockey teams.

As the league would scarcely be viable without their seventh team, the other owners were keen to help Mr Barr relocate the Eagles.

Enter Belfast Giants' managing director, **Bob Zeller,** who made a success out of starting up the Giants. The 60-year-old Canadian, a minority shareholder in the Giants, was especially motivated to help. Giants have the most to lose if the league ever folds as it would leave Northern Ireland's only professional hockey club without any opposition.

Mr Zeller set up Eagles Hockey Ltd to handle the team's marketing while Bill Barr continued as the club's owner and franchise holder through his company, Ice Hockey Services Ltd.

It was a win-win-win situation. A win for the league to guarantee its survival for at least for one more season, a win for Bill Barr and the Eagles as their fans would have only a half-hour's drive to their new home, and a win for the sport which finally gained a state-of-the-art arena in one of the country's largest cities.

• **Scottish Eagles**, the team's new name, is frowned on by the world governing body. (Eagles entered the Continental Cup before announcing their new home.) The IIHF prefer the name of a town or city as a prefix. Our Scottish friends insist that a team can be marketed more effectively in Scotland if no town is mentioned.

This seems to be borne out by the fact that the other North American sports north of the border use only the prefix 'Scottish'. The US football team is the Scottish Claymores and the basketball team (which also plays at Braehead) is known as the Scottish Rocks.

• **The Braehead Arena** is part of a £285 million leisure and retail complex in the Glasgow suburb, located next to the M8 motorway in central west Scotland. Opened in September 1999 for the World Curling Championships, it holds 4,000 for hockey and has a 60 by 30 metres main ice pad, a circular leisure pad, and a 50 by 35 metres curling pad on the first floor overlooking the River Clyde.

■ **Paisley tie-up** Braehead is 30 miles north of Centrum but it's only five miles or so from Paisley's Lagoon Centre, the former home of the BNL's Pirates. So Eagles arranged practice time there, linked up with the junior teams and were to play their first game - a friendly against BNL champions, Dundee Stars - at the Lagoon.

• **Who's running the Giants?** Chairman and majority shareholder, **Albert Maasland**, 42, a Dutch-Canadian retired merchant banker and former University of Toronto goalie. He said he was happy to take a more active role in the club, though he will continue to live with his family in the London area.

• **Too much, too soon?** Eagles lost a quarter of their fans after winning the Grand Slam in their second season, 1997-98. Crowds at the Centrum dwindled from an average of 2,400 to 1,800 last season.

• The smart, modern, 2,745-seat **Centrum** had closed as we write, with no news of when or if it might re-open. The best hope of its survival is the £500,000 grant that Mr Barr received from the lottery in 1996 to help him complete the building work. This was made on condition that Centrum remains an ice rink for at least 20 years.

• **'Mr Hockey'** - Apart from his two UK club interests, Bob Zeller is the deputy chairman of Superleague, a director of the governing body, Ice Hockey UK, and a member of the IIHF committee looking into the feasibility of a European League.

• **Clash of interests** Superleague issued the following statement in July 2002 as Bob Zeller's

shareholding in the Giants left him with a potential clash of interests.

'...the following will take effect so far as relates to the transfer of players between the two clubs and their scheduled fixtures.

'No transfer (permanent or temporary) of any player will be allowed to take place between Belfast Giants and Scottish Eagles or vice versa, either directly or via another club or clubs, in any league, from the period beginning with the first date of registration for a season for either of the clubs until the end of that relevant season.

'In addition, all possible steps will be taken to prevent the clubs meeting in any ISL competition as the last fixture of any series of any competition, except in the knock-out stages where they are pre-drawn.

'The above restrictions are the same as those imposed upon Manchester Storm and Nottingham Panthers following the changes to their shareholding interests last season. [Ed's Note - Panthers' **Neil Black** has a minority shareholding in the Storm.]

'ISL Corporate Rules allow persons to have an interest in more than one ISL club, so long as they only have control of one club at any time.'

DUBLIN DRUIDS
DIAL 'I' for Irish

When **Ian Taylor**, Superleague's outgoing chief executive, told the press at the 2002 Playoff Finals that he would shortly be introducing "the Manchester United of ice hockey", the yawns were nearly audible.

Yes, Ian, muttered the heard-it-all-before hacks, of course you will.

On behalf of our friends in the fourth estate, *The Ice Hockey Annual* would like to apologise to the former chief exec. It seems you were right this time, Ian. Pity your colleagues on the Superleague Board didn't see things your way.

The *Annual* learned during the summer that a consortium which included several world-class organisations was refused the league's (southern) Ireland franchise.

The consortium, known as DIAL for Dublin International Arena Ltd, was put together by **Martin Kenney**, a Canadian lawyer and former netminder who is president of the Irish Ice Hockey Association. DIAL have tendered for the 15,000-seat arena which is proposed as part of the government-backed Sports Campus Ireland. (See *The Ice Hockey Annual 2000-01*.)

The principal partner in DIAL is **Harry Harkimo**'s *Jokerit Oy*, the owners of Finland's Hartwall Arena, Europe's most successful arena and home of Finnish élite league team, Jokerit Helsinki. Mr Harkimo built the Hartwall and is currently constructing a 16,000-seater in Hamburg, Germany.

The other partner is *Clearchannel/SFX*, one of the world's biggest venue operators and event promoters, who operate Sheffield Arena.

DIAL also joined forces with an Australian consortium led by *Bovis Lend Lease*, a multi-national construction and development company, and had support from the *NHL* and the *NHL Players Association*.

So the league bit their hands off, eh? Don't be silly. When the Board came to consider the two short-listed bids for the franchise in May 2002, we understand that Harry Harkimo's ill-fated involvement with Newcastle Jesters counted against him. And after last summer's debacle in Sheffield, *Clearchannel* weren't the league's flavour of the month, either.

While the league have refused to comment publicly, we understand that the franchise was awarded instead to a successful American real estate developer, **Burke McHugh** of Colorado.

Though his plans for an arena on the campus of Dublin City University in the north of the city are not nearly as advanced as DIAL's, Mr McHugh named his team Dublin Druids.

This was the situation in July 2002. The Irish government were expected to have the final say on which arena is eventually built when they announce their plans later in the year for Sports Campus Ireland. This mega-complex - which could cost anything up to £1.2 billion - was designed to include an 80,000-seat national football stadium and an Olympic Park as well as the arena.

• For more on this story, read *News Rinks News* elsewhere in the *Annual* and go to the Irish Ice Hockey Association's website at www.iiha.org.

A third Irish team?

The Irish are determined that the Emerald Isle should become a new hotbed of ice hockey.

Bangor businessman **Allan Moore**, the former commercial director of the Belfast Giants, unveiled plans in May 2002 for a British National League team in the 1,500-seat Dundonald Ice Bowl in the Belfast suburbs.

According to a report in the Belfast *Sunday Life* newspaper, Moore has signed ten players for the team - to be called the Ice Warriors - ready for season 2003-04. A coaching appointment was expected later.

There are plans for a major refurbishment of the Ice Bowl, including new seating and a new roof, costing a substantial six-figure sum.

With his partner, **John Lyttle**, the chairman of the Northern Ireland Ice Hockey Association, Moore hopes the team will play some BNL games in the Giants' Odyssey Arena as well.

Gary Stefan, the BNL's general manager, said he is delighted that a Belfast side has applied to join the league. "I think the new club and the Belfast Giants can exist successfully side by side," he told the paper.

News from the flagship

London Knights, described on their formation in 1998-99 as Superleague's 'flagship' franchise, are to move to the Millennium Dome - once New Labour's own 'flagship'.

Knights' parent company, the Anschutz Entertainment Group (AEG), are part of a consortium who in May 2002 signed a 20-year deal with the British Government to buy the ill-starred Dome and 200 acres of prime development land on the Greenwich Peninsula.

AEG are a $20 billion US entertainment group, one of the largest private companies in America, owning property and media interests. Subsidiary company, AEG Sports, is the world's largest owner of sports teams, including the NHL's Los Angeles Kings, the Knights and five other European ice hockey clubs.

AEG have taken a 55-year lease on the Dome and will spend £135 million on creating a sports and entertainment complex within the Dome which they claim will rival New York's Madison Square Garden. The centre-piece will be a 20,000-seat arena (flexible seating can reduce that to 7,500) while restaurants, hotels and a casino are also included in the plans.

Detlef Kornett, the European head of AEG, rebuffed critics who pointed out that indoor sports are not as popular in the UK as they are in North America. In their four Superleague seasons, Knights have struggled to attract more than 3,000 to their 10,000-capacity arena.

"Our main focus [at the Dome] will be geared towards concerts," he told *Leisure Management* magazine. "But we will learn from our positive experiences in the US and adapt them for the local market. That is our formula for success."

German-born Kornett, a former head of NFL Europe, added: "Knights will be one of the anchor tenants in the new building and we will be looking to hold world-class events there like the Superleague finals, European competitions and some NHL games."

Meanwhile, Knights' present home has been sold and it was unclear where the team would play until the 'new Dome' opens, probably in time for season 2006-07. Moving out of London Arena will be a relief for many fans as even Kornett agreed that it is not ideal as an entertainment centre. A former warehouse and later boxing venue, it was converted to an ice rink in 1998 at a cost of several millions, but there is little atmosphere at games.

On the ice, London enjoyed success under the two-year reign (1999-2001) of GM-coach **Chris McSorley**. A brother of the NHL's **Marty McSorley**, Chris was a fine publicist for his team and the sport and a big fan favourite. He left in the summer of 2001 for Geneva Eagles, one of AEG's other European hockey clubs, and coached them into the Swiss A league. See *International Round-Up*.

His successor at Knights, **Bob Leslie**, is a Canadian with several years' experience in Europe, latterly as head coach of Cologne Sharks in the German DEL. His parents were born in Britain and Nathan, one of his two hockey playing sons, joined him during the season from the BNL's Dundee Stars.

McSorley's departure was followed by those of **Richard Boprey**, Knights' first and only Director of Marketing, and PR manager, **Paula George**. 'Bopes', a New Yorker and former player, is best known for his commentating partnership on *Eurosport* with **Paul Ferguson**. In April 2002 he joined *Planet Ice* as their marketing man, based in Basingstoke.

Paula, who came from Harwood & Co, the sponsorship managers for Superleague in its first season, was replaced by **Barney Allen**, but he left at the end of the 2001-02 season.

In changes at the top of the club, **Joan Hill**, the former chief executive at Cardiff City FC, took on the same role at Knights, replacing Canadian **Brian Jokat** who remained with AEG in London. Brian, a former Altrincham Aces' player, shared his time between all six of Anschutz' European clubs.

ANSCHUTZ FAMILY GET-TOGETHER

London Knights travelled to Geneva in mid-August 2001 for the *Credit Suisse* Cup (formerly the Gasag Cup) against opposition from their sister teams in the Anschutz family.

Although Knights beat tournament winners, Sparta Prague, they were shutout in their other three games and finished last in the five-team tournament. Knights' goalie, **Trevor Robins**, was selected as the player of the tournament.

The event was the first time Knights' new coach, Bob Leslie, had gone head- to-head with his predecessor, Chris McSorley, now coach at Geneva. Knights used three guests from the Los Angeles Kings' system: defencemen **Jonathon Shockey** and **Steve Shireeffs**, and centreman **Brendan Brooks**. Knights' results:

10 August	Knights-Sparta Prague	**3-1**
11 August	Berlin Polar Bears-Knights	**0-0**
	Berlin won 2-1 on penalties	
12 August	Munich Barons-Knights	**2-0**
	Knights-Geneva Eagles	**0-2**

Superleague's wage cap

The wage cap - the limit on the amount Superleague clubs can spend on players' wages - has been a bone of contention ever since it was introduced in season 1999-2000.

The league ran without any cap for its first three seasons but with some clubs going on a £1 million spending spree, something had to be done as the crowds failed to increase.

The first cap came in at £500,000 but even this was too rich for some teams' blood and it was reduced by ten per cent to £450,000 the very next season. When it was cut another ten per cent to £400,000 last year it produced howls of rage from the coaches who insisted it was impossible to employ 20 players of a decent standard at that price. The coaches were ignored, of course. (See *Quotes of the Year*.)

The league has always been shy of publishing exactly what the cap covers but league secretary, **Brian Storey**, told the *Annual* in 2000 that "it relates to the costs of players' salaries and benefits in kind, excluding housing costs." Players' cars, however, are outside the cap as are payments to the team manager or coach.

You don't have to be Einstein to realise there are loopholes big enough in that definition to drive the proverbial coach and horses through, especially as the cap relies ultimately on trust between the club owners and league HQ.

Mr Storey told the Sheffield fans this past summer that the league was looking into using the North American 'squealer' system. This involves the league paying a reward to any player who 'squeals' on a club that he suspects has broken the cap. If the league proves the breach and fines the club, the 'squealer' will receive a percentage of the fine.

Not very British but the minor leagues in the USA apparently find it quite effective. Watch this space.

Clearing up the Supermess

NEWCASTLE JESTERS

In the last *Annual*, we left you with a cliff-hanger - would the Newcastle Jesters play their opening game before their fans lost the will to live?

There was to be no happy ending as Superleague finally lost patience with the awful **Graham Gutteridge**/Fablon Investments/**Paul Smith**/Eye Group gang that claimed it was capable of running the league's Northumberland and Durham franchise.

(See the 2001-02 *Annual* for more information on this story than you probably need.)

Actually, the league showed remarkable patience - due to having to go through due legal processes, said a league official - as it was not until 24 October 2001 that the group finally had the franchise taken away from them.

Most of the first two months of the season was an extension of the noisily embarrassing arguments between the league and the franchise holders. Smith, previously of Durham Wasps, resigned as club chairman on 7 September 2001 but Gutteridge, the man behind Fablon Investments, a company registered in Gibraltar, clung on to the bitter end.

He was last seen in court facing allegations that money from a Fablon subsidiary, NonLeague Media plc, had ended up in a solicitor's account, enabling Gutteridge's wife to buy a house for £500,000.

He wasn't the only one with egg on his face. The loss of Jesters reduced the league to seven teams and left Jesters' former players owed £150,000 in unpaid wages. The club was believed to have run up debts of around £250,000 in all. Loyal coach **Glenn Mulvenna** was left without a team.

The franchise reverted to Superleague but they had no success in selling it. Riding to the rescue came **Alex Dampier**, the former GB, Sheffield, Nottingham and Murrayfield coach, and his Steelers' coaching partner, **Clyde Tuyl**.

Dampier and Tuyl joined forces with Newcastle speedway co-promoter, **Darryl Illingworth**, a long-time ice hockey fan, and entered a new team, the KBS Vipers, into the British National League.

This was a brave as well as an intriguing move as Vipers will be the first BNL team to play in a large arena. Newcastle's Telewest Arena can hold as many as 7,500 for hockey.

So we leave you with another cliff-hanger. Can Dampier turn Vipers into a money-spinning attraction, or have too many fans lost the will ever to watch ice hockey in Newcastle again?

■ 'Damps' received 52 per cent of the votes in a November poll on the *This Is The North-East* website, which asked the supporters who they would like to see replace Paul Smith.

SHEFFIELD STEELERS

At least the Steelers got back on the ice, but it wasn't until the fourth week of the season that returning coach, **Mike Blaisdell**, was able to put out a full team.

When the strife-torn club was taken over at the start of 2001-02 by **Norton Lea**, the wealthy former owner of Chesterfield FC immediately instituted a regime of austerity which the club may never have seen before in 11 years of mostly spend, spend, spend.

Former GM, **Dave Simms**, returned as PR man, and former NHL defenceman and fan favourite, **Ron Shudra**, was appointed

commercial manager. The delay and the tight budget, however, meant that Steelers were never able to show much of their Grand Slam form. As many as 1,500 fans stayed away, disgusted by the summer-time antics as much as by the under-par displays on the ice.

Their 2002 Playoff victory, though a gutsy one, came too late to win back the lost legions.

While he gained a reputation among his players for being careful with his money, off the ice Mr Lea worked to make peace with his former enemies. He settled his differences with **Andy Cooke**, **Martin Jenkinson** and **Mark Smith**, the so-called CJS consortium with whom he and Superleague had fought a bitter battle for the South Yorkshire franchise in the summer.

In November, the 75-year-old owner acquired the rights to the Steelers' name and logo from CJS and agreed to games between Steelers and Hull Thunder, the BNL team that was bought by Martin Jenkinson from **Darren Brown** in October 2001.

And a month after the end of the campaign, he restructured the club, handing over his shares to the supporters to ensure, as he put it, that the club would never again be sold off to the highest bidder. The new company was called the South Yorkshire Franchise Ice Hockey Club Ltd, and uniquely combined the Steelers' trading entity with the franchise for the first time.

Mr Lea explained that he expected to retire soon and wanted the club to continue under one banner. "I can't be completely hands-on for ever," he told the *Sheffield Star*, "and all those who have worked so hard for the Steelers - the fans - will ultimately run the club."

No doubt he also hoped that it would help to attract many of the fans who had stayed away. Steelers' average crowd in 2001-02 barely topped 4,000, the lowest in their history.

■ Unusually among Superleague owners, Norton Lea appears to be a strong backer of home-grown players. He told the *Star* that his most important objective was to improve the chances of bringing up-and-coming British youngsters into the sport.

"Why does every football club get £138,000 a year grant for youth development and ice hockey gets nothing," he mused. He was reported to be keeping an eye on the new rink being built next door to the arena. *See New Rinks News.*

He signed five under-19s who play at Sheffield's Queen's Road rink - **Stevie Duncombe**, **Dave Lawrence**, **Keith Leyland**, **Lee Morgan** and **Ritchie Oliver**.

■ The associate directors of the SYFIHCL are Norton Lea, Dave Simms, **Stephen Williams**, a partner in a local firm of solicitors, **Catherine Locking**, a director of Spaldings UK, **Tony**

Harthill, a sales manager in the medical supply industry, **Jurgen Morton Hall**, a purchasing executive, and **Allison Jackson**.

Some readers may recall that Mr Williams was a director of the club in the **George Dodds'** era. Tony Harthill is the press officer and a founding member of the National Ice Hockey Supporters Association.

■ Former Steelers' owner, **Darren Brown**, was close to bankruptcy in June 2002, according to the Sheffield press. Creditors of the former photocopier salesman turned down his offer of paying them just a fraction of his £283,506 debts.

Brown, 30, offered to pay back 14.3p for every pound he owes at a bankruptcy hearing in Oldham. If creditors had accepted the offer he would have paid back £34,507 of the debt and avoided bankruptcy. But he was having to come up with an alternative offer to avoid one of his creditors pursuing a bankruptcy order against him.

Brown, who was being investigated by the Serious Fraud Office after leaving Chesterfield FC £1.6 million in the red, owed the British National League £15,000 and Steelers' Dave Simms £12,500.

He may have avoided an investigation into his time at the Steelers as the SFO decided they did not have the resources for this as well. They were keeping the position under review, however.

Ice Hockey UK

Chairman **Jim Anderson** was due to leave the governing body at its AGM in October 2002 after two years, due to changes in his business. Anderson was understood to be relieved at relinquishing his post which the Scot told colleagues involved him in 'too many confrontational situations'.

The organisation's other directors are due to stand for re-election in July 2003 when their four-year term expires.

Stephen Cooper

Coventry Blaze defenceman, **Stephen Cooper**, announced his retirement at the end of the 2001-02 season after a remarkable career spanning 21 years.

Cooper, 12-and-a-half stone (178lbs) of pure muscle on a 5ft 10in frame, is considered one of our all-time greatest home-grown rearguards. The British Ice Hockey Writers Association awarded him their Alan Weeks Trophy as the Best British Defenceman a record nine times, and he's a shoo-in for the Hall of Fame.

He told his local paper, the Coventry *Evening Telegraph*, that there were several reasons for his decision to leave the game he has played since he was a 14-year-old. Travelling is perhaps the main one as he lives in Manchester where he had recently started a new job selling Ferraris. Finishing his career while still injury-free and in good form was also important.

Paul Thompson, his coach at Coventry, said: "It's going to be impossible to replace him. He's been the pedigree defenceman of his generation and there's no British player like him."

Born in Peterlee, Co Durham 35 years ago, Cooper started his career with his home town team, Durham Wasps, alongside his younger brother, Ian. He went on to play 974 major competitive games with Wasps, Cardiff Devils, Manchester Storm, Newcastle Riverkings and Nottingham Panthers before ending his career in the *Findus* BNL with Hull Thunder and Coventry.

Always a big game player, he scored some crucial goals in the BNL playoffs this year and was a key factor in Blaze's success in reaching the finals. His contributions to the GB team were equally important. He was first selected in 1989 when Britain returned to world play after a long absence, and he was a member of the 1994 team that played in the World A Pool against Canada, Russia and other major nations.

In all, he was capped 61 times for GB before stepping down after the 2000 World games in Katowice, Poland.

Thompson said that Blaze would be retiring Stephen's no. 55 jersey at their first home game of the 2002-03 season "not just in recognition of his contribution to hockey in Coventry, but to honour him for his services to hockey in Britain".

McSorley saves the Devils

GB and Geneva Eagles' coach, **Chris McSorley**, finally won control of the Cardiff Devils in July 2002, but only after protracted negotiations with former owner, **Bob Phillips**.

Phillips had alienated most of the Devils' faithful by failing to pay the players and numerous other bills at the end of season 2000-01. He then took the team out of Superleague and put together a makeshift side which finished dead last in the British National League. At times during 2001-02, there were more fans holding 'vigils' outside the Wales National Ice Rink than there were inside watching the game.

McSorley had first expressed an interest in taking over the club in November 2001 when he organised a challenge game between Devils' alumni and his GB team. (See *World Championships*.) His brother, Marty, who played in the NHL mostly as **Wayne Gretzky**'s 'minder', guested for the Devils and was touted as a future Devils' coach.

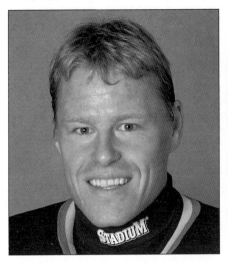 

NAMES IN THE NEWS *clockwise from above left*: **DAVID LONGSTAFF** enjoyed his season in Stockholm, Sweden; Coventry's **STEPHEN COOPER** hung them up after 21 years; **PAXTON SCHULTE** entertained the Belfast crowds; **BOB LESLIE** took over as coach of London Knights.

Photos: Djurgardens IHC, Tony Boot, Mike Smith/Icepix.

But Mr Phillips, who claimed he had lost £250,000 on running Devils in the Superleague, wanted £500,000 for the club and the lease of the WNIR which he owned. Though Chris McSorley apparently knocked him down to £300,000, the negotiations then faltered and the club continued to be run by **Brian Candy**, a former business associate of Bob Phillips.

TOM STEWART WATCH

We thought you'd like to know that **Tom Stewart**, the former owner of Dundee Rockets, and his Birmingham-based associate, **David Huxley**, have been linked with the following ice projects:

❑ **Dundee** - a 200-acre sports complex with four-pad, 13,500-seat arena at Monifieth, Dundee,

❑ **Newcastle** - a new ISL franchise,

❑ **Telford** - a new BNL franchise,

❑ **Cardiff** - bid to become co-owner of the Devils,

❑ **Ambri-Piotta** - bid to become owner of Switzerland's once wealthiest club, (See International Round-Up.)

❑ **Les Chaux-des-Fonds** - part owner of the Swiss A league club,

❑ **Windsor, Nova Scotia** - offered 'seed money' for $600 million project ,

❑ **Paris** - a $700 million project similar to the Dundee one outside the capital.

And that was just last season!

In the summer the pair enquired about acquiring the rights to the IIHF's **Continental Cup** for nine million Euros and putting a new BNL team in **Paisley**. Phew!

As far as we know, the only transaction that was actually completed was the purchase of *Ice Hockey News* by Mr Huxley's firm, Midlands Publishing Holdings Ltd.

• Tom Stewart's 12-year ban from involvement in ice hockey imposed by the BIHA expired along with the governing body in December 1998.

Several people showed interest in the club after that, including former Devils' sponsor, **Martin Barton**, ex-Dundee Rockets' owner, **Tom Stewart** (of course), and **Kevin Tatum**, who had just relinquished control of Peterborough Pirates.

After the season ended McSorley made an offer, according to the local *South Wales Echo*, of £250,000 for the club and the balance of the lease which is due to expire in 2005. He also pledged to pay £70,000 to cover last season's unpaid players' wages.

This was rejected by Mr Phillips, and the club's future looked grim when the bids by Tatum and Barton also collapsed in mid-June.

Two weeks later, however, McSorley and Phillips agreed a deal. Though neither was willing to disclose the financial details, it called for Phillips to remain as the rink's leaseholder, continuing to control the rink's catering, among other things.

The hockey club was to be run independently by a separate company headed by Chris McSorley and some of the fans. This company reached a rent-free agreement with Bob Phillips for matches and training.

The fans went rather quiet at this news. Though it brought them Chris McSorley, whom they respected, it did not remove their bogey man, Bob Phillips. And nothing was said about the outstanding debts from season 2000-01.

Moreover, McSorley made it clear he would have to be an absentee owner. "I have the best hockey coaching job in the world, " he told the Annual, "and I can't risk jeopardising it." And he didn't mean the GB one!

His Geneva team are owned by Anschutz and the Swiss league pays the best salaries in Europe, with considerable tax advantages. After taking Eagles into the Swiss A league in his first season, he has gained considerable respect there, too. (See *International Round-Up.*)

Chris handed over the day-to-day running of the Devils to its managing director **Bill Buglass**, 54, a retired businessman and long-time Devils' fan, former Newcastle Jesters' coach and GB defender, **Glenn Mulvenna**, and general manager, **Paul Sullivan**, who stepped down as chairman of Cardiff Devils Supporters Ltd.

To help win the fans over, McSorley insisted that "Superleague remains our ambition". But the 2,700-seat WNIR is too small to make this viable and plans for an arena in Cardiff Bay's projected Sports Village seem as far away as ever. (See *New Rinks News.*)

■ According to Martin Barton, who has been a club sponsor for many years, Devils lost £900,000 in 1996-97, their first Superleague season. That's around £30,000 a game.

BNL lose three teams

PLANET ICE KILL PIRATES AFTER 20 YEARS

Planet Ice, who took over the management of the Peterborough rink in 1997, created their own team in May 2002 to replace the Pirates and entered them in the English Premier League.

The company, which owns or manages six other rinks in England, refused to continue dealing with Pirates' owners who they claimed had not paid their outstanding debts.

PI's plans initially met strong opposition from Pirates' fans and some of their directors. Eventually, two directors who had been sacked by Pirates came to an agreement with the company.

Phil Wing and **Rob Housden** set up the Phantoms and appointed **Luc Chabot**, Isle of Wight Raiders' player-coach, to the same role with the new club.

Peterborough Pirates' 20 years in ice hockey finished on 24 February 2002 with a 9-1 defeat of Cardiff Devils in the British National League.

Their two decades brought the highs of a British Championship final at Wembley and the coaching of crack ex-NHL players, **Garry Unger** and **Rocky Saganiuk**, as well as the lows of coaching character, **'Heavy' Evason**, relegation and a temporary rink closure.

▪ Pirates' former MD, **Paul McMillan**, later became a director of Cardiff Devils.

MILTON KEYNES NO LONGER BNL KINGS

Similar disagreements occurred at *Planet Ice*'s Milton Keynes rink. The company showed a morbid sense of occasion here, too, as the announcement of Kings' effective demise came only 24 hours after their tenth anniversary game on 11 May 2002.

PI put together a new club, the Lightning, which was accepted into the English Premier League at their AGM on 12 May. Kings' Canadian forward, **Nick Poole**, was appointed coach and English forward, **Simon Howard**, his assistant. Poole first played in Britain in London Knights' opening Superleague season.

The handover was not cordial. A *PI* spokesman told the local paper: "It is no secret that MK Kings Ice Hockey Ltd, the previous company running Kings, has gone into receivership. *Planet Ice* felt that it could no longer do business with that organisation."

Kings' management committee chairman, **Paul Stearman**, said the club had not received written notice to quit, only a verbal indication.

▪ The old Kings, led by **Rick Strachan**, their recently re-appointed player-coach, decided to fight on in the BNL under the ownership of husband and wife pair, **Mike** and **Sue Pack**. The trio reached agreement with the Solihull rink and named the new team, Solihull MK Kings.

▪ The English IHA insist there is no conflict of interest between the three *Planet Ice* teams in their league. Although *PI* own the Isle of Wight Raiders, the Lightning and Phantoms are privately owned, renting their ice-time from *PI*.

▪ *Planet Ice* also own the BNL's Basingstoke Bison through their associate company, Ice Hockey League Ltd. (This company also sponsors the English Premier League.)

Despite the name, **Mike Petrouis**, the managing director of *Planet Ice*, denied on the club's website that either company had plans to create their own league "unless we win the lottery four weeks running".

He agreed, however, that he had rather fallen out with the BNL over the televising of the second leg of the Guildford-Coventry playoff semi-finals. He believed this should have been played at Coventry and not Guildford. Oh, didn't we say? *Planet Ice* run the Coventry Skydome, too, though not the Blaze. *(See TV story later.)*

SLOUGH HIT BY CRIPPLING DEBTS

Slough Jets, formed in 1986 by Anglo-Canadian GB international **Gary Stefan**, discovered at the end of 2001 that the club had debts of around £50,000 .

In a statement the club said: 'The problems started two years ago, when money for tax and National Insurance was taken from our account but not paid to the Inland Revenue by our then accountant. These problems have dogged us ever since and have now come to a head with the Revenue threatening to shut us down.'

The debts were so heavy that Jets managed to finish the 2001-02 season only by releasing some of their better paid players.

A game held to raise money to help stave off the tax man raised a four-figure sum, but the club's suggested schedule of repayments to the Revenue was turned down in court.

Slough Jets Ice Hockey Club Ltd folded and its directors, **Pauline Rost** and **Geoff Cutting**, were not allowed to continue in the BNL because of ice hockey-related debts. Combined with the lack of funds this resulted in Jets entering the English Premier League for 2002-03.

For a change, however, there was a happy ending as **Warren Rost**, the club's commercial manager, secured a five-figure sponsorship from *Invesco Perpetual*, the UK's second largest retail fund managers.

Slapshot VI - Yawn, or six fights and you're out

"I am still concerned about the safety of the players in this league. I said it last year and I am saying it again this year." *Enio Sacilotto*.

Few fans agreed with the coach of Superleague's Bracknell Bees when he made this comment to *Ice Hockey News* in October 2001.

The cause of this season's controversy was the new 'six fights and you're out' ruling from the league. This read -

'A player, on reaching a total of six fighting penalties [unspecified], is automatically suspended for one game and fined £250. The

player will also be referred to the ISL's disciplinary committee who may take further action. Once a player has received six fighting penalties, each time he receives a subsequent fighting penalty, he will be suspended for one game and fined a further £250.'

The league explained that this was introduced to create a higher quality of game, etc. etc. In the eyes of those many fans who, rightly or wrongly, prefer a rugged, physical game, all it did was turn ice hockey into figure skating with attitude.

It certainly seemed odd for a professional league that imports most of its players from North America, to penalise them because they play like North American professionals.

The rule was amended, though only slightly, in the off-season.

THE USUAL SUSPECTS

There were few surprises in our notes of the some of the season's unsavoury incidents with the clubs' designated hitters, or 'goons', being most often mentioned in dispatches.

- Belfast's **Paxton Schulte** was the first to be fined and suspended under the 'six fights' rule - on 16 October! Unlike many others, 'Paxo' didn't let some silly rule stop him enjoying himself and his last fight didn't come until his last game of the season.

That was when Giants were knocked out of the playoffs in London during the controversial ending of the quarter-finals. (*See Superleague section.*) Schulte had his automatic one-game suspension doubled for his threatening behaviour towards referee **Simon Kirkham**.

In the same incident, Giants' coach **Dave Whistle**, who also threw out his toys, was suspended for two games and fined £500.

- Panther **Clayton Norris** was suspended for ten games (reduced to seven on appeal) and fined £250 for cross-checking London's **Ian McIntyre** in the team's 6-6 draw at Nottingham on 6 October.

- Sheffield's captain, **Paul Kruse**, nearly started an international incident when he gave a Russian defenceman a two-handed whack across the thigh during a brawl near the end of a televised 'un-friendly' against the touring Moscow Dynamo.

Reports differ as to whether the attack was made with his stick or his opponent's helmet. He received two games and a £250 fine which left Steelers' PR man, **Dave Simms**, seething.

"We must have the only league body in world ice hockey to ban a player for two domestic games for an incident in a friendly. Could you see the Russian Elite League taking a player out of the line up after a friendly in England?" he whined to the local *Star* newspaper. He also rambled on about it all being the fault of Newcastle Jesters, but we rather lost him there.

- Nottingham's **Barry (Tarzan) Nieckar** appeared to have stopped fighting after receiving his fifth major penalty in mid-season. Our notes may just be incomplete, of course, but it would explain the drop-off in fighting - and entertainment value, some would say - in the second half of the season.

- Goalies may have a reputation for being excitable, but they're never 'goons'. Nottingham's **Danny Lorenz** was a case in point. He allegedly attacked referee **Andy Carson** with 'a sumo wrestler-type belly-flop' after the stripey allowed Sheffield's third goal in their 4-0 shutout of Panthers in Sheffield on 1 December.

As he was quick to apologise to Carson and followed it up in writing, he escaped with an automatic two-game suspension.

The game produced 71 minutes in penalties, and provoked Panthers' coach **Paul Adey** into a mild diatribe against the ref., but it was quiet compared to some Steelers-Panthers derbies.

Overall, season 2001-02 was a feeble vintage. One of their nine meetings, on 13 January, set some kind of record, being worth only 12 minutes. That 'six fights' rule again, we guess.

BNL DON'T DO THINGS LIKE THIS

When the *Findus* British National League threw out Hull Thunder's own 'goon', **Rob McCaig** [*see panel on next page*] for ten weeks for 'incidents during the game at Slough on 13 October' they took the opportunity to stress that they have a stricter discipline code than their big brothers in Superleague.

That didn't answer the question on most people's minds - how the heck did Thunder ever receive permission to ice this nutter in the first place?

Paisley Pirates went out of the BNL not with a whimper but with a brawl. On 3 February in a 7-3 home defeat to Scots rivals, Fife Flyers, nine players - including both netminders - received game misconducts, mostly for fighting. Pirate **Mark Biesenthal** was clobbered the heaviest, with a ten-minute misconduct and a gross on top.

EPL OWNER BANNED FOR A YEAR

Croatian **Zoran Kosic** of Haringey Greyhounds was banned for a year by the EIHA after allegedly striking Romford's **Marc Long** with his stick during an English Premier League game in the north London rink on 27 October.

The ban threw the club into turmoil as the 31-year-old forward from Belgrade, who lives and works in London, was effectively the club's owner. He put a substantial amount of money into Greyhounds during the summer of 2001.

A former Yugoslav international, Kosic was also the team's top scorer in each of the two seasons he spent with the club. In 2000-01, he was voted their Most Valuable Player.

Greyhounds had won just one of their nine games before the incident which resulted in the team having to play the rest of the season as genuine amateurs. (*See Club Report.*)

Super Brit Watch

'LOBBY' IN SWEDEN

Great Britain's skipper, **David Longstaff**, signed for Superleague's Manchester Storm in the summer of 2002 after playing a full season with Swedish élite league club, Djurgardens IK.

Superleague's first English player of the year in 2000-01 was the first Brit to compete professionally in Sweden. He was offered a contract to return to Stockholm but reluctantly declined as he and his wife, Michelle, want their two young sons to be educated in England.

'Lobby', 27, joined Djurgardens after his best British season to date when he was the top scorer on Sheffield Steelers' Grand Slam-winning side. He scored nine goals and 20 points in 45 league games for Djurgardens, a team which regularly has its best players taken by NHL clubs.

Though he has never been considered a 'dirty' player in Britain, his penalty total of 55 minutes was the fourth highest in the Swedish club.

Djurgardens finished fourth in the league - considered a poor season by the standards of the perennial Swedish champs - and after they won only one playoff game their coaches were sacked as their revolutionary 'torpedo' system was deemed to be a failure. 'Lobby' had been one of the team's two 'torpedoes'

Apart from a few missed games with a leg injury, David's only personal disappointment came at the start of the season when Djurgardens' game against the reigning Stanley Cup champs, Colorado Avalanche, was called off following the tragedy of 11 September. The game was sponsored by *American Airlines*.

His biggest blow, of course, came in Britain's World Championship games in Hungary when he was hospitalised for 12 days with deep vein thrombosis. Thankfully he made a full recovery. (See *World Championships.*)

SHIELDS IS TOP SNIPER, ROOKIE IN MAINE

Glasgow-born **Colin Shields** was voted Rookie of the Year with his American college side, University of Maine Black Bears, in season 2001-02. The 21-year-old was also voted to his league's All-Rookie squad when the Bears ended as runners-up in Hockey East and reached the final of the NCAA's Frozen Four.

The GB forward was Bears' highest goal scorer with 29, nine more than the next best player on the team and sixth best in USA college hockey. His 46 points were good enough for third in Bears' scoring.

The one-time Paisley Pirate, whose parents still live in the Glasgow area, is only the second British-born player after **Tony Hand** to be drafted by an NHL team, an honour which had an unexpectedly practical benefit. As he had been forced to sit out a season due to a technicality in his college eligibility, his two weeks at Philadelphia Flyers' training camp in September 2001 helped him to shake off the rust.

Colin went on to become the second highest scorer with his national team in Hungary. (See *World Championships.*)

■ For Colin's full career history, see *The Ice Hockey Annual 2000-01.*

TOP GOON

Wichita - The Central Hockey League (CHL) today [2 April 2002] suspended Thunder defenseman **Rob McCaig** for the entire 2002-03 CHL season.

McCaig, a nine-year veteran, received the one-year ban for initiating physical contact with a fan late in the third period of Wichita's season finale at the Amarillo Rattlers on Sunday, 17 March.

McCaig was issued a game misconduct for the incident. "There is no justification for becoming involved with fans, regardless of the scope of instigation by those fans," said CHL Director of Hockey-Compliance, **Rod Pasma**.

"The onus is on the coach and the players not to become involved with fans who may become antagonistic."

A native of Innisfail, Alberta, McCaig picked up four points and 140 penalty minutes in 28 games for the Thunder this past season.

In 353 career pro games, the 30-year-old McCaig has a whopping 2,140 penalty minutes.

Wichita Thunder press release on the former Hull Thunder player who was suspended by the BNL five months before the North American ban.. (See adjoining story.)

*In Britain, McCaig racked up 493 penalty minutes in 48 games with Lee Valley, Newcastle and Hull. While with Cobras he was fined £1,000 and banned for four months by Superleague after allegedly biting linesman **Moray Hanson** on the arm.*

ISL DOWN TO FIVE REGULARS - JUST

Only five British born and trained players - all members of the GB national team - took a regular shift in Superleague last season - and that's only if we look on the bright side.

In truth, only Ayr's Englishman **Jonathan Weaver** played in every one of his team's games. **Joe Watkins** (Bracknell) and **Stevie Lyle** (Manchester) are goalies and naturally shared their duties. Watkins was usually number two to **Brian Greer**.

Nottingham's **Ashley Tait** learned much of his hockey as a kid in Canada, and **David Clarke** managed only 12 games with London Knights as he spent most of his season with the BNL's Milton Keynes Kings.

Three teenagers mostly sat on Superleague benches while playing for BNL clubs in a 'development programme'. Panthers' **Paul Moran** was really an MK King, Ayr's **Patrick** (**Paddy**) **Ward**, 17, iced with Edinburgh Capitals, and Bracknell defenceman **James Morgan**, 19, also appeared with Guildford Flames.

Sheffield Steelers' **Steve Duncombe**, 17, and **Keith Leyland**, 16, were usually seen at the city's Queen's Road rink, though they played in some Best of British games with Coventry Blaze.

Just 200 minutes on the telly

Yes, British ice hockey was on our national TV screens for just three hours, 20 minutes in season 2001-02 - two hours on ***ITV***, 20 minutes on ***BBC*** and 60 minutes on ***Sky Sports 3***.

If you're an NHL fan you were lucky, since good old ***Channel 5*** broadcast live weekly games from the Show and every Stanley Cup final contest, albeit at an ungodly hour. And the Beeb brought us wide coverage of February's Winter Olympics from Salt Lake City.

But that was it for the British game.

The success of Belfast Giants no doubt helped to persuade the ***BBC*** that Superleague's Challenge Cup final in the Odyssey Arena was worth a live showing on Sunday *Grandstand* - but only in Northern Ireland. Mainland fans had to be content with about 20 minutes of highlights.

Sadly, Giants' lop-sided 5-0 defeat would have done little for the viewing figures, likewise the poor camera positions up in the gods.

Commentators were ice hockey journalist, **Simon Crosse** (play-by-play), and Nottingham Panthers' director of hockey, **Alex Dampier**. Panthers' **PC Drouin** and London's **David Clarke** were the studio experts.

The early rounds of the Olympics were difficult to find on the Beeb, often being shown late at night with no warning. But we caught the final with commentary from the BBC's **Bob Ballard** and Utah Grizzlies coach, **Gary Mouser**. (The hockey games were held in the Grizzlies' rink.)

In the studio were the self-styled former French Olympic hockey player and Millennium Dome showman, **PY Gerbeau**, plus a snappily dressed Dampier again. Screened at peak time on a Sunday evening, we heard that the BBC were very pleased with the audience figures.

Personally, we admit to preferring the wall-to-wall coverage of the Games on *Eurosport* with commentary by the under-rated (by every other TV station) **Paul Ferguson** and **Richard Boprey**.

ITV have not done ice hockey for a few years and we have to say it showed when they brought us highlights of the British National League's playoffs, courtesy of league sponsors, *Findus*. Seemingly geared to fans rather than casual viewers - not a good idea - we thought the presentation was sloppy and uninformed.

However, all the ITV areas showed the games and even though the first broadcast clashed with the Grand National over on the BBC, viewing figures peaked at a not shabby 660,000, according to the league. The Dundee-Fife final a week later did even better with an 880,000-viewer peak rating.

The two broadcasts in April, each of an hour's duration, were shown two weeks after the games were played. Commentators were **Phil Simmonds** (play-by-play) and BNL general manager, **Gary Stefan**. Phil, who is best known as the match announcer for the Basingstoke Bison, was making his commentating debut.

The games in the first programme were the two-leg semi-finals between Coventry Blaze and Guildford Flames, and Fife Flyers and Dundee Stars. The league took a lot of flak from Coventry when their home advantage in the second leg of the semi was surrendered to their opponents, to satisfy the needs of TV.

With the best action expected in the second leg and the camera crews based in Southampton, the venue was switched to Guildford. There was only one camera at Coventry for the first leg so most of the hockey in the first TV show came from Guildford.

Camera crews are expensive, the league explained to us, and even with sponsors, *Findus*, helping out, there was not enough money in the kitty for full coverage of the final and both semis.

Equinox Productions - the company owned by Manchester Storm's co-owner, **Gary Cowan** - and Nottingham Panthers' trade union sponsor, ***GMB***, were behind the semi-documentary coverage of Moscow Dynamos' Christmas tour of England shown on ***Sky Sports 3*** in January. (See *Touring Teams*.)

The games were preceded by shots of Moscow and the Dynamos' training camp, where their assistant captain admitted being surprised about going to England. "We don't know much about English hockey," he said. "We just know lots of Canadians play there." Thanks, Sergei.

Commentators were Storm's PR man, **Andy Costigan**, and Radio Sheffield's **Seth Bennett**.

Season 2001-02 was *Channel 5*'s fourth year of NHL coverage as they have patiently built up a loyal following. The studio presenters were **Nick Halling**, **Jonathan Gould** and someone who knew a bit about the game, London Knights' backroom boy, **Russell Chamberlain**.

Finally, the unhappy saga of greed and bad luck, known as the million-pound contract with *NTL*-owned Premium TV, came to an end with Superleague accepting an out-of-court settlement in early 2002 after no games had been shown.

No details of the settlement were released but the *Annual* understands a six-figure sum was involved. *NTL* are the $20 billion, multinational cable telecoms giants who barely managed to survive the dramatic loss of confidence in such businesses on the stockmarket.

As recorded in last year's *Annual*, the TV contract was originally with both Superleague and the BNL, but Superleague later struck a separate deal with Premium.

The BNL's decision to stick with the original contract turned out to be a shrewd move as Premium eventually sold the league's playoffs to ITV (see above). Superleague had apparently been promised that their games would be shown on a new sports channel, *British Sport*, but it never materialised.

The worst part of this story is that Superleague sacrificed their valuable *Sky Sports*' contract because of the silly money offered by NTL/Premium.

LYNN POLLOCK CUP, MAY 2003
For details of Scotland's biggest junior tournament go to
www.lynnpollockcup.com

Ice Hockey News closes

Ice Hockey News, Britain's longest running ice hockey magazine, closed after their issue of 27 April 2002. The colour weekly was founded in 1981 by **Vic Batchelder** as the fortnightly *Ice Hockey News Review*. Vic sold the magazine in 1999 to Pinegen of Croydon who kept it going for three years under two different editors, **Peter Oakes** and Tony Hoare.

Pinegen, who produce a number of publications, including speedway's only weekly, blamed the closure on unsustainable losses due to the lack of co-operation from ice rinks, and unpaid debts when three Superleague clubs ran into financial problems in 2000-01.

Vic Batchelder, who died in October 2001 (see *Obituaries*), built the *News Review* into the sport's publication of record, selling nearly 6,000 copies a fortnight. It went weekly only after its sale to Pinegen.

■ *It's that man again!* We understand that the subscribers' list and goodwill of *Ice Hockey News* was purchased by Midlands Publishing Holdings Ltd, a Birmingham-based company run by **David Huxley**, a long-time colleague of former Dundee Rockets' owner, **Tom Stewart**.

■ Former *IHN* editor, Peter Oakes, writes regularly on ice hockey in the *Daily Star* and the Scottish *Sun*.

■ After ten years and 344 issues in sole charge, *Powerplay* editor, **Simon Potter**, sold his weekly magazine to its printers, Keyprint of Peterborough, in January 2002. Keyprint publish the weekly basketball magazine, *Tip Off*. Simon remained as editor.

Varsity Match 2002

Cambridge University's campaign for an ice rink received a boost when the Light Blues beat their bitter opponents, Oxford University, 8-1 in the 82nd annual Varsity Match on 10 March 2002.

The victory gave Cambridge the Patton Cup for the second straight year and the fourth time in five attempts. The series, which dates back to 1900, is Europe's longest running hockey rivalry.

Defeat was doubly embarrassing for the Dark Blues as it was held in their home rink which was filled by 1,200 mostly Oxford fans.

Andrew Ashcroft was the man of the match with three goals and two assists. **Chris Murawsky** and **Hari Kunduri** tallied two apiece and **John Millar** chipped in the other. Ashcroft, an engineering student from Sudbury, Ontario, also had a hat-trick in last year's contest.

The game was tied at 1-1 until the halfway mark after Oxford's **Stephan Wagner** cancelled out Ashcroft's fourth minute opener. Oxford's **Joe Place** received a major and a game misconduct after a particularly bad check from behind on Ashcroft which left the Cambridge skipper winded on the ice for several moments.

The victory was Cambridge's 26th while Oxford have won 54 times. Two games have been drawn. (The full list of early results is in *The Ice Hockey Annual 1986-87*.).

■ The Patton Cup was donated by **Major B M (Peter) Patton**, one of the early pioneers of hockey in this country, who was recently inducted into the IIHF Hall of Fame. (See *International Round-Up*.)

■ The Women's Varsity Match was won 2-0 by a mostly British-staffed Oxford team a day earlier.

Major Teams 2001~02

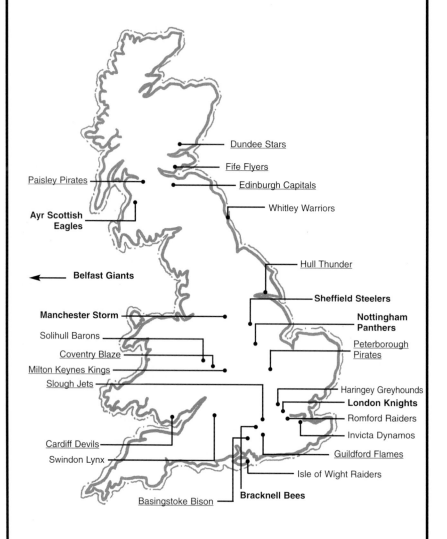

Dundee Stars

Fife Flyers

Paisley Pirates

Edinburgh Capitals

Ayr Scottish Eagles

Whitley Warriors

Belfast Giants

Hull Thunder

Sheffield Steelers

Manchester Storm

Nottingham Panthers

Solihull Barons

Coventry Blaze

Peterborough Pirates

Milton Keynes Kings

Slough Jets

Haringey Greyhounds

London Knights

Romford Raiders

Invicta Dynamos

Cardiff Devils

Swindon Lynx

Guildford Flames

Isle of Wight Raiders

Basingstoke Bison

Bracknell Bees

Superleague   <u>British National League</u>   English/Scottish Leagues

AYR SCOTTISH EAGLES

PLAYER	SEKONDA SUPERLEAGUE					SUPERLEAGUE PLAYOFFS					ALL COMPETITIONS				
Scorers	GP	G	A	Pts	Pim	GP	G	A	Pts	Pim	GP	G	A	Pts	Pim
Ed Courtenay	47	21	30	51	16	7	2	6	8	4	59	25	40	65	20
Rhett Gordon (WP)	48	11	19	30	46	7	2	3	5	8	60	18	25	43	54
Dody Wood (WP)	42	16	15	31	171	7	3	4	7	11	54	21	21	42	194
Shawn Byram	42	11	19	30	85	7	2	2	4	32	54	16	25	41	131
* Jonathan Weaver	47	16	18	34	14	3	2	0	2	2	55	19	21	40	16
Dainius (Dino) Bauba	44	14	17	31	115	7	0	1	1	11	56	14	19	33	130
Johan Silfwerplatz	48	9	17	26	23	7	0	4	4	0	60	9	24	33	25
Alan Schuler	48	3	23	26	28	7	0	2	2	0	60	3	29	32	30
Mike Jickling	48	10	11	21	19	7	3	4	7	2	60	13	17	30	23
Cam Bristow (WP)	48	6	12	18	111	7	4	1	5	4	60	10	15	25	123
Ian Herbers (WP)	41	2	13	15	106	7	0	4	4	4	53	5	19	24	116
Mike Harding	32	9	12	21	43	3	0	0	0	4	35	9	12	21	47
Johan Molin	8	2	2	4	2	7	3	5	8	2	20	8	8	16	4
Ryan Risidore (WP)	41	4	5	9	80	7	0	2	2	8	53	4	7	11	96
Anders Hillstrom	48	1	6	7	26	7	0	1	1	2	60	1	7	8	30
Erik Norbak	7	0	7	7	2	-	-	-	-	-	7	0	7	7	2
Joaquin Gage (N) (WP)	41	0	4	4	14	7	0	2	2	2	52	0	6	6	16
Phil Crowe	20	1	1	2	71	7	2	0	2	33	32	3	1	4	106
Colin Ryder (N) 1	8	0	1	1	0	-	-	-	-	-	9	0	1	1	0
* Paddy Ward 2	24	0	0	0	0	2	0	0	0	0	30	0	0	0	0
Bench Penalties					24					4					28
TEAM TOTALS	48	136	232	368	996	7	23	41	64	133	60	178	304	482	1191
Netminders	GPI	Min	SOG	GA	Sv%	GPI	Min	SOG	GA	Sv%	GPI	Min	SOG	GA	Sv%
Joaquin Gage (WP)	41	2459	1140	104	90.9	7	420	210	15	92.9	52	3124	1478	125	91.5
Colin Ryder 1	8	421	187	21	88.8	-	-	-	-	-	9	481	220	24	89.1
Empty Net Goals			5	5				0	0				5	5	
TEAM TOTALS	48	2880	1332	130	90.2	7	420	210	15	92.9	60	3605	1703	154	91.0

Shutouts: Gage (4) - league: 26 Oct at Sheffield Steelers (29 saves),
10 Nov at Manchester Storm (21 saves),
23 Jan at Nottingham Panthers (33 saves),
3 March at Belfast Giants (23 saves)

Also played for: 1 Belfast Giants; 2 Edinburgh Capitals

All Competitions = league, playoffs, Challenge Cup and Ahearne Trophy

No Joaquin, Gage is the man!

RONNIE NICHOL

Paul Heavey started his first full season in charge of Eagles with a squad showing few changes from the previous year.

The Glaswegian, who was joined on the coaching staff by ex-London Knights' assistant, **Scott Rex**, has always preached team defence and his major signings were on the blueline.

Big **Ryan Risidore** and **Ian Herbers**, along with the welcome return of **Alan Schuler** as team captain, were his key rearguards.

Offensively, the only new faces were centre **Mike Jickling** and ex-NHL hard man, **Dody Wood**. Heavey's biggest capture, however, was between the pipes where he was willing to wait until late in the summer for the right man to come along in **Joaquin Gage**.

The former Edmonton Oiler signed up after being unable to find a team in North America, even though he had iced in the 'show' the previous season. This was a real coup.

Despite being shut out at home against Belfast in their Superleague opener, Eagles started the season well, helped by the scoring pace set by former San Jose teammates, **Ed Courtenay** and - to everyone's surprise - Dody Wood.

Eagles were in the top two with Belfast right through to the turn of the year.

After a mental switch-off in October when they shipped 13 goals at Belfast (2-7) and Bracknell (3-6), they went on a six-game undefeated run. But then the vagaries of ISL's scheduling left them without a game for 13 days and on resumption their momentum had been lost.

And how! During their next 16 games, Eagles posted just home and away wins over Nottingham.

But after "getting their heads together", as Heavey put it, they upped their performance levels to those of earlier in the season, ousting Panthers in the Challenge Cup semi-finals and securing second spot in the league.

But the big moment of the year was reserved for Sunday 3 March when Eagles went into Belfast and played arguably their greatest ever domestic game to secure the Challenge Cup with a 5-0 blanking of the hosts.

Totally fired up, Eagles skated through the Playoffs in some style, dropping only a solitary point against Nottingham on their way to topping the group standings.

They travelled to Nottingham for the weekend finals as favourites, but sadly the magic had gone. Aided by an inspired display from Manchester, Eagles bowed out at the semi-final stage for the second year in a row.

PLAYER AWARDS
Player of the Year   Joaquin Gage

LEADING PLAYERS
Joaquin Gage *born 19 September 1973*
When he brought him over, coach Paul Heavey said: "He's likely to win games on his own for us." He did just that.

Arguably the best goaltender to play in this country in the modern era and well worthy of the title of Superleague's Player of the Year.

Alan Schuler *born 21 September 1968*
Back 'home' to Ayr after two years in Cardiff, this time as skipper, he was inspirational on the blueline. He led by example and was never anything other than highly consistent.

A consummate professional and one of the most popular players in the community.

Darin (Dody) Wood *born 8 May 1972*
Signed by Heavey "to allow our skilled players to do what they do best", Eagles gained a bonus as they ended up with one of the smartest and most respected players in the league. Able to look after his team-mates as well as contributing in a major way at both ends of the ice.

FACT FILE 2001-02
Sekonda **Superleague**:   Runners-up
Playoffs: Semi-finalists
Challenge Cup: Champions

HISTORY
Founded 1996. Previous Ayr clubs were Raiders (1991-92 and 1939-55) and Rangers (1962-65) at Beresford Terrace and Bruins (1974-91, 1969-72, 1966-67) at Limekiln Road.
Leagues Scottish Eagles - Superleague 1996-2002; Raiders - British League 1991-92, 1954-55, Scottish National League 1939-54; Bruins - British League (Premier Div) 1982-91; Scottish National League 1981-82; Northern League 1974-82, 1969-72, 1966-67.
Honours Eagles - 2001-02: Challenge Cup; 1997-98: grand slam of league, *B&H* Cup, playoffs & *Express* Cup; Bruins - British Championship finalists 1989; Raiders - Scottish National League 1952-53.

AYR SCOTTISH EAGLES *left to right, back row:* Paul Heavey (coach), Johan Silfwerplatz, Paddy Ward, Ian Herbers, Anders Hillstrom, Ryan Risadore, Mike Harding, Cam Bristow, Dino Bauba, Scott Rex (asst. coach); *front row:* Joaquin Gage, Dody Wood, Rhett Gordon, Ed Courtenay, Alan Schuler, Mike Jickling, Jonathan Weaver, Colin Ryder.

BASINGSTOKE BISON

PLAYER	FINDUS BRITISH NATIONAL LEAGUE					FINDUS PLAYOFFS					ALL COMPETITIONS				
Scorers	GP	G	A	Pts	Pim	GP	G	A	Pts	Pim	GP	G	A	Pts	Pim
Dru Burgess (I)	44	31	37	68	10	6	1	3	4	0	57	34	46	80	10
Mike Ellis	40	26	25	51	38	6	2	4	6	0	52	33	35	68	38
Richard Little	38	23	19	42	16	6	1	2	3	4	51	36	24	60	22
Gary Clarke	44	30	14	44	10	6	2	0	2	0	57	35	23	58	12
Derek Higdon	29	14	22	36	20						36	17	31	48	20
Chris Brant (I) 1	22	11	25	36	34						29	13	32	45	40
Jimmy Andersson (I)	44	5	30	35	14	6	2	1	3	0	57	10	34	44	18
Jake Armstrong	44	11	11	22	24	5	0	1	1	0	56	15	18	33	28
Neil Liddiard	43	12	15	27	113	6	0	1	1	12	56	14	19	33	170
James Manson	44	3	15	18	32	6	1	1	2	8	57	5	18	23	46
Dustin Lattery (I)	14	10	10	20	19	4	1	1	2	0	18	11	11	22	19
Rob Lamey 4	29	4	14	18	6	6	1	1	2	0	35	5	15	20	6
Matt Cote	43	6	9	15	38	5	0	0	0	2	55	7	11	18	50
Chris Crombie (I) 2	12	5	7	12	18	6	2	2	4	8	18	7	9	16	26
Nick Cross 2	12	5	6	11	14	6	0	3	3	2	18	5	9	14	16
Ryan Aldridge	44	3	4	7	34	6	0	0	0	20	57	4	6	10	58
Joe Baird	34	1	5	6	14	6	0	1	1	4	41	1	6	7	18
Richard Hargreaves 3	12	0	0	0	8						18	1	5	6	20
Andy Morgan	27	0	1	1	2						34	1	3	4	2
Andy Pickles 3	19	0	3	3	8						26	0	3	3	12
Neil Leary	39	1	0	1	2	5	0	0	0	0	49	1	0	1	2
Adam Greener 2	20	0	1	1	10	4	0	0	0	4	30	0	1	1	18
Bench Penalties					10					4					16
TEAM TOTALS	44	201	273	474	494	6	13	21	34	68	57	255	359	614	669
Netminders	GP	Mins	SOG	GA	Sv%	GP	Mins	SOG	GA	Sv%	GP	Mins	SOG	GA	Sv%
Dean Skinns	7	350	155	13	91.6						9	420	178	14	92.1
Robert Schistad (I)	39	2266	1204	132	89.0	6	369	212	18	91.5	46	2705	1452	154	89.4
Stephen Foster 5	1	60	30	4	86.7						6	340	152	18	88.2
Andy Murray											1	10	3	1	66.7
Empty Net Goals		2	2	2			1	1	1			3	3	3	
TEAM TOTALS	44	2678	1391	151	89.1	6	370	213	19	91.1	57	3478	1788	190	89.4

Shutouts: Foster (1) - cup: 15 Sept at Slough Jets (22 saves);
Schistad (2) - league: 27 Oct v Peterborough Pirates (28 saves),
*9 Jan v Cardiff Devils (2 saves)
Skinns (1) - league: *9 Jan v Cardiff Devils (15 saves).   * shared

Also played for: 1 Bracknell Bees, Sheffield Steelers; 2 Slough Jets; 3 Isle of Wight Raiders;
4 Guildford Flames; 5 Hull Thunder, Milton Keynes Kings

Also appeared: Alec Field (N)

All Competitions = league, playoffs and Findus Cup

BASINGSTOKE BISON *left to right*, *back row*: Alan Parrott (equipment), Neil Leary, Jim Anderson, Joe Baird, Neil Liddiard, Richard Little, Chris Crombie, Nick Cross, Rob Lamey, James Manson, Dustin Lattery, Ryan Aldridge, Charlie Colon (coach); *front row*: Dean Skinns, Gary Clarke, Mike Ellis, Harry Robinson (*Wella*), Dru Burgess, Jake Armstrong, Robert Schistad.

Photo: David Taylor

Bison get a Dustin

GRAHAM MERRY

Wella Bison appeared to have their strongest side since joining the *Findus* BNL, but instead they had to settle for fourth in the league, their worst ever finish. They also missed out on the rest of the silverware.

For the start of the campaign, **Chris Brant** returned from Bracknell and was joined by fellow Canadian **Derek Higdon**. On the British side of the roster, former Beaver, **Andy Pickles**, donned a Bison jersey for the first time along with his Isle of Wight team-mate, **Richard Hargreaves**.

MK Kings' top scorer, **Gary Clarke**, completed the quintet of newcomers but he was the only one to complete the season.

In the winner-takes-all *Findus* Challenge Cup clash with Slough Jets, 16-year-old **Dean Skinns** made a dream debut when he shared a shutout with first choice keeper, **Stephen Foster**. The 3-0 win booked Bison a place in the semi-final.

But the following weekend was the last for 'Fozzie'. The fans were stunned when he was axed and replaced by Canadian **Robert Schistad**, a former Norwegian international.

LATTERY FIND OF SEASON

The semi-final of the FCC was by far the most disappointing game of the season. Though without injured captain **Mike Ellis** and cup-tied **Rob Lamey**, Bison led Coventry Blaze 3-0 at 41.11. Then they collapsed and lost in a penalty shootout.

With the Herd's league form indifferent, Brant was released after Christmas and Higdon soon after. In their place came former fan favourite, **Chris Crombie**, along with British forward **Nick Cross**, both from cash-strapped Slough.

But it was Canadian **Dustin Lattery** who was the find of the season. He had come to Britain simply looking for a team. This trio helped Bison to see off local rivals, Guildford Flames and Hull Thunder, and eventually clinch fourth place.

On the opening weekend of the playoffs there was good news and bad news — Bison doused Flames 3-2 in Guildford but lost Lattery due to a concussion. And in the return in Basingstoke, their Surrey rivals gained sweet revenge with a 3-0 victory, thanks to an awesome display by their goalie **Mark McArthur**.

The Herd heavily outshot their visitors again but they were unable to convert their chances. It was the story of their season in a nutshell.

PLAYER AWARDS

Players' Player	**Matt Coté**
Supporters' Player	**Matt Coté**
Coach's Award	**Dru Burgess**
Captain's Award	**Ryan Aldridge**
Most Improved British Player	**Dean Skinns**

LEADING PLAYERS

Dru Burgess *born 7 December 1974*

Back to his best after a season dogged by injury, the Canadian once again showed his silky smooth stick handling skills and ended the season as the team's leading goal scorer.

Matt Coté *born 19 January 1966*

This rock of the Bison defence had an outstanding season, his second in a Bison uniform. The British-Canadian's trademark shot-stopping ability was recognised with a hatful of awards.

Dustin Lattery *born 20 November 1976*

Although the Canadian forward arrived late in the season he made a big impact, scoring on his debut. He was always in the thick of the action until forced to sit out the end of the season with a concussion.

FACT FILE 2001-02

Findus **British National League**:	Fourth
Findus **Playoffs**:	Third in group
Findus **Challenge Cup**:	Finalists

HISTORY

Founded 1988 as Beavers. Name changed to Bison in May 1995.

Leagues British National League 1998-2002; Superleague 1996-98; British League, Premier Div 1993-96; British League, Div One 1990-93; English League 1988-90.

Honours: British League, Div One & playoffs 1992-93; English League (promotion) playoffs 1989-90. *Benson and Hedges* Plate 1999-2000 & 2000-01.

BELFAST GIANTS

PLAYER	SEKONDA SUPERLEAGUE					SUPERLEAGUE PLAYOFFS					ALL COMPETITIONS				
Scorers	GP	G	A	Pts	Pim	GP	G	A	Pts	Pim	GP	G	A	Pts	Pim
Sean Berens (WP)	42	21	34	55	48	6	7	3	10	2	53	31	41	72	52
Kevin Riehl (WP)	48	22	37	59	16	4	2	0	2	10	57	25	39	64	26
Jason Ruff	42	17	31	48	48	6	1	5	6	38	51	19	37	56	90
Jeff Hoad	46	16	23	39	50	6	4	3	7	0	57	21	26	47	54
Paxton Schulte (WP)	46	20	17	37	133	6	1	3	4	42	57	21	24	45	179
Colin Ward	48	20	21	41	32	6	0	3	3	2	59	21	24	45	34
Rod Stevens	48	18	21	39	38	6	1	3	4	4	59	20	24	44	42
Rob Stewart	48	6	23	29	18	6	0	4	4	0	59	7	29	36	22
Curtis Bowen	48	12	16	28	83	6	1	1	2	6	59	16	19	35	93
Chad Allan (WP)	48	4	20	24	33	6	1	4	5	2	59	5	26	31	37
Dave Matsos	40	8	12	20	16	6	0	2	2	0	51	11	16	27	20
Todd Kelman	48	9	10	19	48	6	1	0	1	4	59	10	10	20	68
Jason Bowen (WP)	31	4	8	12	105	6	0	1	1	10	42	5	11	16	123
Terran Sandwith	48	0	13	13	92	6	0	0	0	2	59	0	14	14	96
Shane Johnson (WP)	43	0	6	6	30	6	2	2	4	4	54	2	10	12	36
Mike Bales (N)	34	0	3	3	10	5	0	0	0	0	42	0	3	3	10
Mark Cavallin (N)	16	0	1	1	0	3	0	0	0	0	20	0	1	1	0
Colin Ryder (N) 1	-	-	-	-	-	-	-	-	-	-	2	0	0	0	0
Bench Penalties					22					20					42
TEAM TOTALS	48	177	296	473	822	6	21	34	55	146	59	214	354	568	1024

Netminders	GPI	Min	SOG	GA	Sv%	GPI	Min	SOG	GA	Sv%	GPI	Min	SOG	GA	Sv%
Mike Bales	34	1996	965	77	92.0	5	206	115	10	91.3	42	2346	1149	96	91.6
Mark Cavallin	16	884	435	40	90.8	3	154	68	8	88.2	20	1074	526	50	90.5
Colin Ryder 1	-	-	-	-	-	-	-	-	-	-	2	125	47	7	85.1
Empty Net Goals			2	2				1	1				3	3	
TEAM TOTALS	48	2880	1402	119	91.5	6	360	184	19	89.7	59	3545	1725	156	91.0

Shutouts: Bales (3) - league: 2 Sept at Ayr Scottish Eagles (20 saves),
12 Jan v London Knights (36 saves);
playoffs: 8 March v Nottingham Panthers (29 saves)

Also played for: 1 Ayr Scottish Eagles

All Competitions = league, playoffs, Challenge Cup and Ahearne Trophy

Giants are for Riehl

STUART McKINLEY

THE short history of the *Harp Lager* Belfast Giants has been nothing short of spectacular.

They started life with 16 consecutive away games before their first contest in the spanking new Odyssey Arena was played in front of a sell-out 7,300 crowd in December 2000.

Since then almost every game has attracted full houses and 16 months after first taking to the ice they were crowned Superleague champions.

Dave Whistle kept ten of the 18 players who finished the inaugural season and added six top quality skaters before the season got underway. Just one, **Curtis Bowen**, joined from another Superleague club, Manchester Storm.

The season got off to the worst possible start, with a 9-3 loss at home to London on the opening night. It would have taken a brave man to predict championship glory that night for anyone but the visitors.

Twenty-four hours later, however, things took a turn for the better when Whistle's side took the short trip across the sea to Ayr and returned home 5-0 victors. Goalie **Mike Bales** was outstanding for his shutout.

Four road games without a win followed before Whistle completed his roster with the signing of **Sean Berens**. The American formed a talented top line with **Kevin Riehl** and **Jason Ruff**, and enjoyed a dream debut against Nottingham with two goals and an assist.

The trio would go on to be recognised by the Writers Association as the best in the league.

As the season wore on it became a matter of when rather than if the Giants would be crowned champions as a 16-game unbeaten run took them to the title.

When they were, there were only a couple of hundred of their fans to witness it. With 'Riverdance' taking over their Odyssey home, Giants faced five consecutive away games with the league certain to be won on the road.

A 4-1 away win at Sheffield on January 19 left Giants needing just a point to take the title in Bracknell. They almost blew it, having to come back from 2-0 down to clinch the game with the tying goal in the third period coming from the unlikely source of defenceman **Chad Allan**.

Giants went on to reach the Challenge Cup final which had been switched to their Odyssey Arena home. But Ayr spoilt the party running away with a 5-0 win to put the brakes on Giants' treble chase.

Two wins and a draw weren't enough to take them to the Playoff finals, but all involved with the team were happy with their season's work.

PLAYER AWARDS

Most Valuable Player:	**Mike Bales**
Player's Player:	**Jason Ruff**
Coach's Award:	**Kevin Riehl/Mark Cavallin**
Top Goalscorer (Harp Lager *award*):	
	Kevin Riehl
Fans' Player of the Year:	**Mike Bales**

LEADING PLAYERS

Mike Bales born 6 August 1971

The former NHLer with Ottawa and Boston was one of the best goaltenders Superleague has seen, ending the season with a league-leading 92.0 save percentage and two shutouts. Voted to the Writers' first All-Star team.

Sean Berens born 6 April 1976

The league's second highest scorer was the last piece in Whistle's jigsaw, but probably the most important. Linking the right-winger with **Kevin Riehl** (centre) and **Jason Ruff** was an inspirational move by the coach as the trio formed the league's most feared offence.

The only American on the squad, Sean also entertained the fans off the ice as a guitar player and song writer.

Jason Ruff born 27 January 1970

Though rough by nature as well as by name, the left-winger's fights were few and far between.

Instead, he hurt the opposition with his skill and vision, scoring and providing a number of goals. Never had a bad game all season.

FACT FILE 2001-02

Sekonda **Superleague**:	Winners.
Playoffs:	Fifth.
Challenge Cup:	Finalists.

HISTORY

Founded: 2000.
Leagues: *Sekonda* Superleague 2000-02.
Honours: *Sekonda* Superleague 2001-02.

BELFAST GIANTS *left to right, back row:* Alex von Hasselberg, Sean Berens, Rob Stewart, Shane Johnson, Chad Allan, Paxton Schulte, Jason Bowen, Jason Ruff, Curtis Bowen, Todd Kelman, Dave Matsos, Kevin Reihl, Tom Blatchford; *front row:* Mark Cavallin, Colin Ward, Rob Stewart, Dave Whistle (coach), Jeff Hoad, Terran Sandwith, Mike Bales.

Photo: Michael Cooper.

BRACKNELL BEES

PLAYER	SEKONDA SUPERLEAGUE					SUPERLEAGUE PLAYOFFS					ALL COMPETITIONS				
Scorers	GP	G	A	Pts	Pim	GP	G	A	Pts	Pim	GP	G	A	Pts	Pim
Dan Ceman (WP)	48	19	26	45	26	6	2	3	5	0	58	21	32	53	30
Mark Cadotte (WP)	47	18	23	41	18	6	0	3	3	4	57	21	27	48	26
Sam Ftorek (WP)	47	18	15	33	36	6	1	2	3	2	57	20	22	42	40
Blake Knox	46	7	19	26	56	6	1	1	2	6	55	12	21	33	76
Mark Turner	48	11	20	31	24	6	0	0	0	6	58	11	22	33	30
Brad Peddle (WP)	48	8	21	29	62	6	0	2	2	6	58	8	23	31	72
Darren Hurley	45	12	9	21	83	6	1	2	3	6	55	13	11	24	114
Mike McBain (WP)	45	4	16	20	36	6	0	0	0	4	55	5	18	23	52
Blair Scott	44	4	15	19	98	6	0	1	1	9	54	5	17	22	117
Steve O'Rourke	41	8	11	19	59	6	0	0	0	2	49	8	11	19	61
Doug Stienstra	44	4	10	14	8	6	1	0	1	2	54	5	11	16	10
Daniel Goneau	15	6	9	15	14	-	-	-	-	-	18	6	9	15	14
Todd Goodwin (WP)	26	7	7	14	16	-	-	-	-	-	26	7	7	14	16
Joe Ciccarello	12	6	2	8	2	6	1	0	1	8	22	8	2	10	10
Mark Matier	47	1	5	6	70	6	0	2	2	24	56	1	7	8	121
Eric Bertrand	8	4	3	7	4	-	-	-	-	-	8	4	3	7	4
Tuomo Kyha	9	1	3	4	0	6	1	0	1	2	19	2	4	6	6
* James Morgan 3	46	0	5	5	14	6	0	0	0	0	55	0	5	5	39
Chris Brant 1	2	2	2	4	2	-	-	-	-	-	2	2	2	4	2
Jari Torkki	4	0	1	1	0	6	1	0	1	2	10	1	1	2	2
Ryan Moynihan 2	8	0	1	1	2	6	1	0	1	0	17	1	1	2	2
Likit Andersson	3	0	1	1	6	-	-	-	-	-	3	0	1	1	6
Brian Greer (N)	34	0	1	1	8	5	0	0	0	0	40	0	1	1	8
Warren Tait 2	1	0	0	0	0	-	-	-	-	-	1	0	0	0	0
* Joe Watkins (N)	18	0	0	0	4	2	0	0	0	0	23	0	0	0	6
Bench Penalties					30					0					30
TEAM TOTALS	48	140	225	365	678	6	10	16	26	83	58	161	258	419	894

Netminders	GPI	Min	SOG	GA	Sv%	GPI	Min	SOG	GA	Sv%	GPI	Min	SOG	GA	Sv%
Brian Greer	34	1923	1106	98	91.1	5	275	168	18	89.3	40	2258	1318	121	90.8
* Joe Watkins	18	957	534	58	89.1	3	85	60	8	86.7	24	1222	696	77	88.9
Empty Net Goals			2	2				0	0				3	3	
TEAM TOTALS	48	2880	1642	158	90.4	6	360	228	26	88.6	58	3480	2017	201	90.0

Shutouts: Greer (2) - league: 11 Oct at London Knights (27 saves),
                      25 Nov v Manchester Storm (17 saves).

Also played for: 1 Basingstoke Bison, Sheffield Steelers; 2 Peterborough Pirates; 3 Guildford Flames

All Competitions = league, playoffs, Challenge Cup and Ahearne Trophy

BRACKNELL BEES *left to right*, *back row*: Andreas Larssen (physio), Charlotte Hilligsoe, Jari Torkki, Blair Scott, James Morgan, Sam Ftorek, Steve O'Rourke, Mike McBain, Mark Matier, Tuomo Kyhä, Doug Stienstra, Ryan Moynihan, Mark Turner, Mark Cadotte, Brian Miller (equipment), Dave Kelly (trainer), Gary Montgomery (equipment); *front row*: Joe Watkins, Joe Ciccarello, Dan Ceman, Enio Sacilotto, Blake Knox, Darren Hurley, Brad Peddle, Brian Greer.

Year of two halves

ALAN MANICOM

The difference between the Bracknell Bees' side that began the 2001-02 campaign and the one that finished it was as stark as it was alarming.

Around the turn of the year, coach **Enio Sacilotto** looked set to improve on last season's third place. Bees were flying high in second spot, bolstered by the superb form of netminder **Brian Greer** who had enjoyed two shutouts.

At the other end, centreman **Mark Cadotte** had won the *Sekonda* Face To Watch award for October after topping Superleague's scoring charts with an impressive nine goals and 11 assists from just seven games.

Bees even bounced back from a 9-1 thrashing at Ayr and an 8-2 debacle at home to Storm with a run that saw them lose only once in 13 games.

But in the New Year, they won just two of 28 games in all competitions and their fall from grace was encapsulated by Cadotte. The little left winger struggled to recapture his early season form and ended up being benched by Sacilotto in the club's final few outings.

The problems, though, had begun early in December when the hugely influential **Todd Goodwin** suffered a season-ending knee injury, ironically playing against Belfast Giants, the club he had left in the summer.

Although fans didn't realise it at the time, that 3-1 defeat was also the last appearance of power forward **Eric Bertrand**. His departure to Cologne Sharks in the German DEL a month after joining was a huge loss for Bees who were never to replace his physical presence.

Veteran **Chris Brant** returned to play two games after his summer move to the BNL's Basingstoke Bison didn't work out, and he scored in both matches. But 'Chief', as the native North American Indian is affectionately known to his fans, was allowed to slip away to Sheffield Steelers, whom he helped to Playoff success.

Then came the unsettling saga of **Daniel Goneau**. The Montrealer was axed six weeks after being made to honour a contract to join Bees from Ingolstadt in Germany's Bundesleague. A former team-mate of **Wayne Gretzky** at New York Rangers, he had arrived with high expectations, but he left with Bees sliding down the table to fifth place on the back of seven successive defeats.

Although that depressing run ended with a 4-4 draw at London, Bees' final league game, there was another nose dive in the Playoffs. Bees lost all six matches, culminating in an embarrassing 8-2 disaster at home to Manchester.

PLAYER AWARDS

Players' Player:	**Mike McBain**
Coach's Award:	**Dan Ceman**
Supporters' Player:	**Blake Knox**
Best Forward:	**Dan Ceman**
Best Defensive Player:	
	Mike McBain/Brad Peddle

LEADING PLAYERS

Eric Bertrand   *born 16 April 1975*

The power forward that Sacilotto had been searching so hard for. A big physical presence with a strong work ethic, the ex-NHL left-winger could skate, hit and score.

He made a big impact when he joined but unfortunately he was only around for a month before moving on to the lucrative DEL.

Dan Ceman   *born July 25 1973*

Described by Sacilotto as 'the league's most under-valued player', the centreman was the club's top scorer with 21 goals and 32 assists from 58 games. Exceptionally hard-working and Bees' most consistent performer.

Mike McBain   *born January 12 1977*

A good all-round defenceman who his coach reckoned was "the best in Superleague".

The Kimberley, BC native who played 64 games with the NHL's Tampa Bay Lightning joined a few weeks into the season but straight away demonstrated that he is a class act.

FACT FILE 2001-02

Sekonda **Superleague:**	Fifth
Playoffs:	Seventh
Challenge Cup:	Semi-finalists

HISTORY

Founded: 1987.

Leagues: Superleague 1996-2002; British League, Premier Div. 1991-95; British League, Div. One 1995-96, 1990-91; English League 1987-90.

Honours: *Sekonda* Superleague 1999-2000, Promotion Playoffs 1991-92, English League 1989-90.

CARDIFF DEVILS

PLAYER	FINDUS BRITISH NATIONAL LEAGUE					ALL COMPETITIONS				
Scorers	GP	G	A	Pts	Pim	GP	G	A	Pts	Pim
Lee Cowmeadow	39	21	10	31	33	45	24	13	37	37
Jerry Keefe (I)	9	5	10	15	2	14	9	17	26	8
Albie O'Connell WP	11	7	6	13	0	16	11	11	22	2
Marc Twaite 2	13	6	2	8	12	18	9	9	18	18
Neil Francis	44	4	11	15	62	50	5	13	18	68
Bryan Blair (I) 7	13	8	6	14	8	19	10	7	17	12
Mike Nicholishen WP	12	3	10	13	12	18	4	13	17	28
Jason Stone 5	36	1	16	17	10	36	1	16	17	10
Stuart Potts 7	31	8	8	16	4	31	8	8	16	4
Jamie Visser (I)	44	8	7	15	10	50	8	7	15	10
Darren Houghton (I) 6	13	4	7	11	16	19	7	7	14	26
Paul Sample 7	28	6	6	12	8	28	6	6	12	8
Matt Myers	32	5	3	8	8	37	6	3	9	8
Andrew Sande	14	1	5	6	35	20	1	5	6	53
Mark Hazlehurst	38	0	4	4	42	44	0	6	6	72
Joe Miller	20	2	3	5	0	20	2	3	5	0
Dan Madge	42	0	4	4	12	45	0	4	4	14
David Owen	33	1	1	2	2	39	1	2	3	2
Rhodri Evans	33	0	3	3	34	38	0	3	3	59
Barry Hollyhead (N) 1	3	0	1	1	0	1	1	1	2	0
Philip Hill	2	0	1	1	0	8	0	1	1	0
Tom Noble (N) WP	13	0	1	1	26	18	0	1	1	26
Chris Deacon	17	0	1	1	26	23	0	1	1	28
Wesley Spencer	21	0	1	1	4	26	0	1	1	6
Chris Bailey 8	26	0	1	1	16	26	0	1	1	16
David James	26	0	1	1	2	31	0	1	1	27
Dan Wood (N)	37	0	1	1	0	37	0	1	1	0
Bench Penalties					16					16
TEAM TOTALS	44	90	130	220	414	50	113	161	274	558

Netminders	GP	Mins	SOG	GA	Sv%	GP	Mins	SOG	GA	Sv%
Dean Crossland (I) 3	5	281	256	29	88.7	5	281	256	29	88.7
Tom Noble WP	13	751	518	58	88.8	17	991	629	73	88.4
Jason Crossland (I) 4	2	120	123	18	85.4	2	120	123	18	85.4
Dan Wood	23	1273	1042	163	84.4	25	1393	1128	179	84.1
Barry Hollyhead 1	2	80	54	11	79.6	2	80	54	11	79.6
Mike Brabon	4	104	94	22	76.6	4	104	94	22	76.6
Nathan Craze	1	31	35	11	68.6	1	31	35	11	68.6
TEAM TOTALS	44	2640	2122	312	85.3	50	3000	2319	343	85.2

Also played for: 1 Coventry Blaze; 2 Peterborough Pirates, Sheffield Steelers; 3 London Knights, Paisley Pirates, Slough Jets; 4 Edinburgh Capitals, Swindon Lynx; 5 Guildford Flames 6 Hull Thunder; 7 Milton Keynes Kings; 8 Paisley Pirates

All Competitions = league and Findus Cup

Season of protest

ANDREW WELTCH

A season which looked like it might never happen turned into one which most Cardiff hockey fans will want to forget.

After an uncertain summer, Swansea businessman **Brian Candy** emerged as the new chairman, taking Devils into the *Findus* British National League, the first time the Welsh club had dropped a level in their 16-year history.

Two weeks before their first scheduled game, Canadian **Ken Southwick** arrived as coach, and worked frantically to assemble a team.

For their opening game - a challenge against old rivals, Peterborough, on 1 September - Devils featured some familiar faces from the British scene, including **Marc (Smurf) Twaite**, **Mark Hazelhurst**, **Bryan Blair** and **Bobby Brown**. Impressive newcomer **Mike Nicholishen** was appointed captain.

Making up the rest of the squad were Cardiff products who had already proved themselves with previous Devils sides - **Neil Francis, Lee Cowmeadow, Richard Townsend**, and the only survivor from the previous year's Superleague Devils, **Rhodri Evans**.

When Devils lost 11-4 to Pirates, the game was played in front of an estimated 400 fans, the smallest crowd ever at a Devils' game.

A similar number remained outside, protesting at former chairman **Bob Phillips'** continued involvement and the unpaid players' wages and expenses from the previous campaign.

Southwick boosted the squad with ex-Hull goalie **Tom Noble**, former Belfast Giant **Jerry Keefe** and Basingstoke's top scorer **Albie O'Connell**. But even the likeable coach, a committed Christian who greeted Cardiffians with a cheery "good morning" on his daily jogs around Roath Park, could not win over the protesters.

Attendances dropped further, the local media virtually ignored the club and there was little interest from sponsors. Within weeks, Southwick was released as a cost-cutting measure, with Hazelhurst taking over as player-coach.

The best hope for a resolution came when GB coach **Chris McSorley** and his NHL star brother, **Marty**, emerged as potential buyers. Chris even brought the national team for a mid-week game against a Cardiff Select featuring Devils' players past and present. The match drew the biggest crowd of the season but the deal failed and the season got worse.

Keefe, O'Connell and the rest of the imports were released to save money, and the team was inevitably outclassed week after week.

PLAYER AWARDS

Players' Player	**Dan Madge**
Most Improved Player	**Dan Madge**
Defenceman of the Year	**Jason Stone**
Top Points Scorer	**Lee Cowmeadow**

LEADING PLAYERS

Lee Cowmeadow *born 24 August 1974*

The versatile Welshman returned home after eight years of travels, and landed himself the captaincy, once the imports had gone. He led by example, worked his socks off and topped the club scoring table by a mile.

Dan Madge *born 1 August 1982*

Cardiff had to do a lot of defending and that suited teenager Madge just fine. The junior international moved up from the under-19s and thrived under the pressure, collecting two awards into the bargain.

Jason Stone *born 30 December 1972*

The long-serving Devils' defenceman came back to Wales after a season at Guildford and proved a vital presence on the blue line. This was unlike any Cardiff side he had played on, but he remained his dependable self and contributed a useful tally of assists, too.

FACT FILE 2001-02

Findus **British National League:** 12th
Findus **Playoffs:** Did not qualify
Findus **Challenge Cup:** Third in group

HISTORY

Founded 1986.

Leagues *Findus* British National League 2001-02; *Sekonda* Superleague 1996-2001; British League, Premier Div. 1989-96; British League, Div. One 1987-89; British League, Div. Two 1986-87.

Honours *Sekonda* Superleague Playoff Champions in 1999; League and Championship winners in 1993-94, 1992-93, 1989-90; League winners in 1996-97; *Benson and Hedges* Cup winners 1992

MARK HAZELHURST, who took over as coach of Cardiff Devils halfway through their most difficult season to date. *Photo*: Chris Valentine

COVENTRY BLAZE

PLAYER	FINDUS BRITISH NATIONAL LEAGUE					FINDUS PLAYOFFS					ALL COMPETITIONS				
Scorers	GP	G	A	Pts	Pim	GP	G	A	Pts	Pim	GP	G	A	Pts	Pim
Claude Dumas	43	30	46	76	24	10	7	10	17	2	61	43	64	107	44
Steve Chartrand	44	32	34	66	39	10	7	4	11	2	62	45	47	92	47
Shaun Johnson	43	20	36	56	10	10	2	17	19	2	61	24	60	84	20
Steve Roberts (I) 3	37	39	25	64	52	10	10	7	17	0	49	50	33	83	54
Hilton Ruggles	44	25	33	58	68	10	6	6	12	28	62	37	45	82	106
Steve Carpenter	42	18	34	52	102	10	1	8	9	30	60	22	49	71	140
Stephen Cooper	44	9	34	43	79	10	6	6	12	10	62	17	47	64	107
Tom Watkins	44	16	20	36	30	10	4	5	9	0	62	26	28	54	34
Mike Shewan	44	4	32	36	8	10	1	8	9	2	61	7	42	49	12
Michael Tasker	41	12	12	24	85	10	5	1	6	16	59	18	17	35	107
Kurt Irvine	44	8	5	13	105	10	0	3	3	14	62	10	9	19	129
Mathais Soderstrom (I)	44	3	9	12	85	10	0	4	4	8	60	3	15	18	95
Michael Knights	29	3	5	8	36	10	0	2	2	4	45	4	9	13	67
Rob Eley	42	1	4	5	4	10	2	0	2	0	60	4	5	9	6
Shaun Yardley	40	3	0	3	8	10	0	0	0	0	58	4	1	5	16
Andrew McNiven (I)	1	2	0	2	2						3	2	3	5	2
James Pease	42	0	4	4	8	8	0	0	0	2	58	0	4	4	14
Russell Cowley 2	20	2	0	2	2	4	0	1	1	2	26	2	1	3	4
Ian Burt (N) (I)	44	0	3	3	4	10	0	0	0	2	62	0	3	3	6
Jordan Shields (I) 4	5	0	2	2	0						5	0	2	2	0
Barry Hollyhead (N) 1	42	0	1	1	2	10	0	0	0	0	60	0	1	1	2
Bench Penalties					10					2					14
TEAM TOTALS	44	227	339	566	765	10	51	82	133	126	62	318	485	803	1028
Netminders	GP	Mins	SOG	GA	Sv%	GP	Mins	SOG	GA	Sv%	GP	Mins	SOG	GA	Sv%
Barry Hollyhead 1	7	389	140	14	90.0	2	80	22	1	95.5	10	529	175	15	91.4
Ian Burt (I)	38	2289	927	103	88.9	9	520	217	20	90.8	54	3234	1280	139	89.1
Empty Net Goals		2	1	1								2	1	1	
TEAM TOTALS	44	2680	1068	118	89.0	10	600	239	21	91.2	62	3765	1456	155	89.4

Shutouts: Hollyhead (2) - cup: 6 Sept v Solihull Barons (13 saves),
league: 5 Jan v Cardiff Devils (8 saves)

Burt (3) - cup: 15 Sept at Guildford Flames (28 saves), league: 2 Feb at Milton Keynes
Kings (19 saves); playoffs: 3 March v Fife Flyers (20 saves)

Also played for: 1 Cardiff Devils; 2 Swindon Lynx; 3 Hull Thunder; 4 Peterborough Pirates
Also appeared: Ricky Ashton (N), Les Millie.

All Competitions = league, playoffs and Findus Cup

COVENTRY BLAZE *left to right*, *back row:* Phil Hadley (trainer), Steve Small (manager), Tom Watkins, Steve Carpenter, Claude Dumas, Andrew McNiven, James Pease, Rob Eley, Mike Shewan, Michael Knights, Mathias Soderstrom, Shaun Yardley, John Crook (equipment); *front row:* Ian Burt, Shaun Johnson, Stephen Cooper, Hilton Ruggles, Paul Thompson (coach), Steve Chartrand, Kurt Irvine, Michael Tasker, Barry Hollyhead.

Bridesmaids times three

ANTONY HOPKER

Bridesmaids in all three competitions, the *High and Mighty* Coventry Blaze can still look back at a season of progress on and off the ice.

A physical presence was added in **Steve Carpenter** from Superleague's Sheffield Steelers, while support at the Skydome steadily grew, hitting a record 2,624 in the final game.

Two young recruits from Cornell University showed promise: power forward **Andrew McNiven** impressed, but suffered a recurrence of a concussion and soon returned home; netminder **Ian Burt** improved throughout the season but was prone to letting in soft goals.

Hard-shooting **Steve Roberts** arrived in October and set Blaze alight with bags of goals. But Coventry developed a habit of needing overtime, or Blaze-time as it became known, to secure the points.

They recorded their first ever win in Fife to start a sweep of the Flyers in the league, but November proved the cruellest month. After fighting their way back from 3-0 down against Basingstoke to eventually win on penalties in the semi-finals of the *Findus* Challenge Cup, Coventry were brushed aside by Fife in the final.

The forwards lost form, prompting coach **Paul Thompson** to switch his lines around. "We can't tic-tac-toe it up the ice and walk it into the net - we're not good enough. We need to get in hard on the net and score those ugly goals," he said.

Roberts was put alongside **Shaun Johnson** and **Claude Dumas**, and they rained in goals. **Hilton Ruggles** also returned to form after playing through a hand injury that had sapped him early in the season.

The league slipped away, but Coventry breezed through the playoff groups before a heated semi-final against Guildford. When Blaze lost home advantage for the second leg, apparently at the insistence of the TV company filming the game, it stoked the passions for the first match.

Flames took the lead but a superlative performance from rock steady **Stephen Cooper** put Coventry back in charge. It was to be his penultimate home game as he announced his retirement at the end of the season.

"I'm fed up with coming second," said Thompson after a 7-4 home defeat to Dundee. "Some of our players didn't show up at all," he later complained.

Coventry nearly clawed their way back in the return leg - in front of 500 travelling fans - but a 3-1 scalp wasn't enough, and the trophy cabinet remained unordered.

PLAYER AWARDS

Players' Player	**Mathias Soderstrom**
Player of the Year	**Mathias Soderstrom**
Coach's Player	**Hilton Ruggles**
Best Forward	**Claude Dumas**
Best Defenceman	**Steve Carpenter**
Most Improved Player	**Shaun Yardley**
Best British Player	**Shaun Johnson**

LEADING PLAYERS

Stephen Cooper *born 11 November 1966*
A big game player to the last. His knack of scoring crucial goals at key moments almost single-handedly got Coventry into the playoff final. His steady play and vision kept Blaze afloat throughout the season.

Hilton Ruggles *born 1 June 1963*
His shooting may not be what it was, but he worked tirelessly around the boards and was the team's top penalty killer and scorer of game-winning goals.

The winger was forced to reinvent his game when he played through the early months with a hand injury that would have kept many others off the ice.

Michael Tasker *born 10 July 1973*
The engine room of the team and fearless leader of a third line that frequently made the difference between Blaze and other sides. A fans' hero after flooring Peterborough's hard man **Jesse Hammill**, the GB centreman was one of the best winners of face-offs and scored some big goals.

FACT FILE 2001-02

Findus **British National League**: Runners-up
Findus **Playoffs**: Finalists
Findus **Challenge Cup**: Finalists

HISTORY

Founded: 2000, after club moved from Solihull.
Leagues: *Findus* British National League 2000-02.

DUNDEE STARS

PLAYER	FINDUS BRITISH NATIONAL LEAGUE					FINDUS PLAYOFFS					ALL COMPETITIONS				
Scorers	GP	G	A	Pts	Pim	GP	G	A	Pts	Pim	GP	G	A	Pts	Pim
Tony Hand	44	25	79	104	18	10	7	17	24	4	60	39	106	145	28
Teeder Wynne WP	44	44	50	94	14	10	12	16	28	2	60	65	71	136	18
Scott Young	44	35	49	84	167	8	5	6	11	20	58	41	62	103	205
Jan Mikel WP	44	27	58	85	62	10	2	10	12	48	59	32	71	103	114
Patrick Lochi (I)	40	36	24	60	41	10	5	8	13	2	56	46	38	84	45
Martin Wiita (I)	43	17	49	66	6	10	2	4	6	0	59	23	60	83	6
Mikko Inkinen (I)	42	26	42	68	40	10	2	2	4	10	54	30	46	76	50
Paul Berrington	44	13	37	50	54	10	2	1	3	6	56	16	38	54	64
Craig Nelson (I)	43	17	21	38	50	10	0	2	2	10	59	19	28	47	74
Scott Kirton (I)	22	18	14	32	53						22	18	14	32	53
Slava Koulikov	42	12	11	23	38	10	0	1	1	0	58	16	14	30	38
Dominic Hopkins	38	13	7	20	10	10	0	1	1	2	54	14	8	22	12
Andy Finlay	44	4	10	14	12	10	1	1	2	2	60	5	11	16	28
Nate Leslie (I) 1	4	2	1	3	3						10	4	9	13	9
Stephen Murphy (N)	44	0	6	6	0	10	0	2	2	0	60	0	8	8	0
Gary Dowd	44	0	3	3	22	10	1	0	1	0	60	1	5	6	24
Trevor Doyle WP	1	0	0	0	4	10	3	2	5	24	11	3	2	5	28
Stewart Rugg (N)	44	0	2	2	2	10	0	0	0	0	60	0	2	2	2
Bench Penalties					24					2					32
TEAM TOTALS	44	289	463	752	620	10	42	73	115	132	60	372	593	965	832
Netminders	GP	Mins	SOG	GA	Sv%	GP	Mins	SOG	GA	Sv%	GP	Mins	SOG	GA	Sv%
Stephen Murphy	43	2359	1018	91	91.1	10	600	281	15	94.7	59	3285	1435	115	92.0
Stewart Rugg	10	289	98	10	89.8						12	323	113	12	89.4
TEAM TOTALS	44	2648	1116	101	90.9	10	600	281	15	94.7	60	3608	1548	127	91.8

Shutouts: Murphy (8) - cup: 15 Sept at Paisley Pirates (19 saves); league:* 27 Oct v Cardiff Devils (15 saves), *21 Nov v Paisley Pirates (21 saves), 2 Dec v Coventry Blaze (32 saves), *26 Jan at Cardiff Devils (3 saves); playoffs: 3 March v Milton Keynes Kings (14 saves), 9 March at Milton Keynes Kings (17 saves), 17 March v Guildford Flames (31 saves).

Rugg (3) - league: * 27 Oct v Cardiff Devils (5 saves), * 26 Jan at Cardiff Devils (12 saves), 3 Feb v Cardiff Devils (14 saves)   * shared

Also played for: 1 London Knights

Also appeared: Andrew Affleck, Tom Miller, Martyn Ford, Wayne Maxwell

All Competitions = league, playoffs and Findus Cup

Stars of their first season

IAN ROACHE, The Courier

So successful were Dundee *Texol* Stars in their rookie season, that even when they lost they won.

By the time they came to face-off in the second leg of the playoff final against Coventry Blaze at Dundee Ice Arena on 31 March, **Tony Hand**'s team had already claimed two crowns.

No one could touch them in the *Findus* BNL title race, with 40 wins out of 44, while the Caledonia (Scottish) Cup was in the trophy room thanks to a comfortable two-legged win over local rivals, Fife Flyers.

Only the *Findus* Challenge Cup eluded them but that was entirely excusable as the team had only been created in the summer.

When the men behind the formation of the club - brothers **Charlie, Mike** and **Steve Ward** - paraded Hand as their new player-coach it was a brave gamble. The Edinburgh native - one of Britain's all-time great players - had never coached at senior level before.

> "It's like playing with a bunch of your friends, the atmosphere is so good." *Stephen Murphy, Stars' goalie.* The Courier (Dundee).

He repaid their confidence by putting together a select, 15-man roster of talented skaters, many of whom he had played alongside at Superleague level.

There was **Teeder Wynne**, a former team-mate at Ayr and Sheffield, and defencemen **Scott Young** and skipper **Jan Mikel**, both from Eagles.

Much travelled forward **Paul Berrington** was a dual national 'find' and defender **Craig Nelson** and goalie **Stephen Murphy** came over from Fife Flyers. All three went on to international honours with GB. Local lads **Gary Dowd** and **Andy Finlay** were given regular shifts along with GB under-20 blueliner, **Dominic Hopkins** from Guildford Flames.

Another former Eagle, hard man **Trevor Doyle**, was signed as reinforcement for the playoffs when a 7-4 success in the Midlands set the scene for the climactic second leg of the final in the City of Discovery.

Dundee nerves were jangling as Blaze took a 3-1 lead and just needed one more strike for glory. Blaze battled away bravely but Murphy was the hero for the home side and Stars collected the newly minted John Brady Bowl.

PLAYER AWARDS

Players' Player:	**Martin Wiita**
Player of the Year:	**Scott Young**
Most Valuable Player:	**Stephen Murphy**
Top Points Scorer:	**Tony Hand**
Top Goal Scorer:	**Teeder Wynne**
Club Website Award:	**Scott Young**

LEADING PLAYERS

Tony Hand born *15 August, 1967*

It's still sinking in that the country's most talented player has all the tools to become one of its finest coaches. His deep understanding of the game and talent for picking the right players were his secrets. After a slow start, Stars rarely lost a game. We don't have room to mention here all the individual awards he collected.

Jan Mikel born *14 April, 1975*

Hand chose the 6ft, 2in former Czech international defender to captain the Stars as the pair played together at Superleague's Ayr. He proved his coach's faith in him with sound, all-round play, garnering 58 assists, third highest in the league, and a berth on the All-Star team.

Stephen Murphy born *11 December, 1981*

Only 20, but already in his fourth full senior season, he is one of the country's most exciting young talents. His value to the team could not be over-estimated as a barrow-load of man-of-the-match awards testified.

FACT FILE 2001-02

Findus **British National League:**	Winners
Findus **Playoffs:**	Champions
Findus **Challenge Cup:**	2nd in group
Caledonia Cup:	Winners

HISTORY

Founded: 2001.

Leagues: *Findus* British National League 2001-02.

Honours: *Findus* British National League 2001-02; *Findus* Playoffs 2001-02; Caledonia Cup 2002.

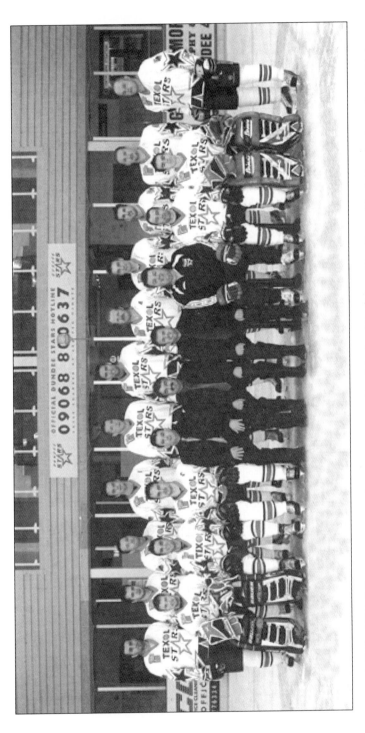

DUNDEE STARS *left to right, back row:* Patrick Lochi, Slava Koulikov, Paul Berrington, Craig Nelson, Trevor Doyle, Dominic Hopkins, Scott Young, Mikko Inkinen, Teeder Wynne, Martin Wiita, Gary Dowd; *front row:* Stewart Rugg, Andy Finlay, Jan Mikel, Mike Ward (director), Charlie Ward (director), Steven Ward (director), Roger Hunt (asst. coach), Tony Hand, Stephen Murphy.

Photo: Godfrey Mordente

EDINBURGH CAPITALS

PLAYER	FINDUS BRITISH NATIONAL LEAGUE					FINDUS PLAYOFFS					ALL COMPETITIONS				
Scorers	GP	G	A	Pts	Pim	GP	G	A	Pts	Pim	GP	G	A	Pts	Pim
Jason Lafreniere (I)	44	38	50	88	32	6	3	2	5	6	52	41	52	93	52
Noel Burkitt (I) 5	31	28	29	57	74	6	2	5	7	14	37	30	34	64	88
John Downes	42	17	29	46	8	6	3	2	5	12	54	20	32	52	22
Steven Lynch	44	14	27	41	34	6	0	5	5	6	56	16	36	52	42
Roland Carlsson (I)	43	12	27	39	44	6	2	2	4	16	49	14	29	43	60
Chris Dearden (I)	43	7	19	26	41	6	1	5	6	6	55	8	24	32	57
Rob Trumbley WP 4	28	13	14	27	67	4	0	2	2	38	32	13	16	29	105
Laurie Dunbar	44	11	15	26	9	6	0	1	1	2	50	11	16	27	11
Alan Hough	35	7	17	24	46	4	0	1	1	6	42	8	18	26	52
Craig Wilson	42	7	11	18	22	6	1	3	4	2	54	10	15	25	28
David Fry (I)	25	8	14	22	36						28	9	14	23	38
Mikko Koivunoro (I) 1	12	1	16	17	6						12	1	16	17	6
Andrew Coleman (I)	44	2	14	16	24	6	0	0	0	0	54	2	14	16	26
Samuli Mykkanen (I) 6	8	3	3	6	0	6	3	1	4	0	14	6	4	10	0
Gerad Adams (I)	17	6	4	10	99						17	6	4	10	99
Paddy Ward 8	33	0	7	7	10	4	0	0	0	0	38	0	7	7	12
Ron Shudra 2	7	3	1	4	2						9	3	1	4	4
Rob Simnor (I) 5	4	2	1	3	0						4	2	1	3	0
Steven Francey	8	0	0	0	0						14	1	1	2	4
Ross Hay	29	0	1	1	2	3	0	0	0	0	38	1	1	2	4
Ian Simpson	30	1	1	2	2	4	0	0	0	0	40	1	1	2	4
Neil Abel											2	0	1	1	2
Laurie Dunbar											6	0	1	1	4
David Beatson	3	0	0	0	0						9	0	1	1	4
Neil Hay	7	0	0	0	0	1	0	0	0	0	12	0	1	1	6
Bench Penalties															
TEAM TOTALS	44	180	300	480	576	6	15	29	44	114	56	203	340	543	760
Netminders	GP	Mins	SOG	GA	Sv%	GP	Mins	SOG	GA	Sv%	GP	Mins	SOG	GA	Sv%
Pasi Raitanen 7						6	360	243	29	88.1	6	360	243	29	88.1
Jason Crossland (I) 3	15	907	519	59	88.6						21	1237	745	97	87.0
Ryan Ford	27	1524	842	125	85.2						29	1554	863	129	85.1
Alastair Flockhart	5	214	119	25	79.0						5	214	119	25	79.0
Ken Forshall	1	14	1	0	100						1	14	1	0	100
Empty Net Goals		3	3	3								3	3	3	
TEAM TOTALS	44	2662	1484	212	85.7	6	360	243	29	88.1	56	3022	1731	254	85.7

Shutouts: Ford (2) - league: 11 Nov v Paisley Pirates (34 saves), 16 Dec v Cardiff Devils (20 saves).

Also played for: 1 Guildford Flames; 2 Sheffield Steelers; 3 Cardiff Devils, Swindon Lynx;
4 Hull Thunder; 5 Romford Raiders; 6 Solihull Barons; 7 Peterborough Pirates;
8 Ayr Scottish Eagles

Also appeared: Tristian Rogers (N), M Cooke, Alan Ward, Scott Neil, Scott Robertson,
Ricky Ashton (N), Mark McRae, Daniel McIntyre, Gary Hughes, Graeme Brown,
Fraser Croall (N), John Wilson, Sean Lamb, Gordon Nelson.

All Competitions = league, playoffs and Findus *Cup*

EDINBURGH CAPITALS *left to right, back row:* Ryan Ford, John Downes, Laurie Dunbar, Pasi Raitanen, Chris Deardon, Noel Burkitt, Roland Carlsson, Samuli Mykkanen, Andrew Coleman, Jason Lafreniere, Rob Trumbley; *front row:* Ian Simpson, Steven Lynch, Craig Wilson, Paddy Ward.

Photo: Jan Orkisz.

EDINBURGH CAPITALS

Steelers' Jason boosts Caps

Edinburgh Capitals bowed out of the season with a disappointing *Findus* British National League playoff defeat at home to arch-rivals, Fife Flyers.

But the fans witnessed another positive year for their favourites with improved attendances, boosted gate receipts and the best team seen at Murrayfield for some time.

Capitals achieved their objective of making the playoffs by claiming seventh spot in the 12-strong league table. But general manager **Scott Neil** was disappointed that they won only one of their six playoff games, ironically a 6-3 road victory at Hull Thunder.

"We were in a really tough group," he said. "We'd not beaten Coventry Blaze either home or away, and we'd only beaten Fife Flyers once, so it was always going to be difficult."

Neil stressed that the side were always competitive and that was his theme throughout a season in which he introduced former NHL forward, **Jason Lafreniere**, to Murrayfield.

LAFRENIERE JOY TO WATCH

The veteran Quebec, Tampa Bay and New York Rangers' playmaker - who was with Sheffield Steelers in their first Superleague season - was a joy to watch, his power, allied to his subtlety, lifting the team up the table.

His line-mates, **John Downes** and **Noel Burkitt**, certainly profited from having a player of his quality alongside them. And it was no surprise that the trio were the side's top three points scorers.

On the blueline, the retention of cultured **Roland Carlsson** after a loan spell from Superleague side, Newcastle, was an undoubted plus: the defenceman scored a number of crucial goals for the team.

Success was also achieved by the club's Scottish National League team who won the Grand Slam of league, Autumn Cup, Scottish Cup and Spring Cup.

Coach **Jock Hay**, the former Murrayfield legend, was in charge of the all-Scottish squad and he developed a strong pool of talented young players.

Sean Lamb, Jock's sons **Neil Hay** and his brother **Ross**, plus Stevie Francey and Mark McRae scored well over 100 goals between them, and goaltenders, **Ali Flockhart** and **Fraser Croall**, performed creditably.

PLAYER AWARDS
Players' Player — Jason Lafreniere
Player of the Year: — Jason Lafreniere
Supporters' Player: — Jason Lafreniere

LEADING PLAYERS
Roland Carlsson *born 7 July 1971*
A steady influence on defence and a key player in their league campaign. A blend of skill and experience, he was respected for his committment and professional attitude. Popular both with his teammates and the fans.

John Downes *born 26 May 1977*
A reliable and hard working forward, he played on Lafreniere's wing in his first season with Capitals and established himself as one of the league's best British players.

Jason Lafreniere *born 6 December 1966*
Skilled ex-NHLer who helped raise the game of his teammates and led the team in scoring. His worth was recognised by the Writers' Association who voted them to their second All-Star team - and from a team placed seventh in the league.

FACT FILE 2001-02
Findus **British National League:** Seventh
Findus **Playoffs:** 4th in group
Findus **Challenge Cup:** 2nd in qual. group
Scottish National League: Winners
Scottish Autumn Cup: Winners
Scottish Spring Cup: Winners
Scottish Cup: Winners

HISTORY (first team)
Founded: 1998. Known as Murrayfield Royals 1995-98 and 1952-66, Edinburgh Racers 1994-95 and Murrayfield Racers 1966-94.
Leagues: Capitals - *Findus* British National Lge 1998-2002; Royals - British National Lge 1997-98, Northern Premier Lge 1996-97, British Lge, Div One 1995-96, British Lge 1954-55, Scottish National Lge 1952-54; Racers - British Lge, Premier Div 1982-95, Northern Lge 1966-82.
Past Honours: Racers - See *The Ice Hockey Annual 1998-99.*

FIFE FLYERS

PLAYER	FINDUS BRITISH NATIONAL LEAGUE					FINDUS PLAYOFFS					ALL COMPETITIONS				
Scorers	GP	G	A	Pts	Pim	GP	G	A	Pts	Pim	GP	G	A	Pts	Pim
Todd Dutiaume (I)	44	32	48	80	96	8	3	6	9	4	52	35	54	89	100
Russell Monteith WP	42	44	40	84	6						42	44	40	84	6
Karry Biette (I)	42	27	37	64	80	8	6	6	12	10	50	33	43	76	90
Steven King	42	12	48	60	48	8	3	4	7	4	50	15	52	67	52
Frank Morris	44	25	25	50	32	8	3	4	7	8	52	28	29	57	40
Mark Morrison (I)	42	23	24	47	32	8	2	2	4	6	50	25	26	51	38
Mark Dutiaume (I) 1	30	21	26	47	26						30	21	26	47	26
Iain Robertson	43	15	22	37	26	8	2	5	7	8	51	17	27	44	34
Gary Wishart	44	7	15	22	10	8	1	2	3	2	52	8	17	25	12
Bob Quinnell WP	8	6	3	9	34	8	3	8	11	6	16	9	11	20	40
Derek King	43	3	10	13	32	8	0	0	0	0	51	3	10	13	32
Andy Samuel	44	2	9	11	6	8	0	1	1	0	52	2	10	12	6
Daryl Venters	43	2	6	8	12	8	2	0	2	2	51	4	6	10	14
Kyle Horne	43	3	4	7	16	8	0	1	1	2	51	3	5	8	18
Nick Poole 2	2	0	2	2	2	8	2	4	6	0	10	2	6	8	2
Shawn Silver (I) (N)	44	0	3	3	22	8	0	0	0	0	52	0	3	3	22
Chad Reekie	5	0	2	2	0	1	0	0	0	0	6	0	2	2	0
Gavin Holmes	18	0	1	1	25	1	0	0	0	0	19	0	1	1	25
Bench Penalties					2					0					2
TEAM TOTALS	44	222	325	547	507	8	27	43	70	52	60	298	430	728	647

Netminders	GP	Mins	SOG	GA	Sv%	GP	Mins	SOG	GA	Sv%	GP	Mins	SOG	GA	Sv%
Shawn Silver (I)	43	2478	1222	101	91.7	8	490	272	30	89.0	59	3429	1716	144	91.6
Colin Grubb	7	184	64	7	89.1						9	203	72	8	88.9
Empty Net Goals		2	2	2								2	2	2	
TEAM TOTALS	44	2664	1288	110	91.5	8	490	272	30	89.0	60	3634	1790	154	91.4

Shutouts: Silver (3) - league: 3 Nov v Slough Jets (17 saves), *15 Dec v Cardiff Devils (4 saves), * 22 Dec at Cardiff Devils (6 saves).

Grubb (2) - *15 Dec v Cardiff Devils (6 saves), *22 Dec at Cardiff Devils (7 saves).

Also played for: 1 Sheffield Steelers; 2 Peterborough Pirates

Also appeared: Tom Muir, Adam Walker, Paul Wood.

All Competitions = league, playoffs and Findus Cup

Missing Monty

ALLAN CROW

Another season and more silverware, but for Fife Flyers there was the nagging feeling that it could have yielded more.

Mark Morrison returned for a ninth consecutive season in Kirkcaldy and bolstered his team with proven hockey players - the evergreen **Frank Morris**, the razor-sharp **Todd Dutiaume** and the outstanding **Russell Monteith**.

Three times Grand Slammer, **Karry Biette**, was added late in the summer and switched to defence, while Dutiaume's younger brother, Mark, joined his London Knights' team-mate, **Shawn Silver**, north of the border.

The season started with a capacity crowd and the rebirth of the Fife-Dundee derby which has a pedigree spanning six decades.

Fife won 3-2, but Stars were to be their nemesis as the season reached its climax, taking the Caledonia Cup from them, and eliminating them from the semi-finals of the playoffs.

MORRISON WINS COACHING BATTLE

Flyers scored one win on Dundee ice - the only team to do so - to dump Stars out of the *Findus* Challenge Cup, and in November they went to the Cup final and produced their finest hour, crushing Coventry Blaze 6-3.

Morrison won the coaching battle while his on-ice leader, the never-say-die Biette, produced a stunning solo goal to set the Nottingham Ice Centre alight.

In the league Fife were always in the top three, but, like everyone else, found Stars' consistency just too hot to handle.

Their four-man defence put in some sterling work with **Derek King** immense and Morris a model of consistency, while Silver enjoyed a solid season between the pipes.

Mark Dutiaume was cut mid-season and went to Sheffield, while blueliner **Bob Quinnell** was added. Fife remained on course for the playoffs .. until a knee injury in a nothing league game in Milton Keynes ended Monteith's season.

Playmaker **Nick Poole** had already signed up for the post-season schedule, and after watching him skate many fans were left wondering how well he would have complemented 'Monty'.

In the end the loss of the league's best centreman was too much for the team to overcome.

PLAYER AWARDS
No details supplied

LEADING PLAYERS

Karry Biette *born 24 February 24 1973*
Every team needs an on-ice leader like Karry - tenacious, tough, talented and willing to skate for every second of every shift. The converted defender made the *Findus* Challenge Cup final the 'Biette final' with an inspirational goal. Knows what it takes to win.

Derek King *born 5 June 1970*
A cornerstone of the team, he played through the pain barrier last season and turned in a string of excellent performances.

One of the league's most experienced home-based defencemen, he is a fine exponent of the dying art of the poke check.

Frank Morris *born 22 March 1963*
The super-fit 38-year-old rearguard breezed through the season with dedication and commitment. After 15 seasons in Britain, he still finds the net and reads the game superbly from the blue line.

He's enjoying his hockey more now than ever, so expect him to play on as long as he can bend down to lace up his skates!

FACT FILE 2001-02
Findus **British National League**: Third
Findus **Playoffs**: Semi-finalists
Findus **Challenge Cup**: Winners
Caledonia Cup: Finalists

HISTORY
Founded: 1938.

Leagues: (*Findus*) British National League (BNL) 1997-2002; Northern Premier League (NPL) 1996-97; British League 1982-96, 1954-55; Northern League (NL) 1966-82; Scottish National League (SNL) 1981-82, 1946-54, 1938-40.

Major Honours:
British Champions 1985. *Leagues*: BNL 1999-2000; NPL 1997-98, 1996-97; British Lge, Div. One 1991-92; NL 1976-78; SNL 1951-52, 1939-40. *Playoffs*: BNL 1999-2000, 1998-99. *Findus* Challenge Cup: 2001-02; *Autumn Cup*: 1978, 1976, 1975; Scottish - 1950, 1948. *Scottish Cup*: 2001, 2000, 1999, 1998, 1995, 1994.

FIFE FLYERS *left to right*, *back row*: Derek King, Daryl Venters, Karry Biette, Iain Robertson, Mark Morrison; *middle row*: Alan Wishart (trainer), Allan Anderson (asst. coach), Mark Dutiaume, Russell Monteith, Todd Dutiaume, Gavin Holmes, Paul Wood, Alan Grubb (equipment); *front row*: Shawn Silver, Steven King, Frank Morris, Andy Samuel, Ricky Grubb.

Photo: Nikki McLeod

GUILDFORD FLAMES

PLAYER	FINDUS BRITISH NATIONAL LEAGUE					FINDUS PLAYOFFS					ALL COMPETITIONS				
Scorers	GP	G	A	Pts	Pim	GP	G	A	Pts	Pim	GP	G	A	Pts	Pim
Mikko Koivunoro (I) 1	29	17	44	61	36	8	0	5	5	20	37	17	49	66	56
Derek DeCosty (I)	40	36	24	60	36	3	0	0	0	0	43	36	24	60	36
Todd Wetzel (I)	38	24	31	55	60	7	2	3	5	4	45	26	34	60	64
John Haig	44	20	29	49	16	8	1	4	5	4	52	21	33	54	20
Nicky Chinn	38	11	38	49	94	8	0	1	1	24	46	11	39	50	118
Jason Dailey WP	44	18	15	33	52	8	3	2	5	8	52	21	17	38	60
David Smith	44	10	17	27	20	8	2	2	4	2	52	12	19	31	22
Rick Plant	43	7	17	24	67	8	1	2	3	0	51	8	19	27	67
Scott Campbell (I)	26	5	18	23	67	7	1	3	4	20	33	6	21	27	87
Jason Jennings (I)	12	8	9	17	6	8	5	4	9	2	20	13	13	26	8
Greg Burke (I) 6	30	9	15	24	76						30	9	15	24	76
Tony Redmond	39	8	10	18	10	8	1	0	1	18	47	9	10	19	28
Kent Nobes (I)	15	9	5	14	2						15	9	5	14	2
Mitch Grant (I) 2	12	6	4	10	2	7	0	1	1	0	19	6	5	11	2
Paul Dixon	26	1	9	10	16	8	1	0	1	8	34	2	9	11	24
Stan Marple	24	4	5	9	88	6	0	0	0	4	30	4	5	9	92
Robert Lamey 3	15	1	6	7	4						15	1	6	7	4
Ian Defty 7	15	1	4	5	22	6	0	0	0	2	21	1	4	5	24
Regan Stocco	21	1	2	3	26						21	1	2	3	26
Michael Plenty	6	0	2	2	0	3	0	0	0	0	9	0	2	2	0
Jason Stone 5	4	1	0	1	32						4	1	0	1	32
Mark Galazzi	32	1	0	1	2	8	0	0	0	2	40	1	0	1	4
James Morgan 4	7	0	1	1	14						7	0	1	1	14
Mark McArthur (I) (N)	44	0	1	1	32	8	0	0	0	4	52	0	1	1	36
TEAM TOTALS	44	198	306	504	780	8	17	27	44	122	57	240	368	608	1012
Netminders	GP	Mins	SOG	GA	Sv%	GP	Mins	SOG	GA	Sv%	GP	Mins	SOG	GA	Sv%
Mark McArthur (I)	42	2551	1395	132	90.5	8	488	275	23	91.6	55	3339	1834	166	90.9
Grant King	2	120	44	8	81.8						2	120	44	8	81.8
Empty Net Goals		4	4	4								4	4	4	
TEAM TOTALS	44	2675	1443	144	90.0	8	488	275	23	91.6	57	3463	1882	178	90.5

Shutouts: McArthur - league: 4 Nov v Cardiff Devils (26 saves),
23 Dec v Milton Keynes Kings (26 saves);
playoffs: 9 March at Basingstoke Bison (51 saves)

Also played for: 1 Edinburgh Capitals; 2 Slough Jets; 3 Basingstoke Bison; 4 Bracknell Bees;
5 Cardiff Devils; 6 London Knights; 7 Hull Thunder

Also appeared: Mike Thomas, Chris Wiggins, Jamie Hepburn, Mike Timms, Alex Field (N).

All Competitions = league, playoffs and Findus Cup

GUILDFORD FLAMES *left to right, back row:* Mike Urquhart (asst coach), Michael Timms, Mark Galazzi, Todd Wetzel, Regan Stocco, Ricky Plant, Greg Burke, Kent Nobes, Jason Dailey, Stan Marple, Adrian Jenkinson (trainer/medic/equipment); *front row:* Mark McArthur, David Smith, Derek DeCosty, Paul Dixon, Malcolm Norman (managing director), Nicky Chinn, Rob Lamey, John Haig, Grant King.

Fifth after five

GARY CHAPPELL

After arguably their most successful season since their formation in 1992, Guildford Flames shockingly ended up empty-handed.

On paper they should have added yet more silverware to their growing trophy cabinet after securing the Triple in 2000-01, but head coach, **Stan Marple**, admitted his *Findus* BNL side, packed with former Superleague stars, under-achieved.

Marple - back for his fifth season in the coaching hot-seat - was up against it from the word go. The fans had been given a taste of success and were expecting more.

But the Surrey side had strong competition, especially new club, Dundee Stars, whose coach, **Tony Hand**, had recruited many top ISL players.

Coventry Blaze were always going to be tough, too, so Marple set about signing some big name players himself.

Perhaps his key acquisition was Finnish hotshot, **Mikko Koivunoro**, as Flames benefited from the demise of ISL's Newcastle Jesters.

But Guildford had lost two veteran players through retirement at the start of the campaign. First was 'Mr Guildford', **Ryan Campbell**, then **Wayne (Reggie) Crawford** called it a day at the age of 40.

Marple's new crop of players did not live up to expectations and frustrations began to show. Even returning netminder, **Mark McArthur**, was having a nightmare season after impressing in his debut year.

There were many inconsistent results, with Flames losing at home 4-3 to rejuvenated Paisley Pirates, 6-4 to the surprising Edinburgh Capitals, and 3-0 to local rivals, Slough Jets.

Marple's cause was not helped when he lost **Jason Jennings** to a freak domestic accident - while cutting down a tree in his garden, he almost sliced off a finger.

The club's top scorer in the 2000-01 playoffs refused treatment and flew home to Canada. Though not expected back, he recovered in time to return and help Flames secure their best run of the season, reaching the semi-finals of the league playoffs.

There, though, Guildford were paired with Dundee, one of their fiercest rivals, who had won the league title. Flames lost 3-2 at home and 3-0 at Camperdown.

Marple, who chose to watch the Superleague finals in Nottingham rather than the Dundee-Coventry *Findus* BNL final, said he had learned more about personnel this season than in his whole career as a coach.

PLAYER AWARDS
Players' Player — **Paul Dixon**
Best British Trained Player — **Paul Dixon**
Most Sportsmanlike Player — **Tony Redmond**
Top Points Scorer — **Derek DeCosty**
Supporters' Player of the Year — **Jason Dailey**
Supporters' British Player — **John Haig**

LEADING PLAYERS
Jason Dailey   born 15 February 1976
Marple targeted the blueliner after his dazzling debut season with rivals, Slough Jets. His belief in the player paid off as he bagged 38 points, including 21 goals, in 52 games.

Derek DeCosty   born 4 January 1968
One of Guildford's most consistent and popular forwards, he proved it again by netting 36 goals in 43 matches and was beaten to the league scoring crown by just one point. Deco's experience and leadership were badly missed when injury kept him out of the playoffs.

Paul Dixon   born 4 August 1973
Mr Reliable on the blueline picked up two club awards and was selected for his eighth consecutive World Championships.

"Second place is first place for losers." **Stan Marple**, agreeing with his critics that Flames had a disappointing season. Ice Hockey News.

FACT FILE 2001-02
Findus **British National League**: Fifth
Findus **Playoffs**: Semi-finalists
Findus **Challenge Cup** 2nd in group

HISTORY
Founded: 1992.
Leagues: (*Findus*) British National League (BNL) 1997-2002; Premier League (PL) 1996-97; British League, Div. One 1993-96; English League 1992-93.
Honours: BNL and Playoffs 2000-01, 1997-98; *ntl* Cup 2000-01; B&H Plate 1998-99.

HARINGEY GREYHOUNDS

PLAYER	ENGLISH PREMIER LEAGUE					ALL COMPETITIONS				
Scorers	GP	G	A	Pts	Pim	GP	G	A	Pts	Pim
Rob Cole	23	7	20	27	20	30	11	23	34	26
Danny Farren	22	5	21	26	26	28	7	26	33	26
Zoran Kozic	8	9	5	14	68	11	10	6	16	68
Sergejs Kravchenko	19	7	8	15	34	26	7	9	16	34
Alexei Eskine (I)	16	4	6	10	41	21	4	11	15	41
Gary Dodds	21	6	4	10	2	29	9	4	13	8
Nicholas Burton	9	7	2	9	14	11	8	3	11	14
Stephen Fullan (I)	22	5	4	9	40	30	5	5	10	46
Glenn Hammer (I) 1	12	3	5	8	56	18	3	5	8	101
Andrew Sillitoe	14	2	4	6	45	21	2	5	7	49
Ryan Mair (I)	6	3	0	3	92	8	6	0	6	92
Jan Bestic	18	3	2	5	0	21	4	2	6	0
Kwabina Oppong-Addai	10	2	2	4	28	14	3	3	6	36
Anthony Child 2	4	2	3	5	87	5	2	3	5	87
Roger Black	24	1	4	5	26	32	1	4	5	26
Ian Clark	24	1	1	2	89	31	1	2	3	89
Brian Clark	25	0	1	1	51	33	0	3	3	55
Grim Grastad (I)	3	1	0	1	2	5	1	1	2	2
Bradley Beck-Hill	2	0	2	2	0	3	0	2	2	0
Timo Ojasto (I)	8	0	2	2	2	9	0	2	2	2
Deavon Clayton	10	0	2	2	22	11	0	2	2	22
Michael Palin						1	1	0	1	0
Michael Savaria						1	0	1	1	0
James Grimstead 2	2	0	0	0	8	5	0	1	1	8
Tom Wills (N) (I)	9	0	0	0	0	10	0	1	1	0
TEAM TOTALS	25	68	98	166	797	33	85	124	209	944
Netminders	GPI	Min	SOG	GA	Sv%	GPI	Min	SOG	GA	Sv%
Tom Wills (I)	8	408	416	54	87.02	8	408	416	54	87.02
Robert Sheldrake	3	120	84	11	86.90	3	120	84	11	86.90
Chris Douglas 2	2	120	93	10	89.25	3	134	111	15	86.49
Nathan Lawrence	10	449	402	77	80.85	15	719	630	119	81.11
Damien Orr 3	8	403	281	59	79.00	12	599	467	94	79.87
TEAM TOTALS	25	1500	1276	211	83.46	33	1980	1708	293	82.84

Also played for: 1 Invicta Dynamos; 2 Romford Raiders; 3 Isle of Wight Raiders

Also appeared: Gary Organ, James Hatfull, Mark McDonald (I), Tom Clark.

All Competitions = league and Premier Cup

Back in the Black

MARTIN BENTLEY

Haringey Greyhounds began the 2001-02 season with a 5-2 win over the Lions in Nottingham back in early September.

Unfortunately, that was as good as it got. A disastrous season saw them lose every other game to finish bottom of the Premier League.

Things had started in a blaze of optimism as player-coach and team owner, **Zoran Kozic**, had put together a sponsorship package aimed at making the amateur Greyhounds competitive.

In came high profile signings such as ex-Chelmsford and Swindon forward **Ryan Mair**, Norwegian duo **Glenn Hammer** and **Grim Grastad**, and British players of the quality of **Anthony Child** and ex-Milton Keynes' winger **Danny Farren**.

However, the team failed to gel and Greyhounds suffered heavy defeats against the Isle of Wight (4-12) and Invicta (4-9). Moreover, in the early season they went through bench coaches faster than most teams go through stick tape, with **Erskine Douglas** and **Lenny Cole** each lasting barely a fortnight.

Then a series of disasters in October and November endangered the club's very existence. An horrendous 17-1 home defeat by Romford in the cup was swiftly followed by the departure of Child, **James Grimstead** and goalie **Chris Douglas** to their local rivals.

Three weeks later Kozic, Greyhounds' most talented player, received a 12-month ban for slashing Romford's **Marc Long** during the teams' next encounter. A couple of weeks later he announced that there was no more finance available, and left.

For a few horrible days it looked as though the team would join the depressing list of clubs to have gone belly-up in mid-season.

But new owner, defenceman **Roger Black** - a cousin of Nottingham Panthers' owner **Neil Black** - signed former Greyhounds, Canadian goalie **Tom Wills** and Finn **Nick Burton**, and they began the long climb back to respectability.

Wills, 35, performed miracles against superior opposition, the new first line of Burton, Farren and **Rob Cole** began to trouble teams at the other end of the rink, and club stalwarts **Steve Fullan**, the Clark brothers and **Gary Dodds**, were models of consistency.

They were unable, however, to stem the never-ending procession of defeats, and the wooden spoon position was confirmed three games from the end of the season.

PLAYER AWARDS

Most Valuable Player　　　　　Danny Farren

LEADING PLAYERS

Danny Farren *born 5 February 1979*
Talented British winger who stuck by his team while players were quitting left, right and centre. Formed part of a decent first line later in the season with **Nick Burton** and **Rob Cole**, and always played the game with a smile on his face.

Steve Fullan *born 24 February 1968*
In his fourth and, sadly, final season as a Greyhound, Steve was once again a model of unobtrusive consistency on the blue line.

He also captained the team, helped out with the coaching and still found time to score a two-minute hat-trick in a game on the Isle of Wight!

Tom Wills *born 16 September 1966*
When the team's fortunes were at their lowest ebb, they sent once again for the amiable 35-year-old former University of Toronto keeper to help them out. Though he couldn't single-handedly stop their losing run, he kept the scores respectable when the team looked in danger of a hammering.

FACT FILE 2001-02

English Premier League:	8th
Playoffs:	Did not qualify
English Premier Cup:	5th in group

HISTORY

Founded: 1990. (Haringey Racers were Alexandra Palace's senior team in 1990-92).
Leagues: English (Premier) League 1994-2002; English Conference 1991-94; English Div. Three 1990-91.
Honours: English Div. One South 1999-2000.

HARINGEY GREYHOUNDS *left to right, back row:* Loretta Wroe (official), Martin Bentley (official), Roger Black, Glenn Hammer, Ryan Mair, James Hatfull, Deavon Clayton, Sergejs Kravchenko, Alexei Eskine, Ian Clark, Tom Clark, Andrew Sillitoe, A Muckle (equipment), Harvey Wroe (club sec.), Sarah Harris (physio); *front row:* Damien Orr, Brian Clark, Danny Farren, Anthony Child, Zoran Kozic, Rob Sheldrake, Gary Dodds, Grim Garstad, Steve Fullan, Jan Bestic, Nathan Lawrence.

HULL THUNDER

PLAYER	FINDUS BRITISH NATIONAL LEAGUE					FINDUS PLAYOFFS					ALL COMPETITIONS				
Scorers	GP	G	A	Pts	Pim	GP	G	A	Pts	Pim	GP	G	A	Pts	Pim
Corey Lyons	41	31	46	77	20	6	3	3	6	2	52	36	52	88	34
Steve Smillie 7	36	34	37	71	38	4	4	3	7	8	40	38	40	78	46
Daryl Lavoie (I)	40	8	56	64	102	6	1	2	3	35	51	10	59	69	153
Anthony Johnson	42	18	31	49	36	6	2	4	6	10	53	23	38	61	50
Eric Lavigne WP	42	14	35	49	163	5	0	1	1	8	48	14	36	50	171
Mark Florence	38	15	19	34	8	6	1	2	3	0	46	16	21	37	8
Oleg Synkov WP 9	23	10	13	23	2	6	2	2	4	2	29	12	15	27	4
Stephen Johnson	34	3	17	20	40	6	2	1	3	4	45	7	20	27	60
Darren Houghton (I) 5	27	10	11	21	22	3	1	1	2	2	30	11	12	23	24
Doug McEwen 2	11	7	10	17	6	6	1	2	3	2	17	8	12	20	8
Stephen Wallace	40	11	3	14	10	6	0	0	0	2	51	14	4	18	12
Mike Bishop (I)	29	6	9	15	44	6	1	0	1	16	38	8	10	18	68
Michael Bowman	42	6	6	12	6	5	0	1	1	0	52	7	11	18	6
Anthony Payne	19	6	8	14	66						24	6	12	18	74
Ryan Lake	31	3	3	6	16	6	0	1	1	2	41	4	4	8	24
Ian Defty 8	21	1	6	7	30						26	1	7	8	48
Karl Hopper	44	3	1	4	36	6	0	0	0	12	55	3	2	5	50
Steve Roberts (I) 3	2	3	1	4	0						2	3	1	4	0
Rob McCaig (I)	5	1	0	1	79						10	3	1	4	137
Stephen Foster (N) 6	35	0	3	3	4						36	0	3	3	4
Paul Wallace	11	0	1	1	30						16	0	2	2	46
Andrew Munroe	41	0	2	2	12	6	0	0	0	0	52	0	2	2	14
Bench Penalties					14										2	16
TEAM TOTALS	44	190	318	508	788	6	18	23	41	107	57	224	364	588	1061
Netminders	GP	Mins	SOG	GA	Sv%	GP	Mins	SOG	GA	Sv%	GP	Mins	SOG	GA	Sv%
Stephen Foster 6	35	2116	1224	115	90.6						36	2176	1263	118	90.7
Bill Russell (I) 10	4	243	123	14	88.6						4	243	123	14	88.6
Greg Rockman	4	240	159	18	88.7						4	240	159	18	88.7
Clint Owen (I) 9						6	370	235	33	86.0	6	370	235	33	86.0
Andy Moffat 1	1	60	43	8	81.4						5	300	169	27	84.0
Sam Roberts	1	10	2	1	50.0						1	10	2	1	50.0
Empty Net Goals		5	5	5								5	5	5	
TEAM TOTALS	44	2674	1556	161	89.7	6	370	235	33	86.0	57	3344	1956	216	89.0

Shutouts: Foster - league: 26 Jan v Peterborough Pirates (29 saves);
Rockman - league: 23 Feb at Slough Jets (34 saves)

Also played for: 1 Isle of Wight Raiders; 2 P'borough Pirates; 3 Coventry Blaze; 4 Edinburgh Capitals;
5 Cardiff Devils; 6 Basingstoke Bison, Milton Keynes Kings; 7 Milton Keynes Kings
8 Guildford Flames; 9 Paisley Pirates; 10 Slough Jets

Also appeared: Scott Robertson, Karl Holmes, Rob Trumbley WP (4), Kenny Johnson (N),
Tristan Rogers (N), Phil Miles (N), Paul Windridge, Ben Milhench

All Competitions = league, playoffs and Findus *Cup*

HULL THUNDER *left to right, back row:* Vanessa Brown (physio), Ryan Lake, Andy Munroe, Steve Smillie, Karl Hopper, Mike Bishop (coach), Eric Lavigne, Corey Lyons, Stephen Wallace, Michael Bowman, Mark Florence, Al Cross (sponsor), Terry Ward (bench coach); *front row:* Andy Moffat, Anthony Payne, Stephen Johnson, Martin Jenkinson (director), Anthony Johnson, Mike O'Connor (director), Ian Defty, Daryl Lavoie, Stephen Foster.

Photo: Arthur Foster.

Thunder at new dawn?

CATHY WIGHAM

Hopefully the 2001-02 campaign marked a watershed in Hull ice hockey's turbulent history. After years of false financial dawns, the senior team finally seemed to have got its act together.

On the face of it, finishing sixth in the league and without a playoff semi-final place was hardly a great deal to crow about. In fact, Thunder appeared to be in exactly the same position as they were in the 2000-01 season.

However, that's like saying chalk is like cheese. The uncertainty and financial disharmony of 2000-01 gave way to calm and order in 2001-02. For starters there were on-time pay cheques, no embarrassing scenes of players demanding cash on match nights and a full team to finish the season.

The optimism was palpable, thanks largely to new owner, **Martin Jenkinson**, and his sidekick, **Mike O'Connor**. They only arrived after a tortuous summer ownership wrangle involving rival bids from then owner **Darren Brown**, general manager, **Mike Grantham**, and local player, **Anthony Payne**.

With Brown at the helm the season started a week late due to an argument over an unpaid bill belonging to former general manager, **Glenn Meier**. Even so there was optimism with a handful of imports - **Daryl Lavoie, Rob McCaig**, newly installed player-coach, **Mike Bishop**, and **Corey Lyons** - plus Brits like **Johnson** brothers, **Anthony** and **Stephen**, Anthony Payne, **Stephen Wallace, Mike Bowman, Ian Defty, Karl Hopper and Andy Munroe**.

It was just like the good old days with bust-a-gut Brits battering away at import-laden teams. **Stephen Foster** replaced **Eoin McInerney**, who had defected to Sheffield before signing on the dotted line, and **Steve Smillie** also arrived mid-season.

In between, Jenkinson and O'Connor replaced the outgoing Brown. By the end of October McCaig's lengthy suspension had led to his sacking and by Christmas, Defty and Payne were replaced by **Oleg Synkov** and **Darren Houghton**.

On paper the signings did strengthen the team, but on the ice the results were mixed. Dundee proved too tough a nut to crack, although Thunder did rattle off victories over Coventry, Basingstoke and Guildford - and there was a loss to Cardiff.

Thunder's playoff ambitions were wrecked by an unfortunate knee injury to Foster and they bowed out at the group stages.

PLAYER AWARDS

Player of the Year	**Stephen Foster**
Coach's Player	**Anthony Johnson**
Best Forward	**Steve Smillie**
Best Defenceman	**Daryl Lavoie**
Most Improved Player	**Ryan Lake**
Spirit of the Game	**Ryan Lake**

LEADING PLAYERS

Stephen Foster *born 1 January 1974*
Saved Thunder's bacon on too many occasions for comfort, when an AWOL defence hung him out to dry. Consistent game in, game out, the affable Durham-born keeper's signing was a Godsend in October.

Anthony Johnson *born 4 January 1969*
The sun might be setting on a 'been there, seen it, done it, got the T-shirt' career domestically and internationally, but the forward is still a key player. Started slowly, but then got better and better, making up in heart what he lacked in height.

Daryl Lavoie *born 10 January 1974*
An outstanding campaign from the Canadian who signed in the close season from Superleague's Nottingham.

Thunder's defenceman of the year, whose silky skating skills, stick handling and speed reminded Thunder watchers of former fans' favourite **Kelly Reed**. Made Thunder tick both in defence and in attack.

FACT FILE 2001-02
***Findus** British National League:* 6th
***Findus** Playoffs:* 3rd in qr-final group
***Findus** Challenge Cup:* 3rd in group

HISTORY
Founded: February 1999. The first club in Hull was Humberside Seahawks 1988-96 (known as Humberside Hawks 1993-96). Second club was Kingston Hawks 1996-99 (briefly Hull City Hawks 1998-99).
Leagues: *Hull* - British National League 1999-2002; *Kingston* - British National Lge 1997-99, Premier Lge 1996-97; *Humberside* - British Lge, Premier Div. 1991-96, British Lge, Div. One 1989-91, English Lge 1988-96.
Honours: British League, Div. One 1990-91; English League 1988-89.

INVICTA DYNAMOS

PLAYER	ENGLISH PREMIER LEAGUE					PLAYOFFS					ALL COMPETITIONS				
Scorers	GP	G	A	Pts	Pim	GP	G	A	Pts	Pim	GP	G	A	Pts	Pim
Matt Beveridge (I)	26	25	34	59	10	6	3	2	5	2	50	41	51	92	24
Mikko Skinnari (I)	26	21	37	58	8	6	1	6	7	0	47	29	58	87	14
Duane Ward (I)	20	20	24	44	50	6	2	4	6	10	43	38	42	80	131
Andy Hannah	23	18	27	45	66	6	3	0	3	16	47	37	32	69	170
Mike Kindred	24	14	16	30	14	6	2	5	7	0	48	23	36	59	22
Elliot Andrews	25	18	17	35	14	6	1	4	5	2	48	24	32	56	40
Phil Chard	25	9	19	28	22	6	1	2	3	2	49	10	29	39	30
Jake French	26	6	3	9	34	6	1	3	4	2	50	9	12	21	48
Sean Clement	21	4	9	13	32	5	1	1	2	12	39	8	12	20	70
Carl Greenhous	22	4	9	13	20	6	1	0	1	2	45	6	13	19	32
Paul Hume	26	6	3	9	8	6	1	0	1	2	50	8	7	15	18
Kevin Parrish	25	0	4	4	4	6	0	0	0	0	47	2	5	7	8
Peter Korff	25	1	3	4	4	6	0	0	0	0	49	1	5	6	69
Jonathan Gray	23	1	3	4	2	3	0	0	0	0	42	2	3	5	6
Greg Hales	26	2	0	2	0	6	0	0	0	0	50	2	0	2	4
Matt van der Velden (N)	24	0	2	2	2	6	0	0	0	0	48	0	2	2	2
TEAM TOTALS	26	149	210	359	298	6	17	27	44	50	50	240	339	579	688
Netminders	GPI	Min	SOG	GA	Sv%	GPI	Min	SOG	GA	Sv%	GPI	Min	SOG	GA	Sv%
Matt van der Velden	16	930	527	60	88.61	6	360	189	11	94.18	38	2226	1295	124	90.42
Adam Noctor	11	630	297	32	89.23						14	774	371	38	89.76
Empty Net Goals														1	1
TEAM TOTALS	26	1560	824	92	88.83	6	360	189	11	94.18	50	3000	1667	163	90.22

Shutouts: van der Valden - playoffs: 10 March v Romford Raiders (34 saves)

Also played for: 1 Haringey Greyhounds

Also appeared: Glenn Hammer (I) 1

All Competitions = league, playoffs, Premier Cup and Findus Challenge Cup

Nothing for 10 years, then two come along at once

ANDY BRADLEY

Polishing silverware has become an occupational therapy for the Dynamos after they completed a pleasing double for the first time in their history.

They thrilled crowds at the Ice Bowl, Gillingham, by winning the English Premier League crown and then the Playoffs to emerge as true champions.

The Kent club had never won either title before though their predecessors, the Medway Bears, did the same double just ten years ago.

But Dynamos' hopes of completing the treble came to grief when they were pipped 9-7 on aggregate by their local rivals, Romford Raiders, in the Premier Cup final.

"Right from the start we set our sights on the treble and we came close to achieving our target," reflected team captain, **Phil Chard**.

"We had our backs against the wall on more occasions than I can remember, yet we still came up with the results when it mattered most, apart from the very last game."

While retaining the cream of the previous season's crop, four new players were added to the roster. And thanks to the sponsorship provided by *Kelly Packaging,* they were not run-of-the-mill journeymen but seasoned and accomplished craftsmen.

Andy Hannah returned to the Ice Bowl from Chelmsford, **Jake French** and import **Duane Ward** were also former Chieftains, and **Carl Greenhous** was signed from Romford.

This quality quartet improved the team's ability on defence and in attack. Many players were now capable of sticking the puck in the net and one night in November they did, in a sensational 11-4 home victory over the Isle of Wight.

The game set a new club scoring record as they netted four times in the space of 54 seconds midway through the second period.

Winning at home and picking up as many road points as possible was Dynamos' recipe for success, exactly as their player-manager, **Sean Clement**, had predicted. It looked like they would do just that until they were humbled 6-2 in the Ice Bowl by main title rivals, Solihull Barons, in January.

The result briefly opened up possibilities for the other teams but, although five had an interest in the championship chase, it eventually boiled down to a straight two-horse race between Solihull and the Dynamos. The Kent side ultimately clinched the crown by winning 5-2 at Haringey in their penultimate fixture.

PLAYER AWARDS

Players' Player:	Mike Kindred
Best Forward:	Matt Beveridge
Best Defenceman:	Matt Van Der Velden
Supporters' Player:	Mikko Skinnari
Booster Club Player:	Carl Greenhous
Best British Player:	Jake French
'Mr Dynamo':	Phil Chard

LEADING PLAYERS

Carl Greenhous born *28 October 1972*
The ex-Romford and Chelmsford player was one of the reasons Invicta were stronger on defence. In his debut season at the Ice Bowl he produced consistently solid displays.

Mikko Skinnari born *14 September 1975*
The popular Finnish forward returned for a fourth successive season and was more impressive than ever. Recognised as a genuine maker and taker of chances, he notched nearly 90 points in all competitions with dazzling bursts of speed and slick stickwork.

Matt van der Velden born *21 August 1979*
The young British netminder, signed from Romford two years ago, established himself as one of the best in the league. From Christmas onwards he hardly made a mistake and was a major reason Dynamos conceded so few goals.

FACT FILE 2001-02

English Premier League: Winners
Playoffs: Champions
English Premier Cup: Finalists

HISTORY

Founded: 1997. Previous club was Medway Bears 1984-97.
Leagues: English (Premier) League 1997-2002, 1991-92 & 1984-86; Premier League 1996-97; British League, Div. One 1992-96 and 1986-91.
Honours: English Premier League and playoffs 2001-02; English League & (promotion) playoffs 1991-92; British League, Div. Two 1985-86.

INVICTA DYNAMOS *left to right*, *back row: (standing)*: Jackie Mason (club secretary), Jake French, Eliot Andrews, Kevin Parrish, Greg Hales, Sean Clement, Phil Chard, Mikko Skinnari, Bernard Sealy, Andy Mason (manager); Carl Greenhous, Mat van der Velden, Matthew Beveridge, Paul Hume, Jon Gray, Peter Korff, Duane Ward, Andy Hannah, Adam Noctor; *front:* Eamonn Connolly (stick boy).

Photo: David Trevallion.

ISLE OF WIGHT RAIDERS

PLAYER	ENGLISH PREMIER LEAGUE					PLAYOFFS					ALL COMPETITIONS				
Scorers	GP	G	A	Pts	Pim	GP	G	A	Pts	Pim	GP	G	A	Pts	Pim
Kyle Amyotte (I)	26	43	31	74	32	6	5	5	10	0	40	57	43	100	32
Darcy Cahill	25	26	47	73	62	5	5	8	13	14	37	35	62	97	78
Luc Chabot	26	16	32	48	11	6	3	5	8	6	40	25	43	68	47
Brendon Knight (I)	26	18	26	44	10	6	2	3	5	8	40	23	41	64	18
Peter Nyman	24	9	30	39	10	6	1	8	9	4	37	11	41	52	43
Jason Coles	24	14	15	29	118	6	3	4	7	4	38	25	26	51	124
Mark Levers	25	16	16	32	42	6	4	3	7	4	38	23	21	44	56
Tony Blaize	25	13	15	28	57	6	2	0	2	4	39	16	19	35	61
Richard Hargreaves 3	14	6	7	13	36	6	3	4	7	8	27	13	18	31	46
Scott Carter	26	7	14	21	30	6	0	2	2	2	40	9	18	27	36
Gareth Owen	25	8	9	17	70	5	0	1	1	0	38	9	15	24	94
Andy Pickles 3	7	1	6	7	8	6	3	1	4	4	19	6	9	15	30
Steve Gannaway	25	3	9	12	30	4	0	0	0	2	36	3	11	14	38
Richard Thornton	23	3	6	9	38	6	0	1	1	2	35	3	8	11	44
Paul Sanderson	20	4	6	10	2						27	4	6	10	2
Michael Hargreaves	26	1	4	5	30	6	0	0	0	0	40	2	6	8	40
Matt Wynn	23	0	3	3	0	5	0	0	0	0	32	2	4	6	4
Craig Wynn (N) 2	18	0	2	2	2						22	0	2	2	2
Danny Baldwin	1	1	0	1	0						1	1	0	1	0
Damien Orr (N) 1	3	0	0	0	0	6	0	0	0	0	10	0	1	1	0
Damon Larter	12	0	0	0	2	2	0	0	0	0	16	0	1	1	2
Andy Moffat (N) 4	8	0	1	1	2	6	0	0	0	2	19	0	1	1	4
TEAM TOTALS	26	189	279	468	598	6	31	45	76	64	40	267	396	663	829

Netminders	GPI	Min	SOG	GA	Sv%	GPI	Min	SOG	GA	Sv%	GPI	Min	SOG	GA	Sv%
Damien Orr 1	1	20	11	1	90.91						2	50	20	1	95.00
Andy Moffat 4	8	400	177	18	89.83	6	360	232	14	93.97	18	1000	571	49	91.42
Toby Cooley	4	184	85	9	89.41						4	184	85	9	89.41
Craig Wynn 2	16	896	599	75	87.48						19	1076	692	85	87.72
Matt Evans	2	60	23	1	95.65						3	90	39	5	87.18
TEAM TOTALS	26	1560	895	104	88.38	6	360	232	14	93.97	40	2400	1407	149	89.26

Shutouts: Moffat (2) - league:* 5 Jan v England under-18 (4 saves),
playoffs: 16 March v Nottingham Lions (35 saves);
Evans (1) - league: *5 Jan v England under-18 (15 saves)
* shared

Also played for: 1 Haringey Greyhounds, Paisley Pirates; 2 Swindon Lynx; 3 Basingstoke Bison;
4 Hull Thunder

Also appeared: Adam Greener, Dale Herridge

All Competitions = league, playoffs and Premier Cup

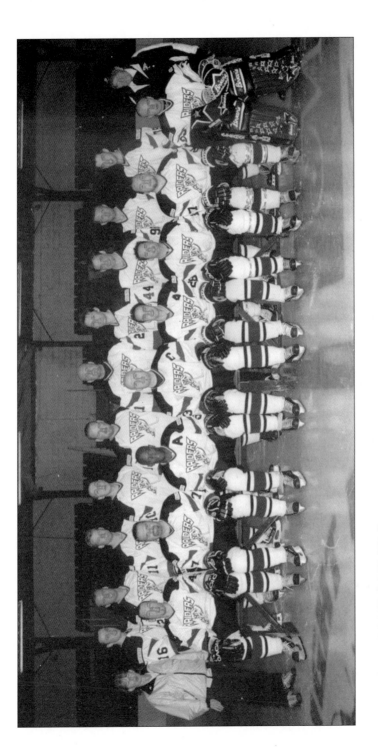

ISLE OF WIGHT RAIDERS *left to right, back row:* Mavis Siddons (secretary), Mark Levers, Andy Pickles, Brendon Knight, Ritchie Thornton, Matt Wynn, Peter Nyman, Paul Sanderson, Luc Chabot, Steve Gannaway, Michael Hargreaves, Ted Chappell (manager); *front row:* Richard Hargreaves, Darcy Cahill, Tony Blaize, Jason Coles, Gareth Owen, Scott Carter, Kyle Amyotte, Andy Moffat.

So near, so far away

CLARE WALL

The Isle of Wight Raiders, sponsored by *Steve Porter Transport Group*, failed to live up to the expectations of many fans following the successes of the previous season.

Though their third place finish was an improvement on 2000-01, with only three points separating the top three teams, many felt the Island side could have topped the table.

Goalie problems in the early part of the season and a lack of away points in the latter part did most to deny **Luc Chabot**'s team the title.

When first choice netminder **Craig Wynn** returned to Swindon, former GB under-20 international **Andy Moffat** replaced him from the BNL's Hull Thunder. Though the Scot arrived too late to retrieve his new team's league position, he shone in the playoffs.

Up front, Chabot made perhaps his best signing in Canadian sniper **Kyle Amyotte**. The former top scorer with Romford repeated his feat on the Island just pipping his fellow countryman, **Darcy Cahill**. Between them the pair scored over a third of Raiders' league goals.

The other new import, **Brendon Knight**, was the king-pin on Raiders' line with **Gareth Owen** and another GB under-20 international, **Marc Levers** from Nottingham Lions.

The playoffs were a bitter disappointment. After demolishing league rivals, Solihull Barons, and the all-British Lions in the first round, Raiders faced league champs, Invicta Dynamos, in the two-legged final.

Playing at home in the first leg, they were hit by two Dynamos' goals in the first period but **Andy Pickles** scored in the last session to set up a thrilling return in Gillingham next day.

Dynamos went 3-1 up early on, reminding Raiders how they had struggled to win points there all season, but **Jason Coles** and Knight levelled the aggregate score in the second period. Then in a deadly four-minute spell late in the game, Invicta beat Moffat three times to put paid to Wight's hopes of a trophy.

They had already lost the chance of defending their Premier Cup (formerly Millennium Cup) after failing to qualify from their group.

Overall, Raiders' powerplay was weak and they found it hard to gain good results against the bigger clubs, especially the dark horse Solihull Barons who surprisingly took five league points off them.

The crowds dropped off as well which left Chabot with too little revenue for reinforcements.

PLAYER AWARDS

Players' Player	**Jason Coles**
Player of the Year:	**Darcy Cahill**
Best Forward:	**Darcy Cahill**
Best Defenceman:	**Peter Nyman**
Most Improved Player:	**Marc Levers**

LEADING PLAYERS

Brendon Knight *born 15 February 1977*
Arriving from SUNY Potsdam University in New York, the Canadian was one of the quickest skaters in the league and possessed an excellent shot. His points tally doesn't reflect the effort he put in game after game.

Marc Levers *born 30 June 1981*
The promising GB international forward finished as the team's top British scorer, blending well with **Gareth Owen** and import **Brendon Knight**. The trio were a formidable attacking force.

Andy Moffat *born 9 May 1982*
The 19-year-old netminder from Fife in Scotland spent only half the season with Raiders but he earned the respect of his team-mates and the fans. He won his first game as a Raider and with only one bad performance, proved to be the team's saviour.

MUTTY'S BEQUEST
Raiders were left over £15,000 in the will of longtime fan, **Helmut (Mutty) Wucherpfennig**, who died in August 2000.

FACT FILE 2001-02
English Premier League:	3rd
Playoffs:	Finalists
English Premier Cup:	3rd in group

HISTORY
Founded: 1999. The first club on the Island in 1991 was Solent Vikings. The team was known as *Wightlink* Raiders 1992-99.
Leagues: English (Premier) League 1991-2002.
Honours: English Premier Cup 2001; English League 1993-97.

LONDON KNIGHTS

PLAYER	SEKONDA SUPERLEAGUE					SUPERLEAGUE PLAYOFFS					ALL COMPETITIONS				
Scorers	GP	G	A	Pts	Pim	GP	G	A	Pts	Pim	GP	G	A	Pts	Pim
Mike Barrie (WP)	48	20	24	44	140	5	1	1	2	39	55	21	27	48	206
Vezio Sacratini	45	11	22	33	52	7	4	1	5	8	54	15	26	41	62
Ian McIntyre (WP)	48	15	18	33	56	7	1	5	6	4	57	17	23	40	60
Maurizio Mansi	48	14	23	37	32	7	1	1	2	4	57	15	25	40	36
Kim Ahlroos	48	14	15	29	20	7	3	3	6	2	57	17	20	37	22
Mark Kolesar	48	5	20	25	48	7	3	3	6	18	57	10	23	33	66
Paul Rushforth	46	8	12	20	127	7	1	4	5	8	54	9	16	25	135
Trevor Roenick (WP)	30	13	9	22	20	-	-	-	-	-	30	13	9	22	20
Rich Bronilla (WP)	46	3	12	15	18	7	0	4	4	8	55	4	16	20	26
Dave Struch (WP)	29	3	11	14	18	7	0	3	3	6	36	3	14	17	24
Rob Donovan	41	1	13	14	96	7	0	2	2	2	50	1	15	16	100
Sean Blanchard (WP)	35	6	6	12	14	7	0	1	1	8	44	6	8	14	22
Nate Leslie 1	38	6	3	9	25	7	1	0	1	4	47	7	4	11	29
Steve Thornton	15	3	7	10	8	-	-	-	-	-	15	3	7	10	8
Gerad Adams	21	2	1	3	92	7	3	2	5	10	30	5	3	8	102
Dominic Amodeo	8	1	5	6	2	5	0	0	0	0	15	2	6	8	2
Mike Ware	35	2	4	6	33	-	-	-	-	-	35	2	4	6	33
Greg Burke 4	8	0	1	1	8	7	1	2	3	6	17	2	3	5	18
* David Clarke 2	10	2	1	3	0	1	0	0	0	0	12	2	1	3	0
Doug Searle	23	1	2	3	15	-	-	-	-	-	23	1	2	3	15
Trevor Robins (N) (WP)	15	0	1	1	2	-	-	-	-	-	15	0	1	1	2
Dave Trofimenkoff (N)	30	0	1	1	2	7	0	0	0	0	39	0	1	1	2
Domenic DeGiorgio (N) 2	1	0	0	0	0	-	-	-	-	-	1	0	0	0	0
Dean Crossland (N) (I) 3	2	0	0	0	0	-	-	-	-	-	2	0	0	0	0
Scott Bailey (N) (I)	1	0	0	0	2	-	-	-	-	-	3	0	0	0	2
Bench Penalties					12					0					12
TEAM TOTALS	48	130	211	341	842	7	19	32	51	127	57	155	254	409	1004
Netminders	GPI	Min	SOG	GA	Sv%	GPI	Min	SOG	GA	Sv%	GPI	Min	SOG	GA	Sv%
Domenic DeGiorgio (I) 2	1	60	32	2	93.8	-	-	-	-	-	1	60	32	2	93.8
Trevor Robins (WP)	15	889	438	42	90.4	-	-	-	-	-	15	889	438	42	90.4
Dave Trofimenkoff	30	1751	897	88	90.2	7	420	166	17	89.8	39	2233	1085	107	90.1
Dean Crossland (I) 3	2	120	55	6	89.1	-	-	-	-	-	2	120	55	6	89.1
Scott Bailey (I)	1	60	25	5	80.0	-	-	-	-	-	3	123	53	7	86.8
Empty Net Goals			2	2				1	1				3	3	
TEAM TOTALS	48	2880	1449	145	90.0	7	420	167	18	89.2	57	3425	1666	167	90.0

Shutouts: Robins - league: 23 Sept at Bracknell Bees (15 saves)

Also played for: 1 Dundee Stars; 2 Milton Keynes Kings;

3 Cardiff Devils, Paisley Pirates, Slough Jets; 4 Guildford Flames

All Competitions = league, playoffs, Challenge Cup and Ahearne Trophy

Knights in casualty

SIMON CROSSE

Though the regular season is best forgotten, the Knights finished well, coming a goal short of a Playoff final appearance.

Knights' fans will never know what impact a fully fit squad would have had on Superleague.

"Our injury list is unprecedented in sports. We have had eight surgeries!" said frustrated coach, **Bob Leslie**, at the end of his debut season.

Trevor Robins, Steve Thornton, Trevor Roenick, Mike Ware and **David Struch** all went under the knife. Put another way, the franchise player, the projected top scorer, the hot new signing, the enforcer and the captain were all gone for most of the season.

The team made a spectacular start putting 14 goals past Belfast in the opening two matches. Five signings from Cardiff Devils gave Leslie some instant partnerships but Struch was injured eight minutes into the season and 15 games later, Thornton went down.

London didn't cope well with the injury disruption and won only twice in December and not at all in January. Their winless streak lasted from Christmas through to 7 February.

HARD WORKING LESLIE

Thornton had made a comeback during the Continental Cup semi-final round in Oslo, but **Mike Barrie**'s ejections and suspensions along with the salary-capped short bench meant that while their performances did the UK proud they were unable to match last season's outstanding silver medal finish.

It was continental opposition, though, that gave the club its stretch run boost. The Ahearne Cup matches against Schwenningen and Hanover saw the Knights turn a corner.

While still short of bodies, and with the so-called 'extra forwards', **Greg Burke** and **Nate Leslie**, pushed into full time action, the club saved their best for last.

Coach's son Leslie, an early season signing from Dundee, improved game on game and his hard working performances became a highlight.

Also noteworthy was the first half play of **Trevor Roenick** (brother of the NHL's **Jeremy**), the tireless efforts of fans' player of the year, **Mark Kolesar**, and the playoff performances of Robins' 'back-up', **Dave Trofimenkoff**.

However, rarely has a club's top scorer been as unpopular as the ill-disciplined Barrie who missed the Playoff finals after another suspension.

PLAYER AWARDS

Most Valuable Player	Maurizio Mansi
Players' Player:	Ian McIntyre
Coach's Player:	Dave Trofimenkoff
Fans' Player of the Year:	Mark Kolesar

LEADING PLAYERS

Mark Kolesar *born 23 January 1973*
The team's inspirational leader. Hard working and tenacious, the centreman was capable of spectacular goals and flashes of brilliance in front of the net.

The former Toronto Maple Leaf improved under Leslie after a disappointing year under previous head coach, **Chris McSorley**, and was the team's brightest spark during their mid-season slump.

Maurizio Mansi *born 3 September 1965*
An unheralded signing from Dusseldorf, the veteran Italian international proved an inspired bit of business by Leslie. The converted forward led the league's defencemen in scoring and finished second top scorer.

Dave Trofimenkoff *born 20 January 1975*
For the second season running, the former Manchester Storm stopper found himself propelled into the starting role for the second half of the campaign.

A season-ending injury to Robins gave 'Troffi' his chance and he repelled the threat of deadline signing, **Scott Bailey**, with a string of impressive performances.

FACT FILE 2001-02

Sekonda **Superleague**:	Sixth
Playoffs:	Semi-finalists
Challenge Cup:	Sixth

HISTORY

Founded:	1998
League:	*Sekonda* Superleague 1998-2002
Honours:	*Sekonda* Superleague Playoffs 1999-2000.

LONDON KNIGHTS *left to right, back row:* Jason Ellery (equipment), Vezio Sacratini, Kim Ahlroos, Trevor Roenick, Ian McIntyre, Rich Bronilla, Mike Barrie, Nate Leslie, Steve Thornton, Rob Donovan, Sean Blanchard, Karen Levers (therapist); *front row:* Trevor Robins, Doug Searle, Maurizio Mansi, Joan Hill (chief exec.), Dave Struch, Bob Leslie (coach), Mark Kolesar, Paul Rushforth, Mike Ware, Dave Trofimenkoff.

MANCHESTER STORM

PLAYER	SEKONDA SUPERLEAGUE					SUPERLEAGUE PLAYOFFS					ALL COMPETITIONS				
Scorers	GP	G	A	Pts	Pim	GP	G	A	Pts	Pim	GP	G	A	Pts	Pim
Trevor Gallant	47	9	34	43	42	8	4	5	9	0	57	14	40	54	42
Mark Bultje	46	15	26	41	58	8	2	6	8	4	56	17	34	51	64
Joe Cardarelli	48	13	21	34	6	8	7	6	13	2	58	22	28	50	8
Ivan Matulik (WP)	46	15	14	29	78	8	4	5	9	8	56	20	20	40	86
Russ Romaniuk (WP)	46	17	14	31	14	7	1	0	1	0	55	19	14	33	14
Joe Busillo	48	9	14	23	94	7	1	5	6	0	57	10	21	31	94
Kris Miller (WP)	47	3	15	18	40	8	0	4	4	4	57	3	20	23	44
Dan Preston (WP)	47	5	10	15	28	8	3	2	5	0	57	8	13	21	28
Rob Wilson	30	5	11	16	66	8	2	3	5	2	40	7	14	21	70
Kayle Short (WP)	48	4	12	16	62	8	1	2	3	8	58	5	15	20	70
Dwight Parrish (WP)	48	9	8	17	50	8	0	1	1	17	58	9	9	18	69
Pierre Allard	48	7	6	13	24	8	0	3	3	2	58	8	9	17	28
Paul Ferone	45	3	6	9	82	8	1	5	6	8	55	4	11	15	92
Mike Morin	48	2	3	5	28	8	3	2	5	4	58	5	5	10	32
Mike Torchia (N)	23	0	2	2	2	5	0	1	1	4	29	0	4	4	6
Justin Hocking (WP)	19	1	1	2	22	-	-	-	-	-	19	1	1	2	22
* Stevie Lyle (N)	30	0	2	2	4	3	0	0	0	0	34	0	2	2	4
Russell Richardson	15	0	0	0	2	-	-	-	-	-	15	0	0	0	2
Bench Penalties					22					2					24
TEAM TOTALS	48	117	199	316	724	8	29	50	79	65	58	152	260	412	799
Netminders	GPI	Min	SOG	GA	Sv%	GPI	Min	SOG	GA	Sv%	GPI	Min	SOG	GA	Sv%
Mike Torchia	23	1211	678	57	91.6	5	305	155	16	89.7	29	1581	871	78	91.0
* Stevie Lyle	30	1669	806	81	90.0	3	180	117	9	92.3	34	1914	958	91	90.5
EN Goals/GW Shots			3	3				1	1				4	4	
TEAM TOTALS	48	2880	1487	141	90.5	8	485	273	26	90.5	58	3495	1833	173	90.6

All Competitions = league, playoffs, Challenge Cup and Ahearne Trophy

MANCHESTER STORM *left to right, back row:* Paul Ferone, Dan Preston, Dwight Parrish, Joe Cardarelli, Russ Romaniuk, Justin Hocking, Kayle Short, Joe Busillo, Pierre Allard, Russ Richardson; *front row:* Stevie Lyle, Mark Bultje, Mike Morin, John Crawley (equipment), Ivan Matulik, Daryl Lipsey (coach), Kris Miller, Trevor Gallant, Mike Torchia.

Photo: Dominique Paul

Zeroes to heroes

ANDY COSTIGAN

The popular **Daryl Lipsey** succeeded **Terry Christensen** as coach of the Storm but his debut season turned into a nightmare.

Then, after six months of heartache, a shock 8-2 win in Bracknell propelled Superleague's wooden spoonists into the Playoff finals.

After a seventh place finish in 2000-01, Storm started the new campaign under a new owner, local businessman **Gary Cowan**, and a considerably revamped roster. Only **Trevor Gallant** returned from Storm's top ten scorers and in came Bracknell's high scoring **Joe Cardarelli** and **Mark Bultje** and the impressive but homeless Cardiff Devil, **Ivan Matulik**.

Another Devil, **Dwight Parrish**, signed on defence along with Sheffield's **Kayle Short**, while **Stevie Lyle** - also fresh from the Cardiff disaster - and **Mike Torchia**, from Grand Slammers Steelers, were arguably the best netminding tandem in the league.

A 6-1 opening night thrashing in Nottingham was just the prelude to a month that yielded only two wins in 11 outings. When matters failed to improve, Lipsey axed former LA Kings' blueliner, **Justin Hocking**, for the experienced GB skipper, **Rob Wilson**.

Perhaps it was an omen that the team were able to resume training in their own MEN Arena in the New Year, rather than the cold and lifeless Blackburn rink.

Storm kept in touch with the teams above them and the highlight of February was their first win over Steelers, 4-3, after a fighting second period comeback from a three-goal deficit. A loss in Nottingham, however, condemned them to another seventh place.

Three defeats was not a good start to the playoffs but a battling tie in Nottingham and another come-from-behind win, this time over the champion Giants, preceded that astonishing night in the Hive. Storm were in the semi-finals for the first time in four seasons.

Torchia was man of the match and skipper Matulik and long-time favourite **Mike Morin** scored the goals they needed to beat the favourites, Ayr Scottish Eagles. But then they had to face their Roses' rivals, Steelers, who in eight league contests Storm had beaten only in that February game.

They held on for a gallant 3-3 draw, which Lipsey understandably insisted was a moral victory for his underdogs, but Lady Luck deserted them in the penalty shootout.

PLAYER AWARDS

Players' Player	**Ivan Matulik**
Fans' Player of the Year	**Ivan Matulik**
Coach's Award (Unsung Hero)	**Stevie Lyle**
Best Forward	**Mark Bultje**
Best Defenceman	**Dan Preston**
Best Road Player	**Mike Torchia**

LEADING PLAYERS

Mark Bultje *born 8 June 1973*
High energy and sheer determination were his hallmarks. Though small in build, he played with great heart and took a lot of physical punishment as he led the first line of forwards.

Ivan Matulik *born 17 June 1968.*
Captain Marvellous led by example in a tough year for his new team. Digging deep during the bad times, his infectious enthusiasm and unashamed emotion kept the heads high. Fans, young and old, took him to their hearts.

Dan Preston *born 2 March 1975*
Joined Storm from Dayton Bombers of the ECHL and after a nervous start proved dependable at the back, bolstering his main role with excellent offensive rushes and blistering shooting. Not the most physical of blueliners, he displayed a commendable temperament.

FACT FILE 2001-02

Sekonda **Superleague**	Seventh
Playoffs	Finalists
Challenge Cup:	Fifth

HISTORY
Founded 1995.
Leagues Superleague 1996-2002; British League, Div. One 1995-96.
Honours *Benson and Hedges* Cup winners 1999-2000; Superleague champions 1998-99, British League Division One champions 1995-96.

MILTON KEYNES KINGS

PLAYER	FINDUS BRITISH NATIONAL LEAGUE					FINDUS PLAYOFFS					ALL COMPETITIONS				
Scorers	GP	G	A	Pts	Pim	GP	G	A	Pts	Pim	GP	G	A	Pts	Pim
David Clarke 1	29	22	23	45	45	5	1	0	1	0	34	23	23	46	45
Jeff Daniels (l)	34	16	25	41	28	6	1	1	2	0	40	17	26	43	28
Rick Strachan	44	2	25	27	28	6	0	2	2	2	55	2	28	30	30
Bryan Blair (l) 4	28	15	11	26	64	6	2	1	3	0	34	17	12	29	64
Mike Breadmore (l)	41	13	10	23	114	6	0	1	1	8	50	16	13	29	130
Janne Ronkainen (l)	33	21	5	26	20	6	1	0	1	2	39	22	5	27	22
Paul Moran 2	44	12	11	23	18	6	0	0	0	8	55	13	12	25	28
Greg Randall	43	8	13	21	26	6	0	1	1	0	54	9	16	25	26
Jonathan Phillips	39	8	7	15	22	6	1	0	1	6	50	12	9	21	30
Danny Meyers	44	7	13	20	24	6	1	0	1	0	55	8	13	21	24
Duncan Patterson (l)	44	2	12	14	107	6	1	1	2	2	55	4	16	20	117
Dwayne Newman WP 5	32	4	10	14	28	6	0	2	2	0	38	4	12	16	28
Simon Howard	41	3	11	14	30	6	0	0	0	4	48	3	11	14	34
Steve Smillie 6	8	6	3	9	4						13	8	5	13	24
Aaron Shrieves (l)	16	3	6	9	44						20	4	9	13	48
Ross Mackintosh	14	0	5	5	10						19	1	7	8	18
Stuart Potts 4	14	1	3	4	6						19	2	3	5	6
Mark McCoy	12	3	1	4	20						15	3	1	4	22
Domenic DeGiorgio (N) (l) 1	41	0	1	1	6	6	0	1	1	2	52	0	2	2	12
Paul Sample 4	14	0	1	1	10						18	0	1	1	12
Bench Penalties					18										22
TEAM TOTALS	44	146	196	342	672	6	8	10	18	34	55	168	224	392	770
Netminders	GP	Mins	SOG	GA	Sv%	GP	Mins	SOG	GA	Sv%	GP	Mins	SOG	GA	Sv%
Domenic DeGiorgio (l) 1	41	2448	1593	141	91.2	6	378	226	21	90.7	52	3125	1990	185	90.7
Stephen Foster 3	2	119	59	7	88.1						2	119	59	7	88.1
Alan Sutton	4	114	56	9	83.9						4	114	56	9	83.9
Empty Net Goals		4	3	3								5	4	4	
TEAM TOTALS	44	2685	1711	160	90.6	6	378	226	21	90.7	55	3363	2109	205	90.3

Shutouts: DeGiorgio - league: 11 Nov at Coventry Blaze (25 saves), 17 Feb at Slough Jets (19 saves), 27 Feb at Paisley Pirates (29 saves).

Also played for: 1 London Knights; 2 Nottingham Panthers; 3 Basingstoke Bison, Hull Thunder; 4 Cardiff Devils; 5 Peterborough Pirates;   6 Hull Thunder.

Also appeared: Ross Piggot, Luke Webb (N), Damien Orr, Andrew McGill, Leanne Dennis (N), Rob Cole, Richard Munnelly, Chris Roberts, Mark Wolfe, Kieron Goody, Paul Jamieson, Leigh Jamieson, Matt Darnell, Alan Sutton (N).

All Competitions = league, playoffs and Findus Cup

The more Kings change...

PAUL BROOKMAN

It was all change for Kings as just six players - all British - remained from the 2000-01 season. But the net result was the same - eighth place in the league, good enough to make the playoffs.

After a gap of six years, former player-coach, **Rick Strachan**, returned to the club in his old role as player-coach and assembled a side built on solid defence while some promising British youngsters were brought in on the forward line.

'Strachs' used the *Findus* Challenge Cup group matches to experiment with his formations and though the results were disappointing, he was not too worried. A famous victory against Guildford Flames early in the league campaign gave cause for optimism but it was soon extinguished by a run of 11 straight defeats.

Strachan made changes and by the beginning of November five players had been axed with **Steve Smillie** making way for **Jeff Daniels** by mid-October. Youngsters **Paul Sample** and **Stuart Potts** went to Cardiff Devils in exchange for Canadian **Bryan Blair** while GB international, **David Clarke**, came over from Peterborough Pirates.

A week later **Mark McCoy** gave way for another Pirate, **Dwayne Newman**, and Finnish forward, **Janne Ronkainen**, successfully came through a trial.

The changes produced an immediate turn around with Kings going on a six-match unbeaten run. After mixed results in December and January, they clinched the final playoff place in the last league game of the season, beating Paisley Pirates 5-0. That midweek match was memorable for not starting until gone 11 p.m. after the visitors were caught up in a motorway accident tailback.

The playoffs were an anti-climax as Kings managed to pick up just one point, finishing bottom of their group. But despite this failure the season will be looked upon as a success as Kings qualified for the playoffs, thanks largely to Strachan's skilful coaching.

The find of the season had to be Ronkainen. In 33 league games he found the net on no less than 21 occasions and became a fans' favourite.

The final game, a charity match to celebrate the club's tenth anniversary, was overshadowed by the news of a redevelopment plan for Kings' Leisure Plaza home, leaving the club's future in doubt for the third time in their short history.

PLAYER AWARDS

Players' Player	**Dwayne Newman**
Most Valuable Player	**Domenic DeGiorgio**
Coach's Award	**Danny Meyers**
Best British Player	**David Clarke**
Top Points Scorer	**Jeff Daniels**
Most Improved Player	**Paul Moran**

LEADING PLAYERS

Domenic DeGiorgio *born 9 January 1977*
The Niagara Falls native came to Kings via Italy and earned the nickname 'the Dominator' for his excellent performances. His 91.2 save percentage was good enough for runners-up spot in the league.

Simon Howard *born 21 September 1973*
Defenceman 'Howie' was an original King in 1990 and returned to the club in 2001. Always Mr Dependable and a model of consistency.

Duncan Paterson *born 11 July 1974*
Big Dunc could always be relied on to lead by example. As team captain he commanded the blue line and was never afraid to go in hard when necessary.

FACT FILE 2001-02
Findus **British National League:**   8th
Findus **Playoffs:**   4th in qr-final group
Findus **Challenge Cup:**   3rd in group

HISTORY
Founded: 1990. Rink closed 1996-98.
Leagues: *Findus* British National League 1999-2002; English League (Premier Div) 1998-99, 1990-91; British League, Premier Div 1994-96; British League, Div One 1991-94.
Honours: English Cup 1998-99; British League, Div. One 1993-94.

MILTON KEYNES KINGS *left to right, back row:* Janne Ronkainen, Paul Jamieson, Dwayne Newman, Danny Meyers, Leigh Jamieson, Bryan Blair, Aaron Shrieves, Matt Darnell, David Clarke, Kieran Goody, Paul Moran; *front row:* Domenic DeGiorgio, Rick Strachan, Jeff Daniels, Simon Howard, Duncan Paterson, Greg Randall, Jonathan Phillips, Mike Breadmore, Allen Sutton.

Photo: Chris Valentine.

NOTTINGHAM PANTHERS

PLAYER	SEKONDA SUPERLEAGUE					SUPERLEAGUE PLAYOFFS					ALL COMPETITIONS				
Scorers	GP	G	A	Pts	Pim	GP	G	A	Pts	Pim	GP	G	A	Pts	Pim
PC Drouin (WP)	48	18	34	52	78	6	2	4	6	4	58	20	39	59	82
Patrik Wallenberg	48	21	26	47	73	6	3	1	4	2	58	24	28	52	77
Lee Jinman	41	9	31	40	78	6	3	4	7	4	51	13	36	49	88
Greg Hadden	46	21	17	38	10	6	0	3	3	0	54	21	22	43	15
Steve Moria	47	14	11	25	14	6	0	1	1	2	57	16	12	28	16
Claude Savoie (WP)	44	12	11	23	31	6	2	2	4	4	54	14	13	27	37
* Ashley Tait	43	6	14	20	31	6	1	1	2	0	53	8	15	23	31
Jimmy Drolet (WP)	48	7	13	20	72	6	0	3	3	8	58	7	16	23	90
Calle Carlsson	48	6	11	17	52	6	0	0	0	4	58	8	12	20	56
Joel Poirier (WP)	45	6	12	18	82	6	0	1	1	2	55	6	14	20	84
Christian Sjogren	18	2	9	11	63	6	0	1	1	14	27	3	11	14	81
Clayton Norris (WP)	41	4	5	9	165	6	1	1	2	19	51	5	8	13	194
Brent Pope	48	1	12	13	63	6	0	0	0	4	58	1	12	13	71
Barry Nieckar (WP)	45	5	6	11	222	6	0	0	0	2	55	5	7	12	230
Frank Evans (WP)	36	3	6	9	53	-	-	-	-	-	36	3	6	9	53
Randall Weber	40	1	4	5	6	6	1	0	1	0	47	2	4	6	6
Darren Maloney	41	2	3	5	14	6	0	0	0	2	47	2	3	5	16
Anthony (AJ) Kelham	15	2	1	3	0	2	0	0	0	0	19	2	2	4	0
Jimmy Paek	5	0	0	0	4	6	0	1	1	4	14	1	3	4	8
Danny Lorenz (N)	46	0	1	1	24	5	0	1	1	0	54	0	2	2	24
* Paul Moran 1	5	0	0	0	0	1	0	0	0	0	7	0	0	0	0
Pasi Hakkinen (N)	8	0	0	0	0	3	0	0	0	0	12	0	0	0	0
Bench Penalties					60					2					66
TEAM TOTALS	48	140	227	367	1195	6	13	24	37	77	58	161	265	426	1325
Netminders	GPI	Min	SOG	GA	Sv%	GPI	Min	SOG	GA	Sv%	GPI	Min	SOG	GA	Sv%
Danny Lorenz	46	2633	1363	122	91.0	5	278	146	15	89.7	54	3091	1605	145	91.0
Pasi Hakkinen	8	247	125	14	88.8	2	82	43	4	90.7	11	389	202	20	90.1
Empty Net Goals			5	5				1	1				7	7	
TEAM TOTALS	48	2880	1493	141	90.6	6	360	190	20	89.5	58	3480	1814	172	90.5

Shutouts: Lorenz (3) - league: 16 Sept at Manchester Storm (25 saves), 16 Oct at Belfast Giants (25 saves), 20 Jan v London Knights (30 saves).

Also played for: 1 Milton Keynes Kings

All Competitions = league, playoffs, Challenge Cup and Ahearne Trophy

NOTTINGHAM PANTHERS *left to right, back row:* Pete Hunt (equipment), Randall Weber, Paul Moran, Lee Jinman, Claude Savoie, Jimmy Drolet, Ashley Tait, Steve Moria, Alex Dampier (dir. of hockey), Clayton Norris, Brent Pope, Darren Maloney, Calle Carlsson, Frank Evans, AJ Kelham, Patrick Wallenberg; *front row:* Adam Goodridge (equipment), PC Drouin, Greg Hadden, Danny Lorenz, Gary Moran (GM), Paul Adey (coach), Andy Worth (sponsor), Pasi Hakkinen, Joel Poirier, Barry Nieckar, Vincent Haywood (physio).

Jersey raised, spirit Damp-ened

MICK HOLLAND, Nottingham Evening Post

Thirteen fresh faces from the previous disappointing season - a mix of experience and potential - brought renewed hopes for a major turnaround in Panthers' fortunes.

With **Alex Dampier** and rookie coach **Paul Adey** at the helm, those hopes looked well founded - until the later stages of the campaign.

The new-look squad had got to grips with winning on the road again, so fourth place and failure to reach the Playoff finals (once again on their own ice) left the fans feeling let down.

With attacking hopes resting largely on the shoulders of sharp-shooter **Greg Hadden** and the classy **PC Drouin**, this time Panthers had help in the shape of newcomers **Lee Jinman**, **Claude Savoie** and **Joel Poirier**, formerly captain of Newcastle.

But the surprise of the year was Swede **Patrik Wallenberg**, who came over unsung but went back home with his reputation fully enhanced after finishing sixth in league scoring.

At the back, the unflappable **Darren Maloney** and ex-Bracknell stalwart **Jimmy Drolet** were undoubted successes, while **Danny Lorenz** added needed stability between the pipes.

Among the other new faces were ex-Cardiff trio, **Clayton Norris**, **Steve Moria** and **Frank Evans**, though the latter left for Canada at Christmas for family reasons.

His departure made room for the return of double Stanley Cup winner, **Jimmy Paek** from Anchorage Aces, who proved to be just as popular with the supporters as the previous year.

His arrival helped Panthers towards their hopes of a best ever second place behind the runaway leaders, Belfast. But the lack of goals from key players in crucial games brought a late slump.

And it didn't really come as a surprise when their bid to pip bottom club, Manchester, to that last Playoff spot failed to materialise, even though they tried to shake up the players by axing Dampier with just three games left.

Beneath the disappointment, the supporters at least had something to smile about. In the last game of the season, **Randall Weber** became the first player since the club was formed in 1946 to have his no. 10 shirt officially retired.

After a 17-year career with the club, he had been playing on a game-by-game basis after "retiring" the previous season.

The 33-year-old deputy general manager at the Nottingham Ice Centre, said: "The players say the only reason they're raising my shirt in the arena is so I can't reach it to carry on playing!"

PLAYER AWARDS

Players' Player:	**Danny Lorenz**
Most Valuable Player:	**Danny Lorenz**
Most Consistent Player:	**Patrik Wallenberg**
Sponsors' Player:	**Lee Jinman**
Most Entertaining Player:	**Barry Nieckar**
Supporters' Player:	**Patrik Wallenberg**
Team Spirit (Gary Rippingale Award):	**Randall Weber**

LEADING PLAYERS

Lee Jinman *born January 10, 1976*
One of the most skilful players in the league, the Toronto-born forward soon became a firm favourite with the fans. His ability to create chances from nothing also made him a marked man with the opposition.

Danny Lorenz *born March 10, 1972*
The popular Canadian was the calming influence the team had missed since moving to the National Ice Centre. Faced more rubber than any other goalie in the league.

Patrik Wallenberg *born 4 January 1977*
The surprise package of the Superleague, the unassuming Swede impressed with his skill, speed and knack of scoring key goals. Ran **PC Drouin** close as the club's top scorer.

LIFE BEGINS AT....

Steve Moria scored his 200th Superleague point on 3 February 2002 which, according the *Annual's* records and contrary to what you may have read elsewhere, was his 41st birthday.

FACT FILE 2001-02

Sekonda **Superleague**	Fourth
Playoffs	Sixth
Challenge Cup	Semi-finalists

HISTORY
Founded 1946. Re-formed 1980. Club suspended operations 1960-80. Purchased by Aladdin Sports Management in 1997.

Leagues Superleague 1996-2002; British Lge (BL) (Premier Div) 1982-96 and 1954-60; English Nat Lge (ENL) 1981-82 and 1946-54; Inter-City Lge 1980-82.

Honours: British Champions 1989; League - BL 1955-56, ENL 1953-54 and 1950-51; Autumn Cup winners 1998, 1996 & 1994 *(B&H)*, 1991, 1986, 1955; Ahearne Trophy 1956.

PAISLEY PIRATES

PLAYER	FINDUS BRITISH NATIONAL LEAGUE					ALL COMPETITIONS				
Scorers	GP	G	A	Pts	Pim	GP	G	A	Pts	Pim
Domenic Parlatore (I)	44	43	52	95	114	50	49	56	105	130
Jeff White (I)	44	24	45	69	56	50	25	48	73	74
Oleg Synkov WP 1	25	15	29	44	14	31	16	36	52	16
Ken Ruddick (I)	21	9	19	28	30	21	9	19	28	30
Jon Cameron (I) 2	16	9	15	24	12	16	9	15	24	12
Jimmie Ronnback (I)	16	9	9	18	2	22	11	12	23	2
Markus Juvanowski (I)	29	8	12	20	8	35	10	13	23	12
Mark Biesenthal (I)	15	6	16	22	74	15	6	16	22	74
Graeme Lester	38	7	11	18	24	44	8	12	20	28
Jussi Eloranta (I)	14	8	7	15	8	14	8	7	15	8
Antii Boman (I)	18	7	8	15	28	18	7	8	15	28
Raphiel Protopapas (I)	15	9	4	13	30	15	9	4	13	30
Murray Johnstone	43	1	8	9	16	49	1	8	9	16
Robert Johanesson (I)	17	2	4	6	12	17	2	4	6	12
James Clark	33	1	4	5	194	39	1	4	5	214
Mark Steele	43	1	4	5	36	49	1	4	5	42
Chris Conaboy	30	1	1	2	152	36	1	2	3	196
Clint Owen (N) (I) 1	14	0	3	3	32	14	0	3	3	32
Kenny Redmond	8	0	1	1	6	14	1	1	2	10
Chris Bailey 3	21	1	0	1	36	21	1	0	1	36
Jaakko Suomalainen (N) (I)	19	0	1	1	12	19	0	1	1	12
Bjorn Bohm (I)	14	0	1	1	16	20	0	1	1	30
Bench Penalties					34					36
TEAM TOTALS	44	161	254	415	986	50	175	274	449	1142

Netminders	GP	Mins	SOG	GA	Sv%	GP	Mins	SOG	GA	Sv%
Jaakko Suomalainen (I)	17	1001	683	66	90.3	17	1001	683	66	90.3
Dean Crossland (I) 4	2	120	91	9	90.1	2	120	91	9	90.1
Clint Owen (I) 1	14	845	480	61	87.3	14	845	480	61	87.3
Damien Orr 5	1	29	30	4	86.7	1	29	30	4	86.7
Jan Sundstrom	2	115	113	23	79.6	7	358	276	46	83.3
Chris McGarvey	13	549	456	96	78.9	16	666	544	107	80.3
TEAM TOTALS	44	2659	1853	259	86.0	50	3019	2104	293	86.1

Also played for: 1 Hull Thunder; 2 Slough Jets; 3 Cardiff Devils; 4 Cardiff Devils, London Knights, Slough Jets; 5 Haringey Racers, Isle of Wight Raiders; 6 Whitley Warriors

Also appeared: John Russell, Alan Haig, Martin Ford, John Churchill, Simon Leach (6), Andy Watt, Jamie Williamson, Stuart Steel (N), Stuart McCaig, Gareth Downie, Myles Watson, Colin Nelson, Tom Miller, Alan Campbell, Stuart Swiatek, Gordon Nelson, Robert Henderson, Colin McMillan, Gary Morris.

All Competitions = league and Findus Cup

Three coaches and Pirates' funeral

STEWART DAVIDSON

Even by their previous standards, last season was a remarkably bad one for Paisley Pirates, who contrived to lose three coaches (including a wheeled one!) on their way to a ninth place finish in the *Findus* BNL.

The team started off with the experienced **Jim Lynch**, but he left before winter set in following an apparent disagreement over team selection with **Alex Whelan**, the club's major sponsor.

His departure was a shock as it came after a run of seven successive wins, something that the ever-decreasing Lagoon faithful had not come close to seeing in half-a-decade.

This unfortunate decision was followed by a truly inexplicable one when, despite his previous discipline record, Canadian **Doug Marsden** was brought in for his third spell as coach.

Marsden had played for Pirates on and off since their first season and was their top scorer in 1996-97. But he walked out on the team a few weeks into 2000-01 after they had sportingly reinstated him following his sacking in 1997-98 for driving his sponsored car while disqualified.

His first move was to replace Lynch's Scandinavians with North Americans, most controversially allowing the best of the goalies, Finn **Jaakko Suomalainen**, to leave.

The turnover of players during the campaign was huge with 44 players, including 17 imports and four netminders, appearing in Pirates' colours. And almost half of them played four or less games, including several local players.

It was hardly surprising when the directors - all of whom had day jobs as well - found that the club's troubles were affecting their health and resigned, leaving only Marsden and Whelan to keep the club going.

The third coach, this one with the team in it, broke down en route to the midweek game at Milton Keynes. The players hitched a lift on the supporters' bus but this was then caught up in a 15-mile tailback and the face-off was delayed for three hours. When the final whistle sounded at 1 a.m. Pirates had lost 5-0.

Then came the news that the Inland Revenue, who were owed a sum of around £20,000, were taking the club to court. They were declared insolvent and after ten years the name of Paisley Pirates looked likely to disappear.

The final straw came when it was revealed that Marsden was being sought by police after money in a Save the Pirates fund had gone missing. But he had already left the country.

PLAYER AWARDS

Player of the Year	**Jeff White**
British Player of the Year	**Graeme Lester**

LEADING PLAYERS

Graeme Lester *born 15 September 1978*
One of the few quality Brits, the forward could fit into any team in the *Findus* BNL. Missing only six games, he played on through injury and must have been the most committed player at Paisley, as well as the longest-serving.

Dominic Parlatore *born 18 February 1978*
Despite the team's lowly placing, the Canadian centreman finished runner-up in the league scorers' chart. With 114 PIMs he also knew how to handle himself and was probably the club's best player in recent seasons.

Jeff White *born 11 April 1976*
Along with Parlatore, the defenceman played in every game, not a common occurrence with Paisley imports in the past few years. With 73 points, he finished second in Pirates' scoring and was effective in assisting others to score.

FACT FILE 2001-02

Findus **British National League**:	9th
Findus **Playoffs**:	Did not qualify
Findus **Challenge Cup**:	3rd in group

HISTORY

Founded: Current team in 1992, original team at the East Lane arena 1946-70. Known as Mohawks 1966-77, playing games at Glasgow's Crossmyloof rink after East Lane closed.

Leagues: British National Lge 1997-2002, Northern Premier Lge 1996-97, British Lge, Div. One 1993-96, Scottish Lge 1992-93 & 1996-97, Northern Lge (NL) 1971-77 & 1966-70, Scottish Lge (SL) 1962-65, British Lge (BL) 1954-60, Scottish National Lge (SNL) 1946-54.

Honours: *Pirates* - Scottish Cup 1996-97; BL 1958-59; SNL and Scottish Autumn Cup 1953-54; SNL & playoffs 1950-51; Scottish Autumn Cup 1947-48. *Mohawks* - NL 1968-69; Grand Slam of Icy Smith Cup, NL, Spring Cup and Northern Autumn Cup 1967-68; NL 1966-67; SL 1964-65.

PETERBOROUGH PIRATES

PLAYER	FINDUS BRITISH NATIONAL LEAGUE					ALL COMPETITIONS				
Scorers	GP	G	A	Pts	Pim	GP	G	A	Pts	Pim
Nick Poole 6	33	21	34	55	24	40	24	42	66	32
Darren Cotton	43	20	21	41	22	50	24	31	55	24
Jon Cotton	41	13	25	38	48	48	18	34	52	62
Doug McEwen 1	32	11	20	31	20	37	15	23	38	30
Ryan Moynihan WP 11	21	18	18	36	10	21	18	18	36	10
David Clarke 3	10	4	5	9	24	16	15	9	24	75
Jesse Hammill	31	8	7	15	154	37	10	12	22	180
Jani Mertanen (I)	29	4	12	16	24	30	4	13	17	26
Jason Porter	37	2	12	14	28	43	2	12	14	28
Warren Tait 4	33	9	4	13	20	34	9	4	13	20
Craig Britton	43	3	6	9	68	50	4	8	12	84
Jordan Shields (I) 7	6	1	3	4	4	12	3	7	10	18
Lewis Buckman	42	4	2	6	16	47	7	2	9	20
Markus Juvanowski (I)	12	5	4	9	6	12	5	4	9	6
Pete Morley	42	1	7	8	58	49	1	8	9	68
Rob Coutts 9	16	3	5	8	6	16	3	5	8	6
Dwayne Newman WP 8	10	0	1	1	4	16	2	4	6	16
Geoff O'Hara	44	3	2	5	36	51	3	2	5	38
Jason Buckman	33	1	2	3	20	40	1	3	4	20
Pasi Raitanen (N) 5	44	0	0	0	10	51	0	4	4	10
Grant Hendry	42	2	0	2	53	47	3	0	3	53
Jon Oddy	4	1	0	1	59	8	2	0	2	63
Bernie Bradford	13	1	1	2	2	13	1	1	2	2
James Ellwood 10	26	1	0	1	20	26	1	0	1	20
Jon Fone	19	0	0	0	4	26	0	1	1	6
James Moore (N)	39	0	1	1	0	46	0	1	1	0
Bench Penalties					36					36
TEAM TOTALS	44	136	192	328	778	51	175	248	423	955
Netminders	GP	Mins	SOG	GA	Sv%	GP	Mins	SOG	GA	Sv%
Pasi Raitanen 5	42	2447	1656	189	88.6	48	2780	1853	211	88.6
James Moore	8	249	127	18	85.8	11	336	184	23	87.5
Empty Net Goals		1	1	1			1	1	1	
TEAM TOTALS	44	2697	1784	208	88.3	51	3117	2038	235	88.5

Also played for: 1 Hull Thunder; 2 Cardiff Devils, Sheffield Steelers; 3 London Knights, Milton Keynes Kings; 4 Bracknell Bees; 5 Edinburgh Capitals; 6 Fife Flyers; 7 Coventry Blaze; 8 Milton Keynes Kings; 9 Slough Jets; 10 Solihull Barons; 11 Bracknell Bees

Also appeared: Ross Mackintosh, Marc Twaite (2), Dan Jennings

All Competitions = league and Findus Cup

PETERBOROUGH PIRATES

Pirates walk the plank

STEVE JUDGE

Pirates began their season with a celebration - it was their 20th year in ice hockey. Sadly, it also proved to be their last.

After an embarrassingly one-sided defeat in their August challenge against local *Findus* BNL rivals, Coventry Blaze, it was clear that last season's high of reaching the playoff semi-finals was unlikely to be repeated.

Still, aided by a favourable draw in the *Findus* Challenge Cup, Pirates qualified for the semis with a perfect record.

It was not until the league programme opened that problems came to light. Following home defeats by perennial whipping boys, Paisley and Edinburgh, imports **John Oddy** and **Jordan Shields** were released.

Before he returned to Australia, Oddy revealed that the players were on the verge of mutiny due to coach **Doug McEwen**'s brand of leadership.

Meetings were held between directors, players and coach and the crack was papered over, but a new one regarding shortages of money would not go away.

DEFEAT TOO PAINFUL TO RECALL

The cash problems led to the departures of Canadian skipper **Dwayne Newman** and GB international **David Clarke** to Milton Keynes, leaving Pirates with just five imports by the time they faced Scottish powerhouse, Fife Flyers, in the Cup semi-final at Nottingham.

Their 10-2 thrashing is too painful to recall and it proved to be the final curtain for McEwen who was asked to step down a week later. Surprisingly, though, he chose to stay on as a player under new man **Glenn Mulvenna** who had started the season with Superleague's never-to-play outfit, Newcastle Jesters.

Results and form improved under Mulvenna who had help from American **Ryan Moynihan**, a former college forward who averaged almost two points a game. Unfortunately, he joined Superleague Bracknell on deadline day.

Outside hopes of a playoff place ended early in February but with Mulvenna committing himself for the following season, at least the fans could look forward to the new campaign.

That was until **Phil Wing** and **Rob Housden** were sacked as directors and then resurfaced with a new team. Pirates, who reached the British Championship final at Wembley in 1991, were out of Peterborough after two roller coaster decades.

PLAYER AWARDS

Player of the Year	**Pasi Raitanen**
Best British Player	**Darren Cotton**
Best Young Player	**Lewis Buckman**
Clubman of the Year	**Nick Poole**
Maggie MacFarlane Award	**Pasi Raitanen**

LEADING PLAYERS

Craig Britton *born 24 September 1976*
One of the few players to gain some credit in the *Findus* foul-up, the consistent stay-at-home defenceman never allowed his head to drop in a season of lows.

Nick Poole *born 11 July 1973*
Offered to play for Pirates for nothing when they hit troubled times, but still performed like $1 million. The highly skilled, lightning quick forward covered more ice in a night than Scott of the Antarctic did in a lifetime.

Pasi Raitanen *born 13 May 1971*
The Finn claims he doesn't care if he lets in six goals in every game, as long as the team scores seven. Unfortunately, in his third season with the team, Pirates did not have the firepower to match his excellent netminding.

FACT FILE 2001-02
Findus **British National League:** 10th
Findus **Playoffs:** Did not qualify
Findus **Challenge Cup:** Semi-finalists

HISTORY
Founded: 1982.
Leagues: British National Lge 1997-2002; Premier Lge 1996-97; British Lge, Div One 1995-96, 1986-87, 1982-85; British Lge, Premier Div 1987-95, 1985-86.
Honours: (*Heineken*) British Championship finalists 1991; Christmas Cup 1999; British Lge, Div. One playoffs 1987-88; British Lge, Div. One 1986-87, 1984-85.

PETERBOROUGH PIRATES *left to right*, *back row*: Jani Mertanen, Darren Cotton, Lewis Buckman, Jason Buckman, Danny Valentine, Geoff O'Hara, James Ellwood, Bernie Bradford, Warren Tait, Doug McEwen; *middle row*: Rob Horspool (equipment), Rob Coutts, Craig Britton, Jesse Hammill, Pete Morley, Grant Hendry, Jon Fone, Ryan Moynihan, Steve Fagan (physio); *front row*: James Moore, Dave Llewellyn (bench coach), John Avery (Specsavers), Jon Cotton, Michael Avery (Specsavers), Glenn Mulvenna (manager/coach), Billy Glover (equipment), Pasi Raitanen.

ROMFORD RAIDERS

PLAYER	ENGLISH PREMIER LEAGUE					PLAYOFFS					ALL COMPETITIONS				
Scorers	GP	G	A	Pts	Pim	GP	G	A	Pts	Pim	GP	G	A	Pts	Pim
Danny Marshall	26	29	30	59	10	4	2	6	8	2	47	52	48	100	16
James Duval (I)	25	20	35	55	20	4	1	2	3	4	44	34	54	88	44
Jason Rushton (I)	11	17	24	41	96	4	2	2	4	12	23	35	36	71	116
Rob Simnor (I) 2	21	12	23	35	30						31	15	31	46	38
Daniel Cabby	20	13	16	29	72	2	0	1	1	2	37	17	28	45	82
Jamie Randall	26	13	10	23	6	4	1	2	3	0	48	19	24	43	12
Timo Kauhanen (I)	16	13	17	30	6	3	0	0	0	0	27	16	22	38	61
Marc Long (I) 3	13	11	14	25	22						22	17	20	37	58
Adam Collins (I)	22	6	10	16	12	4	0	2	2	2	44	9	24	33	28
Jaakko Komulainen (I)	22	6	17	23	8	3	0	0	0	2	35	8	23	31	10
Stuart Low	25	8	11	19	30	4	0	1	1	0	45	10	17	27	64
Andrew Fox (I)	22	3	11	14	26	4	1	2	3	4	37	5	19	24	32
Noel Burkitt (I) 2	5	3	4	7	2						13	11	9	20	10
Tyrone Miller	24	4	7	11	44	4	1	0	1	8	46	6	11	17	87
Anthony Child 1	19	2	10	12	60	3	1	1	2	6	31	4	13	17	80
Chad Brandimore (I)	3	3	1	4	0	4	5	2	7	0	15	9	7	16	0
Jani Lehtovaara (I)	23	1	10	11	51						27	2	12	14	57
Ben Pitchley	25	1	5	6	48	4	0	0	0	8	47	2	10	12	76
Grant Taylor	20	2	3	5	2	4	0	0	0	0	39	2	4	6	10
Tom Looker	26	2	2	4	0	3	0	0	0	0	45	3	2	5	14
Jon Beckett	3	0	1	1	0						9	1	3	4	6
Colin O'Hara	3	0	0	0	32						10	0	3	3	64
Thomas Spinks	1	0	2	2	0						2	0	2	2	0
Jim Wonnacott	5	0	0	0	36						7	1	0	1	36
James Grimstead 1	6	0	1	1	4						8	0	1	1	4
Chris Goddard	13	0	1	1	0	2	0	0	0	0	22	0	1	1	0
Chris Douglas (N) 1	18	0	1	1	2	2	0	0	0	0	27	0	1	1	2
Simon Smith (N)	25	0	1	1	0	4	0	0	0	0	47	0	1	1	53
TEAM TOTALS	26	169	267	436	631	4	14	21	35	50	48	278	426	704	1060
Netminders	GPI	Min	SOG	GA	Sv%	GPI	Min	SOG	GA	Sv%	GPI	Min	SOG	GA	Sv%
Chris Douglas 1	10	528	250	23	90.80						12	648	309	28	90.94
Simon Smith	16	872	414	43	89.61	4	240	138	13	90.58	33	1833	990	107	89.19
Carl Ambler	2	100	39	7	82.05						4	127	48	7	85.42
Mathieu Davidge	1	60	48	6	87.50						5	272	161	27	83.23
TEAM TOTALS	26	1560	751	79	89.48	4	240	138	13	90.58	48	2880	1508	169	88.79

Shutouts: Smith (3) - league: 14 Oct v Nottingham Lions (18 saves), 10 Nov v England under-20 (11 saves), 11 Nov at Nottingham Lions (9 saves)
Douglas (2) - league: 25 Nov v Haringey Greyhounds (19 saves), 2 Dec v Nottingham Lions (14 saves)

Also played for: 1 Haringey Greyhounds; 2 Edinburgh Capitals; 3 Slough Jets

Also appeared: Andy Martin, Ian Robinson.

All Competitions = league, playoffs, Premier Cup and Findus Challenge Cup

ROMFORD RAIDERS *celebrating their English Premier Cup win* **left to right**, *back row:* Chad Brandimore, Jaakko Komulainen, Tyrone Miller, Jamie Randall, Chris Goddard, Ian Robinson; *third row:* Tom Looker, Adam Collins, Carl Ambler, Thomas Spinks, Andrew Fox; *second row:* Timo Kauhanen, Ben Pitchley, Grant Taylor, Stuart Low, Anthony Child; *front row:* Simon Smith, James Duval, Jason Rushton.

Photo: Alan White

Mac's back, with a cup

'ROB RAIDER'

Romford Raiders won silverware for the second successive season after beating the all-conquering Invicta Dynamos in the English Premier Cup final.

While this was not perhaps the club's preferred trophy, it gave them some consolation after their hopes of defending their playoff championship were dashed by the league winners.

Consistency was one problem, as exemplified by their record against league runners-up, Solihull Barons: Raiders had a 100 per cent success rate at Hobs Moat Road but lost both home league fixtures.

This and a last-second home defeat by the Isle of Wight and the loss of leads against Invicta, left them always looking for playoff qualification rather than a place at the top of the pile.

When the playoffs came, they clawed back a two-goal deficit against Dynamos within 20 minutes but let the lead slip again to end any dreams of back-to-back championships.

There were major changes at the beginning as **Shaun McFadyen** made the short trip 'back home' from Chelmsford, this time as head coach.

The Scot hired **James Duval**, an English-born American recommended by former Romford hero **Andy Heinze**, and recruited **Adam Collins**, **Jamie Randall** and goalie **Simon Smith** from his old club, which was now in a lower division.

Canadian Collins was Chelmsford's player of the year in 2000-01, but Romford's unsung hero turned out to be Englishman Randall who had an outstanding campaign.

Ex-NHL draftee **Colin O'Hara** had looked to be the steal of the season but he disappointed and was soon on a plane home. His fellow Canadians, **Noel Burkitt**, **Marc Long** and **Rob Simnor**, also failed to stay the distance. Stepping in were **Andrew Fox** - another Heinze suggestion - and former Romford favourites, **Timo Kauhanen** and **Jaakko Komulainen**, two of the club's top scorers in 1999-2000.

Hard-hitting, high scoring Canadian **Jason Rushton** grabbed the headlines in the first few weeks with fights, suspensions and a hatful of goals. Life with Rushton was never dull!

While all of this was happening, skipper **Danny Marshall** was quietly re-writing the numbers and by the end of the campaign, the centreman had even passed local legend, **Marc Chartier**, on the club's all-time scoring list.

In the cup final victory over Invicta - after two pulsating games that were a credit to the Premier - Duval's game-winning goal sent the fans happy into the summer break.

PLAYER AWARDS

Players' Player	**James Duval**
Coach's Player	**Jamie Randall**
Best Forward	**James Duval**
Best Defenceman	**Tyrone Miller**
Supporters' Player	**Jamie Randall**
Rookie of the Year	**Carl Ambler**
Outstanding Achievement	**Danny Marshall**

LEADING PLAYERS

Danny Marshall *born 14 May 1977*
Stat-buster Marshall ended the season holding every British scoring record for Romford. Promoted to captain, the 25-year-old hit 'import numbers' including five consecutive hat-tricks and a century in points.

Puzzlingly, though, he again failed to attract the attention of the GB selectors.

Jamie Randall *born 5 February 1975*
"My best hire", according to coach McFayden, his dedication and industry was an example to all. The Doncaster-born forward graduated to the first line and scored some key goals, including a tremendous hat-trick at Solihull.

Simon Smith *born 31 July 1979*
Always reliable, occasionally outstanding, he made the starter's slot his own despite the return of **Chris Douglas**. Often the difference between victory and defeat, he became a crowd favourite.

FACT FILE 2001-02

English Premier League:	4th.
Playoffs:	Finalists.
English Premier Cup:	Winners.

HISTORY

Founded: 1987. (Withdrew from Div One midway through 1994-95 for financial reasons.)
Leagues: English (Premier) League 1995-2002, 1989-90; British League, Div One 1990-94 and 1988-89; British League, Div Two 1987-88.
Honours: English Premier Cup 2001-02; English National League, Premier Div playoffs 2000-01; British League, Div Two 1987-88.

SHEFFIELD STEELERS

PLAYER	SEKONDA SUPERLEAGUE					SUPERLEAGUE PLAYOFFS					ALL COMPETITIONS				
Scorers	GP	G	A	Pts	Pim	GP	G	A	Pts	Pim	GP	G	A	Pts	Pim
Rick Brebant	42	13	30	43	36	8	1	8	9	13	52	16	40	56	49
Scott Allison	46	22	23	45	50	8	3	3	6	8	56	25	29	54	58
Chris Lipsett (WP)	46	24	18	42	67	8	5	2	7	2	56	30	20	50	69
Paul Kruse (WP)	44	12	16	28	152	8	2	2	4	20	54	15	19	34	172
Brad Lauer (WP)	47	13	13	26	62	7	1	3	4	6	56	15	17	32	70
Jason Mansoff (WP)	41	8	19	27	26	8	1	2	3	6	51	9	22	31	32
Marc Laniel (WP)	48	6	18	24	30	8	2	3	5	0	58	8	22	30	30
Kevin Miehm (WP)	19	9	20	29	10	-	-	-	-	-	19	9	20	29	10
Brent Bobyck	47	6	14	20	16	8	1	4	5	2	57	7	19	26	18
Peter Leboutillier	46	6	13	19	146	8	1	1	2	6	56	7	15	22	164
Chris Brant 1	18	3	7	10	12	8	2	2	4	13	28	7	9	16	25
Jeff Sebastian	48	4	10	14	42	8	0	0	0	10	58	4	11	15	52
Jeff Brown	48	3	11	14	84	8	0	0	0	6	58	3	11	14	92
Ron Shudra 4	25	4	6	10	10	8	1	0	1	0	35	5	6	11	10
Mark Dutiaume 3	8	0	6	6	4	8	1	2	3	6	18	1	9	10	14
Bob Maudie	31	5	4	9	10	-	-	-	-	-	31	5	4	9	10
Cal Benazic (WP)	23	0	5	5	82	3	0	0	0	0	27	0	5	5	98
Ryan Bach (N)	27	0	2	2	24	8	0	1	1	0	37	0	3	3	24
* Steve Duncombe	2	0	0	0	0	-	-	-	-	-	2	0	0	0	0
Marc Twaite 2	2	0	0	0	0	-	-	-	-	-	2	0	0	0	0
* Keith Leyland	5	0	0	0	0	-	-	-	-	-	5	0	0	0	0
Eoin McInerney (N)	24	0	0	0	10	-	-	-	-	-	24	0	0	0	10
GW Penalty Shot	-	-	-	-	-	-	1	-	1	-	-	1	-	1	-
Bench Penalties					40					0					40
TEAM TOTALS	48	138	235	373	913	8	22	33	55	98	58	167	281	448	1047
Netminders	GPI	Min	SOG	GA	Sv%	GPI	Min	SOG	GA	Sv%	GPI	Min	SOG	GA	Sv%
Eoin McInerney	24	1326	637	60	90.6	-	-	-	-	-	24	1326	637	60	90.6
Ryan Bach	27	1554	723	80	88.9	8	485	262	12	95.4	37	2159	1034	102	90.1
Empty Net Goals			4	4					1	1				5	5
TEAM TOTALS	48	2880	1364	144	89.4	8	485	263	13	95.1	58	3485	1676	167	90.0

Shutouts: McInerney (2) - league: 22 Sept v Manchester Storm (23 saves),
1 Dec v Nottingham Panthers (24 saves).
Bach (1) - playoffs: 23 March v Bracknell Bees (35 saves).

Also played for: 1 Basingstoke Bison, Bracknell Bees; 2 Cardiff Devils, Peterborough Pirates;
3 Fife Flyers; 4 Edinburgh Capitals

All Competitions = league, playoffs, Challenge Cup and Ahearne Trophy

Playoff miracle

DAVE HAWKINS

Victory in the Playoff final was only fitting for a side whose most valuable player, **Rick Brebant**, has become a byword in British ice hockey for hard work and commitment.

Steelers were never involved in the league title chase, though they did finish third, but they owned the Playoffs.

Following a season when the club won everything was always going to be a difficult task, but in the summer of 2001, living up to expectations was the least of the club's worries. Instead of celebration and recollecting momentous achievements, there was a bitter struggle for control of a franchise with a bad business name.

It was as late as 22 September when a hastily assembled roster, under the ownership of businessman **Norton Lea**, finally iced. With coach **Mike Blaisdell** back behind the bench, Sheffield's 2001-02 team was the gritty one expected of 'Blaiser', although it wasn't the all-guns-blazing style of the previous year.

Nevertheless, their steady efforts produced a run of nine games with only one loss, pleasing the fans who returned to the arena, though they were much reduced in numbers. This good spell ended with the Continental Cup trip to France when the team's sub-standard treatment in Anglet led to their exit at the first hurdle.

Soon after, Injuries to several key players, including centre **Kevin Miehm**, the league's leading points-per-game scorer at the time, were the main cause of Steelers' inability to defend their league and Challenge Cup titles.

Frankly, some players failed to perform. Centreman **Bob Maudie**, a New York Rangers' draft pick and Canadian national team player, found it particularly difficult to fit in.

Among those who impressed were **Eoin McInerney**, who carried the goaltending load early on when first choice, **Ryan Bach**, struggled. But 'impact' players, **Brad Lauer** and **Paul Kruse**, took time to adjust to the size of the ice, and sniper **Chris Lipsett** tore a hole in the goal charts only after his personal choice in sticks arrived with barely two months left.

Returning veteran **Ron Shudra** and the signings of **Mark Dutiaume** from Fife and **Chris Brant** from Basingstoke were the catalysts for the revival that eventually ended in Nottingham.

But the star of the show was the 38-year-old Brebant. When Steelers won the Playoffs for the second year straight, it was the third time in as many years that the GB veteran had been on the winning side in the last game of the season.

PLAYER AWARDS

Players' Player:	Ryan Bach
Coach's Player:	Rick Brebant
Best Road Player:	Rick Brebant
Kids of Steel Player:	Scott Allison

LEADING PLAYERS

Ryan Bach born 21 October 1973
Struggled early on when defence was a forgotten word in Sheffield. But when they got it together, he was almost a one-man show. Led all Playoff goalies with a save percentage of 95.4 and goals against ratio of 1.48.

Rick Brebant born 21 February 1964
Tenacious, resilient, talismanic, committed - and that's just in practice. Worked both ends of the ice tirelessly and finished in the top ten points scorers. If the league measured plus/minus figures, they would be called the Brebant Statistic.

Chris Lipsett born 24 September 1974
If ever a player was an advert for why owners should buy players their tailored equipment then Lipsett is that player. An out-and-out goal scorer who, with hands like his, should be in a better league.

FACT FILE 2001-02

Sekonda **Superleague**	Third
Playoffs	Champions
Challenge Cup	Seventh

HISTORY

Founded: 1991. Franchise purchased from liquidators in 1999 by a consortium led by **Darren Brown**. His Sheffield Steelers Ice Hockey Club Ltd was wound up in April 2001 and four months later **Norton Lea** took control of the team. In May 2002, Lea set up a company, South Yorkshire Franchise Ice Hockey Club Ltd, to own both the team and the franchise.

Leagues: Superleague 1996-2002; British League, Premier Div 1993-96; British League, Div One 1992-93; English League 1991-92.

Honours: Superleague Playoff Champions 2001-02 & 1996-97; Challenge Cup 1999-2000 & 1998-99; British League and Championship 1995-96 & 1994-95.

SHEFFIELD STEELERS *celebrating their Superleague Playoff win* **left to right**, *back:* Marc Laniel, Jason Mansoff, Chris Brant, Ian Pearce (physio), Geoff Butcher (doctor), Ron Shudra, Paul Kruse; *middle:* Brad Lauer, Jeff Sebastian, Mark Dutiaume, Scott Allison, Cal Benazic, Peter Leboutillier, Jeff Brown, Rick Brebant; *front:* Chris Lipsett, Ryan Bach, Brent Bobyck, Eoin McInerney.

Photo: Mike Smith/Icepix

SLOUGH JETS

PLAYER	FINDUS BRITISH NATIONAL LEAGUE					ALL COMPETITIONS				
Scorers	GP	G	A	Pts	Pim	GP	G	A	Pts	Pim
Mitch Grant (I) 1	33	19	11	30	10	39	25	17	42	10
Nick Cross 3	33	10	20	30	70	38	11	23	34	76
Jon Cameron (I) 4	29	10	14	24	42	35	14	17	31	64
Chris Crombie (I) 3	29	10	11	21	52	35	13	15	28	70
Norman Pinnington	32	8	13	21	66	38	10	14	24	120
Rob Coutts 5	31	7	15	22	36	35	7	17	24	36
David Heath	40	8	9	17	6	46	9	12	21	8
Adam Lamarre (I)	29	2	11	13	28	35	5	16	21	34
Joe Stefan	26	7	12	19	47	26	7	12	19	47
Adam Bicknell	44	5	11	16	69	50	6	13	19	81
Jason Reilly	38	6	11	17	4	38	6	11	17	4
Marc Long 6	15	8	7	15	32	15	8	7	15	32
Scott Moody	42	1	10	11	36	48	1	11	12	42
Warren Rost	35	2	7	9	126	40	2	7	9	154
Matt Foord	43	3	2	5	28	49	4	2	6	30
Ricky Skene	43	0	4	4	20	49	0	5	5	30
Terry Miles	18	4	0	4	6	22	4	0	4	6
Chris McEwen	44	2	2	4	8	45	2	2	4	8
Adam Greener 3	7	0	2	2	31	7	0	2	2	31
Matt Towalski	4	0	1	1	0	5	0	1	1	0
Barry Skene	6	0	1	1	2	6	0	1	1	2
Tommy Brooks (N)	7	0	1	1	0	7	0	1	1	0
Chris Babbage	8	0	1	1	2	8	0	1	1	2
Russell Stevens	17	0	1	1	2	23	0	1	1	4
David Hurst (N)	44	0	1	1	0	50	0	1	1	0
Bench Penalties					42					42
TEAM TOTALS	44	112	178	290	769	50	134	210	344	941
Netminders	GP	Mins	SOG	GA	Sv%	GP	Mins	SOG	GA	Sv%
Adam Dobson	2	40	39	3	92.3	2	132	39	3	92.3
Dean Crossland (I) 2	18	1045	537	62	88.5	24	1453	696	75	89.2
Bill Russell 7	13	719	432	60	86.1	13	805	432	60	86.1
Dave Hurst	20	818	487	80	83.6	22	942	504	80	84.1
Tommy Brooks	3	60	45	9	80.0	3	140	45	9	80.0
Empty Net Goals		2	2	2			2	2	2	
TEAM TOTALS	44	2684	1542	216	86.0	50	3474	1718	229	86.7

Shutouts: Crossland - league: 10 Nov v Cardiff Devils (23 saves); 11 Nov at Guildford Flames (39 saves)

Also played for: 1 Guildford Flames; 2 Cardiff Devils, London Knights, Paisley Pirates;
   3 Basingstoke Bison; 4 Paisley Pirates; 5 Peterborough Pirates; 6 Romford Raiders; 7 Hull Thunder.

Also appeared: Danny Hughes, Kevin Murphy, Carl Graham.

All Competitions = league, playoffs and Findus Cup

Slough debts

DICK BELLAMY

This was the club's worst season since their formation as they finished second from last in the *Findus* BNL and failed to make the playoffs for only the second time ever.

Yet they had a good team on paper at the beginning of September. Returning coach **Joe Stefan** decided to concentrate on his bench duties and only ice himself in the event of injury to one of his players.

Rob Coutts and **Adam Lamarre** returned after intervals elsewhere, and new signings **Chris Crombie**, **Dean Crossland** and **Jon Cameron** gave the team a promising look. Stefan also left a place open for **Jason Reilly** who had been banned for failing a drug test.

Jets never lived up to these expectations, however. They struggled to score goals and rapidly became borderline contenders for the playoffs.

Netminder Crossland, signed from Edinburgh Capitals, enjoyed back-to-back shutouts in November but he was inconsistent and unpopular with his team-mates. After warnings, he was sacked and replaced with **Bill Russell** who had hoped to play for Superleague's ill-fated Newcastle team.

On defence, the inexperience of youngsters **Scott Moody**, **Ricky Skene** and **Chris McEwen** put too much on the shoulders of **Warren Rost** and **Rob Coutts**. Cameron showed he had a good hockey brain with strong showings in the *Findus* Challenge Cup, but then he faded.

In losing a majority of their league games, Slough felt robbed of points by the new winner-takes-all rule for overtime draws. The lowest point came at struggling Cardiff Devils just before Christmas when Jets could manage only a 3-3 draw. Ironically, Crossland was guesting for Devils.

Perhaps the result was understandable considering the news that had rocked the club two days earlier. The directors revealed a £27,000 debt to the Inland Revenue which had built up over the previous two seasons. Several contracts were terminated and the players who remained were forced to take large pay cuts.

Back-up **Dave Hurst** stepped into the netminding breach and several under-19 and English League players were promoted. Joe returned to the ice and signed Romford's **Marc Long** as his only import. Long and **Terry Miles** became fan favourites and the team showed more commitment, but they remained largely uncompetitive.

PLAYER AWARDS

Players' Player	Dave Hurst
Supporters' Player of the Year	Joe Stefan
Supporters' British Player	Chris McEwen
Coach's Award	Warren Rost

LEADING PLAYERS

Marc Long *born 12 November 1979*
Canadian forward came to help the club at the start of its player crisis in January and showed a passion and determination which had been lacking from his countrymen earlier on.

Chris McEwen *born 5 October 1982*
The former captain of Swindon's successful under-19 team played his first year of senior hockey in Slough. The defender's commitment to his new team earned him the Best British Player award from the fans.

Terry Miles *born 10 January 1984*
Promising forward who graduated from Slough's under-19s on the departure of Jets' imports. Looks set to mature into a good all-round player. Won a bronze medal with the GB under-19s.

FACT FILE 2001-02

Findus **British National League**:	11th
Findus **Playoffs**:	Did not qualify
Findus **Challenge Cup**;	2nd in group

HISTORY

Founded: 1986.
Leagues: (*Findus*) British National Lge 1997-2002; Premier Lge 1996-97; British Lge, Premier Div 1995-96; British Lge, Div One 1986-95.
Honours: British National League 1998-99; *Benson and Hedges* Plate 1997-98; British League, Div One 1994-95 (and Playoffs), 1993-94 (south), 1989-90.

SOLIHULL BARONS

PLAYER	ENGLISH PREMIER LEAGUE					PLAYOFFS					ALL COMPETITIONS				
Scorers	GP	G	A	Pts	Pim	GP	G	A	Pts	Pim	GP	G	A	Pts	Pim
Duncan Cook (I)	26	41	50	91	83	4	2	6	8	6	43	64	66	130	127
Kevin Conway	23	27	34	61	24	4	2	3	5	2	41	46	48	94	38
Dan Prachar	26	24	25	49	40	4	0	4	4	12	44	25	49	74	58
Samuli Mykkanen (I) 2	22	31	27	58	20						26	35	31	66	24
Neil Adams	23	14	13	27	24	4	2	1	3	6	41	24	23	47	40
Antti Makikyro (I)	25	8	16	24	32	4	3	2	5	2	43	15	23	38	46
Daniel Mackriel	20	9	24	33	16						28	11	29	40	18
Michael Wales	19	6	15	21	84	4	0	2	2	6	37	9	29	38	102
Andrew Howarth	25	9	5	14	24	4	2	3	5	6	43	17	15	32	34
Aaron Shrieves (I) 1	7	5	10	15	39	3	5	3	8	4	15	13	18	31	43
Russell Plant	17	11	11	22	4						24	12	15	27	4
Phil Lee	25	5	6	11	24	3	1	0	1	0	41	8	12	20	65
Don Breau	20	2	11	13	14	3	0	0	0	2	33	2	16	18	52
Russell Coleman	24	5	3	8	16	4	0	0	0	0	40	7	4	11	20
Joel Pickering	10	2	7	9	61	3	0	0	0	4	17	3	8	11	81
Andrew Ayers	23	1	1	2	8	4	0	1	1	8	41	6	4	10	18
Jon Rodway	23	2	4	6	16	4	1	1	2	0	38	3	7	10	18
Colum Chadwick	25	0	3	3	4	4	0	0	0	0	42	1	7	8	16
Rhys McWilliams	14	1	2	3	2	4	0	0	0	0	26	2	3	5	2
Richard Taylor	2	0	0	0	0	2	0	0	0	2	8	2	0	2	8
Phil Knight	15	0	1	1	0	3	0	0	0	0	24	0	2	2	2
Mark Williams	17	0	1	1	82	4	0	0	0	12	26	0	2	2	94
Tom Ayers (N)	26	0	2	2	4	4	0	0	0	2	43	0	3	3	8
James Ellwood 3	5	0	1	1	0						9	0	1	1	0
Stephen Doyle	13	0	1	1	92						18	0	1	1	94
David Whitwell (N)	25	0	1	1	6	3	0	0	0	0	42	0	1	1	6
TEAM TOTALS	26	203	274	477	763	4	18	26	44	74	44	305	417	722	1193
Netminders	GPI	Min	SOG	GA	Sv%	GPI	Min	SOG	GA	Sv%	GPI	Min	SOG	GA	Sv%
David Whitwell	17	887	554	65	88.27	2	120	54	14	74.07	29	1386	819	115	85.96
Tom Ayers	13	673	351	52	85.19	2	120	82	10	87.80	27	1254	705	104	85.25
Empty Net Goals			1	1										1	1
TEAM TOTALS	26	1560	906	118	86.97	4	240	136	24	82.35	44	2640	1525	220	85.57

Also played for: 1 Milton Keynes Kings; 2 Edinburgh Capitals; 3 Peterborough Pirates

Also appeared: Barry Evans, Ross Mackintosh, Tim Lockyer, Jason Price, Adam Brittle.

All Competitions = league, playoffs, Premier Cup and Findus Challenge Cup

SOLIHULL BARONS *left to right, back row:* Andy Ayers, Daniel Mackriel, Jon Rodway, Russell Coleman, Stephen Doyle, Neil Adams, Marc Williams, Colum Chadwick, Samuli Mykkanen, Antti Makikyro, Andrew Howarth, Phil Knight, Russ Plant, Rhys McWilliams; *front row:* David Whitwell, Phil Lee, Brian Chadwick (director), Michael Wales, Kevin King (coach), Dan Prachar, Jeff Porter (man. director), Duncan Cook, Paul Walker (team manager/director), Don Breau, Tom Ayers.

Photo: Adrian Woolley

Barons hard-up

TONY MacDONALD

In another bitter-sweet season, Barons achieved success on the ice, but little joy away from it as the financial problems which have dogged them over the past decade returned to haunt them.

They came within a slap-shot of winning the English Premier League but their achievements failed to capture the imagination of the public and the crowds rarely topped 300.

This left financial backers, **Paul Walker** and **Jeff Porter**, disillusioned ...and considerably lighter in the pocket!

Said Walker: "We felt we put a good product on the ice and were quite pleased to finish second. Maybe the delays in refurbishing the rink put the fans off, but no matter how well we played they still wouldn't come."

Under the guidance of new coach, **Kevin King**, Barons recruited an intriguing cocktail of youth and experience. Veterans **Kevin Conway**, **Don Breau**, **Dan Pracher** and **Phil Lee** returned from the previous campaign and new acquisitions included Canadian sniper **Duncan Cook**, ex-Blackburn forward **Daniel Mackriel** and Finnish pair, defenceman **Antti Makikyro** and forward **Samuli Mykkanen**.

The arrival of young goalie **Dave Whitwell** from Peterborough to partner **Tom Ayers**, allowed former cageman, **Steve Doyle**, to switch to an unfamiliar attacking role.

A surprise *Findus* Cup win at BNL side, Milton Keynes Kings, emphasised the potential of the new team and, despite a couple of early home reverses, their impressive road form kept them hot on the heels of the early pacesetters.

They climbed to second spot in late November with a 5-2 victory over leaders, Isle of Wight, and when high-riding Invicta arrived at Hobs Moat prior to Christmas the title race was wide open.

Barons twice held five-goal leads in the bitter encounter in which a mixture of indiscipline and controversial refereeing allowed the visitors to snatch an 8-8 tie.

The dropped point proved costly. Though they bounced back to close the campaign with nine straight wins, including two over Dynamos, their Medway rivals took the title - by just one point.

Further disappointment followed in the playoffs, and with Walker and Porter indicating their reluctance to continue bankrolling the team, the season ended gloomily.

Said Walker: "I'm certain senior hockey will continue in Solihull, but whether Jeff or myself are involved is open to question."

PLAYER AWARDS

Players' Player:	**Duncan Cook**
Supporters' Player:	**Antti Makikyro**
Best Forward:	**Duncan Cook**
Best Defenceman:	**Antti Makikyro**
Best British Player:	**Michael Wales**
Most Improved Player:	**Andrew Howarth**

LEADING PLAYERS

Duncan Cook *born 5 June 1977*

An instant hit with the fans, the 6ft 2in Canadian made a big impression during his debut season. A natural goal poacher, he used his shooting skills to good effect and led the league in scoring.

Andrew Howarth *born 18 May 1978*

After making a full recovery from a career threatening injury, the locally trained forward continued to improve during his second season on the roster. Always a handful for opposing defences.

Antti Makikyro *born 23 April 1978*

The popular Finn enjoyed a solid rookie season on the blue line and scored some big goals, too. Turned up to play every night and proved particularly effective on the power-play.

FACT FILE 2001-02

English Premier League:	2nd
Playoffs:	2nd in group
English Premier Cup:	Semi-finalists

HISTORY

Founded: 1965, reformed 2000. Disbanded 1996 with heavy debts and replaced by new club, the Blaze, who moved to Coventry in 2000.

Leagues: English Premier League 2000-02; British Lge, Div. One/Two 1993-96 & 1982-86; English Lge 1991-93; British Lge, Premier Div. 1986-91; Inter-City Lge 1978-82; Southern Lge 1972-78.

Honours: English League 1992-93; British Lge, Div. One 1985-86, Div. Two 1983-84; Southern League 1977-78.

SWINDON LYNX

PLAYER	ENGLISH PREMIER LEAGUE					PLAYOFFS					ALL COMPETITIONS				
Scorers	GP	G	A	Pts	Pim	GP	G	A	Pts	Pim	GP	G	A	Pts	Pim
Merv Priest	26	40	42	82	51	4	5	4	9	4	43	56	61	117	57
Ken Forshee (I)	26	27	22	49	24	4	3	7	10	6	43	37	36	73	50
Robin Davison	19	14	30	44	46	3	3	1	4	2	31	20	37	57	116
Gareth Endicott	23	13	15	28	79	4	1	3	4	4	40	25	20	45	91
Sean Tarr (I)	26	7	20	27	52	4	1	0	1	2	43	10	32	42	78
Bryan Larkin	22	5	13	18	40	4	0	1	1	8	36	8	18	26	60
Wayne Fiddes	22	3	16	19	18	4	0	1	1	4	39	3	20	23	28
Russell Cowley 3	9	8	13	21	2						12	8	14	22	2
Lee Brathwaite	18	3	13	16	61	4	1	3	4	12	33	4	18	22	87
Rob Johnston	24	6	8	14	18	4	0	1	1	8	38	8	12	20	42
Grant Bailey	23	8	3	11	16	3	0	2	2	2	38	11	7	18	56
Michael Smith	25	8	6	14	8	4	0	0	0	2	42	10	8	18	10
Simon Keating	24	3	7	10	103	4	0	0	0	34	41	4	9	13	171
Drew Chapman	15	3	5	8	22	3	0	0	0	2	24	4	5	9	28
Jani Eskola (I)	15	2	1	3	0						23	3	3	6	22
Mark Richardson	6	3	1	4	0	3	0	0	0	0	11	3	1	4	0
Nick Eden	15	0	3	3	4	4	0	0	0	0	26	0	3	3	6
Adam Andrews	18	0	0	0	4						28	1	0	1	6
Craig Wynn (N) 1	10	0	1	1	0	4	0	0	0	0	17	0	1	1	0
Andrew Shurmer	17	0	1	1	2	2	0	0	0	0	24	0	1	1	2
TEAM TOTALS	26	153	220	373	562	4	14	23	37	92	43	215	306	521	923

Netminders	GPI	Min	SOG	GA	Sv%	GPI	Min	SOG	GA	Sv%	GPI	Min	SOG	GA	Sv%
Dan Shea	1	60	31	2	93.55						1	60	31	2	93.55
Ken Wotherspoon	10	496	221	22	90.05						10	496	221	22	90.05
Jason Crossland (I) 2	3	180	117	15	87.18						6	360	205	21	89.76
Alec Field	6	304	212	25	88.21						8	424	291	30	89.69
Ron Bertrand (I)											5	300	188	20	89.36
Craig Wynn 1	9	520	294	34	88.44	4	239	132	17	87.12	16	940	548	67	87.77
Empty Net Goals								1	1					1	1
TEAM TOTALS	26	1560	875	98	88.80	4	239	133	18	86.47	43	2580	1485	163	89.02

Shutouts: Wotherspoon (3) - league: 24 Nov v Haringey Greyhounds (19 saves),

1 Dec v England under-20 (11 saves),

16 Feb v England under-18 (17 saves)

Also played for: 1 Isle of Wight Raiders; 2 Cardiff Devils, Edinburgh Capitals; 3 Coventry Blaze

Also appeared: Dean Mills, Gary Slevin, John Dewar, Lee Richardson.

All Competitions = league, playoffs, Premier Cup and Findus Challenge Cup

Goalie missing Lynx

MICHAEL PHILLIPS

The new Swindon *Innogy* Lynx battled all season to retain their English Premier League title but were beset by goalie problems which prevented them from settling into a winning rhythm.

The defending champion Phoenix had been denied the opportunity to retain their crown after a legal challenge over the use of the name. Instead, the team became the Lynx, though they were consoled by sponsorship from the giant Swindon-based energy provider, Innogy plc.

Despite the new name, the team remained essentially the same as the previous year with coach **Bryan Larkin** adding just one new face to his roster in Finn **Jani Eskola**. The *Innogy* Lynx began well in the pre-league *Findus* Challenge Cup, providing a stiff challenge for their BNL opponents. Narrow defeats at home to Peterborough and away to Hull - both by one goal in three - were topped by an impressive home victory over Cardiff Devils.

The team were shaping up well for a repeat performance of their league championship year. But their plans were dealt an early blow when doubts began circulating about the validity of star netminder **Ron Bertrand**'s passport credentials. After weeks of checking and counter-checking it became clear that the Canadian's UK stamp had expired and he was forced to leave the country.

As Larkin had built his team round last season's player of the year, his departure ripped the heart out of the team. Still, early results went their way, with wins at home to Romford, Solihull and eventual champions Invicta, backed up with a superb away win over the Barons.

Larkin had brought in **Alec Field** from Basingstoke to replace Bertrand, sharing the duties with **Ken Wotherspoon**, and briefly, Lynx topped the table. But results eventually dipped as the players realised they had relied too heavily on their goalie in the past.

Changes were made again, but though Field was replaced by Canadian **Jason Crossland**, signed from Edinburgh Capitals, results continued to fluctuate though they remained in touch with the leaders. By the time **Craig Wynn** took over from Crossland as the team's fourth no. 1 goalie, Lynx were still in with a chance at the title. Their hopes were only finally dashed when they lost a crucial game at Invicta in March and had to settle for fifth place.

The team narrowly lost out in the first round of the remaining competitions. In the playoffs, Romford and league champs, Invicta, beat them on goal difference; in the Premier Cup, only two points separated Lynx from the group's top side.

PLAYER AWARDS

Player of the Year	**Merv Priest**
Best Defender	**Lee Brathwaite**
Best Forward	**Merv Priest**
Best Newcomer	**Russell Cowley**
Most Improved Player	**Mark Richardson**

LEADING PLAYERS

Lee Brathwaite *born 17 July 1978*
A rock in Swindon's defence again, he's only 23 though considered a veteran by some onlookers. Continues to play quality hockey despite a full-time career as a fire-fighter.

Bryan Larkin *born 2 February 1967*
The player-coach was the heart of the Lynx as he had been with the league-winning Phoenix in 2000-01 and as captain of the league and playoff-winning IceLords in 1996-97.

His solid defensive play has made him a crowd favourite in Swindon since his arrival to play for the Wildcats in 1991. Decided to retire at the end of the season to concentrate on his blossoming hockey equipment business.

Merv Priest *born 2 August 1973*
Club's top scorer for second straight year and just missed out on being the league's leading pointsman. Showed good leadership qualities when deputising for his coach.

FACT FILE 2001-02

English Premier League:	Fifth
Playoffs:	3rd in qr-final group
Premier Cup:	4th in group
Findus Challenge Cup:	4th in group

HISTORY

Founded: 2000 as Phoenix. Name changed to Lynx in 2001. The town's team was the Chill in 1997-2000, IceLords in 1996-97 and Wildcats in 1986-96.

Leagues: Lynx and Phoenix - English (Premier) League 2000-02; Chill - English League 1997-2000; IceLords - Premier League 1996-97; Wildcats - British League, Div One 1986-96.

SWINDON LYNX *left to right, back row:* Wayne Fiddes, Ian Smith (equipment), Nick Eden, Gary Slevin, Adam Andrews, Mick Smith, Drew Chapman, Andrew Shurmer, Dean Mills; *front row:* Ken Wotherspoon, Ken Forshee, Sean Tarr, Lee Brathwaite, Phil Jefferies (manager), Bryan Larkin, Robin Davison, Gareth Endicott, Ron Bertrand.

WHITLEY WARRIORS

PLAYER	ENGLISH NATIONAL LEAGUE NORTH					PLAYOFFS					ALL COMPETITIONS				
Scorers	GP	G	A	Pts	Pim	GP	G	A	Pts	Pim	GP	G	A	Pts	Pim
Karl Culley	17	31	36	67	48	4	4	7	11	2	32	47	58	105	54
Andrew Carter	17	24	34	58	85	4	8	4	12	12	32	42	57	99	119
Stuart Lonsdale	18	16	19	35	31	4	1	4	5	2	33	29	39	68	39
Andrew Tindale	17	17	25	42	8	4	2	4	6	6	31	27	36	63	16
Paul Graham	18	10	18	28	13	4	1	5	6	0	31	19	27	46	15
Darren Taylor	8	6	7	13	29	4	3	3	6	6	19	17	23	40	80
Kevin Bucas	18	8	17	25	111	4	3	2	5	14	31	15	24	39	190
Lee Baxter	9	7	8	15	12	4	5	4	9	2	21	17	21	38	26
James Hutchinson	18	10	12	22	14	3	0	0	0	4	31	12	16	28	24
Ray Haslam	16	7	9	16	38						24	13	10	23	46
Paul McGinnety	11	3	10	13	41	3	0	1	1	36	20	3	15	18	103
Daniel Ord	11	5	9	14	40	1	0	0	0	41	19	6	11	17	87
Simon McGinnety	2	0	1	1	18	4	1	5	6	6	11	2	9	11	64
Daniel Good	12	7	0	7	0	4	1	0	1	0	24	9	1	10	0
Paul Willis	10	2	4	6	16	3	1	0	1	6	17	3	7	10	28
Bobby Bradley	6	2	3	5	80						8	3	4	7	84
Dale Howey	16	0	4	4	34	4	1	0	1	0	30	1	6	7	40
Neil Bainbridge	16	2	2	4	2	2	1	0	1	0	25	4	2	6	27
Scott Taylor	6	2	4	6	0						6	2	4	6	0
Richard Dunn	10	1	3	4	0	4	1	0	1	25	21	2	3	5	25
Stephen Wall (N)	16	0	3	3	0	4	0	2	2	0	30	0	5	5	48
Simon Leach 1	1	0	2	2	8						2	0	4	4	10
Rob Wilson	11	2	0	2	10	2	0	0	0	0	20	2	0	2	18
TEAM TOTALS	18	162	230	392	659	4	33	41	74	162	33	275	382	657	1143
Netminders	GPI	Min	SOG	GA	Sv%	GPI	Min	SOG	GA	Sv%	GPI	Min	SOG	GA	Sv%
Anthony Markham	2	120	56	5	91.07						3	164	74	7	90.54
Stephen Wall	14	760	428	44	89.72	3	180	95	9	90.53	27	1460	796	78	90.20
Rory Dunn	1	20	15	2	86.67	1	60	22	4	81.82	3	90	41	6	85.36
Stephen Hoult	2	100	34	5	85.29						2	100	34	5	85.29
Gordon Ford	3	80	24	4	83.33						6	166	61	10	83.61
TEAM TOTALS	18	1000	533	60	89.23	4	240	117	13	88.89	33	1980	1006	106	89.46

Also played for: 1 Paisley Pirates

Also appeared: Bryan Dunn, David Creed, Paul Sample, Peter Winn

All Competitions = league, playoffs and English Cup

WHITLEY WARRIORS *left to right, back row:* David Shearer (equipment), Andrew Tindale, Dale Howey, Ray Haslam, Kevin Bucas, Paul Sample, Paul Willis, Rob Wilson, Neil Bainbridge, James Hutchinson, Daniel Ord, Richard Dunn, Paul McGinnety, Michael Winn (manager); *front row:* Stephen Winn, Stephen Wall, Paul Graham, Stuart Lonsdale, Karl Culley, Peter Winn (coach), Andrew Carter, Lee Baxter, Scott Taylor, Gordon Ford.

Four wins for Winn

DAVID HALL

Warriors achieved an unusual Quadruple in 2001-02 - a belated second successive English National League Championship in November followed by a third at the end of the season which completed their first Grand Slam of league, cup and playoff championship.

No wonder their coach, **Peter Winn**, was over the moon. "We achieved everything we set out to do and I couldn't be happier," he said after the 6-1 home defeat of Basingstoke Buffalo in the (second) championship final.

With the bulk of the previous season's squad to call on, Winn needed only to tweak defence and attack and he signed **Andrew Tindale** and **James Hutchinson** from neighbours, Sunderland Chiefs.

Usually slow starters, Warriors were quick out of the trap this time, dropping just one point in their opening 11 games, before going down 3-1 at Blackburn in a mid-November cup game.

Their response was to demolish Billingham Eagles 10-1 in the long delayed second leg of the 2000-01 championship final, a victory that gave Whitley the rare distinction of winning the same title twice in the same campaign.

Though Warriors were proving to be the dominant force in the Northern Conference, their clash at Altrincham at the beginning of February was crucial to their title ambitions.

A titanic struggle in which Aces triumphed 6-5 was only Warriors' second league or cup defeat since the season started, but in a close race runners-up place loomed for the third year in a row. They finally captured the trophy a couple of weeks later after Aces fell at Kingston.

The finals of the English Cup and the playoff championship against Telford Wild Foxes and Basingstoke respectively provided plenty of entertainment, the highlight being the fight back from a five-goal deficit in the cup against a determined Telford.

Their only other defeats came in challenge games against Premier League runners-up, Solihull Barons, when Warriors pushed the Midlands outfit close on both occasions.

The performances helped to persuade Barons to vote for Warriors to move up to the Premier League at the summer meetings - but sadly, they were the only club to support the move.

Distance was an obvious stumbling block, but after overwhelming the National League in 2001-02, the club could hardly be blamed for believing that they deserved to be elevated to a higher standard of competition.

PLAYER AWARDS

Hillheads' Player of the Year
Stewart Lonsdale
Players' Player **Andrew Tindale**
Most Valuable Player **Andrew Tindale**
Supporters' Player **James Hutchinson**
Most Improved Player **Stephen Wall**
Rookie Of The Year **Dale Howey**

LEADING PLAYERS

Karl Culley *born 1 June 1978*
Played a major role in the team's success with a 100-point campaign - for the second year in a row. The first captain to lift every trophy the club competed for, his blistering speed and excellent stick handling made him a difficult opponent.

Dale Howey *born 2 May 1985*
An unflappable blueliner, who rarely allowed the opposition to pass him, the teenager shone in his first season in the senior squad after stepping up from the under-16s.

Andrew Tindale *born 22 October 1980*
A graduate of Newcastle Jesters' 'academy', his play-making skills were the ideal foil to **Andrew Carter** and Culley on the potent first line.

FACT FILE 2001-02

English National League:
Northern Conference winners
Playoff Championship: Winners
English Cup: Winners

HISTORY

Founded: 1956. Known as Newcastle Warriors in 1995-96, playing part of the season in Newcastle's *Telewest* Arena.

Leagues: English (National) League 1997-2002; Northern Premier League 1996-97; British League, Premier Division 1982-96; Northern League 1966-82.

Honours: English National League playoff champions 2001-02 & 2000-01; English National League North and English Cup 2001-02; English League, Div One playoffs 1999-2000; Scottish Cup 1992; Northern League 1973-75; Icy Smith Cup 1972-73 & 1973-74.

LEAGUE ORGANISATION

Organised ice hockey in 2001-02 was divided into three leagues, each run independently of the other.

The seven-team **Superleague** is a commercial organisation run under the auspices of a limited liability company, Ice Hockey Superleague Ltd (ISL), with each member club having a director on the ISL board.

The players are professionals recruited worldwide but mostly from North America. There was a £400,000 wage limit on players' salaries (a reduction of ten per cent compared with the previous season), and team rosters were limited to 20 skaters plus two netminders.

A proportion of the league's players require work permits (WP) and the guidelines on the origin and number of WP players are agreed jointly between Superleague, the Dept of Employment (overseas labour section), the governing body, Ice Hockey UK, and the Ice Hockey Players Association (GB).

For 2001-02, the guidelines were that this category of players should not exceed one-third of a team's roster with the remainder holding European Union passports.

North Americans should have played in a league at East Coast Hockey League (ECHL) level or above; Europeans must have played on a team from a country which competed in World A Pool the previous season.

The semi-pro **British National League** (BNL), (also a limited company) comprised 12 teams. The clubs had an agreement that at least 50 per cent of each team's players should be British trained and eligible to play for the national team. There was a wages guideline of £100,000 per club per season.

The **English Leagues**, which are run by the English Ice Hockey Association, comprise a wide range of clubs from the virtually amateur to those with budgets as large as the smaller BNL clubs. The teams with the most ice time and largest budgets competed in the Premier League and the remainder played in one of the National League's two regional conferences.

Each Premier team had to have at least three players on the ice who had completed two years training in England at under-19 level. The number of imported players depended only on a club's finances. The wages budget in the Premier League was around £75,000 per team.

Manchester Storm's **ROB WILSON** unleashes a bullet past Sheffield Steeler **PETE LEBOUTILLIER** in the Superleague Playoff Final at Nottingham Arena. *Photo: Kieran Galvin.*

SEKONDA SUPERLEAGUE

FINAL STANDINGS

	GP	W	L	D	GF	GA	Pts	Pct.
(/-6) Belfast Giants BEL	48	31	9	8	177	119	70	72.9
Home	24	20	2	2	98	53	42	87.5
Away	24	11	7	6	79	66	28	58.3
(5-5) Ayr Scottish Eagles AYR	48	20	19	9	136	130	49	51.0
Home	24	13	7	4	83	60	30	62.5
Away	24	7	12	5	53	70	19	39.6
(2-1) Sheffield Steelers SHE	48	18	18	12	138	144	48	50.0
Home	24	12	5	7	83	64	31	64.6
Away	24	6	13	5	55	80	17	35.4
(6-8) Nottingham Panthers NOT	48	19	20	9	140	141	47	48.9
Home	24	13	7	4	76	63	30	62.5
Away	24	6	13	5	64	78	17	35.4
(1-3) Bracknell Bees BRK	48	15	20	13	140	158	43	44.8
Home	24	10	8	6	72	68	26	54.2
Away	24	5	12	7	68	90	17	35.4
(4-4) London Knights LON	48	14	21	13	130	145	41	42.7
Home	24	9	7	8	70	64	26	54.2
Away	24	5	14	5	60	81	15	31.3
(3-7) Manchester Storm MAN	48	13	23	12	117	141	38	39.6
Home	24	9	8	7	63	61	25	52.1
Away	24	4	15	5	54	80	13	27.1

Pct. = Percentage of points gained to points available

Figures in brackets are the last two seasons' league positions (1999/2000-2000-01)

LEADING POINTS SCORERS

		GP	G	A	Pts	Pim
Kevin Riehl	BEL	48	22	37	59	16
Sean Berens	BEL	42	21	34	55	48
PC Drouin	NOT	48	18	34	52	78
Ed Courtenay	AYR	47	21	30	51	16
Jason Ruff	BEL	42	17	31	48	48
Patrik Wallenberg	NOT	48	21	26	47	73
Scott Allison	SHE	46	22	23	45	50
Dan Ceman	BRK	48	19	26	45	26
Mike Barrie	LON	48	20	24	44	140
Rick Brebant	SHE	42	13	30	43	36
Trevor Gallant	MAN	47	9	34	43	42

LEADING NETMINDERS

		GPI	Min	SOG	GA	Sv%
Mike Bales	BEL	34	1996	965	77	92.0
Mike Torchia	MAN	23	1211	678	57	91.6
Brian Greer	BRK	34	1923	1106	98	91.1
Danny Lorenz	NOT	46	2633	1363	122	91.0
Joaquin Gage	AYR	41	2459	1140	104	90.9

Qualification: 960 minutes

KEY MEN

clockwise from above left: Belfast Giants' goalie **MIKE BALES**, had the league's best save percentage; **MIKE BARRIE** was London Knights' top scorer and highest penalty taker; **CHRIS 'THE CHIEF' BRANT** and **'ROCKET' RON SHUDRA** helped Sheffield Steelers to win the Playoffs.

Photos: Michael Cooper, Tony Boot, Mike Smith/Icepix

POWERPLAY

Powerplay percentages	Adv.	PPG	Pct.
Ayr Scottish Eagles	204	41	20.1
Bracknell Bees	229	42	18.3
Sheffield Steelers	204	36	17.6
Belfast Giants	189	31	16.4
Manchester Storm	220	36	16.4
London Knights	213	30	14.1
Nottingham Panthers	232	32	13.8
LEAGUE TOTALS	1491	248	16.6

Adv. - Times with man advantage
PPG - powerplay goals scored
Pct. - percentage of goals scored to powerplays.

TOP POWERPLAY GOAL SCORERS

Ed Courtenay AYR 11; Scott Allison SHE, Paxton Schulte BEL 10; Ivan Matulik MAN 8; Dan Ceman BRK, Russ Romanuik MAN 7.

PENALTY KILLING

Penalty killing percentages	TSH	PGA	Pct.
Bracknell Bees	198	26	86.9
Belfast Giants	215	30	86.0
Ayr Scottish Eagles	228	37	83.8
London Knights	180	31	82.8
Nottingham Panthers	254	44	82.7
Manchester Storm	203	36	82.3
Sheffield Steelers	213	44	79.3
LEAGUE TOTALS	1491	248	83.4

TOP SHORT-HANDED GOAL SCORERS

Dody Wood AYR 4, Mark Cadotte BRK 3.

FAIR PLAY

Team Penalties	GP	Pim	Ave
Bracknell Bees	48	678	14.1
Manchester Storm	48	724	15.1
Belfast Giants	48	822	17.1
London Knights	48	842	17.5
Sheffield Steelers	48	913	19.0
Ayr Scottish Eagles	48	996	20.8
Nottingham Panthers	48	1195	24.9
LEAGUE TOTALS	168	6170	18.4

SIN-BIN

Player Penalties	GP	Pim	Ave
Barry Nieckar NOT	45	222	4.93
Gerard Adams LON	21	92	4.38
Dody Wood AYR	42	171	4.07
Clayton Norris NOT	41	165	4.02
Cal Benazic SHE	23	82	3.56
Phil Crowe AYR	20	71	3.55
Christian Sjogren NOT	18	63	3.50
Paul Kruse SHE	44	152	3.45

PAST WINNERS

2000-01	*Sheffield Steelers
1999-00	Bracknell Bees
1998-99	Manchester Storm
1997-98	Ayr Scottish Eagles
1996-97	Cardiff Devils

* exceeded £450,000 wage cap

PAST SCORING CHAMPIONS

2000-01	Greg Bullock MAN
1999-00	Ed Courtenay SHE
1998-99	Paul Adey NOT
1997-98	Tony Hand SHE
1996-97	Dale Junkin BRK

OFFICIAL SUPERLEAGUE WEBSITE
www.iceweb.co.uk

WE ARE NUMBER ONE!

Belfast Giants **COLIN WARD,** *left,* coach **DAVE WHISTLE,** *centre,* and captain **JEFF HOAD,** celebrate their Superleague title win with the Monteith Bowl. *Photo:* Michael Cooper.

Giants dwarf league

Superleague 2001-02 belonged to *Belfast Giants* who, in their first full season, clinched the league title as early as 19 January.

Dave Whistle's squad went to the top of the table on 28 September and stayed there - apart from a brief spell in October.

Their All-Star line of **Kevin Riehl-Sean Berens-Jason Ruff,** ended 1-2-6 in scoring as the team racked up a staggering 26 per cent more goals than their highest scoring opponents.

Giants' defence was also the stingiest, allowing only 2.31 goals a game, and goalie **Mike Bales**' personal save percentage was the league's best.

In contrast, there was a fine old tussle for second place which wasn't decided until the last weekend of the season.

Ayr Scottish Eagles gave a lot of the credit for their runners-up spot to two former NHLers, goalie **Joaquin Gage** and forward **Dody Wood**.

Right behind were **Mike Blaisdell**'s defending champion *Sheffield Steelers*, who once again defied the odds, this time caused by an enforced three-week delay to the start of their season.

One point further away were *Nottingham Panthers* led by fan favourite **PC Drouin** and newcomer, Swede **Patrik Wallenburg**.

Apart from Giants, this was a highly competitive league race with far fewer points (11) between the second and seventh teams, than between Giants and Eagles (21).

Bracknell Bees suffered from an unusual number of player problems. After a strong start, led by **Mark Cadotte,** who had 15 goals and 24 points by November, Bees faded.

Pity poor **Bob Leslie** whose *London Knights* lost five key players to injury for much of his first Superleague season, including one of Europe's best goalies, **Trevor Robins**. **Mike Barrie,** their top scorer, also incurred the refs' displeasure far too often.

Even with a new owner, and a new coach in long-time assistant, **Daryl Lipsey,** *Manchester Storm* could not improve on 2000-01's seventh place finish. Indeed, they never rose above fifth all season, although it was no fault of goalie **Mike Torchia,** who boasted the league's second best save percentage.

RESULTS CHART

	AYR	BEL	BRK	LON	MAN	NOT	SHE
AYR	**	0-4 2/9	7-3 5/9	3-2 8/9	2-4 6/10	3-1 30/9	3-3 23/9
Scottish	**	2-5C 26/9	4-1C 13/10	5-1 16/9	2-3C 23/12	3-3C 24/10	3-1 14/10
Eagles	**	3-5 30/12	9-1 4/11	2-2C 8/12	1-1 19/1	5-2 9/12	5-2C 11/11
	**	1-5 13/1	7-3 10/2	5-2 1/3	3-2 30/1	4-2 27/2	1-2 24/2
BELFAST	3-1 21/9	**	4-2 28/9	3-9 1/9	3-1 29/9	4-2 20/9	5-1C 8/11
Giants	7-2C 18/10	**	4-1C 1/11	4-3 4/10	2-1 19/10	0-1 16/10	6-3 5/12
	4-2 20/12	**	4-3 10/11	4-3C 19/12	6-2C 3/11	5-4C 21/11	8-1 4/1
	3-3 23/2	**	5-2 23/11	3-0 12/1	4-2 30/11	6-3 2/3	1-1 8/2
BR'CKNELL	6-3 21/10	1-1 15/9	**	0-1 23/9	2-1 9/9	5-2 28/10	5-2 30/9
Bees	2-1 1/12	1-3C 9/12	**	5-2C 25/10	4-0C 25/11	2-8C 11/11	7-3C 18/11
	4-4 5/1 CC	2-2 9/1	**	3-3 27/12	3-3 2/12	3-3 12/1	3-2 6/1
	1-3 20/2	2-5 24/2	**	1-2 7/2	5-4 20/12	2-4 3/2	3-6 24/1
LONDON	4-3 18/9	5-2 6/9	0-5 11/10	**	3-6 30/9	3-1 13/9	5-1C 4/11
Knights	1-2C 7/10	6-3 14/10	2-4C 6/12	**	1-3C 1/11	3-5 4/12	3-1 2/12
	5-2 29/11	1-3C 30/10	4-2 21/2	**	4-4 6/1	2-2C 18/12	2-2 10/1
	1-1 17/1	5-2 11/11	4-4 3/3	**	2-2 3/2	2-2 27/1	2-2 31/1
M'CHESTER	2-2 7/9	2-2 13/9	1-4 2/9	4-1 20/9	**	0-1 16/9	3-4C 24/11
Storm	0-2C 10/11	1-4C 21/10	3-1C 14/10	1-1C 18/11	**	3-3 27/9	1-2 30/12
	4-2 12/12	2-2 16/12	3-3 13/1	7-2 9/12	**	2-4C 4/11	4-3 10/2
	4-3 20/1	3-1 27/1	3-3 1/2	5-3 24/2	**	3-1 5/1	2-7 3/3
NOTT'HAM	3-4 15/9	4-3 8/9	2-3 22/9	6-6C 6/10	6-1 1/9	**	1-2 3/10
Panthers	2-1C 24/11	3-2C 27/10	5-5C 3/11	2-3 20/10	4-2 12/10	**	3-1C 8/12
	2-3 6/1	1-7 17/11	4-2 16/1	2-1 13/11	4-2C 22/12	**	2-1 16/12
	4-1 2/2	4-5 2/12	4-4 26/1	2-0 20/1	4-2 23/2	**	2-2 13/1
SHEFFIELD	1-1 29/9	3-3 10/10	3-3 7/10	5-3 26/9	3-0 22/9	6-4 13/10	**
Steelers	0-1 26/10	8-1C 28/10	3-5C 29/12	4-4 10/11	4-4C 15/12	4-0C 1/12	**
	3-5C 3/11	1-4 17/1	1-1 27/1	1-3C 2/12	4-2 26/12	5-4 23/12	**
	4-1 12/1	5-5 3/2	4-3 12/2	4-3 2/2	4-2 26/1	3-2 19/1	**
	AYR	BEL	BRK	LON	MAN	NOT	SHE

C = points count towards Challenge Cup

Second figure is date of game

PLAYOFFS

All Superleague teams entered the Playoffs. The first, qualifying round was played as a single round-robin.

The match-ups were allocated according to the final league positions with the league winners rewarded with home advantage over the teams immediately below them.

The top four teams qualified for the semi-finals.

QUALIFYING ROUND

	GP	W	L	D	GF	GA	Pts
Ayr Scottish Eagles	6	5	0	1	22	13	11
Sheffield Steelers	6	4	1	1	15	8	9
London Knights	6	4	2	0	17	15	8
M'chester Storm	6	2	3	1	24	21	5
Belfast Giants	6	2	3	1	21	19	5
Nottingham Panthers	6	1	3	2	13	20	4
Bracknell Bees	6	0	6	0	10	26	0

Positions of teams tied on points decided by (1) wins, (2) goal difference.

RESULTS

	AYR	BEL	BRK	LON	MAN	NOT	SHE
AYR	-	3-1				4-4	4-2
BEL	3-5	-				6-0	1-1
BRK		4-5	-	2-3	2-8		
LON	1-3	4-2		-	5-4		
MAN	2-3	5-4			-		1-3
NOT		3-1	1-3	4-4		-	
SHE		4-0	3-1		2-1		-

SEMI-FINALS

at the Nottingham Ice Centre

Sat 30 March	Ayr-Manchester	1-2
	Sheffield-London	3-2

FINAL

at the Nottingham Ice Centre

Sun 31 March Sheffield-Manchester 3-3ot
STEELERS won 4-3 on penalties

Storming finish

Superleague's insistence that every team should qualify for the Playoffs flies in the face of ice hockey's most treasured tradition.

Only once, in season 2000-01, has the league's quirky tradition been broken. But this year a new Playoff format at least helped to produce an exciting, if clumsy climax with the semi-finalists not known until the last weekend of the qualifying games.

What's more, last placed Manchester Storm made it through to the Final Four at the expense of league champs, Belfast Giants.

That outcome seemed unlikely after the early games as Storm predictably lost at home to Ayr and Sheffield, while Giants drew with the fired-up Steelers and **Mike Bales'** 29 saves helped Belfast to shutout Panthers 6-0 in the province.

Giants' last game in the Odyssey did not send their fans home happy, though, so it was perhaps as well that it drew one of their lowest crowds of the season. After **Mike Jickling** and **Jonathan Weaver** had given Ayr a 2-0 lead after two minutes, Bales was replaced by **Mark Cavallin**. Things went downhill after that with high scoring **Jason Ruff** being sent off for fighting and Giants eventually losing 5-3.

But the race stayed wide open when a few days later Storm tied in Nottingham and Belfast edged old rivals, Bracknell, by a goal.

So to the final week and the showdown in the MEN. Storm's sharpshooter **Joe Cardarelli** saved his team from oblivion with the winning goal four minutes from time in a 5-4 victory over Belfast. Everyone got a bit edgy now.

On the final day, Giants lost 4-2 in London, in a game that started *an hour before* Manchester's contest in Bracknell, where Bees had already been eliminated. The time difference gave Storm a comfort zone of knowing just how many they needed to win by.

Daryl Lipsey's underdogs duly trounced Bees 8-2 for a tie-breaking plus-3 goal difference compared to Belfast's plus-2.

Was Giants' captain, **Jeff Hoad**, upset? You bet he was. "I don't mean this to sound like sour grapes," he told the *Belfast Telegraph*, "but the outcome was decided by a team [Bees] that didn't care. But we're not mad at them. We lost ourselves when we had our fate in our hands."

Whistle had already blown his top, outside the London Arena dressing room of referee **Simon Kirkham**, who had given him a gross misconduct.

The whole affair was horribly reminiscent of Whistle's 1999-2000 season at Bracknell when the league winners were knocked out of the Playoffs.

PLAYOFF SEMI-FINALS

Nottingham Arena

Saturday 30 March 2002

AYR SCOTTISH EAGLES	1	(0-1-0)
MANCHESTER STORM	2	(1-1-0)

First Period
0-1 MAN Matulik (Busillo, Cardarelli) 10.47
Penalty minutes: Eagles 6, Storm 6.
Second Period
0-2 MAN Morin (Allard, Ferone) 32.21
1-2 AYR Bristow (Wood, Silfwerplatz) 38.04
Penalty minutes: Eagles 2, Storm 2.
Third Period
No scoring.
Penalty minutes: Eagles 9, Storm 7.
Shots on Goal
Gage AYR   11-10- 2 23   (*save - 95.6%*)
Torchia MAN   4-14-10 28   (*save - 92.9%*)
Man of the Match: Mike Torchia MAN.
Referee: Mike Rowe   *Linesmen*: Hicks, Pirry.
Attendance: 6,945.

SHEFFIELD STEELERS	3	(1-2-0)
LONDON KNIGHTS	2	(2-0-0)

First Period
0-1 LON Adams (Bronilla, Rushforth) 2.12
0-2 LON Ahlroos (Rushforth, Bronilla) pp 4.39
1-2 SHE Allison (Brebant) pp 10.39
Penalty minutes: Steelers 10, Knights 8
Second Period
2-2 SHE Shudra (Lauer) 33.31
3-2 SHE Lipsett (Brebant, Bobyck) 35.55
Penalty minutes: Steelers 4, Knights 4.
Third Period
No scoring.
Penalty minutes: Steelers 4, Knights 0.
Shots on Goal
Bach SHE   12- 6-11 29 (*save 93.1%*)
Trofimenkoff LON   3-11- 3 17 (*save 82.4%*)
Man of the Match: Ryan Bach SHE.
Referee: Andy Carson.
Linesmen: Craig, Staniforth.
Attendance: 6,945.

PLAYOFF FINAL

Nottingham Arena

Sunday 31 March 2002

SHEFFIELD STEELERS	3	(1-1-1-0)
MANCHESTER STORM	3	(2-1-0-0)

After OT. Steelers won 4-3 after penalties

First Period
1-0 SHE Kruse (Allison, Lauer) 1.11
1-1 MAN Gallant (Bultje) pp 11.23
1-2 MAN Morin (Allard, Miller) 16.36
Penalty minutes: Steelers 4, Storm 2.
Second Period
1-3 MAN Ferone 22.06
2-3 SHE Kruse 39.27
Penalty minutes: Steelers 0, Storm 4.
Third Period
3-3 SHE Lipsett (Bobyck, Mansoff) 57.50
Penalty minutes: Steelers 2, Storm 0.
Overtime
No scoring.
No penalties.
Penalty shots

1	MAN	Cardarelli	save	0-0
2	SHE	Lipsett	save	0-0
3	MAN	Romanuik	save	0-0
4	**SHE**	**Lauer**	**score**	**1-0**
5	MAN	Bultje	save	1-0
6	SHE	Brebant	save	1-0
7	MAN	Gallant	save	1-0
8	SHE	Shudra	save	1-0
9	MAN	Preston	save	1-0

Shots on Goal (ex penalties)
Bach SHE   12- 8-13-3 36   (*save 91.7%*)
Torchia MAN 13-12-12-3 40   (*save 92.5%*)
Man of the Match: Paul Kruse SHE
Referee: Nigel Boniface.
Linesmen: Coenen, Folka
Attendance: 7,126.

GREATER THAN THE GREATEST THING EVER

'The Playoff Finals will generate an atmosphere that - if you could could bag it and sell it - would make you a millionaire...'

From Superleague's press release announcing the Nottingham Arena as the Playoff venue. The release also managed to use the words 'delighted', 'magnificent', 'perfect', 'prestigious', 'weekend to remember', 'fantastic', 'spectacular', 'extremely positive', 'fabulous', 'absolutely delighted', 'bigger and better than ever', 'ideal', and 'superb' twice.

Blimey! What would they have said about Wembley?

THE FINAL FOUR

AYR SCOTTISH EAGLES
Joaquin Gage, Colin Ryder; Ian Herbers, Anders Hillstrom, Ryan Risidore, Alan Schuler (capt), Johan Silfwerplatz; Dino Bauba, Cam Bristow, Shawn Byram, Ed Courtenay, Phil Crowe, Rhett Gordon, Mike Harding, Mike Jickling, Johan Molin, Jonathan Weaver, Dody Wood.
Coach: Paul Heavey. *Manager*: Kenny MacLeod.
Asst coach: Scott Rex.

LONDON KNIGHTS
Dave Trofimenkoff, Scott Bailey; Gerard Adams, Sean Blanchard, Rich Bronilla, Greg Burke, Rob Donovan; Kim Ahlroos, Dominic Amodeo, David Clarke, Mark Kolesar, Maurizio Mansi, Ian McIntyre, Paul Rushforth, Vezio Sacratini, David Struch (capt), Nathan Leslie.
Manager-coach: Bob Leslie.

MANCHESTER STORM
Stevie Lyle, Mike Torchia; Kris Miller, Dwight Parrish, Dan Preston, Kayle Short, Rob Wilson; Pierre Allard, Mark Bultje, Joe Busillo, Joe Cardarelli, Paul Ferone, Trevor Gallant, Ivan Matulik (capt), Mike Morin, Russ Romanuik.
Manager-coach: Daryl Lipsey.

SHEFFIELD STEELERS
Ryan Bach, Eoin McInerney; Cal Benazic, Jeff Brown, Marc Laniel, Jason Mansoff, Jeff Sebastian, Ron Shudra; Scott Allison, Brent Bobyck, Chris Brant, Rick Brebant, Paul Kruse (capt), Brad Lauer, Peter Leboutillier, Chris Lipsett, Marc Dutiaume.
Head coach: Mike Blaisdell.
Asst coach: Rick Brebant.

SIN-BIN

Players' penalties	GP	Pims	Ave
Mike Barrie LON	5	39	7.80
Paxton Schulte BEL	6	42	7.00
Jason Ruff BEL	6	38	6.33

PAST FINALISTS

2001 **Sheffield** **Steelers** beat London Knights 2-1 at Nottingham Arena.
2000 **London** **Knights** beat Newcastle Riverkings 7-3 at the *MEN* Arena, Manchester.
1999 **Cardiff** **Devils** beat Nottingham Panthers 2-1 at the *MEN* Arena, Manchester.
1998 Ayr Scottish Eagles beat Cardiff Devils 3-2 at the *Nynex* Arena, Manchester.
1997 Sheffield Steelers beat Nottingham Panthers 3-1 at the *Nynex* Arena, Manchester.

LEADING PLAYOFF SCORERS

	GP	G	A	Pts	Pim
Joe Cardarelli MAN	8	7	6	13	2
Sean Berens BEL	6	7	3	10	2
Trevor Gallant MAN	8	4	5	9	0
Ivan Matulik MAN	8	4	5	9	8
Rick Brebant SHE	8	1	8	9	13

LEADING PLAYOFF NETMINDERS

	GPI	Mins	SoG	GA	Sv%
Ryan Bach SHE	8	485	262	12	95.4
Joaquin Gage AYR	7	420	210	15	92.9
Stevie Lyle MAN	3	180	117	9	92.3

Qualification: 160 minutes

No fairy tale ending for Storm

Manchester Storm, who qualified for the Final Four in fourth place, turned their Giant-killing act into an Eagle shoot, upsetting the number one qualifiers in the first semi-final.

It was Storm's fourth game without defeat after losing their opening three Playoff games.

Goals from skipper **Ivan Matulik** and **Pierre Allard** left Ayr playing catch-up. "Our defence was poor in the first period," admitted Eagles' coach, **Paul Heavey**, while his opposite number, **Daryl Lipsey**, tried to look as though this were an everyday occurrence.

In a thrilling second semi, Sheffield's keeper, **Ryan Bach**, was little short of sensational especially in the last period when London poured shots on the former Los Angeles Kings' stopper.

Steelers' fans held their breath five minutes from time when Bach was winded after falling awkwardly, but he refused to go off. "I'd only have replaced him if his pulse rate had gone down to ten," quipped coach **Mike Blaisdell**.

In the final, the unfancied Storm, with a brilliant performance from their keeper, former Steeler **Mike Torchia**, cruised into a 3-1 lead early on against the defending champions. A fairy-tale ending seemed on the cards, but the indomitable Steelers hadn't read the script and **Chris Lipsett**, the league's leading scorer, tied the game two minutes from time.

When five minutes, four-on-four overtime failed to settle the most enthralling Playoff final of the Superleague era, most fans would have accepted the draw as a happy ending.

Sheffield's ex-NHLer, **Brad Lauer**, was the only one of nine players to convert his penalty shot. "I faked it and put it on my backhand," he said while Steelers and their fans celebrated their third Superleague Playoff title and fifth in all.

CHALLENGE CUP

One round of nominated Superleague games counted as the qualifying round of the Cup. (See Superleague Results Chart).

The leading four teams qualified for the semi-finals with first meeting fourth and second playing third, over home and away legs.

The Cup's destination was decided in a one-game final at the Odyssey Arena in Belfast.

The final was televised by BBC Northern Ireland for Grandstand and sponsored by on-line bookies, bluesquare.com.

QUALIFYING ROUND

	GP	W	L	D	GF	GA	Pts
Belfast Giants	12	10	2	0	49	29	20
N'ham Panthers	12	6	2	4	44	35	16
Ayr S. Eagles	12	5	4	3	34	33	13
Bracknell Bees	12	5	5	2	40	41	12
M'chester Storm	12	3	7	2	24	37	8
London Knights	12	2	6	4	29	34	8
Sheffield Steelers	12	3	8	1	35	46	7

All games counted towards Superleague points

SEMI-FINALS
First legs
23 Jan
AYR-NOTTINGHAM　　　**3-0** (0-0,2-0,1-0)
Goal scorers: Gordon 2, Molin.
30 Jan
BRACKNELL-BELFAST　　**1-5** (1-2,0-1,0-2)
Goal scorers: BRK McBain; BEL Matsos 2, Ruff, Bowen, Stevens.

Second legs
5 Feb
BELFAST-BRACKNELL　　**4-5** (1-2,3-1,0-2)
Goal scorers: BEL Berens 2, Bowen, Ward; BRK Knox 3, Cadotte 2.
GIANTS win 9-6 on aggregate.

9 Feb
NOTTINGHAM-AYR　　　**4-4** (1-1,2-1,1-2)
Goal scorers: NOT Paek, Moria, Tait, Carlsson; AYR Byram 2, Wood, Herbers.
EAGLES win 7-4 on aggregate

FINAL
***Odyssey Arena, Belfast**, 3 March 2002*

BELFAST GIANTS	0	(0-0-0)
AYR SCOTTISH EAGLES	5	(2-2-1)

First Period
0-1　　AYR Gordon　　　　　　　　　　　　2.42
0-2　　AYR Courtenay (Silfwerplatz)　　4.48
Penalty minutes: Giants 4, Eagles 4.
Second Period
0-3　　AYR Weaver (Gordon)　　　　　　27.54
0-4　　AYR Gordon (Weaver, Byram)　　36.49
Penalty minutes: Giants 6, Eagles 4.
Third Period
0-5　　AYR Wood (Bristow, Bauba)　　　43.12
Penalty minutes: Giants 0, Eagles 2.
Shots on Goal
Bales BEL　　12- 6-8 26　　　(save 80.8%)
Gage AYR　　　8-11-6 25　　　(save 100.0)
Referee: Simon Kirkham.　　Attendance: 7,100
Linesmen: Staniforth, Norcott.

THE WINNING TEAM
AYR SCOTTISH EAGLES
Joaquin Gage, Colin Ryder; Ian Herbers, Alan Schuler (capt), Johan Silfwerplatz, Anders Hillstrom, Ryan Risidore, Patrick Ward; Dino Bauba, Cam Bristow, Mike Jickling, Dody Wood, Jonathan Weaver, Johan Molin, Shawn Byram, Ed Courtenay, Phil Crowe, Rhett Gordon.
Coach: Paul Heavey. *Manager*: Kenny MacLeod.

Giant killers

Ayr's shutout defeat of Belfast Giants was one of the biggest upsets of the season.

Giants should have been on top form after their Superleague title run - though they might have been a bit jaded after playing Nottingham Panthers in a league game the previous evening - and were performing in front of their usual sell-out crowd. Eagles had not won in the Odyssey all season.

But instead of cruising to victory, Giants were 2-0 down after five minutes and rarely looked like recovering.

As always, a lot depended on the goalies and **Mike Bales**, the league's top netminder, had an off-day while his opposite number, **Joaquin Gage**, was in literally unbeatable form.

It was hard to disagree with **Paul Heavey**, the victorious coach, when he said: "I've never been part of a team who have been in such control of a game. We deserved this win."

■ The Odyssey Arena was awarded the final after London Arena, who won the right to stage the game, withdrew when Knights were knocked out of the competition.

ALL-TIME SUPERLEAGUE RECORDS

LEAGUE STANDINGS

Seasons 1996-97 to 2001-02	S	GP	W	L	D	OL	GF	GA	Pts	Pct.
Cardiff Devils CAR	6	202	118	75	9	13	756	590	282	60.6
Belfast Giants BEL	2	96	54	34	8	9	335	278	142	60.4
Sheffield Steelers SHE	6	250	132	94	24	13	894	783	331	57.6
Ayr Scottish Eagles AYR	6	250	121	105	24	10	865	801	297	53.2
Manchester Storm MAN	6	250	119	110	21	12	840	822	286	51.8
Nottingham Panthers NOT	6	250	115	118	17	12	801	853	269	49.4
Bracknell Bees BRK	6	250	112	117	21	17	902	923	281	49.0
London Knights LON	4	180	72	89	19	11	522	583	192	45.3
Newcastle Cobras/Riverkings/Jesters NEW	5	202	63	133	6	21	580	776	165	32.7
Basingstoke Bison BAS	2	70	16	47	7	9	232	318	48	27.9

LEADING SCORERS

1996-2002	S	GP	G	A	Pts	Ave
Ed Courtenay AYR/SHE	5	199	122	126	248	1.25
Vezio Sacratini LON/CAR	6	237	99	141	240	1.01
*Tony Hand AYR/SHE	5	191	60	160	220	1.15
Greg Hadden NOT	6	225	116	103	219	0.97
Ivan Matulik MAN/CAR	6	244	101	113	214	0.88
Rick Brebant SHE/MAN/LON/NEW	6	208	69	143	212	1.02
Steve Thornton LON/CAR	6	193	77	127	204	1.08
Steve Moria NOT/CAR	6	244	106	97	203	0.83
Blake Knox BRK/NEW/NOT/BAS	6	243	69	124	193	0.79
Shawn Byram AYR/MAN	6	206	63	122	185	0.89

* Left league after 2000-01 season

LEADING NETMINDERS

1996-2002	S	GPI	Mins	SoG	GA	Sav%
Rob Dopson AYR	1	28	1674	885	66	92.5
Jim Hrivnak MAN	1	15	927	515	40	92.2
Mike Bales BEL	1	34	1996	965	77	92.0
Mike Torchia MAN/SHE	2	46	2521	1221	102	91.6
Derek Herlofsky CAR	4	93	5469	2755	235	91.5
Trevor Robins LON/NOT	5	145	8465	4436	397	91.1
Danny Lorenz NOT	1	46	2633	1363	122	91.0
Joaquin Gage AYR	1	41	2459	1140	104	90.9

Qualification: One-third of team's games in a season.

AHEARNE TROPHY

The seven Superleague teams took on seven German DEL (Deutsche Elite League) clubs in a 14-game, six-day tournament during the Winter Olympic break. In a format similar to golf's Ryder Cup, the league whose teams gained most points won the Ahearne Trophy.

The games were the idea of the Anschutz Entertainment Group who own a number of European club sides, including London Knights.

They were devised to promote the idea of a European League, though they were also helpful in filling the gaps in Superleague's schedule caused by the demise of two of their franchises.

The German DEL is rated as the sixth strongest in Europe, so to ensure that the games were as competitive as possible, all bar one of the German clubs - Schwenningen Wild Wings - came from the bottom half of the 16-team DEL.

In addition, the games were staged while many top DEL players were in Salt Lake City.

The Ahearne Trophy was named after **John F (Bunny) Ahearne**, the controversial former president of the British Ice Hockey Association and the International Ice Hockey Federation.

The original trophy was first competed for in 1952. Nottingham Panthers won it in 1956 and the last winner in 1974 was Djurgardens of Stockholm.

The organisers received permission from the Swedish Federation to revive the tournament, though a new trophy was struck for the occasion, hand-crafted by Tyrone Crystal of Northern Ireland.

RESULTS

12 Feb	Belfast-Oberhausen	3-4ot
	Manchester-Iserlohn	1-1ot
13 Feb	Belfast-Hanover	4-3ot
	Sheffield-Oberhausen	3-5
14 Feb	London-Hanover	3-1
	Nottingham-Iserlohn	1-2
16 Feb	Bracknell-Schwenningen	2-4
	Ayr-Berlin Eisbären	2-2ot
	Nottingham-Düsseldorf	3-2
	Sheffield-Frankfurt	4-5
17 Feb	London-Schwenningen	3-3ot
	Manchester-Berlin	5-5ot
	Bracknell-Düsseldorf	3-4
	Ayr-Frankfurt	5-3

FINAL STANDINGS

	GP	W	L	D	GF	GA	Pts
DEL	14	6	4	4	44	42	16
Superleague	14	4	6	4	42	44	12

Superleague Bernd by DEL

Much to the sceptics' surprise, the 'magnificent seven' Superleague teams took their import-dominated German opponents right down to the last day before conceding the newly minted Ahearne Trophy.

The league were already adrift by four points by the Sunday, and when London and Manchester could only draw with their rivals, it left Bracknell needing to beat Dusseldorf to have any chance of pulling off a late victory.

Bees were never ahead of the Germans who took a 3-1 lead at the mid-point. **Blake Knox** and **Joe Ciccarello** tied the game but **Bernd Kühnhauser** scored the winner on a last period powerplay to seal victory for the DEL.

Ayr were the only winning team that day and with their game facing off last, it fell to Eagles' owner, **Bill Barr** OBE, to present the trophy to **Gernot Tripke**, the chief executive of the DEL.

Each of the 14 teams played two games. Belfast Giants, London Knights, Nottingham Panthers and Ayr Scottish Eagles each won a game for the ISL and four matches were drawn.

The top individual points scorers were Sheffield's **Rick Brebant** and Düsseldorf's **Nikolaus Mondt** who each had two goals and four points. **Sean Berens** of Belfast also had four points, three of them assists.

Immediately after the tournament, Superleague gushed in a press release: "We have received wonderful news that the DEL wish to compete for the Ahearne Trophy again next season. We're thrilled that we'll be seeing more of the same next season."

Fan reaction was less enthusiastic with Manchester and Nottingham each attracting fewer than 2,000 for their midweek games.

■ Two German coaches were sacked days before the tournament. Frankfurt Lions released **Doug Bradley** and the Anschutz-owned Berlin Polar Bears fired **Uli Egen**. Frankfurt and Iserlohn Roosters were both battling to avoid relegation out of the DEL.

■ The competition was unsponsored and TV coverage was restricted to highlights shown on a German channel.

■ The games were played under IIHF rules with a five-minute overtime in the event of a draw.

REACTION TO THE FIRST AHEARNE TROPHY FROM PLAYERS AND FANS

THE DIFFERENCES

"I think the main differences in the leagues are, firstly, that the DEL teams have more depth and talent. The first two lines in any ISL team could compete with any DEL team.

"The difference comes when you are able to play four lines or you have injuries. Injuries play a huge role in the Superleague. If hit with injuries, it is difficult for ISL teams to live up to expectations.

"In the DEL, injuries don't play such a big role because the third and fourth line guys are talented as well.

"Overall, I think the main difference between the leagues is the budgets of the teams in the DEL and being able to attract the bigger name players, but not always the better players.

"The difference between the two leagues is not as much as everybody thinks. The Superleague doesn't get the recognition that it deserves here in Europe. "
Jeff Tomlinson, the former Manchester Storm forward who played for Berlin Ice Bears.

"From what I've seen so far the Superleague is a far tougher league. In the DEL they play a more skilled, European style, whereas in the Superleague it's a more Canadian, hard-hitting style of play. Also there is the salary control, they have no limit in the DEL   *Jason Ruff , who joined Belfast Giants from Frankfurt Lions.*

"Playing in the DEL was a different experience. It was more wide open and not as physical. It's more up and down with more skilled players. Their plays consist of more traps, rushes and speed, and the skill level is higher.

"The ISL teams play a very similar style to the American Hockey League. If you look at our rosters a lot of guys come here from the AHL or the East Coast League; it's definitely more of a Canadian style, more hitting, clutching and grabbing."   *Marc Laniel of Sheffield Steelers, who used to play for Schwenningen Wild Wings.*
Quotes taken from Superleague's website.

COMRADES ON SKATES

"It was interesting talking to the people at the DEL. We found out that they have very similar problems to our own." *Martin Weddell, acting chairman of Superleague, at the launch of the Ahearne Trophy.*
Editor's Note - The DEL is a professional league dominated by non-German players.

BAD TIMING

"Playing German sides in a tournament like this is a good experience for us and the guys enjoyed this game, but because they don't really mean anything I don't think the incentive is there.

"Players are gearing themselves up for play-offs now so the tournament has come at the wrong time. Had it been at the start of the season it might be totally different. It could be a great way to warm up for a new season." *Daryl Lipsey, Manchester Storm coach.* Manchester Evening News.

TAKEN FOR A MUG

'I missed my first EVER Storm home game last night. It hurt like hell, but the world didn't end.

I'm not being taken for a mug, and neither will many of the other season ticket holders who are simply going to put their season ticket renewal reminder in the bin when it arrives.'
Storm fan writing on the web in February 2002 after the team's opening contest in the Ahearne Trophy which attracted an all-time low of 1,860 fans to the MEN Arena.

The club asked season ticket holders to pay extra although the games had been arranged in lieu of ISL matches against Newcastle.

FINDUS BRITISH NATIONAL LEAGUE

FINAL STANDINGS

P/pos		GP	W	L	D	GF	GA	Pts	Pct
(/-/)	**Dundee Stars** DUN	44	40	4	0	289	101	80	90.9
(7-4)	**Coventry Blaze** COV	44	33	9	2	227	118	68	77.3
(1-3)	**Fife Flyers** FIF	44	31	12	1	222	110	63	71.6
(3-2)	**Basingstoke Bison** BAS	44	24	18	2	201	151	50	56.8
(2-1)	**Guildford Flames** GUI	44	24	19	1	198	144	49	55.7
(4-6)	**Hull Thunder** HUL	44	23	19	2	190	161	48	54.5
(8-9)	**Edinburgh Capitals** EDI	44	20	23	1	180	212	41	46.6
(9-8)	**Milton Keynes Kings** MIL	44	17	23	4	146	160	38	43.2
(10-10)	**Paisley Pirates** PAI	44	18	25	1	161	259	37	42.O
(5-5)	**Peterborough Pirates** PET	44	11	30	3	136	208	25	28.4
(6-7)	**Slough Jets** SLO	44	7	33	4	112	216	18	20.4
(/-/)	**Cardiff Devils** CAR	44	5	38	1	90	312	11	12.5

Scoring system
Games tied after the regulation 60 minutes went into 10 minutes sudden-death overtime with the winning team taking both points. Teams still tied at the end of overtime shared the points.
P/pos - league position in each of last two seasons, 1999-2000 and 2000-01. First year of competition for Dundee Stars; Cardiff Devils previously competed in the Superleague.
Pct. - percentage of points gained to points available.

LEADING SCORERS

	GP	G	A	Pts	Pim
Tony Hand DUN	44	25	79	104	18
Domenic Parlatore PAI	44	43	52	95	114
Teeder Wynne DUN	44	44	50	94	14
Jason Lafreniere EDI	44	38	50	88	32
Jan Mikel DUN	44	27	58	85	62
Russ Monteith FIF	42	44	40	84	6
Scott Young DUN	44	35	49	84	167
Steve Smillie HUL/MIL	44	40	40	80	42
Todd Dutiaume FIF	44	32	48	80	96
Mikko Koivunoro EDI/GUI	41	18	60	78	42
Corey Lyons HUL	41	31	46	77	20
Claude Dumas COV	43	30	46	76	24

LEADING NETMINDERS

	GPI	Mins	SoG	GA	S%
Shawn Silver FIF	43	2478	1222	101	91.7
Domenic DeGiorgio MIL	41	2448	1593	141	91.2
Stephen Murphy DUN	43	2359	1018	91	91.1
Mark McArthur GUI	42	2551	1395	132	90.5
Stephen Foster BAS/HUL/MIL	38	2295	1313	126	90.4

Qualification: 880 mins

SIN-BIN

Players' Penalties	GP	Pim	Ave
James Clark PAI	33	194	5.88
Chris Conaboy PAI	30	152	5.07
Jesse Hammill PET	31	154	4.97

LEAGUE AWARDS

INDIVIDUAL

Player of the Year	**Tony Hand** DUN
Best Netminder	**Stephen Murphy** DUN
Best Defenceman	**Scott Young** DUN
British Player of the Year	**Tony Hand** DUN
Coach of the Year	**Tony Hand** DUN

ALL-STARS

Goal	**Stephen Murphy** DUN
Defence	**Jan Mikel** DUN
	Scott Young DUN
Forwards	**Tony Hand** DUN
	Teeder Wynne DUN
	Jason Lafreniere EDI

BRITISH ALL-STARS

Goal	**Stephen Murphy** DUN
Defence	**Stephen Cooper** COV
	Neil Liddiard BAS
Forwards	**David Clarke** MIL
	Steven King FIF
	Tony Hand DUN

Selections made by the team coaches, excluding their own team.

FAIR PLAY

Team Penalties	GP	Pim	Ave
Cardiff Devils	44	414	9.4
Basingstoke Bison	44	494	11.2
Fife Flyers	44	507	11.5
Edinburgh Capitals	44	576	13.1
Dundee Stars	44	620	14.1
Milton Keynes Kings	44	672	15.3
Coventry Blaze	44	765	17.4
Slough Jets	44	769	17.5
Peterborough Pirates	44	778	17.7
Hull Thunder	44	788	17.9
Guildford Flames	44	800	18.2
Paisley Pirates	44	986	22.4
LEAGUE TOTALS	264	8169	15.5

PAST WINNERS

2000-01		Guildford Flames
1999-2000		Fife Flyers
1998-99		Slough Jets
1997-98		Guildford Flames
1996-97	*Premier Lge*	Swindon IceLords
	N Premier Lge	Fife Flyers

Stars light years ahead

The league's fifth season belonged to their newest club, **Dundee Stars**, who captured the title in their very first campaign.

The year was also a personal triumph for Stars' player-coach **Tony Hand**. Britain's premier player for the last 20-odd years successfully added coaching to his already formidable array of talents while carrying off the league's points scoring crown and hitting the 1,000th goal of his career.

Stars' Hand-picked team, which included many faces familiar to Superleague fans, lost only four games all season.

Their big Scottish rivals, Fife Flyers, were the only team to get their measure in their own rink, and their only road defeats came at English clubs, Guildford Flames, and league runners-up, Coventry Blaze.

Unsurprisingly, Stars captured all the league's individual awards and all bar one of the first All-Star team berths.

In any other season **Coventry Blaze** would have eaten all the pies, but instead the second year team had to settle for second place.

Coach **Paul Thompson** had a strong team but they lacked consistent goaltending. While Blaze were very good, Stars were excellent.

Shawn Silver, **Fife Flyers'** ex-Superleague netminder, on the other hand was one of the keys to Flyers' third place with a league-leading 91.7 save percentage.

There was little to choose between the next three teams - **Basingstoke Bison**, **Guildford Flames** and **Hull Thunder** - though few would have given odds of those placings before the season.

After a fraught 2000-01, Thunder's new owners signed three players with Superleague experience - **Corey Lyons**, **Daryl Lavoie** and **Eric Lavigne** - and were much better than expected. But Flames, especially goalie **Mark McArthur**, went off the boil after their Triple winning season.

Another ex-Superleague player, **Jason Lafreniere**, helped to bring respectability to perennial sub-.500 team, **Edinburgh Capitals**. Their seventh place finish was the best in their brief history.

Four of the bottom five clubs appeared to be playing their final BNL season. **Milton Keynes Kings** and **Peterborough Pirates** were withdrawn from the league by their rink owners at the end of the season, and **Slough Jets** and **Paisley Pirates** suffered fatal economic crises.

Cardiff Devils struggled through the season with a scratch side, praying for a saviour in 2002-03.

RESULTS CHART

	BAS	CAR	COV	DUN	EDI	FIF	GUI	HUL	MIL	PAI	PET	SLO
BAS	**	8-2 30/12	5-7 29/9	5-6 20/10	6-1 6/10	3-2 (4) 13/10	3-1 10/11	5-2 1/12	4-5 16/12	12-1 18/11	7-0 27/10	1-1ot 21/10
	**	18-0 9/1	1-8 16/2	1-5 29/12	5-3 19/1	3-1 5/1	6-1 9/2	3-4 30/1	2-2ot 3/2	3-4 9/12	7-3 23/2	6-2 12/1
CAR	5-7 11/11	**	3-4 20/10	2-11 17/11	2-5 3/11	0-17 22/12	2-7 14/10	2-4 30/9	3-2 28/10	8-3 7/10	2-6 8/12	3-5 23/9
	2-6 10/2	**	1-3 29/12	0-5 26/1	3-12 2/2	1-7 17/2	3-9 6/1	4-1 25/11	1-2 27/1	1-4 20/1	4-8 29/1	3-3ot 23/12
COV	4-3 4/11	5-1 21/10	**	6-3 18/11	5-2 14/10	3-2 7/10	3-2ot 25/10 (6)	3-5 17/11	0-2 11/11	12-3 23/9	2-2ot 27/12	8-1 30/9
	7-1 24/2	9-0 5/1	**	3-2ot 9/12 (9)	8-3 6/1	2-1ot 20/1 (16)	7-4 17/2	6-4 16/12	2-4 10/2	15-1 23/12	4-3ot 12/1 (15)	10-2 30/12
DUN	4-2 7/10	9-0 27/10	4-0 2/12	**	7-2 8/12	5-6 11/11	4-2 21/10	8-2 6/10	5-2 14/10	13-1 30/9	14-5 4/11	6-1 16/12
	7-5 20/1	13-0 3/2	5-2 13/1	**	7-4 24/2	8-2 10/2	6-3 30/12	5-3 19/1	9-1 6/1	11-0 21/11	9-1 23/12	6-1 2/2
EDI	2-5 23/9	9-1 1/12	3-7 28/10	4-7 13/10	**	5-1 30/9	6-7ot 20/10 (5)	5-7 13/1	4-2 21/10	3-0 11/11	4-2 2/12	2-1 4/11
	6-5ot 23/12 (12)	7-0 16/12	4-6 27/1	2-12 26/12	**	1-6 18/11	2-9 9/12	4-4ot 17/2	6-4 5/2	4-6 10/2	5-2 3/2	4-2 5/1
FIF	8-2 17/11	6-2 22/9	1-3 27/10	1-6 29/9	8-2 10/11	**	7-3 8/12	2-1 20/10	1-6 9/12	5-1 13/1	6-1 6/10	5-0 3/11
	4-1 2/2	8-0 15/12	2-3 26/1	3-5 2/2	9-3 9/2	**	5-2 29/12	5-2 12/1	7-1 23/2	8-1 16/2	9-1 19/1	3-5 6/1
GUI	5-3 30/9	5-0 4/11	4-2 13/10	1-3 22/9	4-2 7/10	3-6 28/10	**	4-1 5/1	7-1 23/9	5-4 2/12	5-2 18/11	0-3 11/11
	4-6 26/1	10-5 13/1	4-2 3/2	4-3ot 22/12 (11)	4-6 20/1	2-3 27/1	**	3-1 2/2	7-0 23/12	3-4ot 23/2 (17)	9-1 16/2	9-1 10/2
HUL	4-2 14/10	9-1 18/11	2-5 10/11	2-5 28/10	6-5 29/12	1-6 23/9	3-2 27/10	**	5-2 7/10	11-5 4/11	5-4ot 9/1 (14)	5-2 9/12
	2-1 6/1	12-1 2/12	3-6 9/2	3-6 27/1	7-2 16/2	1-1ot 23/12	5-6 24/2	**	7-3 20/1	11-7 30/12	5-0 26/1	10-3 3/2
MIL	4-5 2/12	2-3 6/10	4-4ot 8/12	2-6 3/11	1-3 27/10	5-2 4/11	3-1 29/9	4-5ot 22/9 (1)	**	4-5 13/10	6-1 10/11	8-3 17/11
	1-2 15/12	11-2 19/1	0-8 2/2	1-4 12/1	11-3 26/1	2-5 24/2	3-3 24/11	5-3 22/12	**	5-0 27/2	5-3 9/2	4-2 16/2
PAI	4-9 22/9	3-11 29/9	5-15 6/10	2-7 10/11	4-6 17/11	2-5 1/12	4-3ot 3/11 (7)	3-2 21/10	4-2 20/10	**	5-1 16/12	6-1 28/10
	5-4 22/12	10-3 24/11	3-2 19/1	4-7 9/2	3-7 12/1	3-7 3/2	3-6 15/12	6-4 12/2	3-4 5/1	**	4-2 2/2	2-2ot 27/1
	BAS	**CAR**	**COV**	**DUN**	**EDI**	**FIF**	**GUI**	**HUL**	**MIL**	**PAI**	**PET**	**SLO**

FINDUS BRITISH NATIONAL LEAGUE

	BAS	CAR	COV	DUN	EDI	FIF	GUI	HUL	MIL	PAI	PET	SLO
PET	4-7	6-1	2-5	4-7	1-2	3-6	1-6	2-5	6-3	1-2	**	5-4
	28/10	9/12	3/11	23/9	22/9	21/10	17/11	11/11	30/9	14/10		7/10 (3)
	2-3	9-1	2-3ot	2-6	5-7	4-8	4-3	5-3	1-1ot	5-4ot	**	7-1
	27/1	24/2	15/12 (10)	17/2	22/12	12/2	1/12	10/2	13/1	6/1 (13)		20/1
SLO	3-4ot	6-0	4-5ot	2-5	7-4	2-5	3-6	5-1	1-2	4-7	1-1ot	**
	8/12 (8)	10/11	22/9 (2)	1/12	29/9	14/10	6/10	13/10	18/11	27/10	20/10	
	3-4	6-1	2-6	2-3	3-4	3-7	2-10	0-4	0-7	5-10	2-7	**
	13/1	9/2	22/12	15/12	24/11	2/12	19/1	23/2	17/2	26/1	29/12	

OVERTIME WINNERS

Ref	Team	Scorer		Time
(1)	HUL	Daryl Lavoie (A Johnson, S Johnson)		63.05.
(2)	COV	Steve Chartrand (Tasker, Dumas)		61.55
(3)	PET	Jesse Hammill (Porter, Shields)		65.34
(4)	BAS	Gary Clarke (Brant, Manson)		69.26
(5)	GUI	John Haig		68.34
(6)	COV	Claude Dumas (Chartrand, Ruggles) pp		62.45
(7)	PAI	Jeff White (Juvakoski, Parlatore)		60.30
(8)	BAS	Gary Clarke PS		66.19
(9)	COV	Hilton Ruggles (Tasker)		64.12
(10)	COV	Stephen Cooper (Ruggles, Roberts)		60.38
(11)	GUI	Derek DeCosty (Chinn, Koivunoro)		64.29
(12)	EDI	David Fry (Trumbley, Lynch)		63.12
(13)	PET	Jon Cotton		62.31
(14)	HUL	Mike Bishop (Lavoie, Lyons)		67.47
(15)	COV	Hilton Ruggles (Chartrand)	sh	68.37
(16)	COV	Steve Roberts (Cooper, Dumas)	pp	61.29
(17)	PAI	D Parlatore (Johanneson)		67.44

DUCK, IT'S CHRIS McSORLEY! GB internationals **MICHAEL TASKER**, *left*, and **PAUL BERRINGTON** muscle along the boards in the Coventry Blaze-Dundee Stars playoff finals.

Photo: Mike Smith/Icepix.

FINDUS PLAYOFFS

The top eight BNL teams qualified for the championship playoffs. In the quarter-finals the teams were split into two groups of four with the teams finishing 1st, 4th, 5th and 8th in the league going into group A and the others into group B.

The top two teams in each group qualified for the semi-finals with the winner of one group playing a home-and-away, aggregate goals series against the runners-up in the other group.

The winning semi-finalists competed for the title using the same playing format.

QUARTER-FINAL STANDINGS

Group 1	GP	W	L	D	GF	GA	Pts
Dundee Stars	6	6	0	0	24	5	12
Guildford Flames	6	3	3	0	13	13	6
Basingstoke Bison	6	2	3	1	13	19	5
M Keynes Kings	6	0	5	1	8	21	1
Group 2							
Coventry Blaze	6	5	1	0	34	9	10
Fife Flyers	6	4	1	1	24	20	9
Hull Thunder	6	1	4	1	18	33	3
Edinburgh Capitals	6	1	5	0	15	29	2

QUARTER-FINAL RESULTS

Group 1	BAS	DUN	GUI	MIL
Basingstoke Bison	-	2-5	0-3	2-2ot
Dundee Stars	5-1	-	3-0	3-0
Guildford Flames	2-3	2-3	-	2-1ot (1)
Milton Keynes Kings	2-5	0-5	3-4	-
Group 2	COV	EDI	FIF	HUL
Coventry Blaze	-	5-1	7-0	9-2
Edinburgh Capitals	1-5	-	2-4	1-5
Fife Flyers	6-2	6-2	-	6-2
Hull Thunder	1-5	3-6	4-4ot	-

OVERTIME GAME WINNER:
(1) Jason Dailey (Wetzel, Campbell) 68.17.

SEMI-FINALS

23 Mar Coventry-Guildford 6-3 (0-2,3-1,3-0)
24 Mar Guildford-Coventry 1-4 (0-1,0-0,1-3)
COVENTRY win 10-4 on aggregate
23 Mar Fife-Dundee 2-5 (0-1,1-1,1-3)
24 Mar Dundee-Fife 5-1 (4-0,0-1,1-0)
DUNDEE win 10-3 on aggregate

CHAMPIONSHIP FINALS
First leg, Saturday 30 March 2002

COVENTRY BLAZE	4	(1-0-3)
DUNDEE STARS	7	(2-2-3)

First Period
0-1 DUN Lochi (Wynne, Hand)   1.47
1-1 COV Ruggles (Cooper, Tasker) pp   8.51
1-2 DUN Lochi (Wynne, Hand)   pp 12.34
Penalty minutes: Blaze 8, Stars 20 (Doyle 2+10 - check from behind).
Second Period
1-3 DUN Hand (Wynne)   sh 21.50
1-4 DUN Inkinen (Nelson)   29.07
Penalty minutes: Blaze 6, Stars 4.
Third Period
2-4 COV Ruggles (Johnson, Carpenter) 41.26
3-4 COV Chartrand (Watkins, Ruggles) 44.30
3-5 DUN Wynne (Lochi)   46.21
3-6 DUN Lochi (Wynne, Young)   46.56
3-7 DUN Wynne (Hand)   55.44
4-7 COV Cooper (Johnson)   57.30
Penalty minutes: Blaze 4, Stars 2.
Shots on Goal
Burt COV   4-10-9   23   save 69.6%
Murphy DUN 16-13-8   37   save 89.2%
Referee: Gary Plaistow.   Attendance: 2,624
Linesmen: Darnell, Stanley.

Second leg, Sunday 31 March 2002

DUNDEE STARS	1	(0-1-0)
COVENTRY BLAZE	3	(0-2-1)

First Period
No scoring.
Penalty minutes: Stars 2, Blaze 0.
Second Period
0-1 COV Cooper (Johnson, Roberts)   21.10
0-2 COV Dumas (Soderstrom, Johnson) 27.50
1-2 DUN Hand (Murphy, Wynne)   32.30
Penalty minutes:
Stars 14 (Mikel 10-misc), Blaze 12.
Third Period
1-3 COV Chartrand (Watkins, Cooper) 52.30
Penalty minutes: Stars 4, Blaze 6.
Shots on Goal
Murphy DUN 8-10-16 34   save 91.2%
Burt COV   10-10-8 28   save 96.4%
Referee: Michael Evans.   Attendance: 2,700

DUNDEE STARS are champions
8-5 on aggregate

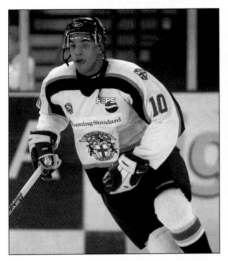 

ALL-STARS *clockwise from top right*: **JAN MIKEL**, captain of Dundee Stars, the Findus BNL playoff winners, with the John Brady Bowl; **STEVEN KING**, Fife Flyers' British All-Star forward; Edinburgh Capital **JASON LAFRENIERE**, the only non-Dundee first team All-Star; **DAVID CLARKE,** Milton Keynes Kings' Superleague and GB forward.   *Photos:* Chris Valentine, Peter Jones.

THE FINALISTS
COVENTRY BLAZE
Ian Burt, Barry Hollyhead; James Pease, Michael Knights, Mathias Soderstrom, Steve Carpenter, Mike Shewan, Stephen Cooper; Tom Watkins, Shaun Johnson, Claude Dumas, Steve Roberts, Steve Chartrand (capt), Kurt Irvine, Rob Eley, Shaun Yardley, Hilton Ruggles, Michael Tasker. *Coach*: Paul Thompson.

DUNDEE STARS
Stephen Murphy, Stewart Rugg; Trevor Doyle, Scott Young, Craig Nelson, Jan Mikel (capt), Gary Dowd, Andy Finlay; Tony Hand, Paul Berrington, Teeder Wynne, Mikko Inkinen, Dominic Hopkins, Patric Lochi, Slava Koulikov, Martin Wiita.
Coach: Tony Hand. *Asst. coach*: Colin Wilson.

LEADING PLAYOFF SCORERS

	GP	G	A	Pts	Pim
Teeder Wynne DUN	10	12	16	28	2
Tony Hand DUN	10	7	17	24	4
Shaun Johnson COV	10	2	17	19	2
Steve Roberts COV	10	10	7	17	0
Claude Dumas COV	10	7	10	17	2
Patric Lochi DUN	10	5	8	13	2
Karry Biette FIF	8	6	6	12	10
Stephen Cooper COV	10	6	6	12	10
Hilton Ruggles COV	10	6	6	12	28
Jan Mikel DUN	10	2	10	12	43

LEADING PLAYOFF NETMINDERS

	GPI	Mins	SoG	GA	S%
Stephen Murphy DUN	10	600	281	15	94.7
Mark McArthur GUI	8	488	275	23	91.6
Robert Schistad BAS	6	369	212	18	91.5

Qualfication: 200 minutes

PAST PLAYOFF WINNERS
2001		Guildford Flames
2000		Fife Flyers
1999		Fife Flyers
1998		Guildford Flames
1997	*Premier Lge*	Swindon IceLords
	N Premier Lge	Fife Flyers

Stars nearly go out
The only pity was that the Playoff final wasn't the best-of-three games.

Dundee Stars and Coventry Blaze - the two strongest teams over the season - each won in the other's rink, but Stars were crowned champions after a nail biting second leg as the rules said aggregate goals decide the winner.

Stars' player-coach, **Tony Hand**, who scored his club's decisive third goal in their 7-4 win in the SkyDome, admitted that Blaze came very close to snatching the title in the return game in Scotland.

"It was touch and go whether we got through," he said after Stars allowed Blaze to pull back to 7-6 through goals from Coventry's 'man of the playoffs' **Stephen Cooper**, and their high-scoring import, **Claude Dumas**.

Again it was Hand who scored the key goal, widening the advantage to 8-6 a few minutes later. The tiring Stars hung on, despite **Steve Chartrand**'s last period effort which left the 600 travelling Blaze fans wishing they hadn't bought that pint in the interval.

'HAND'S GOAL HURT US'
At the final whistle, Hand was relieved, too. "If they'd equalised and we'd had overtime, we'd have been pushed to keep them out," he said.

Blaze coach, **Paul Thompson**, agreed that the series was won in the first game. "We allowed Stars too much freedom," he said. "We know what Tony Hand will do if we let him loose, and his goal was the one that hurt us."

Dundee had less trouble overcoming their Scots rivals, Fife Flyers, in the semis. Flyers made a game of it in the first leg in Kirkcaldy until they were hit by three goals in the last period, and Stars inflicted the killer punch with four more in the first period in Dundee.

The Coventry-Guildford semi was overshadowed by controversy over ITV's insistence that the second game, rather than the first should be held in Guildford.

The change was agreed by league HQ to avoid travelling costs (which would fall on the league) for ITV's southern based camera crew who naturally believed the last leg would be the more important one.

The fuss was not of Blaze's making and they rode out the politics to beat Flames by three goals each time.

Guildford's drive to the semis went through local rivals, Basingstoke Bison, who edged Flames 3-2 in Surrey before goalie **Mark McArthur** blanked Bison 3-0 in Basingstoke.

FINDUS *CHALLENGE CUP*

The new competition, which effectively replaced the Benson and Hedges *Plate*, involved all the Findus *British National League* clubs and the *English Premier League* sides.

The 16 teams in the qualifying round played a round-robin in four regional groupings during September.

The winning team in each group qualified for the final stages in Nottingham Arena in November.

QUALIFYING ROUND RESULTS

Group 1	DUN	EDI	FIF	PAI
Dundee	-	10-1	1-3	11-2
E'burgh	2-8	-	1-8	2-3
Fife	3-2	8-1	-	4-2
Paisley	0-9	5-1	2-7	-

Group 2	COV	GUI	MIL	SOL
Coventry	-	1-3	5-1	11-0
Guildford	0-3	-	7-1	6-2
M Keynes	1-3	3-1 (1)	-	3-6
Solihull	2-10	4-9	3-8	-

Group 3	CAR	HUL	PET	SWI
Cardiff	-	5-1	4-11	7-5
Hull	5-3	-	4-6	2-1
P'boro'	5-1	7-4	-	6-3
Swindon	4-3	0-0 (2)	1-2	-

Group 4	BAS	INV	ROM	SLO
B'stoke	-	7-4	13-2	3-3
Invicta	4-5	-	3-2	2-3
Romford	3-7	4-7	-	2-4
Slough	0-3	7-1	5-2	-

(1) Also a *Findus* league game.
(2) Game not played. Score awarded.

SEMI-FINALS

Nottingham Arena, Sat 24 November 2001
BASINGSTOKE-COVENTRY   **3-3ot**
                    (1-0,1-0,1-3,0-0)
COVENTRY won 4-3 after penalty shots (3-2)
Goal scorers: BAS Higdon, Burgess, Little; COV Dumas, Cooper, Shewan.
Game Winning Penalty Shot: Chartrand.
PETERBOROUGH-FIFE   **2-10**
                    (1-2,0-5,1-3)
Goal scorers: PET Britton, Buckman; FIF Dutuaume 2, Biette 2, Morrison 2, Samuel 2, Wishart, Robertson.

QUALIFYING ROUND STANDINGS

Group 1	GP	W	L	D	GF	GA	Pts
Fife Flyers	6	6	0	0	33	9	12
Dundee Stars	6	4	2	0	41	11	8
Paisley Pirates	6	2	4	0	14	34	4
E'burgh Capitals	6	0	6	0	8	42	0
Group 2							
Coventry Blaze	6	5	1	0	33	7	10
Guildford Flames	6	4	2	0	26	14	8
M Keynes Kings	6	2	4	0	17	25	4
Solihull Barons	6	1	5	0	17	47	2
Group 3							
P'boro' Pirates	6	6	0	0	37	17	12
Hull Thunder	6	2	3	1	16	22	5
Cardiff Devils	6	2	4	0	23	31	4
Swindon Lynx	6	1	4	1	14	20	3
Group 4							
Basingstoke Bison	6	5	0	1	38	16	11
Slough Jets	6	4	1	1	22	13	9
Invicta Dynamos	6	2	4	0	21	28	4
Romford Raiders	6	0	6	0	15	39	0

THE FINAL

Nottingham Arena, Sun 25 November 2001

FIFE FLYERS	**6**	**(2-2-2)**
COVENTRY BLAZE	**3**	**(1-0-2)**

First Period
1-0 FIF Monteith (Dutiaume, Morris) pp   5.21
2-0 FIF Biette (King)   14.23
2-1 COV Dumas (Ruggles)   16.25
Penalties: Flyers 6, Blaze 6.
Second Period
3-1 FIF Biette   26.31
4-1 FIF Dutiaume   34.26
Penalties: Flyers 0, Blaze 2.
Third Period
5-1 FIF Biette (Dutiaume, Morris)   pp   50.05
5-2 COV Dumas (Tasker, Carpenter)   50.21
5-3 COV Roberts   55.48
6-3 FIF Morrison (Monteith)   56.11
Penalties: Flyers 2, Blaze 14 (Dumas 10-misc.)
Shots on Goal
Silver FIF   13-8-9   30   *save* 90.00%
Burt COV   8-7-8   23   *save* 73.91%
Man of Match: Biette FIF.
Referee: Matt Thompson.   *Attendance*: 3,000
Linesmen: Tottman, Darnell.

PAST WINNERS	
***Benson and Hedges* Plate**	
2000	Basingstoke Bison
1999	Basingstoke Bison
1998	Guildford Flames
1997	Slough Jets

THE CUP FINALISTS
COVENTRY BLAZE
Ian Burt, Barry Hollyhead; Mathias Soderstrom, Steve Carpenter, Mike Shewan, Stephen Cooper, James Pease, Russell Cowley; Tom Watkins, Shaun Johnson, Claude Dumas, Steve Roberts, Steve Chartrand (capt), Kurt Irvine, Rob Eley, Shaun Yardley, Hilton Ruggles, Michael Tasker.   *Coach*: Paul Thompson.

FIFE FLYERS
Shawn Silver, Colin Grubb; Derek King, Kyle Horne, Frank Morris (capt), Karry Biette, Gavin Holmes; Daryl Venters, Todd Dutiaume, Steven King, Andy Samuel, Mark Morrison, Mark Dutiaume, Gary Wishart, Iain Robertson, Russell Monteith.   *Coach*: Mark Morrison.

LEADING SCORERS

	GP	G	A	Pts	Pim
Tony Hand DUN	6	7	10	17	6
Karry Biette FIF	8	9	7	16	4
Richard Little BAS	7	12	3	15	2
David Clarke PET	6	11	4	15	51
Steve Chartrand COV	8	6	9	15	6
Teeder Wynne DUN	6	9	5	14	2
Duane Ward INV	6	8	6	14	28
Mark Dutiaume FIF	8	7	7	14	14
Claude Dumas COV	8	6	8	14	18
Jon Cotton PET	7	5	9	14	14

LEADING NETMINDERS

	GPI	Mins	SoG	GA	S%
Shawn Silver FIF	8	461	222	13	94.1
Stephen Murphy DUN	6	326	136	9	93.4
Mark McArthur GUI	5	300	164	11	93.3

Qualification: 120 minutes

SIN-BIN

Player Penalties	GP	Pim	Ave
Rob McCaig HUL	5	58	11.6
David Clarke PET	6	51	8.50
Chris Conaboy PAI	6	44	7.33

Biette Karrys Flyers to cup

A hat-trick from defenceman **Karry Biette** helped Fife Flyers to win the first *Findus* Challenge Cup final against Coventry Blaze.

Biette, who joined Flyers from Guildford Flames in the summer, was voted man of the match with goals in each period, including a spectacular one scored after skating the length of the ice through most of the opposition.

Biette also scored twice in Flyers' overwhelming 10-2 semi-final defeat of cash-strapped Peterborough Pirates. Fife had cruised to a 4-1 lead at the halfway mark.

Coventry, meanwhile, needed overtime and penalties before emerging triumphant from a close semi against Basingstoke Bison.

This and a game against a touring side two days earlier - which coach **Paul Thompson** admitted was a mistake - left Blaze with little in the tank for the final

Coventry failed to get on the scoresheet against Bison until the 48th minute when **Charlie Colon**'s men were already 3-0 up. But they battled hard and three goals in 8.41 from **Claude Dumas**, **Stephen Cooper** and **Mike Shewan** forced the game into overtime.

STARS AND FLAMES MISS JAMBOREE

In the penalty shootout, **Steve Roberts**, **Hilton Ruggles** and finally **Steve Chartrand** all beat **Robert Schistad** in the Basingstoke net to put Blaze into the final.

Dundee Stars were conspicuous by their absence from the Nottingham jamboree weekend which also featured a GB-Romania international. *See World Championships*.

Fife won both their derby games against **Tony Hand**'s team in the qualifying round, which was enough to prevent the new boys from any chance of winning a Grand Slam at their first attempt.

Early season favourites, Guildford Flames, also missed the party. Coventry's **Ian Burt** turned aside 28 Flames' shots for a 3-0 first round shutout, but even worse, **Stan Marple**'s men surprisingly slumped 3-1 in Milton Keynes.

In the spirit of the competition's predecessor, the *Benson and Hedges* Plate, four English Premier League teams were invited to join the party - Romford Raiders, Slough Jets, Solihull Barons and Swindon Lynx.

The foursome lost all their games against the *Findus* BNL sides, apart from Barons' 6-3 victory over local rivals, Milton Keynes, and Swindon's 4-3 defeat of struggling Cardiff Devils. Lynx got a black mark when they failed to play their scheduled home game against Hull Thunder.

ENGLISH LEAGUES

The English leagues - the Premier and the National - comprise the sport's third tier and are designed for clubs with low budgets whose chief aim is developing local players.

The Premier League was first established in 1997-98 to accommodate the non-Superleague clubs who were unable to afford the increasing cost of competing in the British National League (BNL). The league was sponsored by Ice Hockey League Ltd, a Planet Ice company.

The low budget teams now compete in the National League's north and south conferences. There is no automatic promotion to the BNL from the English leagues.

In the Premier League, teams met four times, twice at home and twice away, while the conference sides played each other twice, once home and once away.

LEADING SCORERS

Premier League	GP	G	A	Pts	Pim
Duncan Cook SOL	26	41	50	91	83
Merv Priest SWI	26	40	42	82	51
Kyle Amyotte IOW	26	43	31	74	32
Darcy Cahill IOW	25	26	47	73	62
Kevin Conway SOL	23	27	34	61	24
National League North					
Bobby Haig BLA	17	33	37	70	6
Karl Culley WHI	17	31	36	67	48
Andrew Carter WHI	17	24	34	58	85
Greg Allen ALT	17	30	27	57	8
Nick Chambers GRI	14	22	24	46	61
National Lge South					
Mark Stokes FLI	15	35	29	64	26
Drew Campbell BAS	18	38	20	58	40
Peter Founds FLI	17	22	34	56	71
Derek Flint OXF	17	19	30	49	32
Anthony Page BAS	15	19	28	47	2

FINAL LEAGUE STANDINGS

Premier League	GP	W	L	D	GF	GA	Pts
Invicta Dynamos INV	28	20	5	3	149	92	43
Solihull Barons SOL	28	20	6	2	203	118	42
I of Wight Raiders IOW	28	18	6	4	189	104	40
Romford Raiders ROM	28	18	8	2	169	79	38
Swindon Lynx SWI	28	18	9	1	153	98	37
England u18/20 ENG	28	6	22	0	22	120	12
Nottingham Lions NOT	28	4	23	1	65	196	9
H'gey G'hounds HAR	28	1	26	1	68	211	3
National North							
Whitley Warriors WHI	18	15	1	2	162	60	32
Altrincham Aces ALT	18	15	2	1	158	57	31
Kingston Jets KIN	18	12	4	2	122	78	26
Blackburn Hawks BLA	18	9	7	2	112	81	20
Sh'ffield Scimitars SHE	18	9	8	1	124	91	19
Billingham Eagles BIL	18	7	7	4	84	83	18
Bir'ngham Rockets BIR	18	5	12	1	65	119	11
Grimsby Buffaloes GRI	18	5	13	0	94	177	10
S'derland Chiefs SUN	18	4	13	1	87	114	9
B'ford Bulldogs BRD	18	2	16	0	50	198	4
National South							
B'stoke Buffalo BAS	18	14	4	0	168	82	28
Flintshire Freeze FLI	18	13	4	1	124	91	27
Telford Wild Foxes TEL	18	12	5	1	127	72	25
Oxford City Stars OXF	18	12	6	0	110	75	24
Ch'ford Chieftains CHE	18	10	5	3	100	72	23
MK Thunder MIL	18	8	9	1	77	102	17
Bracknell Hornets BRK	18	5	12	1	66	98	11
Slough H Hawks SLO	18	4	11	3	74	109	11
Invicta Mustangs INV	18	3	13	2	59	123	8
P'boro' Islanders PET	18	2	14	2	69	150	6

Position of teams tied on points decided on results between them.

England under-20 and under-18 games played for double points at opponents' rinks.

LEADING NETMINDERS

Premier League	GPI	Mins	SoG	GA	Sv%
Chris Douglas ROM/HAR	12	648	343	33	90.38
Ken Wotherspoon SWI	10	496	221	22	90.05
Andy Moffat IOW	8	400	177	18	89.83
National Lge North					
Colin Downie BLA	10	600	327	29	91.13
Stephen Wall WHI	14	760	428	44	89.72
Richard Aston ALT	6	289	133	15	88.72
National Lge South					
Daniel Heslop TEL	17	974	583	63	89.19
Paul Wilcock CHE	12	672	413	45	89.10
Allen Sutton MIL	15	900	638	73	88.56

Qualification: 360 minutes

PAST (PREMIER) LEAGUE WINNERS

2000-01	Swindon Phoenix
1999-00	Chelmsford Chieftains
1998-99	Solihull Blaze
1997-98	Solihull Blaze
1996-97	*Wightlink* Raiders
1995-96	*Wightlink* Raiders
1994-95	*Wightlink* Raiders
1993-94	*Wightlink* Raiders
1992-93	Solihull Barons
1991-92	Medway Bears
1990-91	Oxford City Stars
1989-90	Bracknell Bees
1988-89	Humberside Seahawks
1987-88	Romford Raiders

Dynamos' first league crown

Invicta Dynamos emerged as winners after a five-team race for the English Premier League title. The Kent club took the crown exactly ten years after their predecessors. Medway Bears, won the league.

Dynamos, who lost only one game at home and five all season, were backstopped by **Matt van der Velden**, a 22-year-old Brit who helped his team to concede the second fewest goals.

In contrast, *Solihull Barons'* new Canadian forward, **Duncan Cook**, former GB international, **Kevin Conway**, and Finn **Samuli Mykkanen** played crucial roles as Barons out-scored all the opposition and took the runners-up place just one point behind Invicta.

Sadly, the refurbishment of the Solihull rink meant that there was barely room for more than 300 fans to watch the team's free-scoring ways.

FAIR PLAY

Premier League	GP	Pims	Ave
Invicta Dynamos	26	298	11.5
England u20/u18	14	204	14.6
Nottingham Lions	25	493	19.7
Swindon Lynx	26	562	21.6
Isle of Wight Raiders	26	598	23.0
Romford Raiders	26	631	24.3
Solihull Barons	26	763	29.3
Haringey Greyhounds	25	797	31.9
National League North			
Billingham Eagles	16	294	18.4
Sunderland Chiefs	18	340	18.9
Bradford Bulldogs	18	372	20.7
Sheffield Scimitars	18	578	32.1
Kingston Jets	18	594	33.0
Blackburn Hawks	17	571	33.6
Grimsby Buffaloes	18	629	34.9
Whitley Warriors	18	659	36.6
Altrincham Aces	18	679	37.7
Birmingham Rockets	17	868	51.1
National League South			
Basingstoke Buffalo	18	406	22.5
Peterborough Islanders	16	505	31.6
Oxford City Stars	18	569	31.6
Slough Harrier Hawks	17	605	35.6
Flintshire Freeze	18	668	37.1
Milton Keynes Thunder	18	699	38.8
Chelmsford Chieftains	17	710	41.8
Bracknell Hornets	16	718	44.9
Invicta Mustangs	16	721	45.1
Telford Wild Foxes	18	920	51.1

Three points behind Invicta were the *Isle of Wight Raiders*, who had two of the league's top four scorers in Canadians **Kyle Amyotte** and **Darcy Cahill**. Unfortunately, 19-year-old Scot, **Andy Moffat**, one of the league's best netminders, arrived from Hull Thunder too late to improve his team's position.

Romford Raiders snapped up coach **Shaun McFadyen** from Chelmsford Chieftains when the loss of their sponsor forced last year's runners-up to drop into the National League.

But inconsistency and less than sparkling performances from some of their imports, left Raiders five points adrift of first place.

PREMIER LEAGUE RESULTS CHART

	HAR	INV	IOW	NOT	ROM	SOL	SWI	ENG*
HARINGEY	**	4-9	3-11	3-6	3-8	6-8	2-5	1-2
		22/9	21/10	18/11	27/10	20/1	13/1	6/10
Greyhounds	**	2-5	1-10	0-0	5-8	2-15	5-11	1-4
		16/2	6/1	(1)	9/12	9/2	17/2	24/2
INVICTA	5-3	**	5-2	9-1	3-2	9-4	6-4	10-1
	28/10		23/9	9/12	21/10	2/12	14/10	30/9
Dynamos	6-1	**	11-4	2-1	4-2	2-6	6-2	12-2
	27/1		25/11	30/12	23/12	13/1	11/11	10/2
ISLE OF WIGHT	12-4	7-4	**	11-2	6-4	7-8	4-5	14-1
	8/9	27/10		15/9	29/9	6/10	2/12	20/10
Raiders	12-3	4-4	**	8-2	5-5	7-7	3-3	14-0
	15/12	12/1		16/9	24/11	10/11	9/2	5/1
NOTTINGHAM	2-5	2-6	3-9	**	0-10	2-13	2-6	5-2
	2/9	7/10	9/9		11/11	13/10	23/9	28/10
Lions	10-4	4-7	2-8	**	2-4	4-7	1-7	1-5
	4/11	5/1	24/2		27/1	23/12	25/11	17/2
ROMFORD	8-2	3-3	6-7	8-0	**	2-5	5-4	8-0
	7/10	4/11	18/11	14/10		28/10	30/9	10/11
Raiders	10-0	11-3	4-3	13-0	**	1-2	6-4	19-2
	25/11	24/2	20/1	2/12		30/12	6/1	8/12
SOLIHULL	13-3	8-8	5-9	19-2	2-12	**	5-7	12-2
	14/10	22/12	30/9	1/12	16/12		7/10	22/9
Barons	12-3	5-4	7-4	4-2	4-5	**	5-2	9-1
	26/1	6/1	4/11	10/2	29/12		18/11	12/1
SWINDON	10-0	6-3	2-4	13-1	6-2	8-6	**	7-0
	24/11	6/10	13/10	3/11	22/9	29/9		1/12
Lynx	9-2	1-3	3-4	13-8	4-3	4-12	**	7-0
	23/2	19/1	26/1	12/1	5/1	20/10		16/2

* England under-20s played the first game against each other team and England under-18s played the second game. All games played at opponents' rinks for double points.
Second figure is date of game.
(1) Game not played. Score awarded.

NOTES ON NATIONAL LEAGUE GAMES
Games not played, score awarded 0-0: South - Invicta-Bracknell, Invicta-Peterborough, Slough-Chelmsford; North - Billingham-Birmingham, Billingham-Blackburn
In the South, Peterborough-Bracknell awarded 5-0 to Peterborough as Bracknell iced a suspended player. Match statistics expunged.

Dynamos' crown, contd

Swindon Lynx, who won the league in 2000-01 as the Phoenix, ran into work permit trouble over their Canadian goalie, **Ron Bertrand**, and never found the form of the previous campaign.

Nottingham Lions persisted with their all-British policy and while conceding almost 200 goals was unlikely to have improved anyone's game, they did have the satisfaction of twice beating the cash-strapped **Haringey Greyhounds**.

The unfortunate Greyhounds were funded by **Zoran Kozic**, their top scorer in 2000-01, but when he pulled out before Christmas after receiving a punitive 12-month ban for slashing, the London club barely made it through the season.

The second tier National League was dominated by **Whitley Warriors** who won their first Northern Conference title after twice finishing runners-up. **Basingstoke Buffalo** won the league's South Conference after another close five-team battle.

PREMIER LEAGUE PLAYOFFS

At the end of the league games, the top six teams in the Premier League, excluding the England junior sides, qualified for the Playoffs.

The league winner was placed in group A along with the fourth and fifth placed teams, with the remaining sides going into group B.

Each team played the other in their group and the winning teams met in a home and away final.

PRELIMINARY ROUND STANDINGS

Group A	GP	W	L	D	GF	GA	Pts
Invicta Dynamos	4	2	2	0	11	8	4
Romford Raiders	4	2	2	0	14	13	4
Swindon Lynx	4	2	2	0	14	18	4
Group B							
I of Wight Raiders	4	4	0	0	28	8	8
Solihull Barons	4	1	2	1	18	24	3
Nottingham Lions	4	0	3	1	11	25	1

PRELIMINARY ROUND RESULTS

Group A	INV	ROM	SWI
Invicta Dynamos	-	2-0	5-2
Romford Raiders	3-2	-	2-5
Swindon Lynx	3-2	4-9	-
Group B	IOW	NOT	SOL
Isle of Wight Raiders	-	8-0	8-5
Nottingham Lions	1-6	-	4-5
Solihull Barons	2-6	6-6	-

FINALS

First leg, 6 April 2002, Planet Ice Ryde Arena

ISLE OF WIGHT RAIDERS	1	(0-0-1)
INVICTA DYNAMOS	2	(2-0-0)

First Period
0-1 INV Beveridge (Chard, Andrews) pp   7.10
0-2 INV Beveridge (Ward)   14.09
Penalty minutes: Raiders 2, Dynamos 0.
Second Period No scoring.
Penalty minutes: Raiders 2, Dynamos 0.
Third Period
1-2 IOW Pickles (Cahill, Nyman)   42.47
Penalty minutes: Raiders 2, Dynamos 6.
Shots on Goal
Moffat IOW   18-15- 8 41   *save* 95.1%
van der Velden INV   9- 8-11 28   *save* 96.4%
Referee: Kieron O'Halloran.   *Attendance*:
Linesmen: Warman, McShane.   not shown.

Second leg, 7 April 2002, Gillingham Ice Bowl.

INVICTA DYNAMOS	4	(1-0-3)
ISLE OF WIGHT RAIDERS	2	(0-2-0)

First Period
1-0 INV Beveridge (Ward, Andrews)   16.32
Penalty minutes: Dynamos 4, Raiders 4.
Second Period
1-1 IOW Coles (Hargreaves)   27.48
1-2 IOW Knight (Carter, Nyman)   35.52
Penalty minutes: Dynamos 14, Raiders 4.
Third Period
2-2 INV Ward (Andrews, Beveridge)   48.12
3-2 INV Hume (French, Skinnari)   48.47
4-2 INV Hannah (Kindred, Skinnari)   52.25
Penalty minutes: Dynamos 0, Raiders 0.
Shots on Goal
van der Velden INV   7-13-14 34   *save* 94.1%
Moffat IOW   18-15-18 51   *save* 92.1%
Referee: Kieron O'Halloran.
Linesmen: Hastings, Osborne.
Attendance: 503.

INVICTA DYNAMOS are champions
6-3 on aggregate

THE WINNING TEAM
INVICTA DYNAMOS
Matt van der Velden, Adam Noctor; Paul Hume, Peter Korff, Matt Beveridge, Greg Hales, Sean Clement, Mike Kindred, Phil Chard (capt), Jake French, Mikko Skinnari, Elliott Andrews, Duane Ward, Kevin Parrish, Andy Hannah, Carl Greenhous.
Manager: Sean Clement. *Coach*: Andy Hannah.

LEADING SCORERS

	GP	G	A	Pts	Pim
Darcy Cahill IOW	5	5	8	13	14
Kyle Amyotte IOW	6	5	5	10	0
Ken Forshee SWI	4	3	7	10	6
Merv Priest SWI	4	5	4	9	4
Peter Nyman IOW	6	1	8	9	4
Aaron Shrieves SOL	3	5	3	8	4

LEADING NETMINDERS

	GPI	Mins	SoG	GA	Sv%
Matt van der Velden INV	6	360	189	11	94.18
Andy Moffat IOW	6	360	232	14	93.97
Simon Smith ROM	4	240	138	13	90.58

NATIONAL LEAGUE PLAYOFFS

In the National League, the top two teams in each conference qualified for the playoffs.

The top team in the North met the runner-up in the South and the winning South team faced the North runner-up home and away.

The winning teams then met home and away to decide the playoff Championship.

SEMI-FINALS

First semi-final

| 24 Mar | Whitley-Flintshire | 12-2 |
| 7 Apr | Flintshire-Whitley | 4-9 |

Whitley Warriors win 21-6 on aggregate

Second semi-final

| 14 Apr | Altrincham-Basingstoke | 5-9 |
| 20 Apr | Basingstoke-Altrincham | 13-4 |

Basingstoke Buffalo win 22-9 on aggregate

CHAMPIONSHIP FINAL

First leg, 27 April, Planet Ice Basingstoke Arena.
BASINGSTOKE-WHITLEY   6-6 (2-1,2-1,2-4)
Scorers: **Buffalo** - Campbell 2+1; Page 1+3; Newberry, Elliott 1+1; Beere 1g; Broadhurst, Etheridge, Cathcart 1a. **Warriors** - Carter 2+2; Culley 2g; S McGinnety 1+2; Baxter 1g; Taylor 2a; Bucas, Graham, Tindale, Wall 1a.
Shots on Goal: Astill BAS 37, Wall WHI 37.
Penalty minutes: Buffalo 16, Warriors 56 (P McGinnety 2+2+10+game - spearing).
Referee: Kieron O'Halloran.

Second leg, 28 April, Whitley Bay Ice Rink.
WHITLEY-BASINGSTOKE   6-1 (1-0,1-0,4-1)
Scorers: **Warriors** - Carter 2g; Baxter, Good, Tindale, Taylor 1g; Culley, Graham, S McGinnety 2a. **Buffalo** - Page 1g; Campbell, Elliott 1a.
Shots on Goal:
Wall WHI 36, Astill/Bridger BAS 33.
Penalty minutes: Warriors 43 (Dunn 5+game - spearing), Buffalo 8.
Referee: Mick Litchfield.

Whitley Warriors are champions

12-7 on aggregate

THE WINNING TEAM
WHITLEY WARRIORS
Stephen Wall, Rory Dunn; Rob Wilson, Richard Dunn, Dave Howey, Kevin Bucas, Karl Culley (capt), Lee Baxter, Daniel Good, Andrew Carter, Paul McGinnety, Paul Graham, James Hutchinson, Andrew Tindale, Simon McGinnety, Stuart Lonsdale, Darren Taylor.
Coach: Peter Winn.
Paul   Willis replaced ***Paul   McGinnety*** *(suspended) in the second leg.*

Don't break up the Warriors!

After *Whitley Warriors* became one of only two teams in 2001-02 to win the Grand Slam of their league's trophies (Edinburgh was the other), there was a fear that rivals' time-honoured cry of 'break up the Warriors' might actually come true.

The north-east club made a clean sweep of all the competitions they entered - National League North, playoff championship and English Cup - for the first time in their long history.

Whitley attract over 1,000 fans a game and were in the Premier Division of the British League not long ago, but they have balked at the level of wages now being paid by some teams.

They are justly proud of their reputation for developing local players. Defenceman **Dale Howey**, 17, is just one of the new crop who could have a bright future in the sport.

This gave rise to fears in the summer of 2002 that their new neighbour, **Alex Dampier**, may have his eyes on some of the young Warriors for his new BNL team, Newcastle Vipers.

While this was good news for the players as 'Damps' has an unrivalled reputation for bringing out the best in promising youngsters, it would be bad news for Warriors.

Team and rink owners, **Francis Smith** and his sister, **Geraldine Cassidy** (née **Smith**), are the only members of the famous north-east hockey family still in the sport following the demise of **Tom Smith**'s Durham Wasps and the passing of Billingham's **Bill Smith**.

League winners, *Invicta Dynamos*, did the double by capturing the playoff crown but had to hand the Premier Cup to local rivals, Romford Raiders, after a hard fought two-leg final.

Dynamos' key man in the playoffs was Canadian **Matt Beveridge**, a former Paisley, Peterborough and Whitley Bay forward. He scored his side's first three goals and assisted on the fourth as Dynamos beat the Isle of Wight 6-3 in the home and away final.

Warriors added a fourth title during 2001-02 when they beat Billingham Eagles 14-7 on aggregate after the delayed second leg of the **2000-01 English League conference playoffs**. Eagles were without their Canadian defenders, **Andre Malo** and **Brian Perry**, who played in the first leg. Brief details:
17 November 2001, Billingham Forum
EAGLES-WARRIORS 1-10   (1-2,0-3,0-5)
Goal scorers: BIL Payne; WHI Baxter 2, Carter, McGinnety, Ord, Tindale, Hutchinson, Lonsdale, Culley, Willis.
Shots on goal: Snook/Griffiths BIL 40, Hoult WHI 21. *Penalty minutes*: BIL 12, WHI 60.

CUP COMPETITIONS

PREMIER CUP

This competition was open to all teams in the English leagues (excluding the England junior sides), though only Birmingham Rockets and Blackburn Hawks entered from outside the Premier League.

In the preliminary round, the nine teams were divided into two regionalised groups and played the other teams in their group home and away.

The leading team in one group then played the runner-up in the other group home and away and the winning teams met - also home and away - to decide the cup's destination.

PRELIMINARY ROUND STANDINGS

Group A	GP	W	L	D	GF	GA	Pts
Solihull Barons	6	6	0	0	58	12	12
Nottingham Lions	6	4	2	0	36	20	8
B'mingham Rockets	6	1	4	1	17	31	3
Blackburn Hawks	6	0	5	1	9	57	1
Group B							
Invicta Dynamos	8	5	2	1	32	20	11
Romford Raiders	8	5	3	0	52	22	10
I of Wight Raiders	8	4	2	2	47	31	10
Swindon Lynx	8	4	3	1	34	27	9
H'ngey Greyhounds	8	0	8	0	17	82	0

SEMI-FINALS
First semi-final
23 Feb	Solihull-Romford	6-10
17 Mar	Romford-Solihull	9-3

Romford Raiders win 19-9 on aggregate
Second semi-final
3 Mar	Invicta-Nottingham	8-1
17 Mar	Nottingham-Invicta	2-6

Invicta Dynamos win 14-3 on aggregate

FINAL
13 Apr	Romford-Invicta	5-3
14 Apr	Invicta-Romford	4-4

Romford Raiders win Premier Cup
9-7 on aggregate

PAST WINNERS
2000-01	Isle of Wight Raiders
1999-00	Chelmsford Chieftains
1998-99	Milton Keynes Kings

LEADING SCORERS

	GP	G	A	Pts	Pim
Danny Marshall ROM	12	20	11	31	4
Jason Rushton ROM	8	16	10	26	44
James Duval ROM	11	12	13	25	2
Kevin Conway SOL	8	16	7	23	4
Matt Beveridge INV	12	10	11	21	8

LEADING NETMINDERS

	GPI	Mins	SoG	GA	Sv%
Matt vd Velden INV	10	599	376	27	92.8
Greg Rockman BIR	6	360	398	31	92.2
Simon Smith ROM	9	513	298	31	89.6

ENGLISH CUP

Ten of the 20 National League teams entered this competition. Birmingham Rockets and Blackburn Hawks were the only sides to enter both cup tournaments.

PRELIMINARY ROUND STANDINGS

Group A	GP	W	L	D	GF	GA	Pts
Whitley Warriors	8	7	1	0	55	21	14
Altrincham Aces	8	5	3	0	65	28	10
Kingston Jets	8	3	5	0	37	40	6
Blackburn Hawks	8	3	5	0	28	48	6
Birm'gham Rockets	8	2	6	0	23	71	4
Group B							
Telford Wild Foxes	8	6	1	1	55	23	13
Oxford City Stars	8	5	2	1	62	38	11
Ch'ford Chieftains	8	3	2	3	37	38	9
Bracknell Hornets	8	2	6	0	32	53	4
Flintshire Freeze	8	1	6	1	17	51	3

SEMI-FINALS
First semi-final
17 Mar	Whitley-Oxford	15-4

Whitley Warriors win sole leg.
24 Mar	Telford-Altrincham	3-5
31 Mar	Altrincham-Telford	3-8

Telford Wild Foxes win 11-8 on aggregate

FINAL
27 Apr	Telford-Whitley	5-2
28 Apr	Whitley-Telford	8-3

Whitley Warriors win English Cup
10-8 on aggregate

SCOTTISH COMPETITIONS

Grand Slam for Caps

Former Murrayfield Racers' coach, **Jock Hay**, guided Edinburgh Capitals to an unprecedented four titles in the Scottish National League - the league, Scottish, Spring and Autumn Cups.

For readers who may be confused, the Capitals team was not the same one that played in the *Findus* BNL but an all-Scottish side.

The Scottish Cup is now competed for solely by teams in the Scottish National League. From 2001-02, Scotland's Superleague and BNL teams compete for its successor, the Caledonia Cup.

• Despite our strenuous efforts, the *Annual* regrets that we were unable to obtain any further information than that printed here.

SCOTTISH NATIONAL LEAGUE

Winners: EDINBURGH CAPITALS (25 pts)
Runners-Up: **Dundee Tigers** 22 pts; **Kilmarnock Avalanche, Kirkcaldy Kestrels, Paisley Mohawks, Ayr Bruins** 19; **Solway (Dumfries) Sharks** 14; **Perth Panthers** 6; **Inverness Jags** 1.

AUTUMN CUP

FINAL
First leg, 9 December, Murrayfield
EDINBURGH-KIRKCALDY 10-2 (3-2,3-0,4-0)
Goal scoring: Capitals - Francey, N Hay 2; McRae, Wilson, Beatson, Jerome, ?? ; Kestrels - McAndrew, Holmes.
Second leg, 16 December, Kirkcaldy
KIRKCALDY-EDINBURGH 3-5 (0-1,2-3,1-1)
Goal scorers: Kestrels - Annan, Walker, Wishart; Capitals - Francey, N Hay, R Hay, Lamb, McRae.
Winners: **EDINBURGH CAPITALS 15-5** *on agg.*
The first competition of the Scottish season was dogged by controversy.

The first leg of the Autumn Cup was erased from the records after Edinburgh's **Neil Sinclair** was afterwards discovered to be cup-tied.

Kirkcaldy Kestrels were fined £100 after taking 121 minutes in penalties in the second leg.

Players **Steven Wishart** (nine games), **Sean Annan** (7) and **Liam Grieg** (6) were suspended for their behaviour in the various scuffles.

SCOTTISH ICE HOCKEY ASSOCIATION
www.siha.net

CALEDONIA CUP
(formerly Scottish Cup)
SEMI-FINALS
10 Jan **Dundee-Paisley 7-2** (2-1,3-1,2-0)
Goal scorers: Stars - Kirton 3, Hand 2, Mikel, Wynne; Pirates - Biesenthal, Cameron.
15 Jan **Edinburgh-Fife 2-9** *No details.*
FINAL, *First leg*
19 Feb **FIFE-DUNDEE 2-3** (0-2,1-0,1-1)
Goal scorers: Flyers - Morris, Dutiaume; Stars - Lochi, Hand, Wynne.
Second leg
27 Feb **DUNDEE-FIFE 5-3** (1-2,3-0,1-1)
Goal scorers - Stars - Berrington, Wynne, Wiita, Hand, Young; Flyers - Dutiaume 2, Morrison.
DUNDEE STARS won 8-5 on aggregate
In a preview of the *Findus* BNL playoff semi-finals, Dundee Stars won the first Caledonia Cup, fighting back from 2-0 down in the second leg at home to beat bitter rivals Fife Flyers 5-3.

The result gave Stars the trophy after they narrowly won the first leg win at Kirkcaldy, thanks to a **Teeder Wynne** goal in the last 64 seconds.

SPRING CUP
FINAL
19 May **EDINBURGH-DUNDEE 5-3**
More controversy here as Tigers complained bitterly about the appointment of the three Edinburgh-based officials to handle the final.

SCOTTISH CUP
First semi-final
1st leg Ayr Raiders-Dundee Tigers 4-5
2nd leg Dundee Tigers-Ayr Raiders 4-1
Dundee Tigers won 9-5 on aggregate.
Second semi-final
1st leg Edinburgh-Dundee 8-6
2nd leg -Dundee-Edinburgh ??
FINAL
26 May **DUNDEE-EDINBURGH 2-2ot**
***CAPITALS won** penalty shootout 4-2*
Regulation scoring: Capitals - Ian McFarlane, Sean Lamb; Tigers - Niall Stott, Kevin Jenkins.
Penalty shots: Capitals - Lamb, Ross Hay, Steve Francey, Mark McRae; Tigers - Michael Aird, John Robertson.

TOURING TEAMS

After a complete absence of visiting teams in Britain in 2000-01, we were almost over-run by Johnny Foreigner last season.

If Superleague's joust with the German DEL teams for the Ahearne Trophy was the main event [see Superleague section], there was a record number of other European and North American sides spicing up the domestic schedule.

BT TOGETHER BELFAST ICE CUP

Superleague's London Knights won the first international tournament of the 2001-02 season - and the first in Ireland in living memory - at the Odyssey Arena in Belfast.

Knights' netminder, **Trevor Robins**, was voted the player of the tournament, as he had been in London's own pre-season games in Geneva.

FINAL STANDINGS: London 9 pts, Frankfurt 5 pts, Belfast 3 pts, Berlin 1 pt.

24 August

KNIGHTS-FRANKFURT LIONS	4-2
GIANTS-BERLIN POLAR BEARS	6-5
	after OT & penalty shots

25 August

GIANTS-KNIGHTS	2-3
BERLIN-FRANKFURT	2-5

26 August

KNIGHTS-BERLIN	4-2
FRANKFURT-GIANTS	4-3
	after OT & penalty shots

■ Berlin, like London Knights, are part of the Anschutz organisation's stable of European clubs. Before 1992, they were known as Dynamo Berlin and won the two-team East German league title on numerous occasions.

OTHER VISITING TEAMS

AK BARS KAZAN (Russia)
'Snow Leopards Strike West'

26 Aug	Manchester Storm-Ak Bars	0-3
27 Aug	Nottingham Panthers-Ak Bars	1-6
28 Aug	Bracknell Bees-Ak Bars	5-8
30 Aug	Ayr Scottish Eagles-Ak Bars	2-3

Kazan were on their first tour of Britain since meeting and twice losing to Ayr Scottish Eagles in the European League in 1998.

MOSCOW DYNAMO
When the second Russian side came here in December 2001, they stood third in the Russian

League - rated the fourth best in Europe - seven places ahead of Ak Bars Kazan.

Moscow included netminder **Mikhail Shtalenkov**, who played seven seasons in the NHL, and ten others who had either played (three) or been drafted by the big league.

Highlights were later shown on Sky Sports. See *Review of the Year*.

26 Dec	Panthers-Moscow	3-3
27 Dec	Steelers-Moscow	1-5
29 Dec	Storm-Moscow	3-6

■ In a European Hockey League game in 1997-98, Storm held Dynamo 2-2 at home before losing in overtime.
■ Until their EHL contest, Dynamo's previous visit to Britain was in September 1990. They won all of their six games against *Heineken* British League teams during a goodwill tour to celebrate the Golden Jubilee of Durham Wasps.

BORETTI TIGERS, AMSTERDAM
After seeing the results of this tour, Superleague cancelled Amsterdam's game against their All-Star squad!

22 Sept	Isle of Wight Raiders-Tigers	5-3
25 Sept	Basingstoke Bison-Tigers	3-7
26 Sept	Milton Keynes Kings-Tigers	3-5
27 Sept	Coventry Blaze-Tigers	5-3
12 Dec	Hull Thunder-Tigers - *cancelled due to Amsterdam's financial difficulties.*	

■ In season 2000-01, according to the IIHF's official yearbook, Amsterdam finished sixth and last in the Netherlands Superleague under the name of - wait for it - Al Capone's Flames.

HUDDINGE IK (Sweden)
The top side in Sweden's under-20 league are based in the Stockholm suburb where **David Longstaff** lived during the season.

7 Nov	Panthers-Huddinge	10-2
8 Nov	Britain-Huddinge	6-0

See *World Championships* section for details.

ROMANIA
After losing to GB, the Romanians met three club sides.

27 Nov	Fife Flyers-Romania	2-6
28 Nov	Dundee Stars-Romania	5-4
29 Nov	Coventry Blaze-Romania	2-2

US AIR FORCE ACADEMY

19 Nov	Hull Thunder-USAFA	0-5
20 Nov	MK Kings-USAFA	6-4
21 Nov	P'boro' Pirates-USAFA	2-6
22 Nov	Coventry Blaze-USAFA	3-8

YOUTH INTERNATIONALS

Players born 1 January 1983 or later

Nottingham Arena, 31 March 2002

ENGLAND UNDER-19	5	(1-2-2)
SCOTLAND UNDER-19	1	(1-0-0)

Scorers
England - Myers 2g; Wallace 1+2; Towalski, Buckman 1g; Richardson, Miles, Meyers, Moran 1a. **Scotland** - Walker 1g.
Shots on Goal
Ashton/Levers ENG 8- 9- 4 21 *save* 95.24%
Russell SCOT 14-15-15 44 *save* 88.64%
Penalty minutes: England 18, Scotland 12.
Referee: Kevin Biggs. *Linesmen*: Malo, Wilson.

Matt makes his mark

Cardiff teenager **Matthew Myers** scored two goals to help England retain the under-19 championship in the annual clash with their Scottish counterparts.

The feat capped a remarkable season for the talented 17-year-old who played his first senior season with Devils' troubled BNL side and scored twice on his debut for the GB under-18 squad.

Players born 1 January 1985 or later

Hull Ice Arena, 5 May 2002

ENGLAND UNDER-17	5	(0-3-2)
SCOTLAND UNDER-17	4	(1-0-3)

Scorers:
England - Jenner, Butterworth, Good, Smith, Dodwell 1g; Jamieson, Brittle, Bradford, Miller, Burch, Robinson 1a. **Scotland** - Gallacher 2g; Forsyth, Walker 1g; McCaig 2a; McAndrew, McKenzie 1a.
Shots on Goal
Woolhouse/Snook ENG 8- 9-16 33 *save* 87.9%
Arthur/Price SCOT 14-16-12 42 *save* 88.1%
Penalty minutes: England 12 (Miller 10-misc.), Scotland 10.

Scots scare Sassenachs

Scotland, who were heavily beaten in last year's game, took England to the final whistle before conceding. **Euan Forsyth**, **Adam Walker** and a second tally from **Mark Gallacher** in a five-minute spell late in the game brought Scotland to within a goal of their auld enemy. But the English managed to hold on.

THE TEAMS

ENGLAND UNDER-19
Ricky Ashton ALT, Allan Levers NOT; Tom Pope BAS, David Thomas BIL, Rhodri Evans, Matthew Myers CAR, Adam Tercan, Mike Plenty GUI, Stephen Wallace HUL, Leigh Jamieson, Danny Meyers MIL (capt), Chris Colgate, Tom Griffiths, Paul Moran, Adam Radmall NOT, Lewis Buckman PET, Terry Miles, Matt Towalski SLO, Adam Carr SUN, Lee Richardson SWI, James Hutchinson WHI, Dan Hughes (Vasteras, Sweden). *Manager*: Barry Knock. *Coaches*: Dave Ross, Mick Mishener and Mark Beggs.

SCOTLAND UNDER-19
Alistair Flockhart EDI, John Russell PAI; George Murray, Paddy Ward AYR (capt), Scott Welsh DUM, Neil Hay, Sean Lamb, Marc McCrae, Danny McIntyre EDI, Mark McAndrew, Adam Walker FIF, Chad Reekie FIF, Ryan Findlay KIL, Martyn Ford, Stuart McCaig, Thomas Miller, Marrik Shearer PAI.
Manager: Tom Moore. *Coach*: John (Bernie) McCrone.

THE TEAMS

ENGLAND UNDER-17
Michael Snook BIL, Geoff Woolhouse NOT; Kurt Reynolds GUI, Kevin Phillips HUL, Leigh Jamieson MIL, Bernie Bradford PET, Tom Smith SLO, Stephen Duncombe SHE; Andrew Thornton BIL, Joe Miller CAR, Ben Burch, Nick Dodwell, Adam Robinson NOT, Rob Jenner ROM, Simon Butterworth SHE, Mark Richardson SWI, Adam Brittle TEL (capt), Daniel (DJ) Good WHI. *Manager*: Mike Evans CAR. *Coaches*: Terry Ward BIL, Martyn Etheridge NOT.

SCOTLAND UNDER-17
Craig Arthur FIF, Barry Price PAI; Toby Black, Mark Gallacher AYR, Fraser Munro ELG, Euan Forsyth, Scott McAndrew, Scott McKenzie, Chad Reekie, David Robb, Adam Walker (capt) FIF, Alan Campbell, Martin Ford, Stuart McCaig, Thomas Millar, Marrik Shearer PAI, Billy Baxter PER.
Manager: Davey Beatson. *Coaches*: Jock Hay, Gary Smith.

Ben Clements of Chelmsford, the All-Star netminder with the South-East under-15s at the Junior Inter-Conference Championships in Hull, with the Most Valuable Player of the Tournament award, sponsored by The Ice Hockey Annual.

Craze an All Star

England's under-16s won bronze in their 15th straight entry in the Chris Verwijst Tournament which is rated as one of the best in Europe.

Cardiff Devils' goalie, **Nathan Craze**, was the first England player to be voted to the tournament's All Star team after conceding only two goals a game.

The other promising youngsters to keep an eye on are Guildford's **Oliver Bronniman** and Swindon's **Mark Richardson** who topped the team's goal scorers with four apiece.

The 2002 event featured seven national teams plus the home club, Tilburg Trappers, who competed in two groups in the first round.

■ England's youngsters won the gold medal here two years ago as 'Britain' but under the England banner again in 2001, they finished last of the eight teams.

ENGLAND UNDER-16

David Wride BRK, Nathan Craze CAR; Steven Pritchard BIL, Kurt Reynolds GUI, Kevin Phillips HUL, Ben Morgan SHE, Shane Moore SWI, Stuart Bates TEL, Rob Wilson WHI; Peter Traynor ALT, Joe Greener BAS, Oliver Bronniman GUI, Lewis Day HUL, Mark Conway MIL, Stewart Bliss NOT, Simon Butterworth, Greg Wood SHE, Shaun Thompson SLO, John Dewar, Mark Richardson SWI.
Manager: Bob Wilkinson. *Coaches:* Warren Rost, Robert Wilkinson, Paul Simpson.

CHRIS VERWIJST TOURNAMENT
(Players born 1 January 1986 or later)

Tilburg, Netherlands, 22-24 March 2002

ENGLAND RESULTS
22 Mar **Switzerland-England 1-4** (1-0,0-2,0-2)
   England scoring: Bronniman 2g; Richardson, Phillips 1g; Dewar 2a.
   England-Hungary 4-0 (3-0,0-0,1-0)
   England scoring: Greener 2g; Wood, Richardson 1g; Conway, Thompson, Reynolds 1a.
23 Mar **England-Slovenia 2-1** (0-1,2-0,0-0)
   England scoring: Bronniman 1+1; Richardson 1g; Dewar 1a.
Semi-Final
24 Mar **England-Austria 0-4** (0-0,0-1,0-3)
Third Place Playoff
24 Mar **Slovenia-England 4-5** (1-1,1-3,2-1)
   England scoring: Richardson, Bronniman 1+1; Reynolds, Greener, Butterworth 1g; Dewar 2a; Bates, Day 1a.

The juniors also played eight games in Canada:

RIVERSIDE RANGERS BANTAM TOURNEY
Windsor, Canada, 26-30 December 2001
27 Dec **England u16-Tecumseh Eagles 2-2**
   England scoring: Phillips, Traynor 1g; Greener, Day, Wood, Wilson 1a.
28 Dec **England u16-Vipers 0-2**
29 Dec **Essex Ravens-England u16 5-3**
   England scoring: Richardson 1+1; Allinson, Pritchard 1g; Bates, Greener 1a.
(England 1-1-1, failed to qualify for finals)

CHALLENGE GAMES
In Windsor, Canada
27 Dec **England u16-Amherstburg 6-2**
30 Dec **England u16-Windsor 4-0**
31 Dec **England u16-Amherst Ravens 4-1**
2 Jan **Ancaster-England u16 0-6**
In England
17 Nov **Sunderland u19-England u16 2-10**

ENGLAND UNDER-17s *left to right, back row:* Vanessa Brown (physio), Mike Evans (manager), Adam Robinson, Joe Miller, Nick Dodwell, Andy Thornton, Bernie Bradford, Kevin Phillips, Stephen Duncombe, Leigh Jamieson, Simon Butterworth, Ben Burch, Daniel Good, Rob Jenner, Martyn Etheridge (co-coach), Terry Ward (co-coach); *front row:* Geoff Woolhouse, Kurt Reynolds, Adam Brittle, Tom Smith, Mark Richardson, Michael Snook.

WOMEN'S LEAGUE

FINAL STANDINGS

Premier League	GP	W	L	D	GF	GA	Pts
Guildford Lightning	16	15	1	0	81	12	30
Sunderland Scorpions	16	13	2	1	76	22	27
Cardiff Comets	16	9	5	2	50	33	20
Bracknell Queen Bees	16	7	5	4	62	49	18
Kingston Diamonds	16	6	8	2	39	30	14
Swindon Top Cats	16	6	8	2	50	41	14
Slough Phantoms	16	4	10	2	40	63	10
Billingham Wildcats	16	4	11	1	39	69	9
Nottingham Vipers	16	1	15	0	13	131	2

LEADING SCORERS

Premier League	GP	G	A	Pts	Pim
Fiona King GUI	16	16	16	32	2
Lisa King GUI	16	10	19	29	14
Louise Wheeler SLO	11	18	6	24	18
Lynsey Emmerson SUN	14	15	9	24	8
Jane Price SUN	15	10	14	24	12

LEADING NETMINDERS

	GPI	Mins	SoG	GA	Sv%
Vicki Robbins GUI	8	388	173	2	98.8
Pauline Anderson SUN	14	795	270	19	92.9
Dawn Dickinson KIN	15	765	395	28	92.9

Qualification: 320 minutes

CHAMPIONSHIP PLAYOFFS

Premier League

Final	Guildford-**SUNDERLAND**	1-2
3rd place	Bracknell-Cardiff	4-3
Semi-finals	Guildford-Bracknell	9-0
	Sunderland-Cardiff	4-2

Division One

Final	**SHEFFIELD**-Whitley	7-2
3rd place	Romford-Basingstoke	2-3
Semi-finals	Sheffield-Romford	4-3
	Basingstoke-Whitley	2-4

Lightning can't strike twice

Guildford Lightning beat off last season's winners, Sunderland Scorpions, to take their first Premier League title. But they narrowly failed to do the double, losing 2-1 to Scorpions in the playoffs.

Guildford's **Fiona** and **Laura King** (not related), took the scoring honours, though Slough's **Louise Wheeler** potted most goals with 18 in only eleven games. Lightning's first choice goalie, **Vicki Robbins** (no relation to Superleague's Trevor!), allowed only two goals to finish as the top netminder.

In their first season in the Premier, Billingham Wildcats surprisingly beat the 1999-2000 winners, Nottingham Vipers, into last place. Vipers will drop into Division One for next season while the Premier Division is being expanded to ten teams with the promotion of Sheffield Shadows and Basingstoke Lady Bison.

PAST PREMIER LEAGUE WINNERS

2000-01	Sunderland Scorpions
1999-00	Nottingham Vipers
1998-99	Slough Phantoms
1994-98	Sunderland Scorpions
1993-94	Bracknell Queen Bees
1990-93	Oxford City Rockets
1988-90	Oxford/Streatham/Sunderland
	(regional winners)
1987-88	Streatham Strikers
1986-87	Oxford University
1985-86	Streatham Strikers
1984-85	Peterborough Ravens
1983-84	P'boro Ravens/Solihull Vixens
	(joint winners)

IIHF WORLD WOMEN'S CHALLENGE

Hull Arena, 8-10 March 2002

FINAL STANDINGS

	GP	W	L	D	GF	GA	Pts
Italy	2	2	0	0	6	3	4
Britain	2	1	1	0	8	4	2
Belgium	2	0	2	0	0	7	0

RESULTS

8 Mar **Italy-Belgium** **2-0** (0-0,1-0,1-0)

9 Mar **Britain-Belgium** **5-0** (2-0,2-0,1-0)
Scoring: Turner 2+1; Taylor 2g;
Brunning 1g; King 1a.

10 Mar **Britain-Italy** **3-4** (1-3,2-0,0-1)
GB scoring: Oldfield, Lamb, Bicknell 1g;
Bayne, Taylor, Beattie 1a.

BRITAIN

Vicki Robbins GUI, Verity Boome SLO; Tonia Scialdone BIR, Vicky Burton BRK, Kirsten Beattie EDI, Louise Fisher, Alex Von Hasselburg GUI, Susan Hemmerman, Gillian Wyatt KIN, Alice Lamb SLO; Zoe Bayne BIL, Heather Brunning BRK, Fiona King capt, Hannah Young GUI, Angela Taylor PAI (jrs), Gemma Watt PAI (rec), Laura Burke, Emily Turner SHE, Nicola Bicknell SLO, Claire Oldfield WHI.
Coach: Tony Hall (EIHA).
Manager: Alison McCabe.

Late goal knocks out Brits

Emily Turner of Division One's Sheffield Shadows scored twice and assisted on a third as Britain trounced the Belgians 5-0 in this special series of games arranged by the IIHF in lieu of a World Championship in an Olympic year.

Verity Boome had the clean sheet though, in truth, the Slough Phantom keeper was rarely troubled as Britain outshot Belgium 31-16. The Player of the Game was Paisley teenager, **Angela Taylor**, who showed great promise by scoring twice on her international debut.

In the deciding game against Italy, the national team bravely fought back from 3-0 down to tie the game on **Nicola Bicknell**'s goal at 32.38. But they were forced to to settle for second place after a last period tally from Italy's **Sabina Florian**.

HOME INTERNATIONAL

Nottingham Arena, 18 May 2002

ENGLAND	1	(1-0-0)
WALES	4	(3-0-1)

First Period
0-1 WAL Langford (Owen) 3.15
0-2 WAL Hargreaves 16.38
0-3 WAL Pugsley (McMullan) pp 18.03
1-3 ENG Drake 19.51
Penalty minutes: England 8, Wales 2.
Second Period
No scoring.
Penalty minutes: England 4, Wales 4.
Third Period
1-4 WAL Pugsley (Lawton) 54.10
Penalty minutes: England 4, Wales 2.
Shots on Goal:
Hayes ENG 19-6-6 31 *save* 87.1%
Hayman WAL 8-7-4 19 *save* 94.7%
Referee: Joy Tottman.
Linesmen: Ken Reddell, Liz Smith.

The newly formed Wales national side, comprising mostly players from Cardiff Comets, upset the English in the first ever women's home international between the two countries.

Player of the Game was Wales' defender, **Becci Hargreaves**, who skated the length of the ice to score her team's winning goal.

THE TEAMS
ENGLAND
Rhian Hayes BRK, Sasha Martin CAM; Chrissie Newman BAS, Sam Bidmead, Claire Pannell capt, Laura Stark BRK, Emma Stott, Sue Williams, Stacey Wood CHE, Josie Griffiths, Lucy Johnson GUI, Grace Drake INV, Nikki Brock KIN, Natalie Bullen, Kirsty Krater MIL, Jacqui Memmett, Kelly Simpson, Steph Turner SHE, Alice Stanley SLO, Nicki Pattinson, Alex Spooner SUN, Gemma Nichol, Vicki Wood WHI.
Coach: Paul Wilcock CHE.
Manager: Sylvian Clifford CHE.

WALES
Emma Hayman CAR; Sam Hart BAS, Laura Merrick BRI, Laura Burns, Fran Frappell, Becci Hargreaves, Elaine Langford, Lorraine McMullan, Ami Merrick, Shelley Owen, Helen Pugsley CAR, Sarah Audsley GUI, Sam Jones, Sophie Lawton KIN, Oenone Dodwell MIL, Deborah Warwick SOL.
Coach: Mike Pugsley CAR.
Manager: Helen Jefferies CAR.

HALL OF FAME

IAN COOPER

Ian Cooper is presented with a silver salver as the first player in 1996 to play 50 games for his country. Making the presentation is Annette Petrie, the secretary of the GB Supporters Club.

During **Ian Cooper's** long and distinguished career he made many significant contributions to the sport, on and off the ice.

One of the finest players produced in these islands, he helped Durham Wasps and Cardiff Devils to five consecutive league and championship doubles - including two Grand Slams - and made a record 80 World Championship appearances for Britain, playing a key role during their quickfire climb from Pool D to Pool A.

For six years, he devoted many unpaid hours to his duties as chairman of the Ice Hockey Players' Association (IHPA), and was rewarded with a dramatic increase in the number of members.

He represented the IHPA on the council of the British Ice Hockey Association (BIHA), and had a spell on the competitors' section of the British Olympic Committee.

Ian was born on 29 November 1968 at Peterlee, Co Durham. At the age of seven he was so taken with the first ice hockey match he saw that he decided "to have a go with an old stick and a pair of skates" on the newly opened Crowtree (Sunderland) rink.

As he lived halfway between Sunderland and Durham he was able to skate six days a week, playing across two or three age groups.

When he was 15, he topped the scoring with 31 goals and 43 points from 12 games in the northern section of the English Junior League, and his two goals helped Durham Mosquitoes to win the playoffs.

At the same time, he was heading the points scorers with the older Durham Hornets which earned him limited ice-time with the Wasps. He scored three goals in 30 games with Wasps in his first season, 1984-85.

His career took off in the following campaign as he chipped in 38 goals and 36 assists as Durham retained the *Heineken* League, Premier Division title.

Two British Championships at Wembley Arena followed with the Autumn Cup in addition during the second year. With 139 points, Ian earned a place on the Writers' All-Star 'A' team.

In that spring of 1988 he also won the *Ice Hockey News Review*'s Young British Player of the Year award which boasted a prize of a trip to Calgary Flames' NHL training camp.

By now, he and his defenceman brother **Stephen**, who also played for the Wasps, were among the most sought after home-grown players in the game.

But it was still a surprise when **John Lawless's** ambitious Cardiff Devils made the pair probably the biggest offer ever to British trained players at that time.

Though Devils had only just won promotion to Division One, a level below the Premier, the money was enough to persuade the Cooper boys to quit their day jobs and become full-time hockey players.

Lawless's gamble paid off as Devils lifted the Division One title and won the promotion playoffs while Ian again made the All-Star squad.

On his return to the top flight, his points increased again to 163 and Cardiff clinched the Premier Division crown. They added the *Heineken* British Championship after a double overtime, 24-penalty shot victory in a packed Wembley Arena that will live as one of his most enduring memories of the sport.

That summer a chastened Durham offered the brothers full professional wages. In 1990-91, their first season back 'at home' - not entirely coincidentally - Wasps captured the Grand Slam of league, championship and Autumn Cup titles. Ian's points peaked at 178.

After helping Wasps to retain the league and championship, the Cooper boys returned to Cardiff where they and Devils won three league crowns, two championships and an Autumn Cup in six years.

In recognition of Ian's contributions to the sport, in an on-ice ceremony at the 1996 Wembley finals, **Frederick Meredith**, the president of the BIHA, presented him with the prestigious Ahearne Medal.

Ian's 50th senior cap for Britain came in an Olympic qualifier in Holland the following December. He was the first to achieve the half-century in his country's World Championship and Olympic qualifying games.

Looking back, Ian selected Britain's Pool B gold medal in 1993 as being "something special". His coach, **Alex Dampier**, said: "He displays pride when he plays. He gives it his all."

Ian first represented his country in 1985 at under-18 level and collected a gold medal in Pool C in Spain the next season. He also had a five-year stint with the GB under-20s.

He competed in three European Cups. His game-winning goal in Cardiff's 3-2 victory over Kazakhstan gave Devils a place in the 1994 European Cup semi-finals, the first time a British team had progressed that far in the competition.

After Cardiff failed to renew his contract in 1998 he nearly joined Phoenix of the North American West Coast Hockey League before moving to London's Docklands.

There, in a rare privilege for a Brit on an all-import roster, he captained the Knights in their inaugural campaign. But his Superleague career lasted only 18 months as London's new coach **Chris McSorley** arranged for him to move to Guildford Flames of the British National League (BNL).

Two games for the BNL's Basingstoke Bison and a few weeks at English League side, Chelmsford Chieftains, closed out Ian's illustrious career prematurely. He was only 32.

Between 1984 and 2001, he scored 760 goals and 1,620 points in 793 games . He also spent 1,591 minutes in various penalty boxes.

He is now involved in promoting a different sport, athletics, through his job with Harwood & Co, a PR, marketing and event management company, one of whose clients used to be Superleague.

Ian Cooper was one of the modern game's first home-grown players to turn professional. More importantly, he - along with a handful of others like his brother Stephen and **Tony Hand** - displayed a professional attitude which helped to lay the foundation for other true Brits to come into the sport.

CHRIS KELLAND

Chris Kelland was one of the most skilled and dedicated British-Canadians of the game's Modern Era. His hard-nosed defensive play helped his club sides and national teams to numerous honours.

Over two decades, he played 844 games in five different leagues from the English League to Superleague, winning trophies in them all.

He was captain of the GB national squad from 1990 when dual nationals were first permitted until 1994 when he and his team faced the might of Russia and Canada in the World Championship A Pool.

Born on 22 December 1957 at Sault Sainte Marie, Ontario, Chris came to Britain in 1980 and joined Murrayfield Racers, then top dogs in the Northern League under player-coach, **Alex Dampier**. The powerhouse Racers collected several trophies in the 1980s, the most important being the *Heineken* British Championship at Wembley Arena in 1986.

Kelland became a close friend of 'Damps' and in 1991 he moved south to join the coach at Nottingham. The pair helped Panthers to the *Norwich Union* Autumn Cup and runners-up places in the league and championships. He linked up with Alex again in 1993 at Sheffield and Steelers won consecutive league and championships in 1994-95 and 1995-96.

When Dampier was sacked by Steelers in 1998, Chris left, too, though not before he had set some kind of record in his penultimate season by winning a Superleague playoff championship medal at the age of 39 years and 98 days.

The 5ft, 9in, 185 lbs (in his heyday) defender was always super-fit. In his early days here he used to return to Canada for three months every summer to keep his hand in as a lumberjack. So though he joined the Fire Service after leaving Steelers, he still found time and energy to play 30 games with Solihull Blaze as they won the English League and cup double in 1998-99.

The next winter he signed as 'emergency cover' with the BNL's Hull Thunder and in 2000-01 he was in a Coventry Blaze jersey. He now claims to have definitely retired.

NORMAN DE MESQUITA

One of the sport's best known personalities, **Norman de Mesquita** has spread the ice hockey gospel from a variety of angles - as a newspaper reporter (and seller), a radio broadcaster and arena announcer.

He served as chairman of the British Ice Hockey Writers Association for 14 years until 1999 when a serious illness curtailed his activities. The outspoken 'From the Shoulder' column he wrote for his late friend **Vic Batchelder's** *Ice Hockey News Review* made lively reading, and he was ice hockey correspondent of *The Times* from 1985 until 1999.

The Wembley Lions of the post-war years were Norman's first taste of the sport when, as he describes it, "It was love at first sight". While selling copies of the weekly *Ice Hockey World* at three London arenas - Wembley, Haringey and Earls Court - he got to know many of the major figures in the game, including the chief referee, **Ernie Leacock**.

Leacock guided him when he decided to take up refereeing in 1955 and he worked his way up to senior level. He retired in 1968 when the Lions played their last game.

When Detroit Red Wings' owner, **Bruce Norris**, briefly revived the Lions in 1973-74 as London Lions, Norman was sports editor at BBC Radio London. A friend recalled that he was always turning the conversation to ice hockey in his Sunday morning phone-in.

As the possessor of a fine speaking voice and a vast knowledge of the game, he was a natural to become the announcer for Lions' games, and he went on to handle many other major sporting events at the arena.

He looked after Streatham's public address when *Mecca Leisure* took over the rink in 1980; 'the *Mecca* of frozen entertainment in south London' was his introductory catchphrase. He returned to Wembley in 1983 when *Heineken* took the sport back to its 'spiritual home' with the end-of-season championships. 'The Voice of Wembley' stayed at the mike until the last finals were played there in 1996.

It is the cruellest of ironies then that though he otherwise recovered completely from his illness, it left him with a speech impediment. Norman rarely complains, however, nor has it stopped him talking!

Now 70, he still travels regularly to North America, once a year with the London Ice Hockey Nuts Club, a group he formed in 1979. This meant that his comprehensive NHL reports in *Ice Hockey News* (*Review*) were written from first-hand knowledge of the league. Indeed, he proudly claims to have seen a game in every NHL arena.

*Compiled by **Stewart Roberts**. from contributions by **Tony Allen**, **Anthony Beer** and **Martin Harris**.*

HALL OF FAME MEMBERS

The current Hall of Fame was established in 1986 by the British Ice Hockey Writers' Association.

In addition to the members profiled above, the Association have inducted the following:
2001- Jim Lynch. 2000 - Vic Batchelder, Gary Stefan. 1999 - Les Anning, Shannon Hope, Gordon Latto, Roy Shepherd. 1998 - Earl Carlson. 1997- John Lawless. 1996 - Johnny Murray. 1995 - Alex Dampier. 1994 - Mick Curry, Jack Wharry. 1993 - William (Willie) Clark, Nico Toemen, Ian Wight. 1992 - Frank Dempster, Alec Goldstone, Lawrie Lovell. 1991 - Jack Dryburgh, John Rost, Brian Glynne Thomas. 1990 - Alastair Brennan, Sir Arthur Elvin MBE, Willie Kerr Sr. 1989 - George Beach, William Walton (Bill) Booth, Art Hodgins, Peter Johnson, Alfie Miller. 1988 - Patricia Marian (Pat) Marsh, John Cumming (Johnny) Carlyle, *Percy H Nicklin, John Frederick James (Icy) Smith, Alan Weeks. 1987 - Ernest Sidney (Ernie) Leacock, Thomas (Red) Imrie, Terry Matthews, Derek Reilly, Les Strongman. 1986 - *John Francis (Bunny) Ahearne, Robert (Bobby) Giddens, Roy Halpin, Harvey (Red) Stapleford, Sam Stevenson.

*British ice hockey's original Hall of Fame was created in 1950 by **Bob Giddens**, the editor/publisher of* Ice Hockey World, *the sport's only publication from 1935 to 1958.*

The members of the original Hall are listed in The Ice Hockey Annual 2000-01.

OLD-TIME HOCKEY

CHAMPIONS ON ICE
by **Phil Drackett**, published by *Ice Hockey World*

This is just one of the 150 illustrations in *Annual* correspondent, **Phil Drackett**'s latest book about the stars of ice hockey's Superleagues of the 1940s and 1950s.

A sequel to Phil's excellent *Flashing Blades*, it will need no recommendation to those fans who remember those gloomy post-war years being illuminated by the glamour of the world's fastest sport in arenas in London, Nottingham and Scotland.

For newer fans, this is a lively, dramatic and humorous account of the sport's fascinating past from a journalist who was on the spot.

SPECIAL HALF-PRICE OFFER!

A limited number of copies of *Champions On Ice* are available exclusively to readers of *The Ice Hockey Annual* at the special price of £6, post free. (The published price is £12).

To get your copy, just send a cheque or postal order with your address direct to Phil Drackett at 9 Victoria Road, Mundesley, Norwich, Norfolk NR11 8JG.

THE STORY OF HARRINGAY STADIUM AND ARENA
by **Mike Ticher**, published by the Hornsey Historical Society.

Another stroll down Memory Lane for the wrinklies, and perhaps a warning for Superleague club owners of how difficult it is to make Canadian ice hockey work in big arenas in this country!

The 10,000-seat Harringay Arena was the home of two professional, all-Canadian teams between 1936 and 1949. There were also world-class boxing matches while the adjoining stadium was the venue for greyhound racing and speedway. All these events were pioneered in Britain by **Brig-Gen A C Critchley** (*above*), one of sport's greatest promoters.

The changing times - particularly the rise in traffic in London's cramped suburban streets - meant that Harringay became unviable not long after World War 2. The arena was converted to a food warehouse in 1958 before being demolished 20 years later.

The author is a journalist with the *Guardian* newspaper and the football fanzine, *When Saturday Comes*. He lives in Tottenham and was intrigued by the Harringay story which he discovered when he moved to the area. He is keen to have a plaque erected to mark the site in Green Lanes where the buildings once stood.

Copies of the book are available from the Hornsey Historical Society, The Old Schoolhouse, 136 Tottenham Lane, London N8 7EL, price £5, including post & packing.

TRIBUTES

VIC BATCHELDER

Vic Batchelder, who has died aged 61, was the editor and founding publisher of the *Ice Hockey News Review*. the sport's longest running magazine. He started *IHNR* in September 1981 as a four-page pamphlet but long before he edited his last edition in September 1999, the fortnightly publication had expanded to 32 full colour A4 pages.

Vic lived and breathed ice hockey. In many ways, he was fortunate that his magazine coincided with one of the most exciting periods in the sport's history. This was a time of an unprecedented boom in ice hockey teams, fuelled by the largest rink building programme ever seen in Britain; TV coverage; blue-chip sponsors, *Heineken* and *Benson & Hedges;* and the creation of the big-spending Superleague.

None of this prevented him from writing page three editorials bemoaning the state of the game and forecasting its imminent demise unless the authorities - especially BIHA president, **Fred Meredith** - mended their ways.

As he had given up his day job to concentrate on his new creation, his concern was understandable.

Vic built *IHNR* into a magazine of record, covering every aspect of the game - reports from every club, European as well as NHL hockey, a look back to the game's early days, opinion columns from the game's personalities, the junior scene, detailed stats, and much more.

In those pre-internet days, *IHNR* was showered with letters from fans with opinions on every possible topic. But Vic had an opinion on every subject, too, and he typically answered every letter forthrightly. Letter and reply made compulsive reading.

In those days, apart from a strictly limited three paid imports, the players were home-grown and amateur. If Brits were paid, it was a pittance.

So when **John Lawless**, the coach of the new Cardiff Devils, dared to offer good money to Durham Wasps' talented English brothers, **Ian** and **Stephen Cooper**, to join the Devils, Vic's editorial was a howl of anguish, prophesying immediate doom for the sport.

He was given a fair bit of stick the next time he went to a Devils' game. He took it on the chin, but being a staunch traditionalist by nature, he could never quite reconcile himself to professionalism in our sport.

He was very keen, however, on encouraging youngsters into the game and this led him to produce a unique prize for the country's best under-21 player - a trip to an NHL training camp.

In 1985, the Government of Alberta, Air Canada and the NHL's Calgary Flames sponsored the Young British Player of the Year award, which was presented annually until 1994. Many of the players who are now household names in the sport - **Tony Hand**, **David Longstaff**, **Paul Dixon**, the Coopers - won the coveted prize.

Vic came into journalism late after a 'normal' working life, first in the police service (mostly as a dog handler - dogs were one of his other loves), and then with a finance company. Though he was self-taught as a writer, his news sense and reputation for accuracy made his work respected in the highest circles.

He wrote a regular column for the *Guardian* newspaper from the late 1980s until the week before he died, and his passing was greeted with two obituaries in the paper's sports pages, a rarity for a freelance contributor.

If Vic was passionate about ice hockey, he was also passionate about his country. His most treasured memory was undoubtedly ice hockey's finest moment in the modern era - GB winning promotion to the World A Pool in 1993, with mainly home-grown players.

His fellow national newspaper journalist, **Paul Newman**, was sitting beside him in the press seats in Bolzano, Italy when **Tim Cranston** scored GB's winning goal against the Netherlands. "How we cheered," recalled Paul in

Ice Hockey News. "We lost all semblance of press neutrality. Vic was very proud to be British and at that moment he was the happiest I ever saw him." Paul was one of many reporters on *IHNR* who paid tribute to Vic for his help and encouragement in their writing careers.

Vic was born in Ruislip, Middlesex on 27 August 1940 but the family moved to Kidderminster soon after to escape the Blitz. Though he watched ice hockey at Wembley in his teens, his first love was football (he was a life-long Wolves' fan) and after playing in a local league, he worked his way up the officiating ladder until he became a linesman in the Football Combination.

I met him in 1980 when he was living with his wife, Yvonne, and their family in Derby. That's when I found out he was a great family man. He had just re-discovered ice hockey through the return of Nottingham Panthers and having retired as a linesman, he was keen to help his new found sport. He agreed to take on the role of my assistant in the southern-based, amateur Inter-City League.

It was during this time that he realised there was no publication covering the sport and decided he would do one himself. For many years afterwards, he would ring me and think nothing of spending ages on the phone discussing something that had irritated him in the sport. He was always a bit put out that I liked to go to bed before midnight as he was only just getting into his stride around then.

Vic will always have my greatest respect for the vast amount of work he put into *IHNR*, fortnight after fortnight, year after year. But having as a friend a man with honestly held beliefs who loved to argue endlessly about the sport, did make our relationship a tiring one. Partly my fault, of course. I should simply have agreed with him. It made me sympathise - well, almost - with those running the sport to whom he gave such a hard time.

A few months after he was diagnosed with cancer in 1999, Vic sold *IHNR* to his long time printers, Pinegen Ltd, but he carried on writing for his old magazine until only a few days before his death on 11 October 2001.

He was unanimously voted into the British Ice Hockey Writers' Hall of Fame in 2000 for his outstanding service to British ice hockey.

Besides Yvonne, he leaves a daughter, Angie, and two sons, Tony and Allan, a former ice hockey referee and now a supervisor, who helped his father produce the magazine.

■ In memory of Vic, the British Ice Hockey Writers' Association created a new Young British Player of the Year award to be presented in 2003. *Stewart Roberts*

LEO CARREY

Leo Carrey, one of the legends of the original Paisley Pirates at the East Lane rink, has died aged 76. He split his years in Europe from 1946 to 1952 between Paisley, Falkirk Lions and The Hague in Holland, tasting success in both countries.

The Espanola, Ontario native played right wing for Pirates, usually on a line with **Paul Theriault** at centre and **Johnny Vanier** on left wing. He was a member of Scotland's 100 Goal Club, scoring 121 times for Lions and Pirates.

He was an innovator, being one of the first Pirates to wear a protective skull cap, which was very rare in those days of bare-headed players.

During World War Two, he was with the 51st Field Regiment of the Royal Canadian Artillery who were involved in liberating the Hague, capital of the Netherlands. While he was with the Hague club, they won the Western European Cup three years in a row. He coached the Dutch national team to two European championships.

Leo eventually returned to Canada, where he played and coached in the Southern Ontario League until 1965.

He had a terrific love for the game, a total grasp of hockey's history and was a fount of knowledge of the great players over the years. One former coach said: "Wherever Leo played, he was very much the heart and soul of his team."

His hockey connection continued up to his funeral, at which a couple of hockey players acted as pall bearers. His Paisley years seem to have left a lasting impression of Scotland and a bagpipe lament was played.

Leo was pre-deceased by his wife Muriel (Pedlingham), who died in 1995 after 40 years of marriage.

• *The Western European Cup* - Former Hague player, **Jak Herijgers**, now 70, told the *Paisley Daily Express*: "There was a competition in those days, the Lipens Cup, played for by teams from Holland, Belgium and France.

"The cup was presented by a Mr Lipens, a Belgian politician. But he collaborated with the Germans while they occupied Belgium, so the French and Dutch teams refused to play unless the name of the cup was changed and that's how the Western European Cup came about."

Matt Vallance, Paisley Daily Express

ERIC CREGAN

The former Liverpool Leopards and Blackpool Seagulls goalie, who has died aged 51, was a colourful figure in the amateur game.

A forthright Liverpudlian, Eric was an off-beat character with flowing shoulder-length hair (even when it had long since turned grey) who was renowned for his netminding antics and his love of motor-bikes.

> "He was once written about in *The Times* when he played for a team that ended up being hammered 54-0 and Eric, the goalie, was ejected for disputing the 51st!"
>
> **Bob Bramah** on the late **Eric Cregan**
> *Powerplay*

Starting out with a couple of seasons for his home town Leopards, he transferred to Blackpool in 1974, then spent the next nine years moving between the neighbouring clubs.

In 1991-92 he became Seagulls' manager, though he still registered as their reserve netminder, and he later turned out in recreational games for Blackburn Falcons.

A fellow rec. player recalled: "He seemed to have a smile on his face no matter what the score was, and to tell the truth his team was often losing heavily."

Eric was in goal for Falcons on 10 November 2001 at Whitley Bay when he collapsed. He left a wife, Moira, and their two sons.

Martin Harris

CHRIS DILKS

A one-time winger with Ashfield Islanders and Nottingham North Stars recreational teams who played in 19 games for Nottingham Panthers in 1989-94.

Chris died in a motor-cycle accident on 4 September 2001, leaving a wife, Joanne.

JOSEPH (JO-JO) GRABOSKI

Joseph Francis Graboski, always known as Jo-Jo, was one of only two players with sight in one eye known to have competed in pro hockey in England before 1960. The fast skating centreman joined Wembley Lions in 1936-37.

The respected Canadian hockey historian, **Bill Fitsell**, compared Jo-Jo's dazzling play with Ottawa's legendary one-eyed player, **Frank McGee**. A native of Cobalt, Ontario, he lost the sight in 1932 when he was 17 after being struck by an errant hockey stick while practising with the junior Oshawa (Ontario) Generals.

The accident was particularly tragic as he had just received an invitation to try out for the NHL's Chicago Black Hawks.

Jo-Jo claimed that he was the only person to play on a championship team in three different countries - Lions (the 1936-37 English National League winners), Hershey Bears (Eastern American League in 1937-38) and Kirkland Lake (the Canadian Allan Cup titleists in 1939-40).

He nearly didn't make it to the Allan Cup final. He had returned to England in September 1939 to join Nottingham Panthers, and when war was declared he spent a hazardous two weeks dodging U-boats in the Atlantic to get back home.

Graboski died in Sillery, Quebec on 27 January 2002, aged 87.

Martin Harris

JERRY HUDSON

Jerry Hudson, from Gananoque, Ontario, was one of the most consistent scorers and toughest bantamweights to play in Scotland.

Right out of Hollywood's Central Casting, he was pale of face, red of hair and undeterred by the size of his opponents. So much so that when he captained Falkirk Lions and most of the team were about his size, Lions were known as The Little Men of Iron.

Hudson came to Scotland in 1949 and played four seasons with Dunfermline Vikings during which they won the Canada Cup and the Scottish Cup and were runners-up in the league. In those four years, Hudson played 250 games, scoring 128 goals and 171 assists. As any large defenceman who fancied his chances with the little fellow was soon disillusioned, he picked up ten majors.

He was just the type of man that **George McNeil**, the Falkirk coach was looking for to lead his Lions and he recruited him in 1953. The 25-year-old did not let him down, finishing tenth in the scoring with 100 points in 69 games and taking Lions to the Scottish Playoff Championship.

After notching 99 points the following season, Hudson moved to England and helped Nottingham Panthers to their only league and cup double in 1955-56, the last time Panthers won a league title.

Before he retired in the 1960s, he racked up many more points for Paisley Pirates, Edinburgh Royals and Fife Flyers. He died in his adopted Scotland in March 2002, aged 76.

Phil Drackett

JOHN HUNTER

John Hunter, who died aged 38, was a founding player with the Peterborough Pirates.

After picking up the rudiments of the game as an 11-year-old in Canada, John and his older brothers, **Tony** and **Kevin**, attended Pirates' first Sunday lunch-time training session when the East of England rink opened in late 1981.

The trio, who had spent five years in Canada with their parents, helped to build the new team and turned out for Pirates' first game the following May.

John, a rugged centreman, made 69 appearances for Pirates between 1983 and 1987, scoring nine goals and 14 assists with 89 penalty minutes. He played on both their British League, Division One championship sides in 1984-85 and 1986-87. His coach on the first was the legendary **John Lawless**, and for the second, the former NHL Iron Man, **Garry Unger**.

After retiring from the game, Hunter became a Conservative councillor in his adopted city.

A motor cycle engineer by trade, he lost his life in a collision with a lorry on 10 November 2001 while road testing a new bike. He left a wife and children.

Martin Harris

MAUNO (KID) KAUPPI

Kid Kauppi ranked with the best of them, according to his old Wembley captain, **Sonny Rost**. Deceptively quiet and baby-faced, Kauppi was playing his last year of Canadian junior A hockey with Barrie (Ontario) Flyers when the late, great **Lou Bates** recruited him for Wembley Monarchs.

Kauppi, **Les Anning** and **George Steele**, all 19, formed the famous Kid Line in the first season after World War Two. The trio remained friends until Kauppi's death in February 2002, aged 75.

Mauno was the line's playmaker, a heads-up, smooth skater who could take care of himself. He played four seasons with Monarchs and said the highlights were winning the 1948 Autumn Cup and being selected by the fans as their most popular and sportsmanlike player.

In those days, Wembley regularly attracted crowds of 10,000. "The English fans often travelled long distances to see the games," marvelled Kauppi. "They were the very best."

After he returned to Canada, he was at his best with Sudbury (Ontario) Wolves, scoring the overtime goal that took them to the finals of the Allan Cup, the Canadian amateur championship.

Wolves lost in the final to Penticton (BC) Vs who went on to win the 1955 World Championships as Canada.

Kauppi, a native of Coppercliff, Ontario, retired from organised hockey at the age of 27 to look after his growing family and start a building supplies and construction business. A wealthy man by his forties, he bought a motor cruiser in Finland, crossed the Atlantic with his wife and two children, visited the Caribbean and sailed up the Atlantic seaboard back to Canada. He played recreational hockey until he was 68.

Phil Drackett

GEORGE (HERB) KEWLEY

George Kewley, better known as Herb, was a member of a Canadian family who made a big contribution to the sport in the years after World War 2. His father Claude was a Toronto journalist who was asked by the Scottish IHA to recruit players for all the Scottish National League teams. Among his choices were two of his six sons: Keith, who gave up playing after one season to become a successful coach, and Herb, a consistent and high scoring reguard.

They joined Dunfermline Vikings together in the first season after the war and Herb helped Vikings to the league runners-up place and victory in the playoffs.

After Vikings carried off the Simpson knock-out cup the following season, Herb returned to Canada and signed for Sudbury Wolves. He won a World Championship silver medal with Wolves who represented Canada at the 1949 games.

Returning to Scotland, he joined Ayr Raiders with another brother, Hal, and was appointed team captain. During his four seasons he led Raiders to two league titles, one Autumn Cup and a playoff championship.

Only 5ft, 8in tall and weighing 170lbs, he neither smoked not drank. His rushing and blocking style helped him - unusually for a defenceman - to win entry to the 100-Goal Club with 116, plus 178 assists in over 350 competitive games. He was twice selected to the All-Star A team and one of his contemporaries, **Stu Cruikshank**, insisted: "He was good enough to make the NHL." Herb died in his native Ontario on 8 February 2002.

Phil Drackett/Martin Harris/Jimmy Agnew

DUDLEY MOORE

The voice of many sports telephone 'hotlines' died suddenly in January 2002. He was in his late sixties.

A former Fleet Street newspaper reporter, Dudley teamed up with commentator, **Tony Millard**, to provide scores and reports on ice hockey via a premium rate telephone line.

When the service began in season 1987-88, a proportion of the proceeds was donated to the British Ice Hockey Association and was believed to have raised several thousand pounds for the then governing body.

More recently, he worked alongside **Gary Moran** of Nottingham Panthers and eventually they had lines covering 20 ice hockey clubs.

■ Dudley liked to recall a Government of Alberta reception for the Young British Player of the Year award in the 1980s when his name was on the invitation list alongside photographer **Peter Cook** and reporter **Paul Newman**.

The organisers were so taken aback by these apparent A-list celebs that they assumed that Players' Association secretary, **Joanne Collins**, was actually **Joan Collins**, and that Swindon Wildcats' reporter, **Bob Radford**, must be **Robert Redford**.

Stewart Roberts

MIKE PELLETIER

Michael (Mike) Pelletier, a high flyer in commerce and trading, was killed in the terrorist attack on New York's World Trade Centre on 11 September 2001.

Mike, a native of Victoria, BC, in Canada, played for Streatham Redskins in the British League, Premier Division in 1988-89 before being recruited by former Redskins' coach, **Alec Goldstone**, to help save his Division One side, Richmond Flyers, from relegation.

LORNE SMITH

An outstanding defenceman with Nottingham Panthers in the 1950s, **Lorne Smith**, a big, tough man, was almost a one season sensation in the Lace City.

He joined the Panthers from his native Canada in 1952-53 and made the All Star A team, but decided to stay at home for the next campaign. Panthers started the season badly, finished last in the Autumn Cup and sent an SOS to Smith.

He answered the call, came back and Nottingham won the league title. He was to patrol their blueline until the league closed down in 1960 - the last two seasons as player-coach - during which time they won the league again, the Autumn Cup and the Ahearne Trophy.

Smith was no angel - he spent 110 minutes in the cooler in 1954-55 - but in 1957-58 he gave way as Nottingham's bad man to, among others, **Doug Messier**, whose son Mark was to become one of the NHL's all-time greats.

In 424 games for Nottingham (only **Chick Zamick**, **Les Strongman** and **Kenny Westman** played more), he was their all-time penalty king with 534 minutes. But he contributed 85 goals and 149 assists for seventh place in Panthers' pre-1960 goal table and sixth in assists. He was voted to the All Star B team three more times as a defenceman and once as coach.

Smith was born in 1928 at Port Credit, Ontario and turned professional after World War 2 with Baltimore Clippers in the Eastern American Hockey League. After retiring he joined his blueline partner, **Lawson Neil**, in his bookmaking business. He was a guest of honour with Strongman and Zamick at the last Panthers' game in the old Stadium in March 2000.

He passed away peacefully in his Nottingham home on 27 June 2002, sitting in an armchair watching TV and leaving a wife, son and daughter. An indication of the dwindling number of old-time stars is that only two Panthers of Lorne's generation attended his funeral - Strongman and **Harry Todd**.

Phil Drackett

INTERNATIONAL ROUND-UP

Euro League - 'no anonymous teams'

When Swede **Rickard Fagerlund** was appointed by the IIHF to look into the possibility of reforming the European Hockey League, he stressed: "We can't have anonymous teams playing."

The new Euro supremo took up his post when he resigned as president of the Swedish Ice Hockey Federation after the 2002 World Championships in his native land. He had been in the post for 19 years.

The EHL was 'suspended' in 1999 after three seasons and Fagerlund admitted: "It was a compromise and compromises do not last long. Everything was a mish-mash which was not appealing to TV or to the viewers."

He believed that one of the biggest problems with the old set-up was that no one outside the league had ever heard of the champion teams - TPS Turku of Finland, Feldkirch of Austria and Russia's Metallurg Magnitogorsk (twice).

All worthy winners, no doubt, but the first question any TV station or sponsor would ask is where are the representatives from Moscow, Stockholm, Berlin, London, Prague, the continent's major capitals? Internationally recognisable cities like Amsterdam, Munich, Geneva, Belfast and Milan were not involved in the competition at all.

"The new league must be of top quality, with players and teams which are known to the fans," stressed Fagerlund. He added that the IIHF believed strongly in a European league. "It would be very strange if one of the most popular and trendy team sports in the world couldn't create a league in Europe."

To those critics who felt the world governing body should restrict itself to running the annual World Championships and developing the sport, Fagerlund added: "If the IIHF doesn't organise a European league, someone else will."

Among the other issues that Fagerlund addressed were prize money ("we need serious prize money"), and persuading fans whose teams already play 50+ domestic games a season, to care about a European league.

Television and sponsors would be attracted by one deal that the IIHF have negotiated. As reported in last year's *Annual*, the NHL have agreed in principle that the Stanley Cup winner will play the EHL champion for world club supremacy.

KEEP OUR OWN PLAYERS

"At the moment all the best [European] players head to North America and the NHL. What we want to do is come up with a competition that will help European teams to keep those guys here in Europe. Maybe not the very best but certainly the tier below."

Bob Zeller, *Superleague's deputy chairman, on being appointed to an IIHF committee looking into ways of re-creating the European Hockey League.*

Fagerlund said his first job was "to contact all national federations, leagues, top clubs, TV and marketing companies and thoroughly check their interest and commitment." In an interview with the Russian news agency, *Itar-Tass*, in June 2002, he revealed that 'an English firm' was analysing the feedback and was to present its findings to the IIHF in the autumn of 2002.

▪ *Editor's Note* - Some readers will have spotted that London Knights' owner, **Philip Anschutz**, is ahead of the game here. He has already bought, or is building arenas in many of the capital cities mentioned above.

Harkimo and Anschutz link up, move German DEL winners to Hamburg

Wealthy Finnish businessman, **Harry Harkimo**, the former owner of Newcastle Jesters, won the backing of the German Deutsche Elite League (DEL) to move their champion team, Münich Barons, to his new arena in Hamburg.

Harkimo's Jokerit Group are financing, constructing and operating the 13,800-seat Color Line Arena which was due to open in November 2002, replacing the city's old 6,000-seat arena. The total costs of the project were estimated at US$72 million (about £50 million), roughly the same as Manchester's arena when that was built seven years ago.

The arena has been modelled on Harkimo's Hartwall Arena, the home of his Finnish elite league side, Jokerit Helsinki, which he said turned a profit in its first year.

Despite being Germany's second largest city with a population of over ten million, Hamburg has no elite league team, so Harkimo acquired a 30 per cent interest in Münich Barons' DEL licence from the Anschutz Entertainment Group (AEG). The new Hamburg team, the Freezers, was to play in the Color Line Arena in 2002-03.

Barons drew only 3,000 a game in Münich despite winning the DEL in 2001-02. AEG's **Detlef Kornett** said his company invested 15 million Euros (about £10 million) in the Barons but partly due to the city's fanatical attachment to football's Bayern Münich, their losses were "enormous".

In Hamburg, the team expects to draw at least 5,000 spectators a game and has a budget of £5 million. "I want to win the championship in two years," declared Harkimo. In return for his 30 per cent interest, he agreed to drop plans to build a new arena in east Berlin where Anschutz is negotiating to erect a new 16,000-seater for his Eisbären (Polar Bears).

When Freezers join the German elite league, it will give Harkimo an interest in three European teams. In addition to Hamburg and Jokerit Helsinki, the former round-the-world yachtsman has a 40 per cent in AIK Stockholm and he was planning to add an arena in Dublin.

Cologne Sharks win German playoffs

Kölner Haie (Cologne Sharks) upset the form book by winning the German Elite League (DEL) playoffs in April 2002.

In the fifth and deciding game of the final series, Sharks beat defending champs Adler (Eagles) Mannheim 2-1 to capture the eighth German Cup in their history. The team that finished sixth in the league took some notable scalps in the earlier rounds, too. They first swept third place, Krefeld, then knocked out league champs, Münich Barons.

The Haie were also wildly successful at the box office as their average crowd of 11,142 was the second highest in Europe. The Cologne Arena, which held the 2001 World Championships, has a capacity of 18,000.

The achievement did not stop the club from releasing coach, **Rich Chernomaz**, who was brought in as a temporary replacement for sacked head coach **Lance Nethery**. Before the playoffs, the club signed German national team coach, **Hans Zach**, to a two-year contract.

League champions, Münich Barons, as reported above, will move to Hamburg in 2002-03.

Final 2001-02 DEL standings on next page -

DEL standings	W	L	OTW	OTL	GF	GA	Pts
Münich Barons	33	15	10	2	182	138	121
Mannheim Eagles	34	14	6	6	186	135	120
Krefeld Penguins	34	16	6	4	210	162	118
Nuremburg Ice Tigers	31	18	7	4	180	134	111
Kassel Huskies	26	20	6	8	157	147	98
Cologne Sharks	27	24	3	6	173	153	93
Berlin Polar Bears	25	24	6	5	177	166	92
Augsburg Panthers	23	23	8	6	185	189	91
Düsseldorf Metro Stars	23	26	8	3	143	139	88
Hanover Scorpions	21	28	4	7	180	201	78
Frankfurt Lions	20	31	7	2	156	190	76
Iserlohn Roosters	19	28	4	9	154	183	74
Oberhausen Revier Loewen	18	31	5	6	168	187	70
Essen Mosquitos	18	31	3	8	163	195	68
Berlin Capitals	19	30	6	5	168	205	68
Schwenningen Wild Wings	18	30	2	10	134	183	58

All teams played 60 games. Win = 3 points, OT Win = 2 points, OT Loss = 1 point.

Berlin Capitals, who lost the relegation playoffs against Schwenningen, were demoted to the Second Division along with Essen Mosquitoes. Both teams had already had their league licences revoked for financial reasons. The west Berlin club was sold for one Euro in April 2002 but still had debts of almost £3 million.

ERC Ingolstadt were promoted from the Second Division making a 14-team DEL in 2002-03.

Winter Olympics

According to the sports website, sportal.com, a package for a ticket to the men's and women's gold medal ice hockey games plus the closing ceremony cost US$1,560 (approx. £1,100).

One VIP/Corporate package was listed on eBay's Internet auction site for $23,195. The organising committee expected to sell $180 million's worth of tickets.

The Nagano Winter Olympics in Japan in 1998 sold $90 million's worth of tickets. The Salt Lake Olympics shattered that record thanks to an increase in venues and an increase in ticket prices for the most popular events.

Zurich win Continental Cup

Petr Jaks scored twice to help Zurich ZSC Lions of Switzerland retain their Continental Cup title with a 6-1 defeat of Milan Vipers in the final on 13 January 2002. The game was watched by 5,058 fans in Zurich's Hallenstadion.

In third place were HKM Zvolen, the Slovakian champions, who beat Jukurit Mikkeli of Finland 6-3 earlier the same day. Jukurit are the side that effectively knocked London Knights out of the competition in the third round. *See Continental Cup.*

In the semi-finals the previous day, Milan topped Zvolen 4-2 and Lions edged Jukurit 4-3. The total crowds for the four games were 13,796.

"The European talent well is all but dry." *René Fasel, president of the IIHF, lamenting the fact that over 300 Europeans played in the NHL in 2001-02.*

McSorley's Geneva in Swiss A league

GB coach, **Chris McSorley**, successfully guided his club side, Geneva-Servette Eagles, into the Swiss A league in 2001-02.

Helped by a wage-roll of six million Swiss francs (about £2.7 million), the highest in the league, and some experienced players, including French legend **Philippe Bozon**, an ex-NHL forward, the Anschutz-owned team compiled a remarkable 22-game winning streak to reach their target.

First, they took the B league title after winning their last nine league games in a row, then won three best-of-five series in the fewest games possible to clinch the B league playoffs. After all that, Geneva knocked out Chur, the last placed A league club, in four straight games of their best-of-seven promotion series.

Geneva's star forward, **Philippe Bozon**, played in the Olympics for France. But only just. The man who scored the championship winning goal for his Swiss B league club, almost lost his equipment when his luggage was sent from Europe to South America rather than North America.

Apparently, the label read SLC for Salt Lake City, but a short-sighted baggage handler misread it as SDC for Santiago de Chile.

McSorley, a former coach of Superleague's London Knights, will reportedly have another two million francs to play with in 2002-03 to bring Eagles into line with the A league average.

The hard driving McSorley did not take the summer off to bask in the glory. On the contrary. As well as preparing Geneva for the challenge of the A league, he spent considerable time and effort on readying GB for their August internationals, and purchasing and re-stocking Cardiff Devils in the British National League. *See Review of the Year.*

World record crowd

US college rivals Michigan State Spartans and University of Michigan Wolverines played their first game of the season in front of a sell-out crowd of around 74,554 fans.

It was the biggest crowd ever to see an ice hockey game.

The Canadian College Hockey Association contest at Spartans (Football) Stadium on Saturday, 6 October 2001, played under floodlights, beat the previous record by almost 20,000 people.

The old mark was set on 5 March 1957 when an estimated crowd of 55,000 at the World Championships in Moscow's Lenin Stadium watched the Soviet Union draw 4-4 with Sweden.

October's game also ended in a tie with Michigan State holding the University of Michigan 3-3. MSU's **Jim Slater** netted the equaliser with 47 seconds remaining.

Wolverines' Canadian forward, **Mike Cammalleri**, was the star of the historic game recording two goals and one assist.

"It was pretty amazing when we came out of the tunnel," said Cammalleri. "But we had to forget about the crowd when the game started."

Billed as the Cold War, - but renamed the Outdoor Game after the events of 11 September - the event cost around US$500,000 (around £350,000) to stage. The ice pad - an artificial surface similar to those in indoor arenas - and the refrigeration plant were the ones used in the Hollywood hockey movie 'Mystery Alaska'.

The weather was described as partly cloudy with a temperature of 44 degrees Fahrenheit.

NHL legend **Gordie Howe**, who dropped the ceremonial puck prior to the official opening face-off, recalled: "When I was a boy, we played outside and it was always cold. The players will never forget this. This is history."

Another Classic

McGill University beats Oxford University in historic game

Montreal, 10 January, 2002

'A team composed of current and past members of the McGill University Redmen defeated the University Oxford Blues 14-1 in a historic exhibition hockey game today.

'The contest, played at McGill's McConnell Arena, featured two of the oldest hockey teams in the world. McGill - the world's longest established squad - dates back to 1877.

Oxford's Blues, on tour from England, were founded in 1885.

'**François Olivier** and **Carl Bastien**, both from Quebec province, led the Redmen with hat-tricks plus an assist. Defenceman **Scott Giroux**, from Saskatoon, tallied twice. **Patrick Kelly**, the son of NHL Hall of Fame inductee **Red Kelly**, had two assists. '**Jon Drover** of St. John's, Newfoundland, scored the lone goal for Oxford, who dressed five Canadians in their line-up.

'McGill outshot the Blues by a 57-11 margin as Redmen goaltender **Luc Vaillancourt**, a draft pick of the Anaheim Mighty Ducks, made ten saves for the victory. **David Watt** of Edmonton made 43 saves in a losing cause for the Blues. There was only one penalty called in the game, a bench minor to McGill for too many men.

'The Blues have had many illustrious members go on to fame, including Canadian Prime Minister **Lester B. Pearson**, Governor-General **Roland Michener** and long-time NHL president **Clarence Campbell**.

'McGill, often referred to as the birthplace of hockey, has had 12 of its former players inducted into the Hockey Hall of Fame, including **Frank** and **Lester Patrick**.

Our thanks to Earl (the Pearl) Zukerman, McGill communications officer, for this story. Earl brought the McGill Redmen to Britain in 1994-95.

The IIHF admitted Macedonia and Liechtenstein to its family in 2001 bringing the total of affiliated nations to 63. Macedonia, formerly part of Jugoslavia, is one five nations representing the old country on the world governing body, alongside Bosnia-Herzogovina, Croatia, Slovenia and Jugoslavia.

Spengler Cup 2001

HC Davos, the Swiss organising club, won the 75th Spengler Cup with a 4-3 overtime victory over a Canadian Select side.

Lonny Bohonos, a former Vancouver Canucks and Toronto Maple Leafs winger, tallied the unassisted winner just one minute into sudden-death. The win was Davos' second in a row and their tenth since the international tournament began in 1923 when the champions were Oxford University.

Five teams competed for the cup, playing an exhausting schedule of four games in five days between Boxing Day and 30 December, with the winners playing the final on New Year's Eve. The other teams - all club sides - were TPS Turku of Finland, Adler Mannheim of Germany and Czech side, Sparta Prague.

A record total of over 82,000 spectators watched the 11 games.

Tom Stewart watch

Scot **Tom Stewart's** efforts to buy the Swiss A league club, Ambri-Piotta, hit the headlines around Europe during 2001-02.

Stewart, 63, was the owner of Dundee Rockets in the *Heineken* League days of the 1980s and introduced NHL Iron Man **Garry Unger** to Britain. Rockets collapsed after running up heavy debts.

Ambri-Piotta, who have twice won the Continental Cup, could perhaps be compared to Cardiff Devils, a successful club attracting around 2,000 fervent fans, in Ambri's case from the surrounding farming community.

Like Devils, Ambri hit major financial problems and by 2001 they were in urgent need of 2.5 million Swiss francs (about £1 million) if they were to survive.

Step up Mr Stewart's company, Stewart International Marketing Ltd, which also showed interest in investing in a number of struggling British clubs. (See our *Review of the Year*.) SIML were understood to have been prepared to pump a million Swiss francs into Ambri which would have given Stewart a 51 per cent majority share in the club. A partnership with NHL club St. Louis Blues was apparently possible if the deal went through.

The Swiss newspaper, *Blick*, was told that Stewart's company represented a group of USA investors who wanted to put around US$1.5 billion (yes, that's one and a half thousand million) into sports schemes in the USA, England, Scotland, France, Belgium, Poland and Switzerland.

> - Why don't you transfer the promised 2.5 million Swiss francs [about £1 million]?
> - "Because there are delays following the events of 11 September."
> **Tom Stewart** *in an interview with Swiss newspaper,* Blick, *January 2002..*

Among the company's other plans for Ambri were a US$50 million sports academy and a 10,000-seat arena. SIML also wanted to invest in another Swiss club, Les Chaux-des-Fonds.

Stewart gave Ambri a 'letter of credit' but the club eventually gave up hope of receiving any money and instead launched a nation-wide 'Save Ambri' appeal.

Compiled from Blick Online and Eurohockey.net

New arena in Prague for 2004

A brand new multi-purpose arena for 17,000 spectators was to be built in Prague for the 2004 World Championship.

The Czech Republic had been awarded the 2003 World Championship but had to swap with Finland to win time to build the new arena, a condition of their winning the championship bid.

Work on the arena, which is modelled on North American standards, was scheduled to start in June 2002 and take 18 months to complete. Should it not be finished on time, however, Germany and Switzerland were the official stand-by organisers.

• The 2003 World Championships are in Finland - Helsinki, Turku and Tampere; in 2005, Austria will stage the games in Vienna and Innsbruck; and in 2006, the championships will go for the first time to Riga, capital of the Baltic state of Latvia.

> **WE SAID NOT TO MENTION THE WAR**
> Berlin Polar Bears' American forward, **Scott Levins**, enraged German DEL officials and fans when he was alleged to have called an opponent "a ----ing Nazi pig".
> The ex-NHLer admitted the insult, hurled at **Lars Müller** of Iserlohn Roosters while the pair were on the way to the penalty box, but denied accusations that he raised his arm in a Nazi salute and said 'Heil Hitler' to Müller, a criminal offence in Germany.
> Levins, 32, was fined and suspended by his Anschutz-owned club but despite the gravity of the offence, the league fined him only 3,000 Euros.
> The former Winnipeg Jet joined Superleague's Sheffield Steelers for the 2002-03 season.

Obituaries

RAY BAUER, the brother of the late **Bobby Bauer** of Boston Bruins' NHL Kraut Line fame, and former Canadian national team coach, **Father David Bauer**, died on 1 December 2001, aged 81.

Ray Bauer won a gold medal with Canada at the 1949 World Championships and later became the chairman of Bauer Industries, manufacturers of the famous *Bauer* skates.

JAROSLAV DROBNY, who won a World Championship gold medal with Czechoslovakia in 1947, and a silver at the Winter Olympics the following year, died in September 2001 at his home in London. He was 79.

Drobny was an even better tennis player, winning Wimbledon in 1954 when he defeated Australian legend, **Ken Rosewall**, in the final, and won the French Open twice. On the tennis court he wore dark glasses, which he needed as a result of an eye injury he suffered playing hockey.
- *from the newsletter of the Society for International Hockey Research.*

BILLY HARRIS, who coached teams on both sides of the Atlantic, died on 20 September 2001, after a six-year battle with leukaemia. He was 66.

Harris played ten seasons with the Toronto Maple Leafs, appearing on three successive Stanley Cup winning sides in 1962-64. In an NHL career that stretched from 1955 to 1969 and took in stints with Detroit, Oakland and Pittsburgh, he played 769 games, scoring 126 goals and 345 points.

After retiring as a player, he was hired by the Swedish Ice Hockey Federation in 1972 to coach Tre Kronor, the national team. In the Winter Olympics in Sapporo, Japan, Sweden finished fourth behind the powerhouse Soviet Union, Czechoslovakia and the USA, and third in the World Championships in Prague later that spring.

The likeable Harris, who was renowned for his stickhandling ability as a player, also coached the Canadian and Italian national teams and Toronto Toros of the World Hockey Association

CESAR W LÜTHI, the long-time partner of the International Ice Hockey Federation, died on 18 July 2002. He was 71. It was in 1972 that the Swiss-born businessman and avid sports fan founded his own company, Cesar W. Lüthi Marketing and Sales Promotion, and pioneered the so-called rolling board advertising.

A few years later CWL Telesport and Marketing AG was founded; the inaugural contract with the IIHF was created in 1981 for board advertising sales at the World Championships in Sweden and was later extended to cover the television rights.

In 2000 Cesar W. Lüthi sold his company to KirchSport AG, who now hold the World Championship television and advertising rights.

His contributions to ice hockey were recognised by the IIHF when they inducted him into the IIHF Hall of Fame in 1998. He was a recipient of the Olympic Order and an honorary member of the IIHF.

International Hockey Hall of Fame
A former President of the British Ice Hockey Association was among the 2002 IIHF Hall of Fame inductees.

IVAN HLINKA, Czech Republic
Former Czech and Czechoslovak national team player with 256 national team games, 132 goals; 11 IIHF World Championship tournaments (3 gold medals) All-Star in 1978, Olympics in 1972, 1976, coached Czech Republic to Olympic gold in 1998, IIHF World Championship title in 1999, manager of the Czech Olympic team in Salt Lake City.

PETER PATTON, Great Britain
Founding member of the IIHF in 1908; established ice hockey in Great Britain; IIHF President 1914, Vice President 1910-11, 1913-14 and 1923-24; President of British Ice Hockey Association 1914-34. Captain of his team, Princes (London), and long time national team player for England. Played his last national team game in 1930 at the age of 54.

GORDON RENWICK, Canada.
IIHF Vice President from 1978 to 1994. Hon President of Canadian Hockey Association who has spent more than 30 years promoting ice hockey in Canada and internationally. Former president of Galt Hornets, Canadian Amateur champions in 1969 and 1971. Former chairman of IIHF Junior, Old-timers, Statutes and Bylaws, Rules and Marketing Committees.

THAYER TUTT, USA
Former president and vice-president of the International Ice Hockey Federation between 1963 and 1986. Elected to Hockey Hall of Fame in 1978 and received the Lester Patrick Award for services to ice hockey in the United States.

VLADIMIR YURZINOV, Russia
Twice World and European champion as a player. Started coaching in 1974 with Dynamo Moscow, continued with Dynamo Riga, TPS Turku and EHC Kloten, Switzerland. National team assistant coach 1977-1991, several times head coach, also with Latvian national team. An assistant coach on 2002 Russian Olympic team.

A member of the British Ice Hockey Writers' Hall of Fame since 1988, **MRS PAT MARSH,** *the former British Ice Hockey Association secretary, received the IIHF's Paul Loicq Award in 2002. Their citation read:*
'Pat Marsh has dedicated her life to the game of ice hockey, serving in the office of the former IIHF president, **John Francis (Bunny) Ahearne**, for over 20 years. She also served as voluntary international secretary of the BIHA for 18 years and is still active in following the progress of ice hockey in her native Great Britain.'

WINTER OLYMPICS

Salt Lake City, Utah, USA, 9-24 February 2002

FINAL

USA-CANADA	2-5 (1-2,1-1,0-2)

Gold for Wayne

Helped by two goals apiece from **Joe Sakic** and **Jarome Iginla**, **Wayne Gretzky**'s Canada won their first Olympic gold medal for half a century beating the USA in the final of a tournament considered the most entertaining in recent years.

The 2002 Games will also be remembered as the one in which Sweden, one of the favourites, were knocked out in the quarter-finals by the unseeded Belarus when a long shot from **Vladimir Kopat** embarrassingly eluded their New York Islanders' goalie, **Tommy Salo**.

THE WINNING TEAM

Ed Belfour (Dallas), Martin Brodeur (NJ), Curtis Joseph (Toronto); Rob Blake, Adam Foote (Col.), Eric Brewer (Edmonton), Rob Niedermayer (NJ), Al MacInnis, Chris Pronger (St L), Ed Jovanowski (Vancouver); Paul Kariya (Anaheim), Jarome Iginla (Calgary), Joe Sakic (Col.), Joe Nieuwendyk (Dallas), Brendan Shanahan, Steve Yzerman (Detroit), Ryan Smith (Edmonton), Mike Peca (Islanders), Theo Fleury, Eric Lindros (Rangers), Simon Gagne (Phil.), Mario Lemieux (Pitts.), Owen Nolan (SJ).
Head Coach: Pat Quinn (Toronto).
General Manager: Wayne Gretzky (Phoenix).

LEADING SCORERS

	GP	G	A	Pts	Pim
Mats Sundin SWE	4	5	4	9	10
Brett Hull USA	6	3	5	8	6
John Le Clair USA	6	6	1	7	2
Joe Sakic CAN	6	4	3	7	0

LEADING NETMINDERS

	GPI	Mins	SoG	GA	Sav%
Martin Gerber SWI	3	158	95	4	95.8
Mike Richter USA	4	240	132	9	93.2
N Khabibulin RUS	6	359	200	14	93.O

ALL-STARS

Goal:	**Mike Richter** USA
Defence:	**Chris Chelios, Brian Leetch** USA
Forwards:	**John LeClair** USA, **Joe Sakic** CAN
	Mats Sundin SWE.

SEMI-FINALS

Canada-Belarus	7-1 (2-1,2-0,3-0)
Russia-USA	2-3 (0-1,0-2,2-0)

QUARTER-FINALS

Sweden-Belarus	3-4 (1-2,1-0,1-2)
Czech Rep-Russia	0-1 (0-0,0-1,0-0)
USA-Germany	5-0 (1-0,4-0,0-0)
Finland-Canada	1-2 (0-1,1-1,0-0)

FINAL ROUND

Group C	GP	W	L	D	GF	GA	Pts
Sweden	3	3	0	0	14	4	6
Czech Rep.	3	1	1	1	12	7	3
Canada	3	1	1	1	8	10	3
Germany	3	0	3	0	5	18	0
Group D							
USA	3	2	0	1	16	3	5
Finland	3	2	1	0	11	8	4
Russia	3	1	1	1	9	9	3
Belarus	3	0	3	0	6	22	0

QUALIFYING ROUND

Group A	GP	W	L	D	GF	GA	Pts
Germany	3	3	0	0	10	3	6
Latvia	3	1	1	1	11	12	3
Austria	3	1	2	0	7	9	2
Slovakia	3	0	2	1	8	12	1
Group B							
Belarus	3	2	1	0	5	3	4
Ukraine	3	2	1	0	9	5	4
Switzerland	3	1	1	1	7	9	3
France	3	0	2	1	6	10	1

Germany and Belarus qualify for the Final Round

WORLD CHAMPIONSHIPS

Gothenburg, Karlstad, Jonkoping, Sweden, 26 April - 11 May 2002

FINAL
11 May, Scandinavium Arena, Gothenburg
SLOVAKIA-RUSSIA   4-3   (2-0,1-1,1-2)

SEMI-FINALS
9 May, Scandinavium Arena, Gothenburg
RUSSIA-FINLAND   2-2 ot (1-1,1-1,0-0,0-0)
Russia won 3-2 after penalty shoot-out

SLOVAKIA-SWEDEN   2-2 ot (0-1,1-1,1-0,0-0)
Slovakia won 3-2 after penalty shoot-out

WORLD RANKINGS
1 **SLOVAKIA (World Champions)**,
2 Russia,   3 Sweden,   4 Finland, 5 Czech Republic, 6 Canada, 7 USA, 8 Germany, 9 Ukraine, 10 Switzerland, 11 Latvia, 12 Austria, 13 Slovenia, 14 Poland, 15 Italy, 16 Japan.
Poland and Italy relegated to Division I in 2003; Japan must compete in Far East Qualification Tournament.

LEADING SCORERS

	GP	G	A	Pts	Pim
Miroslav Satan SVK	9	5	8	13	2
Kristian Huselius SWE	9	5	6	11	0
Peter Bondra SVK	9	7	2	9	20
Jaromir Jagr CZE	7	4	4	8	2
Richard Lintner SVK	9	4	4	8	22

LEADING NETMINDERS

	GPI	Mins	SoG	GA	Sv%
Ryan Miller USA	4	238	139	7	94.9
Jussi Markinen FIN	7	429	159	10	93.7
Maxim Sokolov RUS	5	291	167	11	93.4

ALL-STAR TEAM
Goal   **Maxim Sokolov** RUS
Defence   **R Lintner** SVK, **T Rhodin** SWE
Forwards   **Niklas Hagman** FIN (C), **Miroslav Satan** SVK (W), **Peter Bondra** SVK (W).
Selected by the media.

Sweet first victory
The world got a brand new champion in 2002.

Slovakia, part of the old Czechoslovakia, upset Russia 4-3 in the final for their first world title in their own right.

The championships have been dominated for the past three years by their former countrymen from the Czech Republic which was formed when Czechoslovakia was split in 1993.

Peter Bondra of the NHL's Washington Capitals gave Slovakia the win when he scored his second goal with a minute and 40 seconds left.   Their other scorers - **Miroslav Satan** (Buffalo) and **Lubomir Visnovsky** (Los Angeles) - were also from NHL clubs.

The Slovaks' victory was all the sweeter for coming on the heels of their failure to qualify for the last eight in the Winter Olympics.

Slovakia iced 11 NHL players in Sweden but because the big league had refused to recognise the Olympic qualfiers, only three NHLers iced in all four Slovakian games in Salt Lake City.

DIVISION I
Group A, Eindhoven, Netherlands, 14-20 April
1   **Belarus**,   2   France,   3   Kazakhstan, 4 Netherlands, 5 Croatia, 6 Korea.
Belarus promoted to World Championship in 2003, Korea relegated to Division II.
Group B, Szeskesfehervar & Dunaujvaros, Hungary, 15-21 April. See next page.

DIVISION II
Group A, Cape Town, S Africa, 31 March-6 April
1 **Estonia**, 2 Belgium, 3 Israel, 4 Australia, 5 South Africa, 6 Turkey.
Estonia promoted to Division I in 2003, Turkey must qualify in Spring 2003.
Group B, Novi Sad, Yugoslavia, 25-31 March
1 **Lithuania**, 2 Yugoslavia, 3 Spain, 4 Bulgaria, 5 Iceland, 6 Luxembourg.
Lithuania promoted to Division I in 2003, Luxembourg must qualify in Spring 2003.

DIVISION I

GROUP B
Szeskesfehervar & Dunaujvaros, Hungary

FINAL STANDINGS

	GP	W	L	D	GF	GA	Pts
Denmark DEN	5	5	0	0	40	10	10
Hungary HUN	5	4	0	0	19	9	8
Norway NOR	5	3	2	0	26	11	6
Britain GB	5	2	3	0	18	16	4
Romania ROM	5	1	4	0	10	31	2
China CHI	5	0	5	0	7	43	0

GB'S WORLD RANKING: 20TH

Denmark are promoted to the World Championships in 2003; China are relegated to Division II.

RESULTS

	DEN	HUN	NOR	ROM	CHI
GB	3-5	1-4	1-2	5-2	8-3
DEN		6-2	4-3	12-2	13-0
HUN			3-1	4-1	6-0
NOR				8-1	12-2
ROM					4-2

GB's BEST PLAYERS
Rob Wilson, Manchester
Paul Berrington, Dundee
Jeff Hoad, Belfast
selected by the GB coaching staff
Darren Hurley, Bracknell
selected by the GB Supporters Club

FAIR PLAY CUP

Penalty minutes per team

Denmark 48, China 64, Hungary 100, Romania 102, Norway 118, **Britain 148**.

BRITAIN'S SCORING

	GP	G	A	Pts	Pim
Tony Hand	5	2	4	6	2
Colin Shields	5	2	3	5	4
David Longstaff	3	1	4	5	2
Darren Hurley	5	4	0	4	39
Jeff Hoad	5	3	1	4	6
Rob Wilson	5	1	2	3	4
Paul Dixon	5	0	3	3	2
Rick Brebant	5	1	1	2	0
Ashley Tait	5	1	1	2	0
Paul Berrington	5	1	1	2	6
Gary Wishart	5	0	2	2	4
Rick Strachan	5	1	0	1	4
Michael Tasker	5	1	0	1	4
Mike Ellis	5	0	1	1	0
David Clarke	5	0	1	1	10
Scott Campbell	5	0	1	1	31
TEAM TOTALS	5	18	25	43	148

BRITAIN'S NETMINDING

	GPI	Mins	SoG	GA	Sv%
Joe Watkins	2	120	67	6	91.04
Stephen Murphy	1	60	17	2	88.23
Stevie Lyle	2	120	50	8	84.00
TEAM TOTALS	5	300	134	16	88.06

THE BRITISH TEAM

Joe Watkins (Bracknell), Stephen Murphy (Dundee), Stevie Lyle (Manchester); Neil Liddiard (Basingstoke), *#Craig Nelson, *Scott Young (Dundee), *Scott Campbell, Paul Dixon (Guildford), *Rob Wilson (Manchester), *Rick Strachan (Milton Keyne); *Mike Ellis (Basingstoke), *Darren Hurley (Bracknell), *#Jeff Hoad (Belfast), Michael Tasker (Coventry), *#Paul Berrington, Tony Hand (Dundee), #Gary Wishart (Fife), David Clarke (Milton Keynes), Ashley Tait (Nottingham), *Rick Brebant (Sheffield), David Longstaff, capt (Djurgarden, Sweden), Colin Shields (Maine Un, USA).
Head coach: Chris McSorley (Geneva, Switz.).
Asst coaches: Paul Thompson (Coventry), Gary Stefan (BNL).
Manager: John Bailey.
* Dual national (10).   # New cap (4)

BRITAIN'S GAME SUMMARIES

14 April 2002, Dunaujvaros

BRITAIN-DENMARK		3-5 (1-0,2-3,0-2)

GB scoring:

Hand (Shields)	4.55	(1-0)
Hurley (Dixon):	24.14	(2-1)
Shields (Longstaff, Hoad)	27.34	(3-1)

Goalies:

Lyle GB	*Shots*: 13-9-7 29	*Save %*: 82.8
Hirch DEN	*Shots*: 9-8-5 22	*Save %*: 86.4
Penalty minutes:	Britain 41, Denmark 8.	
Goals/powerplays:	Britain 0/3, Denmark 3/8.	
GB Man of Match:	Hand.	
Referee:	Kaislehto FIN.	
Attendance:	1,000	

A win in the first game is essential, so is good refereeing. Britain got neither, despite building a 3-1 lead early in the second against the best team in the championships.

McSorley insisted that the cause of GB's downfall was the refereeing. The Finn assessed Britain two minors, a major and a game misconduct after their third goal. "I thought there was a third player out there tonight," he remarked caustically at the post-game press conference. "Shouldn't he be here, too?"

Though Mr Kaislehto seemed determined that GB could do no right, in truth they were often flat and uninspired and Hand admitted that his teammates had not entirely obeyed their coach's instructions not to take unnecessary penalties.

15 April 2002, Dunaujvaros

BRITAIN-HUNGARY		1-4 (1-2,0-0,0-2)

GB scoring:

Shields (Dixon, Hand)	13.32 pp	(1-2)

Goalies:

Watkins GB	*Shots*: 9-10-10 29	*Save %*: 86.2
Szuper HUN	*Shots*: 3- 8- 5 16	*Save %*: 93.7
Penalty minutes:	Britain 14, Hungary 14.	
Goals/powerplays:	Britain 1/6, Hungary 0/6 (1sh).	
GB Man of Match:	Wilson.	
Referee:	Bervensky BEL.	
Attendance:	3,500 capacity.	

Rule two of world championships is to watch out for the home team, no matter how small the country and especially when they have a goalie of the calibre of NHL draftee **Levente Szuper**.

In a fast-paced, intense game, 'Szuper-man' - as his adoring fans chanted - broke the hearts of many GB forwards, especially championship debutant Hoad who was credited with a third of Britain's modest shot total.

Actually, it was GB's Watkins - making his first appearance in goal since 2000 - who faced most shots. Britain's defence, not the strongest aspect of the game at the best of times, was missing defender Young with a recurrence of his back problem.

Brebant had to be helped off the ice at the end of the game after being accidentally kicked in the back of the leg, but fortunately the damage was not serious.

17 April 2002, Szekesfehervar

ROMANIA-BRITAIN		2-5 (1-1,0-1,1-3)

GB scoring:

Hand (Longstaff)	17.39 pp	(1-1)
Wilson (Hand, Longstaff)	37.04 pp	(1-2)
Longstaff (Brebant, Hand)	49.08 pp	(1-3)
Brebant (Tait, Longstaff)	52.21	(1-4)
Hoad (Shields, Dixon)	52.59	(1-5)

Goalies:

Radu ROM	*Shots*: 10-20-15 45.	*Save %*: 88.9
Murphy GB	*Shots*: 7- 5- 5 17	*Save %*: 88.2
Penalty minutes:	Romania 26, Britain 20.	
Goals/powerplays:	Romania 2/8, Britain 3/12.	

GB Man of Match:	Longstaff.
Referee:	Jonak SVK
Attendance:	1,650

A win at last, after two straight defeats, the longest unwanted streak in McSorley's brief stint in charge. But Britain weren't convincing until the last period.

This was the best and worst day of the tournament for 'Lobby' who scored a goal and three assists but was rushed to hospital after the game for treatment to his left leg, later diagnosed as deep vein thrombosis.

In his second senior international Murphy, 20, was not overworked like his counterpart, **Viorel Radu**. GB were credited with 45 shots on the Bucharest netminder and it should have been many more.

Weaver played a couple of shifts at the start but soon retired hurt and did not play again.

19 April 2002, Szekesfehervar

CHINA-BRITAIN		3-8 (0-2,2-3,1-3)

GB scoring:

Hoad (Shields, Campbell)	13.31	(0-1)
Hurley (Ellis, Wishart)	15.18	(0-2)
Hurley	24.12	(0-3)
Strachan (Hand)	36.36 sh	(2-4)
Hoad	39.59	(2-5)
Hurley (Berrington, Wishart)	43.50	(2-6)
Tasker (Clarke)	51.04	(3-7)
Tait (Wilson)	55.14 pp	(3-8

Goalies:

Lyle GB	*Shots*: 5- 6-10 21	*Save %*: 85.7
Geng/Liu CHI	*Shots*: 15-10-13 38	*Save %*: 78.9
Penalty Minutes:	China 12, Britain 20.	
Goals/powerplays:	China 1/6, Britain 1/3.	
GB Man of Match:	Hurley.	
Referee:	Benoist FRA.	
Attendance:	900.	

To struggle as Britain did against the division's weakest side proved how badly GB's game had deteriorated. China trailed only 3-2 at the halfway mark.

The strangest moment came when Brebant was brought down in front of goal and Hand took the penalty shot. Never his strong point, the Dundee player-coach fluffed his opportunity badly.

The game was a personal best for the unassuming Hurley who scored a hat-trick. Not renowned as a sharp-shooter, his effort left onlookers wondering why others couldn't do the same.

20 April 2002, Szekesfehervar

NORWAY-BRITAIN		2-1 (0-0,1-1,1-0)

GB scoring:

Berrington (Wilson)	25.19 pp	(0-1)

Goalies:

Josefsen NOR	*Shots*: 9- 9- 3 21	*Save %*: 95.2
Watkins GB	*Shots*: 6-15-17 38	*Save %*: 94.7

Penalty minutes:
Norway 36 (Svendsberget 2+10 cross-checking),
Britain 53 (Nelson 10misc, Campbell 5+game - spearing).

Goals/powerplays:	Norway 0/8, Britain 1/10.
GB Man of Match:	Berrington.
Referee:	Kaislehto FIN.
Attendance:	1,000

A chippy game between two frustrated teams who could hardly believe they were playing for bronze rather than gold.

Kaislehto, McSorley's 'pal' from game one, was back in the stripes and he didn't disappoint. After the improving Berrington gave GB a 1-0 lead, the Finn dished out five minors, a major and a game misconduct to GB.

However, apart from Campbell's dubious spearing call, these punishments were mostly deserved, and he had been pretty heavy on the Norwegians in the early stages.

BRITAIN *left to right*, *back row:* Paul Dixon, Mike Ellis, Rick Brebant, Neil Liddiard, Michael Tasker, Craig Nelson, Jeff Hoad; *middle row:* Darryl Easson (coaching asst.), Jason Ellery (equipment), Jonathan Weaver, Gary Wishart, David Clarke, Darren Hurley, Paul Berrington, Scott Campbell, Ashley Tait, Colin Shields, Scott Young, Bruce Smart (physio), Phil Hadley (equipment); *front row:* Stevie Lyle, Rob Wilson, David Longstaff, Paul Thompson (asst. coach), Chris McSorley (head coach), Gary Stefan (asst. coach), Rick Strachan, Tony Hand, Stephen Murphy, Joe Watkins.

A flea without spirit

STEWART ROBERTS

As Britain, one of the favourites, were humbled into fourth place in Division I (group B) of the World Championships, chief coach **Chris McSorley** put his finger on the main problem.

After GB were beaten by Norway for the bronze medal, he pointed out how every European nation, except Britain, puts the emphasis on their national team.

"In Britain we believe the domestic leagues are more important," he said. "That's the tail wagging the dog. In fact, it's worse than that. The national team is regarded as the flea in the tail of the dog."

The Canadian who successfully took Geneva Eagles into the Swiss A league has learned a lot from his three seasons in Europe (the first two with Superleague's London Knights).

Most of the leading British clubs are reluctant to release their players for international duty, and that's when they have any players eligible for GB in the first place. McSorley was particularly bothered by Superleague's player policy. "For the elite league to have only six home-grown players is absolutely unacceptable," he blasted.

NEVER PLAYED TOGETHER

This forced indifference to the national programme extends to the lack of preparation time available to GB. The squad that Britain took to Hungary had never played a competitive game as a team. It might have been a different story if they'd had a couple of internationals before the championships, like the Danes did.

The coach was also critical of the style of play practised in the UK which, as he colourfully put it, "turns thoroughbreds into Clydesdales", that is, emphasises intimidation over finesse.

European refs just love that kind of play - not! Then there was the opposition, especially the home team, who were stronger than anyone anticipated. Urged on by fiercely patriotic crowds, Hungary played far above themselves, making it hard to believe that the country has only two indoor rinks.

There's just one thing that can save a team annually charged with this Mission Impossible - chemistry. McSorley reckoned the best way to create team spirit is to win the opening game. Instead, in a game ref'd by a finicky Finn, Britain turned in their most undisciplined performance since 2000 against Germany.

"When you lose that first game," said the coach, "it's like having eleven holes in your boat, and only ten fingers to plug them with."

Of course, this is all written in hindsight. Before the games began, your editor even made a modest wager that GB would win promotion, and I was not alone.

We optimists also failed to reckon without injuries which affected three key forwards - skipper **David Longstaff** (see story alongside), Ayr's **Jonathan Weaver** who travelled but played only a few minutes with a groin pull suffered in the playoffs, and London's **Steve Thornton** whose season-long knee trouble prevented him from joining the team in Hungary.

Defenceman **Rob Wilson** was unable to repeat last year's player of the tournament form after he flew to Canada just before the championships due to a family illness.

Then some of the fit members of the squad turned in sub-par performances, and not just in that wretched first game, either. The chief culprit was **Tony Hand**. He was the first to admit he had a poor tournament - and he was GB's top scorer for the second year running! Who knows how many he might have scored had he not so often thrown away the puck or passed up a scoring chance, looking for the perfect pass.

SEVEN SUPERLEAGUERS

It was obvious that the play of Tony and many of his teammates had suffered by them being in the BNL rather than Superleague. GB used only seven ISL regulars.

Some observers grumbled - after the defeats, of course - about the increase in dual nationals, up to ten from seven in 2001. What's more, of the four new caps, only one was home-grown.

With Britain so confident of winning promotion, it seemed that they changed their risky, Brits-first policy and went for the safer option - experience. One could argue that the team wouldn't have finished any lower had they substituted a couple of young native players for a couple of the older dual nationals.

McSorley's response was that the Brits mostly play in the BNL which simply isn't of a high enough standard for the world championships. Even the purists had to agree that the play of Fife's **Gary Wishart** - the only new home-grown player in the side - rather proved his point.

In the end, though, McSorley took full responsibility for his team's disappointing performances. "The buck stops with me," he conceded after the Hungary debacle. "The team played as well as I could coach them."

Fortunately for the national team, McSorley, despite his obvious reservations, reaffirmed his commitment until 2006.

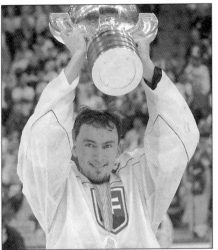

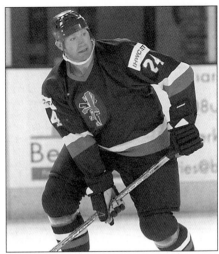

MIROSLAV SATAN, the Slovakian captain, with the World Championship trophy.

MARTY McSORLEY guesting for GB at Coventry. *Photos: Roger Cook.*

BRITAIN'S RECORD 1989-2001

2001 Pool B, Ljubljana, Slovenia
Coach: **Chris McSorley** (London)
Estonia 6-2, Croatia 10-1, Slovenia 3-3,
China 12-1, Kazakhstan 11-2.
World Ranking: **18th.** *Group Standing:* 2nd.

2000 Pool B, Katowice, Poland
Coach: **Peter Woods** (Superleague)
Estonia 5-6, Slovenia 3-3, Netherlands 9-0,
Poland 6-4, Denmark 5-4, Kazakhstan 3-1,
Germany 0-5.
World Ranking: **19th.** *Group Standing:* 3rd

1999 Pool B, Copenhagen, Denmark
Coach: **Peter Woods** (Superleague)
Slovenia 2-1, Kazakhstan 1-0, Germany 2-3,
Estonia 6-2, Poland 4-3, Hungary 4-2,
Denmark 5-5.
World Ranking: **18th.** *Group Standing:* 2nd

1998 Pool B, Ljubljana/Jesenice, Slovenia.
Coach: Peter Woods (Superleague).
Ukraine 1-6, Denmark 7-1, Estonia 4-5,
Slovenia 3-5, Poland 4-3, Norway 3-4,
Netherlands 10-3.
World Ranking: **22nd.** *Group Standing:* 6th

1997 Pool B, Katowice/Sosnowiec, Poland
Coach: **Peter Woods** (Basingstoke)
Poland 3-4, Kazakhstan 2-4, Netherlands 8-2,
Denmark 9-1, Austria 2-2, Switzerland 2-3,
Belarus 2-6.
World Ranking: **18th.** *Group Standing:* 6th

1996 Pool B, Eindhoven, Netherlands
Coach: **Peter Woods** (Basingstoke)
Latvia 5-6, Switzerland 2-7, Poland 4-2,
Netherlands 6-2, Japan 3-3, Denmark 5-1,
Belarus 4-2.
World Ranking: **16th.** *Group Standing:* 4th

1995 Pool B, Bratislava, Slovakia.
Coach: **George Peternousek** (unatt.)
Slovakia 3-7, Romania 0-2, Netherlands 3-2,
Denmark 2-9, Japan 3-4, Poland 4-3, Latvia 4-8.
World Ranking: **19th.** *Group Standing:* 7th

1994 Pool A in Bolzano, Italy.
Coach: **Alex Dampier** (Sheffield)
Russia 3-12, .Germany 0-4, Italy 2-10,
Canada 2-8, Austria 0-10, Norway 2-5.
World Ranking: **12th.** *Group Standing:* 12th

1993 Pool B in Eindhoven, Netherlands.
Coach: **Alex Dampier** (Sheffield).
Poland 4-3, Denmark 4-0, Japan 5-4,
Bulgaria 10-0, Netherlands 3-2,
Romania 10-4, China 14-0.
World Ranking: **13th.** *Group Standing:* 1st

1992 Pool C in Hull, England.
Coach: **Alex Dampier** (Nottingham).
Australia 10-2, S Korea 15-0, Belgium 7-3,
N Korea 16-2, Hungary 14-3.
World Ranking: **21st.** *Group Standing:* 1st

1991 Pool C in Copenhagen, Denmark.
Coach: **Alex Dampier** (Nottingham).
China 5-6, N Korea 7-2, Denmark 2-3,
Belgium 11-0, Hungary 3-3, Bulgaria 4-5,
S Korea 7-1, Romania 6-5.
World Ranking: **21st.** *Group Standing:* 5th

1990 Pool D in Cardiff, Wales.
Coach: **Alex Dampier** (Nottingham)
Australia 14-0, 13-3; Spain 13-1, 17-3.
World Ranking: **26th.** *Group Standing:* 1st

1989 Pool D in Belgium.
Coach: **Terry Matthews** (Whitley Bay).
New Zealand 26-0, Romania 6-6, Belgium 5-6,
Spain 8-4.
World Ranking: **27th.** *Group Standing:* 3rd

'Lobby' in hospital

GB captain, **David Longstaff**, 27, was rushed to hospital after Britain's 5-2 win over Romania when the pain in his left leg became unbearable. It was a measure of the man that he had just played his best game of the tournament, being voted man of the match after scoring a goal and three assists in his 65th international.

When he arrived at the hospital in Szeskesfehervar, an hour's drive south of Budapest, the medics diagnosed deep vein thrombosis, a blood clot which more normally afflicts passengers on long-haul plane flights. If not treated quickly, it can result in serious illness and, in rare cases, death if the clot spreads to major organs.

Fortunately, the doctors did act quickly, ordering 'Lobby' complete bed rest for 12 days with any movement severely restricted, and he was given anti-coagulants or bloodthinners.

With his morale boosted by the presence of his mother and his wife, Michelle - who were flown over by Ice Hockey UK - and **Darryl Easson**, one of the national's team's coaching staff, Longstaff's treatment was effective. His release came exactly 12 days after his admission.

"It happened in the first period of our first game against Denmark," explained the burly forward, "I was slashed behind the left knee and the bruising was huge. **Bruce [Smart**, the team physio] gave me the usual treatment for bruising but it didn't go down like usual and got very painful. That's when they decided they'd better get me to a hospital."

Happily, Lobby made a full recovery and he described the hospital's facilities as first class.

Cut from GB's Nottingham camp
Defence: James Manson BAS, Kyle Horne FIF, *Brent Pope NOT; *forwards*: Nick Cross BAS, Ricky Plant GUI.
Injured and did not travel
*Steve Thornton LON, Tom Watkins COV.

TRIAL GAMES

Britain played six games in UK rinks during 2001-02, in line with Ice Hockey UK's policy of taking the team to meet their fans.

A total of 40 players were seen by the coaches, Chris McSorley, Paul Thompson and Gary Stefan.

According to the governing body, the experiment was a success financially, with around £7,500 being raised for the GB programme, mostly from the Cardiff game.

But as entertainment the games left much to be desired as they were played mostly as passionless exhibitions with no body contact. And the politicking too often left a bad taste.

Plant, Marty star in Cardiff

Coach **Chris McSorley** capped eight new players - all home-grown - in a 25-strong Britain Select which won three games in three nights during the International break in November 2001.

The new men scored 17 points between them, proving to many observers the worth of the decision not to rely on dual nationals as in the past. Three of the five British-Canadians were defenders, brought in to compensate for the dearth of locally trained blueliners.

Guildford's **Ricky Plant**, 23, scored a hat-trick in the most testing match, against an import-heavy Cardiff Select.

GB's other opponents were Coventry Blaze, whose coach **Paul Thompson** is McSorley's assistant with GB, and Huddinge IK, the top Swedish under-20 team from Stockholm. Dundee keeper, **Stephen Murphy**, 19, shutout the Swedes.

The Cardiff game was secondary - at least to some fans - to the appearance of ex-NHLer, **Marty McSorley**, 38, who was making his British debut with the Devils. At the time, the McSorleys were negotiating to buy the team. Next night, Marty guested for GB.

It was Chris McSorley's idea to play games against domestic sides rather than play internationals. "Britain should be the showcase of hockey around the country," he said. Unfortunately, it didn't work out that way.

While the fans flocked to the Wales National Ice Rink, only around 1,500 in all turned up to watch the two contests in Coventry's SkyDome and the coach admitted that the marketing had to be improved. Ice Hockey UK appointed former GB international defenceman, **Mike O'Connor**, as their marketing manager.

☑ The game raised £6,330.43 for the GB programme.

6 November 2001, Coventry SkyDome

COVENTRY BLAZE	**4** (2-1-1)
BRITAIN SELECT	**7** (1-3-3)

Scoring:
COVENTRY - Cowley 2g; Chartrand, Ruggles 1g; Roberts 3a; Carpenter, Eley, Strachan 1a.
GB - Hurley 2+1; Clarke, Ellis 1+1; Berrington, Dixon, Manson 1g; Tait 3a; Hand, Horne, Longstaff, Nelson, T Watkins 1a.
Penalty minutes: Blaze 2, GB 2.
Shots on Goal: Hollyhead COV 40, Lyle/Murphy/J Watkins GB 25.
GB Man of Match: Clarke.
Referee: Simon Kirkham.   *Attendance:* 911

7 November 2001, Wales National Ice Rink

CARDIFF SELECT	**4** (0-2-2)
BRITAIN SELECT	**10** (3-3-4)

Scoring:
CARDIFF - Poulsen 2+1; Matulik 1+2; Moria 1g; Ahlroos 2a; Hazelhurst, McIntyre, Sacratini 1a.
GB - Plant 3+1; T Watkins 1+2; Wishart 1+1; Clarke, Longstaff, Nelson, Tait, Tasker 1g; Young 4a; Weaver 2a; Berrington, Dixon, Hand, Meyers 1a.
Penalty minutes: Cardiff 2, GB 0.
Shots on Goal: Lyle/Noble/Rockman CAR 34, J Watkins/Murphy GB 30.
GB Man of Match: Plant.
Referee: Gary Plaistow. *Attendance:* 2,300 est.

8 November 2001, Coventry SkyDome

BRITAIN SELECT	**6** (2-3-1)
HUDDINGE IK (Sweden)	**0** (0-0-0)

Scoring: GB - Longstaff 2+1; Hand 1+3; Tait 1+1; Ellis, Young 1g; Wilson, Wishart 1a.
Penalty minutes: GB 28 (Liddiard 2+10 check-behind), Huddinge 6.
Shots on Goal: Murphy GB 20, Warren HUD 32.
Referee: Simon Kirkham. *Attendance:* 400 est.

BRITAIN SELECT

Joe Watkins (Bracknell), Stephen Murphy (Dundee), Stevie Lyle (Manchester); *Scott Young (Ayr), Neil Liddiard (Basingstoke), #Steven Lynch (Edinburgh), Kyle Horne (Fife), Paul Dixon (Guildford), *Rob Wilson (Manchester), *Rick Strachan (Milton Keynes); Jonathan Weaver (Ayr), *Mike Ellis, #James Manson (Basingstoke), *Darren Hurley (Bracknell), Michael Tasker, #Tom Watkins (Coventry), #Paul Berrington, Tony Hand, #Craig Nelson (Dundee), #Gary Wishart (Fife), #Ricky Plant (Guildford), #Danny Meyers (Milton Keynes), Ashley Tait (Nottingham), David Clarke (Peterborough), David Longstaff (Djurgarden, Sweden), *Guest at Coventry:* Marty McSorley.

Selected but did not play: *Steve Thornton (London) (injured), #Richard Thornton (Isle of Wight).
Coach: Chris McSorley. *Manager:* John Bailey.
* dual national (5), # new cap (8)

New boys hammer Romania

25 Nov. 2001, Nottingham Arena

BRITAIN SELECT	**6** (3-3-0)
ROMANIA	**1** (0-0-1)

A scratch GB side trounced Romania 6-1 in the first meeting of the nations since 1995.

Man of the match was **Warren Tait**, the 20-year-old brother of Nottingham's Ashley, who was one of 11 new caps in a GB side coached by Basingstoke's **Charlie Colon** in the absence of both head coach, **Chris McSorley**, and his assistant, **Paul Thompson**.

Only three of the 21-man squad were dual nationals, and two of them - Panther **Brent Pope** and Slough's **Scott Moody** - played on defence where the local talent is notoriously thin. Tait's national team debut came after only a handful of matches with Peterborough Pirates after he sustained three concussions in 1999-2000. He had spent the three previous seasons in Canada.

Apart from skipper **Rick Strachan** and Pope, who opened the scoring, all GB's goals came from their rookies. The team's only English National League representative, **Mark Levers** of the Isle of Wight, scored GB's third goal. Dundee's **Stephen Murphy** kept a clean sheet in goal before being replaced in the last period by Coventry's **Barry Hollyhead**.

Romania, who were promoted from World Division II in 2001, were missing four first team players. But the game showed how far GB has come in the last few years. The last time the teams met - in the 1995 World Championship - GB were shutout 2-0 despite icing a heavy dual national content.

Tait was impressed with the standard of Britain's play. "The only difference between this game and the ones I played in Canada," he said, "was that it was a lot more physical over there."

• The game was played as part of the *Findus Challenge Cup* weekend.

Game statistics:
GB scoring: Pope, Strachan, Levers, Randall, W Tait, Twaite 1g; Nelson, Weaver 2a; Liddiard,, Cross, Lamey, Moran, Armstrong 1a.
Penalty minutes: GB 32 (W Tait 2+10 check/behind), Romania 26 (Viorel 10 misc./unsport.).
Shots on Goal: Murphy GB 15, Viorel ROM 39.
GB Man of Match: W Tait.
Referee: Simon Kirkham.   *Attendance:* 1,500.

BRITAIN SELECT

Barry Hollyhead (Coventry), Stephen Murphy (Dundee); Neil Liddiard, James Manson (Basingstoke), Craig Nelson (Dundee), Rick Strachan (Milton Keynes) capt, *#Brent Pope (Nottingham), *#Scott Moody (Slough); Jonathan Weaver (Ayr), #Jake Armstrong, #Joe Baird, #Rob Lamey (Basingstoke), Paul Berrington (Dundee), #Marc Twaite (Guildford), #Mark Levers (I of Wight), #Paul Moran, Danny Meyers, *#Greg Randall (Milton Keynes), Ashley Tait (Nottingham), #Warren Tait (P'boro'), #Nick Cross (Slough).
Coaches: Charlie Colon (Basingstoke) and Gary Stefan (BNL). Manager: John Bailey.
* dual national (3). # new cap (11).

All-Stars break GB's streak

14 Dec 2001, Nottingham Arena

ISL ALL-STARS	8 (1-3-4)
BRITAIN SELECT	5 (3-1-1)

Jonathan Weaver's hat-trick for Britain wasn't enough to prevent the national team from losing their nine-game undefeated streak. "I expect Chris [McSorley] will be on the phone any minute now asking how I managed to lose his record," grinned Coventry's Paul Thompson, who was filling in once again for his boss.

The head man would have had few grounds for complaint. The 20-man team was without several leading players, notably Tony Hand, David Longstaff, Darren Hurley and Steve Thornton (both injured), Mike Ellis and Scott Young.

Instead, in keeping with the national team's policy, GB blooded another new cap - Bracknell/Guildford defender James Morgan, 19. This brought the total of players who had seen GB action during the season to 39 (excluding Marty McSorley, of course).

The All-Stars were also below strength due to injuries which left them with only 19 players, including just four true blueliners. Among the missing were three of their leading goal scorers as well as Trevor Robins, their best netminder.

Officially, the final score was 9-5 with the All-Stars receiving a 'starter' goal for winning the pre-game 'skills competition'.

The winners of this were -
Hardest shot - PC Drouin, All-Stars - 97 mph.
Fastest skater - Mark Bultje, All-Stars, beat GB's Dave Clarke; Paul Berrington, GB, beat PC Drouin; GB's James Morgan beat All-Star Sean Berens.

McQUOTE

On Britain's problems in the World Championships.
"It wouldn't matter if we had [Detroit Red Wings coach] Scotty Bowman over for a two-week training session, the other 30 weeks is what determines how our players progress."
"Our results here are a shot across the bows. They should serve as a wake-up call to our clubs."
Praising the homegrown Brits during the trial games:
"The Longstaffs and Hands of this world - the statesmen if you like - accept the newcomers with class and dignity and make them feel as if they truly belong. That kind of reception makes a massive difference to the new men."
"Something happens to a kid when he pulls on a national jersey. He digs deep within himself and pulls out that extra pound of effort. That gives us, as coaches, something to work with."
"We play more of a system than any of our competitors because the game we play in Britain is vastly different to what is played in international circles."
"Ideally, we'd like to increase our base to 50 or even 75 players. The ripple effect of having that boy's family, son or brother being able to say they are participating in the national team allows everyone to walk a little higher in their shoes. And it opens up opportunities and ambitions for those further down the ladder."
"I didn't realise there was that much depth of talent in British hockey. But it's a long road and each new player still has to prove to us that he can wear the Lion on a regular basis."
"We need to introduce the national programme to the nation. This team seems to have had a hidden identity. I would like to showcase the team around the country to draw attention to the new recruits and give us the chance to generate additonal revenue for the programme."
From an interview with GB head coach, Chris McSorley, by Anthony Beer in Face-Off magazine.

There were two team events -
Puck Control was won by an All-Star squad of Mark Cadotte, Kevin Riehl, Kris Miller and Brian Greer.
Pass the Puck was shared by the teams of Jonathan Weaver, Michael Tasker and Tom Watkins (GB) who beat Eoin McInerney, and All-Stars Shane Johnson, Trevor Roenick and Mike Barrie who faced Joe Watkins.

The game was played in aid of the *NSPCC Full Stop* campaign but the estimated crowd of around 2,000 was unlikely to have left the league with much profit to distribute. However, fans paid a total of £4,113 for 20 All-Star players' jerseys. London's **Mike Barrie** received the highest bid - £350 for his no. 91 shirt.

The league declined to tell the *Annual* where these funds went nor - as in the past - would they reveal how much was raised for the charity.

• GB provided the opposition for the All-Stars after the original opponents, Amsterdam Tigers, had an indifferent tour of Britain in September. *See Touring Teams.*

All-Star Game statistics:

ISL - Roenick 2+1; Hadden 1+3; Drouin, Jickling 1+1; Riehl, Berens, Barrie 1g; Sebastian, Ruff 2a; Mansi, Bultje, Cadotte 1a.

GB - Weaver 3g; Clarke 1+1; Berrington 1g; Tait 3a; Pope, Tasker, Wishart, Wilson 1a.

Penalty minutes: Nil.

Shots on Goal: Greer/McInerney ISL 34, Watkins/Lyle/Murphy GB 45.

GB Man of Match: Weaver.

Referees: Moray Hanson, Nigel Boniface.

Attendance: 2,000 est.

ISL ALL-STARS

Brian Greer (Bracknell), *Eion McInerney (Sheffield); Shane Johnson (Belfast), Maurizio Mansi (London), Kris Miller (Manchester), Jeff Sebastian (Sheffield); *Cam Bristow, *Mike Jickling (Ayr), Sean Berens, Kevin Riehl, *Jason Ruff (Belfast), Mark Cadotte (Bracknell), Mike Barrie, *Ian McIntyre, Trevor Roenick (London), Mark Bultje (Manchester), PC Drouin, Greg Hadden (Nottingham), Chris Lipsett (Sheffield). *Head coach:* Dave Whistle (Belfast), *assistant:* Enio Sacilotto (Bracknell).

*replaced injured players: goal - Robins (London); defence - Silfwerplatz (Ayr), McBain (Bracknell); forwards - Courtenay, Wood (Ayr), Miehm (Sheffield).

BRITAIN SELECT

Joe Watkins (Bracknell), Stephen Murphy (Dundee), Stevie Lyle (Manchester); Neil Liddiard (Basingstoke), #James Morgan (Bracknell/Guildford), *Craig Nelson (Dundee), Kyle Horne (Fife), *Rob Wilson (Manchester), *Rick Strachan (Milton Keynes), *Brent Pope (Nottingham); Jonathan Weaver (Ayr), Rob Lamey, Michael Tasker, Tom Watkins (Coventry), Paul Berrington (Dundee), Gary Wishart (Fife), David Clarke (London/Milton Keynes), Danny Meyers (Milton Keynes), Ashley Tait (Nottingham), Nick Cross (Slough). *Coaches:* Paul Thompson (Coventry) and Gary Stefan (BNL). *Manager:* John Bailey.

* *dual national (4).* # *new cap (1).*

No Odyssey for famous four

7 February 2002, Odyssey Arena, Belfast

BELFAST GIANTS	**2** (2-0-0)
BRITAIN SELECT	**0** (0-0-0)

Politics is never far from any national team and ice hockey is no exception. The war of words over this contest was arguably more entertaining than the low-key game itself, Britain's last before the World Championships.

The clue to the dispute was the huge crowds who follow ice hockey in Belfast. The 5,855 who saw this 'friendly' were the most ever to watch Britain at 'home', exceeding the records set at the 1993 and 1996 Olympic qualifiers in Sheffield.

This provoked a row over how much the governing body should receive from the game and there were lengthy negotiations before Ice Hockey UK sanctioned the contest. Eventually, the governing body told the *Annual* they made a profit of around £4,000, somewhat lower than the reputed asking price.

Though IHUK were happy, some Superleague clubs weren't. Many were suffering from short benches due to injuries and, in any case, they placed more importance on competitive games and especially the Ahearne Trophy tournament which was to be staged the following week.

At least one team claimed they had not been told officially that the game was on and that the players had been informed direct rather than through their team.

> ### CAUGHT IN THE MIDDLE
> "...the way I see it, the national team and the Superleague have problems and I'm caught in the middle." ***Jonathan Weaver**, one of four Superleague players who did not accept their invitations to play for GB against Belfast Giants. The Scottish Sun.*

Only a few days before face-off, four of GB's six Superleague selections made some excuse for turning down the national team's invite - Ayr's **Jonathan Weaver**, Bracknell's **Darren Hurley**, and Manchester's **Stevie Lyle** and **Rob Wilson**.

Only Nottingham's **Ashley Tait** turned out for his country. Bracknell's **Joe Watkins** was excused as GB had sufficient goalies - until Lyle turned down his invite, too.

Ice Hockey UK's chairman, **Jim Anderson**, was furious at this snub to 'his' team and threatened to fine the clubs and refuse to sign any International Transfer Cards for the league. "If they want to behave like a rogue body, we'll have to treat them like one," he stormed.

Martin Weddell, the league's chairman, called the threats "crass stupidity", pointing out that Superleague's rules for releasing players referred only to internationals and not to 'friendlies'.

IHUK promised an investigation into the reasons for the players' absences, saying that if it were proved that any players were messing GB about, they would not be going to Hungary.

While most of the absentees wisely kept quiet, Weaver was surprisingly outspoken about the game in an interview with the Scottish *Sun*.

"I wasn't prepared to play in a useless, pointless game," he said, "when the team that pays my wages and treats me so well was preparing for the biggest game of the season."

He explained that the club had asked him not to play because of their Challenge Cup semi-final that weekend. "Then the authorities came back and threatened all kinds of things," he said. "That's when I decided I didn't want to play, anyway. It was my choice, not Ayr's."

Despite this embarrassing statement, Weaver was invited to play in the championships, along with the other missing trio.

Compared to these fireworks, the game itself was quiet and - with a BNL-based GB side facing the Superleague champs - pretty one-sided. With Nottingham's Tait the only Superleague player in the national side; Guildford Flames filled a couple of the gaps with dual nationals - defenceman **Scott Campbell** and forward **Jason Jennings**.

Britain's best players were both from Dundee Stars, who had just won the *Findu*s BNL title: **Tony Hand** and netminder **Stephen Murphy**, 20, who kicked out 30 of 32 shots on his net. Slough's **Nick Cross** also impressed.

Giants' **Mike Bales** turned away 25 shots for his shutout, including a close-range effort from Hand in the last period which the former NHL keeper deflected onto the far post.

This was the first time GB had been whitewashed since the last game of the 2000 World Championships when they lost 5-0 to Germany, the Pool B winners that year.

Belfast game statistics:

Giants' scoring: Sandwith (Johnson) 16.21, Matsos (Schulte) 17.59.

Penalty minutes: Giants 2, GB 0.

Shots on Goal: Bales BEL 25, Murphy GB 32.

GB Man of Match: Murphy.

Referee: Nigel Boniface.

Attendance: 5,855.

BRITAIN SELECT

Stephen Murphy (Dundee), Barry Hollyhead (Coventry); Neil Liddiard, James Manson (Basingstoke), *Craig Nelson, *Scott Young (Dundee), Kyle Horne (Fife), *Scott Campbell (Guildford), *Rick Strachan (Milton Keynes); *Mike Ellis (Basingstoke), Michael Tasker, Tom Watkins (Coventry), Paul Berrington, Tony Hand (Dundee), Gary Wishart (Fife), *#Jason Jennings, Rick Plant (Guildford), David Clarke (Milton Keynes), Ashley Tait (Nottingham), Nick Cross (Slough).

Coach: Paul Thompson. Manager: John Bailey.

* dual national (6)   new cap (1)

GREAT BRITAIN'S WORLD CHAMPIONSHIP and OLYMPIC PLAYER REGISTER 1989-2002
FORWARDS and DEFENCEMEN

ADEY Paul   b. 28-Aug-63

Club	Year	Comp	GP	G	A	Pts	PIM
Not	1995	OQ	3	1	0	1	0
Not	1996	WC	7	4	4	8	10
Not	1996	OQ	5	3	4	7	0
Not	1997	WC	7	5	1	6	4
Not	1998	WC	7	4	4	8	4
Not	1999	WC	7	3	3	6	2
Milan	1999	WCQ	4	0	0	0	0
Milan	2000	OQ	3	3	1	4	27
Milan	2000	WC	7	2	5	7	14
She	2001	WC	5	3	2	5	4
		Totals	**55**	**28**	**24**	**52**	**65**

BENNETT Ivor   b. 29-Jul-61

Club	Year	Comp	GP	G	A	Pts	PIM
Dur	1989	WC	4	0	1	1	2

BERRINGTON PAUL   b.24-Jan-75

Club	Year	Comp	GP	G	A	Pts	PIM
Dun	2002	WC	5	1	1	2	6

BIDNER Todd   b. 5-Jul-61

Club	Year	Comp	GP	G	A	Pts	PIM
Una	1993	OQ	4	1	1	2	4

BISHOP Mike   b. 15-Jun-66

Club	Year	Comp	GP	G	A	Pts	PIM
Hum	1995	OQ	3	0	0	0	0
Hum	1996	WC	7	1	1	2	22
Not	1996	OQ	5	1	3	4	12
Not	1997	WC	7	2	1	3	45
Not	1998	WC	7	1	0	1	12
Ayr	2000	WC	7	0	3	3	18
		Totals	**36**	**5**	**8**	**13**	**109**

BOBYCK Brent   b. 26-Apr-68

Club	Year	Comp	GP	G	A	Pts	PIM
Not	1999	WCQ	4	0	0	0	0
Not	2000	OQ	3	0	1	1	0
		Totals	**7**	**0**	**1**	**1**	**0**

BOE Vince   b. 23-Dec-70

Club	Year	Comp	GP	G	A	Pts	PIM
Ayr	1999	WC	7	0	2	2	16
Ayr	1999	WCQ	1	0	0	0	4
Ayr	2000	OQ	3	0	1	1	2
		Totals	**11**	**0**	**3**	**3**	**22**

BREBANT Rick   b. 21-Feb-64

Club	Year	Comp	GP	G	A	Pts	PIM
Car	1994	WC	6	1	0	1	8
Dur	1995	OQ	1	0	0	0	0
Man	1998	WC	7	3	5	8	10
Man	1999	WCQ	3	0	1	1	4
Lon	2000	OQ	3	1	2	3	42
Lon	2000	WC	7	4	4	8	14
She	2002	WC	5	1	1	2	0
		Totals	**32**	**10**	**13**	**23**	**78**

CAMPBELL Scott   b. 22-Jan-72

Club	Year	Comp	GP	G	A	Pts	PIM
Lon	1999	WCQ	4	0	0	0	2
Gui	2002	WC	5	0	1	1	31
		Totals	**9**	**0**	**1**	**1**	**33**

CHARD Chris   b. 22-Jun-71

Club	Year	Comp	GP	G	A	Pts	PIM
Bas	1995	OQ	1	0	0	0	0

CHINN Nicky   b. 14-Sep-72

Club	Year	Comp	GP	G	A	Pts	PIM
Car	1993	OQ	2	0	0	0	0
Car	1994	WC	6	0	0	0	0
Car	1995	WC	4	1	2	3	4
She	1995	OQ	1	0	0	0	0
She	1996	OQ	3	1	0	1	2
She	1997	WC	7	1	1	2	29
She	1998	WC	7	1	2	3	31
Car	1999	WC	7	2	3	5	39
Car	2000	OQ	3	0	0	0	4
		Totals	**40**	**6**	**8**	**14**	**109**

CLARKE David   b. 5-Aug-81

Club	Year	Comp	GP	G	A	Pts	PIM
Pet	2000	WC	7	0	0	0	2
New	2001	WC	5	2	0	2	6
Lon	2002	WC	5	0	1	1	10
		Totals	**17**	**2**	**1**	**3**	**18**

CONWAY Kevin   b. 13-Jul-63

Club	Year	Comp	GP	G	A	Pts	PIM
Bas	1992	WC	5	13	10	23	6
Bas	1993	WC	7	8	11	19	8
Bas	1993	OQ	4	1	0	1	6
Bas	1994	WC	6	2	1	3	6
Bas	1995	OQ	3	2	1	3	6
Bas	1996	WC	7	3	2	5	6
Bas	1996	OQ	5	1	0	1	6
Bas	1997	WC	7	2	3	5	0
Bas	1998	WC	7	0	2	2	2
New	1999	WC	7	1	3	4	8
		Totals	**58**	**33**	**33**	**66**	**54**

COOPER Ian   b. 29-Nov-68

Club	Year	Comp	GP	G	A	Pts	PIM
Car	1989	WC	4	4	4	8	8
Car	1990	WC	4	6	5	11	9
Dur	1991	WC	8	4	2	6	16
Dur	1992	WC	5	3	6	9	8
Car	1993	WC	7	4	4	8	6
Car	1994	WC	6	1	0	1	4
Car	1995	WC	2	1	0	1	2
Car	1995	OQ	3	0	0	0	2
Car	1996	WC	7	0	2	2	10
Car	1996	OQ	5	1	2	3	2
Car	1997	WC	7	0	0	0	12
Car	1998	WC	7	3	2	5	38
Lon	1999	WC	7	1	2	3	2
Lon	1999	WCQ	1	0	0	0	0
Gui	2000	WC	7	2	2	4	10
		Totals	**80**	**30**	**31**	**61**	**128**

GREAT BRITAIN'S WORLD CHAMPIONSHIP and OLYMPIC PLAYER REGISTER 1989-2002
FORWARDS and DEFENCEMEN

COOPER Stephen   b. 11-Nov-66

Club	Year	Comp	GP	G	A	Pts	PIM
Car	1989	WC	4	3	4	7	4
Car	1990	WC	4	3	6	9	8
Dur	1992	WC	5	1	4	5	4
Car	1993	WC	7	0	4	4	6
Car	1993	OQ	4	1	0	1	2
Car	1994	WC	6	0	1	1	4
Car	1995	OQ	3	0	0	0	10
Car	1996	WC	7	0	3	3	6
Man	1996	OQ	3	0	0	0	4
New	1999	WC	7	0	0	0	2
Not	1999	WCQ	4	1	1	2	2
Not	2000	WC	7	2	4	6	2
		Totals	61	11	27	38	54

COTE Matt   b. 19-Jan-66

Club	Year	Comp	GP	G	A	Pts	PIM
Brk	1994	WC	6	0	0	0	8
Brk	1995	WC	7	0	1	1	4
Brk	1996	OQ	4	0	0	0	2
Brk	1999	WC	7	0	1	1	2
Brk	1999	WCQ	4	0	0	0	0
Brk	2000	OQ	1	0	0	0	0
		Totals	29	0	2	2	16

CRAPPER Jamie   b. 29-Jan-60

Club	Year	Comp	GP	G	A	Pts	PIM
Brk	1990	WC	4	7	5	12	0
Brk	1991	WC	8	4	1	5	9
Brk	1992	WC	5	1	2	3	25
		Totals	17	12	8	20	34

CRANSTON Tim   b. 13-Dec-62

Club	Year	Comp	GP	G	A	Pts	PIM
She	1993	WC	7	3	1	4	41
She	1993	OQ	4	1	1	2	8
She	1994	WC	6	0	0	0	4
She	1995	OQ	3	0	2	2	6
She	1996	WC	7	4	4	8	14
She	1996	OQ	5	2	2	4	10
She	1997	WC	7	1	3	4	8
		Totals	39	11	13	24	91

DIXON Paul   b. 4-Aug-73

Club	Year	Comp	GP	G	A	Pts	PIM
Dur	1995	WC	5	1	1	2	2
Dur	1995	OQ	2	0	0	0	0
Dur	1996	WC	7	1	1	2	14
New	1996	OQ	2	0	1	1	0
New	1997	WC	7	0	1	1	0
New	1998	WC	4	0	2	2	2
New	1999	WC	7	0	1	1	0
Gui	1999	WCQ	3	0	0	0	2
Gui	2000	WC	7	0	2	2	0
Gui	2001	WC	5	1	2	3	0
Gui	2002	WC	5	0	3	3	2
		Totals	54	3	14	17	22

DURDLE Darren   b. 15-Aug-67

Club	Year	Comp	GP	G	A	Pts	PIM
Ber	1996	OQ	2	0	1	1	2
Ber	1998	WC	6	0	1	1	10
Ber	1999	WC	7	1	0	1	12
Car	1999	WCQ	4	1	2	3	8
Car	2000	OQ	3	1	2	3	4
		Totals	22	3	6	9	36

EDMISTON Dean   b. 12-Feb-69

Club	Year	Comp	GP	G	A	Pts	PIM
Pet	1991	WC	8	2	1	3	13
Med	1992	WC	4	1	3	4	2
		Totals	12	3	4	7	15

ELLIS Mike   b. 21-May-73

Club	Year	Comp	GP	G	A	Pts	PIM
Bas	2000	WC	7	1	1	2	0
Bas	2001	WC	5	0	2	2	10
Bas	2002	WC	5	0	1	1	0
		Totals	17	1	4	5	10

FERA Rick   b. 13-Aug-64

Club	Year	Comp	GP	G	A	Pts	PIM
Bas	1993	WC	7	6	13	19	18
Tra	1993	OQ	4	0	2	2	12
Tra	1994	WC	6	1	2	3	4
		Totals	17	7	17	24	34

GARDEN Graham   b. 2-Jul-70

Club	Year	Comp	GP	G	A	Pts	PIM
Hum	1995	OQ	2	1	0	1	0
Hum	1996	WC	3	1	0	1	4
Deg	1996	OQ	5	0	0	0	2
Deg	1997	WC	7	1	0	1	10
Not	1999	WC	7	2	5	7	10
Not	2000	OQ	3	0	0	0	2
		Totals	27	5	5	10	28

HAND Paul   b. 24-Nov-65

Club	Year	Comp	GP	G	A	Pts	PIM
Mur	1989	WC	4	5	0	5	8
Fif	1990	WC	4	1	3	4	13
Fif	1991	WC	8	1	2	3	14
Mur	1992	WC	2	0	0	0	6
		Totals	18	7	5	12	41

HAND Tony   b. 15-Aug-67

Club	Year	Comp	GP	G	A	Pts	PIM
Mur	1989	WC	4	6	12	18	2
Mur	1990	WC	4	5	8	13	0
Mur	1991	WC	8	9	12	21	12
Mur	1992	WC	5	6	12	18	4
Mur	1993	WC	7	6	8	14	2
Mur	1993	OQ	4	0	2	2	4
Mur	1994	WC	6	0	0	0	0
Ayr	1999	WCQ	4	1	0	1	6
Ayr	2000	WC	7	2	8	10	2
Ayr	2001	WC	5	3	13	16	0
Dun	2002	WC	5	2	4	6	2
		Totals	59	40	79	119	34

HARDING Mike   b. 24-Feb-71

Club	Year	Comp	GP	G	A	Pts	PIM
Man	1999	WCQ	4	1	1	2	0
Man	2000	OQ	3	0	2	2	4
		Totals	7	1	3	4	4

HOAD Jeff   b. 26-Jan-73

Club	Year	Comp	GP	G	A	Pts	PIM
Bel	2002	WC	5	3	1	4	6

GREAT BRITAIN'S WORLD CHAMPIONSHIP and OLYMPIC PLAYER REGISTER 1989-2002
FORWARDS and DEFENCEMEN

HOPE Shannon — b. 25-Nov-62

Club	Year	Comp	GP	G	A	Pts	PIM
Car	1992	WC	2	0	0	0	0
Car	1993	WC	7	0	2	2	4
Car	1993	OQ	4	0	0	0	2
Car	1994	WC	6	0	1	1	14
Car	1995	WC	6	1	1	2	14
Car	1995	OQ	3	0	0	0	6
Car	1996	WC	7	0	1	1	8
Car	1996	OQ	4	0	1	1	28
Car	1997	WC	7	0	2	2	10
Car	1998	WC	7	0	0	0	2
Totals			**53**	**1**	**8**	**9**	**88**

HORNE Kyle — b. 30-Sep-80

Club	Year	Comp	GP	G	A	Pts	PIM
Fif	2001	WC	5	0	2	2	4

HUNT Simon — b. 16-Apr-73

Club	Year	Comp	GP	G	A	Pts	PIM
Not	1995	OQ	3	1	0	1	2
Not	1996	WC	7	2	1	3	24
Not	1996	OQ	1	0	0	0	0
Totals			**11**	**3**	**1**	**4**	**26**

HURLEY Darren — b. 14-Jun-73

Club	Year	Comp	GP	G	A	Pts	PIM
Man	1999	WC	7	1	1	2	8
Man	1999	WCQ	4	0	0	0	29
Car	2000	OQ	3	1	0	1	8
Car	2000	WC	7	1	3	4	32
Brk	2001	WC	5	2	2	4	12
Brk	2002	WC	5	4	0	4	39
Totals			**31**	**9**	**6**	**15**	**128**

IREDALE John — b. 8-Oct-66

Club	Year	Comp	GP	G	A	Pts	PIM
Whi	1989	WC	4	5	4	9	4
Whi	1990	WC	4	0	1	1	4
Whi	1992	WC	5	1	0	1	4
Whi	1993	WC	7	0	3	3	0
Whi	1993	OQ	4	0	0	0	0
Totals			**24**	**6**	**8**	**14**	**12**

JOHNSON Anthony — b. 4-Jan-69

Club	Year	Comp	GP	G	A	Pts	PIM
Dur	1990	WC	4	6	3	9	2
Hum	1991	WC	8	1	1	2	10
Hum	1992	WC	5	5	5	10	0
Hum	1993	WC	7	3	4	7	4
Hum	1993	OQ	4	0	0	0	4
Totals			**28**	**15**	**13**	**28**	**20**

JOHNSON Shaun — b. 22-Mar-73

Club	Year	Comp	GP	G	A	Pts	PIM
Hum	1992	WC	4	1	2	3	2
New	2000	WC	7	0	1	1	0
Cov	2001	WC	5	1	4	5	4
Totals			**16**	**2**	**7**	**9**	**6**

JOHNSON Stephen — b. 19-Jun-67

Club	Year	Comp	GP	G	A	Pts	PIM
Dur	1990	WC	4	2	6	8	0
Hum	1991	WC	8	4	3	7	2
Hum	1992	WC	4	1	0	1	0
Hum	1993	WC	7	3	3	6	4
Totals			**23**	**10**	**12**	**22**	**6**

JOHNSTONE Jeff — b. 21-Sep-75

Club	Year	Comp	GP	G	A	Pts	PIM
Brk	1999	WC	7	4	2	6	4
Lon	1999	WCQ	4	0	1	1	0
Man	2000	OQ	3	0	0	0	2
Totals			**14**	**4**	**3**	**7**	**6**

KENDALL Jason — b. 9-Jul-75

Club	Year	Comp	GP	G	A	Pts	PIM
Brk	2000	OQ	3	0	0	0	0

KELLAND Chris — b. 22-Dec-57

Club	Year	Comp	GP	G	A	Pts	PIM
Mur	1990	WC	4	3	5	8	0
Mur	1991	WC	7	3	2	5	22
Not	1992	WC	5	4	1	5	4
Not	1993	WC	5	0	0	0	4
She	1993	OQ	4	0	0	0	6
She	1994	WC	6	0	0	0	8
Totals			**31**	**10**	**8**	**18**	**44**

KIDD John — b. 22-May-63

Club	Year	Comp	GP	G	A	Pts	PIM
Ayr	1989	WC	4	2	1	3	0

KINDRED Mike — b. 26-May-71

Club	Year	Comp	GP	G	A	Pts	PIM
Mil	1995	WC	5	0	1	1	2

KURTENBACH Terry — b. 14-Mar-63

Club	Year	Comp	GP	G	A	Pts	PIM
Rom	1993	OQ	4	0	1	1	2
Rom	1994	WC	6	1	1	2	2
Gui	1995	WC	7	0	4	4	2
Gui	1995	OQ	3	0	1	1	0
Gui	1996	WC	7	0	0	0	0
Gui	1996	OQ	2	0	0	0	0
Totals			**29**	**1**	**7**	**8**	**6**

LAMBERT Dale — b. 9-Oct-59

Club	Year	Comp	GP	G	A	Pts	PIM
Sol	1993	OQ	4	0	0	0	4

LARKIN Bryan — b. 2-Feb-67

Club	Year	Comp	GP	G	A	Pts	PIM
Swi	1997	WC	7	0	1	1	6

LATTO Gordon — b. 18-Dec-58

Club	Year	Comp	GP	G	A	Pts	PIM
Vas	1976	WC	4	0	0	0	0
Fif	1977	WC	6	0	1	1	2
Fif	1981	WC	7	0	0	0	2
Fif	1989	WC	4	2	1	3	6
Totals			**21**	**2**	**2**	**4**	**10**

LAWLESS John — b. 8-Jan-61

Club	Year	Comp	GP	G	A	Pts	PIM
Car	1990	WC	4	4	8	12	0
Car	1991	WC	8	1	2	3	22
Totals			**12**	**5**	**10**	**15**	**22**

LEE Phil — b. 22-Dec-65

Club	Year	Comp	GP	G	A	Pts	PIM
Sol	1989	WC	4	1	0	1	0
Sol	1990	WC	4	1	0	1	0
Totals			**8**	**2**	**0**	**2**	**0**

GREAT BRITAIN'S WORLD CHAMPIONSHIP and OLYMPIC PLAYER REGISTER 1989-2002
FORWARDS and DEFENCEMEN

LIDDIARD Neil   b. 7-Mar-78

Club	Year	Comp	GP	G	A	Pts	PIM
Pet	2000	OQ	3	0	0	0	0
Pet	2000	WC	7	0	0	0	0
Bas	2001	WC	5	2	2	0	4
Bas	2002	WC	5	0	0	0	8
		Totals	20	2	2	4	12

LINDSAY Jeff   b. 5-Jul-65

Club	Year	Comp	GP	G	A	Pts	PIM
Pet	1995	WC	7	0	0	0	10
Man	1995	OQ	3	0	1	1	4
Man	1996	WC	7	0	0	0	6
Man	1996	OQ	5	0	0	0	2
		Totals	22	0	1	1	22

LITTLE Richard   b. 16-Sep-66

Club	Year	Comp	GP	G	A	Pts	PIM
Bas	1996	OQ	3	2	1	3	4
Bas	1997	WC	7	3	1	4	14
		Totals	10	5	2	7	18

LONGSTAFF David   b. 26-Aug-74

Club	Year	Comp	GP	G	A	Pts	PIM
Whi	1994	WC	6	0	0	0	6
Whi	1995	WC	7	6	1	7	8
New	1995	OQ	1	0	0	0	0
She	1996	WC	7	1	2	3	10
She	1996	OQ	5	1	3	4	6
She	1997	WC	7	1	2	3	8
She	1998	WC	7	4	3	7	8
She	1999	WC	7	2	2	4	4
She	2000	OQ	3	0	1	1	2
She	2000	WC	7	2	3	5	14
She	2001	WC	5	3	7	10	4
Dju	2002	WC	3	1	4	5	2
		Totals	65	21	28	49	72

MacNAUGHT Kevin   b. 23-Jul-60

Club	Year	Comp	GP	G	A	Pts	PIM
Med	1990	WC	4	4	4	8	4
Med	1991	WC	8	3	7	10	10
Med	1992	WC	5	7	5	12	2
		Totals	17	14	16	30	16

MALO Andre   b. 10-May-65

Club	Year	Comp	GP	G	A	Pts	PIM
Bil	1993	WC	7	1	2	3	6
Not	1993	OQ	4	0	0	0	8
Not	1994	WC	5	0	0	0	6
She	1997	WC	7	1	3	4	4
She	1999	WC	7	0	2	2	16
She	1999	WCQ	4	0	0	0	0
She	2000	OQ	3	0	0	0	0
		Totals	37	2	7	9	40

MARSDEN Doug   b. 13-Nov-64

Club	Year	Comp	GP	G	A	Pts	PIM
Pai	1997	WC	7	0	1	1	8

MASON Brian   b. 1-Apr-65

Club	Year	Comp	GP	G	A	Pts	PIM
Slo	1990	WC	4	4	3	7	2
Slo	1991	WC	8	2	2	4	6
Slo	1992	WC	5	3	4	7	29
Mil	1993	WC	7	1	1	2	0
Slo	1993	OQ	4	0	0	0	0
Slo	1994	WC	6	0	0	0	0
		Totals	34	10	10	20	37

McEWEN Doug   b. 2-Oct-63

Club	Year	Comp	GP	G	A	Pts	PIM
Car	1993	WC	7	2	4	6	6
Car	1993	OQ	4	2	1	3	4
Car	1994	WC	6	1	2	3	0
Car	1995	OQ	2	0	0	0	4
Car	1996	WC	7	2	0	2	2
Car	1996	OQ	4	1	1	2	0
Car	1997	WC	7	2	0	2	8
Car	1998	WC	7	2	5	7	4
Pet	2001	WC	5	1	0	1	2
		Totals	49	13	13	26	32

MORGAN Neil   b. 24-Dec-72

Club	Year	Comp	GP	G	A	Pts	PIM
Bla	1995	WC	7	1	2	3	2
Not	1995	OQ	2	0	0	0	0
Not	1996	WC	7	3	1	4	2
Not	1996	OQ	5	1	4	5	2
Not	1997	WC	7	0	1	1	6
Not	1998	WC	7	6	3	9	4
		Totals	35	11	11	22	16

MORIA Steve   b. 3-Feb-61

Club	Year	Comp	GP	G	A	Pts	PIM
Car	1995	OQ	2	0	0	0	0
Car	1996	WC	7	2	1	3	4
Car	1996	OQ	5	4	1	5	2
Car	1997	WC	7	4	2	6	4
Car	1998	WC	7	3	3	6	12
Car	1999	WC	7	2	1	3	2
Car	1999	WCQ	4	0	0	0	0
Car	2000	OQ	3	1	1	2	4
Car	2000	WC	7	6	4	10	2
		Totals	49	22	13	35	30

MORRIS Frank   b. 22-Mar-63

Club	Year	Comp	GP	G	A	Pts	PIM
Mur	1994	WC	6	0	0	0	8
Tra	1995	WC	7	1	1	2	2
		Totals	13	1	1	2	10

MORRISON Scott   b. 12-Aug-64

Club	Year	Comp	GP	G	A	Pts	PIM
Whi	1993	WC	7	10	4	14	2
Whi	1993	OQ	4	0	0	0	0
Whi	1994	WC	4	0	1	1	4
Hum	1995	WC	7	4	2	6	10
Bas	1995	OQ	3	1	1	2	0
		Totals	25	15	8	23	16

MULVENNA Glenn   b. 18-Feb-67

Club	Year	Comp	GP	G	A	Pts	PIM
New	2000	WC	7	0	0	0	18

NEIL Scott   b. 1-Aug-62

Club	Year	Comp	GP	G	A	Pts	PIM
Mur	1981	WC	7	0	0	0	4
Mur	1989	WC	4	5	4	9	0
Mur	1990	WC	4	5	3	8	0
Mur	1991	WC	8	7	1	8	10
Mur	1992	WC	5	6	4	10	4
She	1993	WC	5	0	0	0	0
She	1993	OQ	4	0	0	0	0
		Totals	37	23	12	35	18

NELSON Craig   b. 8-Jul-76

Club	Year	Comp	GP	G	A	Pts	PIM
Dun	2002	WC	5	0	0	0	10

GREAT BRITAIN'S WORLD CHAMPIONSHIP and OLYMPIC PLAYER REGISTER 1989-2002
FORWARDS and DEFENCEMEN

ORD Terry — b. 4-Dec-65

Club	Year	Comp	GP	G	A	Pts	PIM
Whi	1989	WC	4	0	1	1	0

O'CONNOR Mike — b. 12-Dec-61

Club	Year	Comp	GP	G	A	Pts	PIM
Dur	1992	WC	5	3	1	4	10
Dur	1993	WC	7	0	3	3	16
Hum	1993	OQ	4	1	1	2	14
Hum	1994	WC	6	0	0	0	12
		Totals	22	4	5	9	52

PAYNE Anthony — b. 26-Jun-72

Club	Year	Comp	GP	G	A	Pts	PIM
Pet	1995	WC	6	1	0	1	0

PENNYCOOK Jim — b. 12-Jun-57

Club	Year	Comp	GP	G	A	Pts	PIM
Dun	1977	WC	5	1	0	1	0
Mur	1979	WC	7	3	4	7	0
Mur	1981	WC	7	3	1	4	4
Tay	1989	WC	4	3	4	7	0
		Totals	23	10	9	19	4

PENTLAND Paul — b. 11-Nov-64

Club	Year	Comp	GP	G	A	Pts	PIM
Mur	1989	WC	4	0	0	0	0

PICKLES Andy — b. 9-Jun-73

Club	Year	Comp	GP	G	A	Pts	PIM
IOW	2001	WC	5	0	1	1	2

PLOMMER Tommy — b. 26-Aug-68

Club	Year	Comp	GP	G	A	Pts	PIM
She	1995	OQ	3	0	0	0	4
She	1996	OQ	4	3	0	3	0
		Totals	7	3	0	3	4

POUND Ian — b. 22-Jan-67

Club	Year	Comp	GP	G	A	Pts	PIM
Sol	1995	WC	7	0	0	0	10

PRIEST Merv — b. 2-Aug-73

Club	Year	Comp	GP	G	A	Pts	PIM
Bas	1996	WC	7	1	0	1	4
Bas	1996	OQ	3	1	2	3	4
Car	1999	WC	7	1	2	3	10
Car	1999	WCQ	4	0	0	0	2
Car	2000	OQ	2	1	0	1	2
Car	2000	WC	7	2	3	5	8
		Totals	30	6	7	13	30

REID Alistair — b. 15-Jul-63

Club	Year	Comp	GP	G	A	Pts	PIM
Ayr	1989	WC	4	1	2	3	0

RHODES Nigel — b. 19-Jul-67

Club	Year	Comp	GP	G	A	Pts	PIM
Not	1989	WC	4	2	0	2	2

ROBERTSON Iain — b. 2-Jun-69

Club	Year	Comp	GP	G	A	Pts	PIM
Fif	1991	WC	8	0	1	1	2
Fif	1992	WC	5	2	2	4	0
Fif	1993	WC	7	1	0	1	0
Fif	1995	WC	7	1	0	1	0
		Totals	27	4	3	7	2

SAUNDERS Lee — b. 3-Jun-70

Club	Year	Comp	GP	G	A	Pts	PIM
Bas	1995	WC	7	0	1	1	0
Mil	1996	OQ	1	0	0	0	0
		Totals	8	0	1	1	0

SCOTT Patrick — b. 12-Nov-66

Club	Year	Comp	GP	G	A	Pts	PIM
Mil	1993	OQ	4	2	0	2	0
Mil	1994	WC	6	2	0	2	2
Mil	1995	OQ	3	0	1	1	0
Mil	1996	WC	7	1	4	5	2
Bas	1996	OQ	4	1	1	2	2
Bas	1997	WC	7	4	3	7	18
		Totals	31	10	9	19	24

SHIELDS Colin — b. 27-Jan-80

Club	Year	Comp	GP	G	A	Pts	PIM
Una	2001	WC	5	6	2	8	4
UoM	2002	WC	5	2	3	5	4
		Totals	10	8	5	13	8

SMITH Damian — b. 8-Oct-71

Club	Year	Comp	GP	G	A	Pts	PIM
Dur	1992	WC	4	2	2	4	0
Dur	1993	WC	4	1	1	2	0
Dur	1995	WC	6	0	1	1	10
		Totals	14	3	4	7	10

SMITH David — b. 14-Feb-73

Club	Year	Comp	GP	G	A	Pts	PIM
Tra	1995	WC	5	1	0	1	0

SMITH Paul — b. 3-Jul-61

Club	Year	Comp	GP	G	A	Pts	PIM
Dur	1981	WC	7	0	0	0	11
Dur	1989	WC	4	0	1	1	2
		Totals	11	0	1	1	13

SMITH Peter — b. 29-Nov-61

Club	Year	Comp	GP	G	A	Pts	PIM
Pet	1989	WC	4	4	1	5	2
Pet	1990	WC	2	2	0	2	2
Car	1991	WC	8	1	1	2	6
		Totals	14	7	2	9	10

SMITH Stephen — b. 11-Apr-63

Club	Year	Comp	GP	G	A	Pts	PIM
Whi	1989	WC	4	2	1	3	2

STEFAN Gary — b. 23-Jun-59

Club	Year	Comp	GP	G	A	Pts	PIM
Slo	1990	WC	4	4	7	11	8
Slo	1991	WC	8	3	1	4	12
Slo	1992	WC	5	5	2	7	8
		Totals	17	12	10	22	28

STONE Jason — b. 30-Dec-72

Club	Year	Comp	GP	G	A	Pts	PIM
Car	1998	WC	6	0	0	0	0

GREAT BRITAIN'S WORLD CHAMPIONSHIP and OLYMPIC PLAYER REGISTER 1989-2002
FORWARDS and DEFENCEMEN

STRACHAN Rick — b. 27-Mar-63

Club	Year	Comp	GP	G	A	Pts	PIM
Mil	1995	WC	7	0	0	0	2
Bas	1995	OQ	3	0	0	0	0
Bas	1996	WC	7	2	1	3	2
Bas	1996	OQ	5	1	1	2	2
Bas	1997	WC	7	1	4	5	2
Bas	1998	WC	6	0	2	2	2
Bas	1999	WC	7	1	0	1	0
Bas	1999	WCQ	4	0	0	0	2
Bas	2000	OQ	3	0	1	1	2
Bas	2000	WC	7	1	1	2	2
Car	2001	WC	5	0	0	0	0
Mil	2002	WC	5	1	0	1	4
		Totals	66	7	10	17	20

TAIT Ashley — b. 9-Aug-75

Club	Year	Comp	GP	G	A	Pts	PIM
Not	1995	WC	2	0	0	0	4
Not	1995	OQ	3	1	1	2	0
Not	1996	WC	7	1	1	2	10
Kin	1998	WC	7	2	0	2	4
Not	1999	WCQ	4	0	0	0	4
Not	2000	OQ	3	0	0	0	6
Not	2000	WC	7	3	4	7	10
Not	2001	WC	5	2	4	6	4
Not	2002	WC	5	1	1	2	0
		Totals	43	10	11	21	42

TASKER Michael — b. 10-Jul-73

Club	Year	Comp	GP	G	A	Pts	PIM
Cov	2001	WC	5	1	3	4	4
Cov	2002	WC	5	1	0	1	4
		Totals	10	2	3	5	8

THOMPSON Paul — b. 6-May-68

Club	Year	Comp	GP	G	A	Pts	PIM
Gui	1998	WC	6	1	1	2	8

THORNTON Steve — b. 8-Mar-73

Club	Year	Comp	GP	G	A	Pts	PIM
Car	1999	WC	7	2	1	3	0
Car	1999	WCQ	4	0	1	1	2
Car	2001	WC	5	2	8	10	6
		Totals	16	4	10	14	8

WAGHORN Graham — b. 31-Dec-72

Club	Year	Comp	GP	G	A	Pts	PIM
Not	1991	WC	8	0	2	2	10
Not	1993	WC	7	1	1	2	4
Not	1995	OQ	1	0	0	0	2
Not	1996	OQ	3	0	0	0	0
		Totals	19	1	3	4	16

WEAVER Jonathan — b. 20-Jan-77

Club	Year	Comp	GP	G	A	Pts	PIM
New	1998	WC	7	1	5	6	0
Man	1999	WC	7	0	2	2	2
USA	1999	WCQ	4	0	0	0	2
Ayr	2001	WC	5	7	2	9	0
Ayr	2002	WC	3	0	0	0	0
		Totals	26	8	9	17	4

WEBER Randall — b. 2-Sep-68

Club	Year	Comp	GP	G	A	Pts	PIM
Not	1998	WC	7	0	2	2	6

WILSON Rob — b. 18-Jul-68

Club	Year	Comp	GP	G	A	Pts	PIM
She	1998	WC	7	1	4	5	10
She	1999	WC	7	1	3	4	6
New	2001	WC	5	6	7	13	7
Man	2002	WC	5	1	2	3	4
		Totals	24	9	16	25	22

WISHART Gary — b. 28-Aug-81

Club	Year	Comp	GP	G	A	Pts	PIM
Fif	2002	WC	5	0	2	2	4

YOUNG Scott — b. 26-May-65

Club	Year	Comp	GP	G	A	Pts	PIM
Ayr	1999	WCQ	4	0	0	0	10
Ayr	2000	OQ	3	2	1	3	18
Ayr	2000	WC	5	3	3	6	20
Dun	2002	WC	4	0	0	0	8
		Totals	16	5	4	9	56

GOALKEEPERS

COWLEY Wayne — b. 4-Dec-64

Club	Year	Comp	GP	GPI	Mins	GA	GAA
Not	1999	WCQ	3	0	0	0	0.00
Not	2000	WC	7	3	160	10	3.75
		Totals	10	3	160	10	3.75

FOSTER Stephen — b. 1-Jul-74

Club	Year	Comp	GP	GPI	Mins	GA	GAA
Dur	1995	WC	7	6	320	28	5.25
Dur	1995	OQ	2	0	0	0	0.00
Dur	1996	WC	5	3	180	11	3.67
New	1996	OQ	3	0	0	0	0.00
New	1997	WC	5	4	200	12	3.60
New	1998	WC	6	3	155	10	3.87
Ayr	2000	OQ	3	0	0	0	0.00
		Totals	31	16	855	61	4.28

GRAHAM David — b. 24-Oct-59

Club	Year	Comp	GP	GPI	Mins	GA	GAA
Not	1989	WC	4	3	150	12	4.80
Not	1990	WC	3	1	60	1	1.00
Not	1991	WC	3	2	120	5	2.50
		Totals	10	6	330	18	3.27

GREAT BRITAIN WORLD CHAMPIONSHIP and OLYMPIC PLAYER REGISTER 1989-2002
GOALKEEPERS

GRUBB Ricky   b. 3-Mar-77

Club	Year	Comp	GP	GPl	Mins	GA	GAA
Fif	1995	WC	1	1	40	5	7.50

HANSON Moray   b. 21-Jun-64

Club	Year	Comp	GP	GPl	Mins	GA	GAA
Mur	1989	WC	2	1	60	4	4.00
Mur	1991	WC	3	2	120	11	5.50
Mur	1994	WC	4	3	137	17	7.45
		Totals	9	6	317	32	6.06

HIBBERT Jim   b. 8-Feb-75

Club	Year	Comp	GP	GPl	Mins	GA	GAA
New	2000	WC	1	1	20	3	9.00

LYLE Stevie   b. 4-Dec-79

Club	Year	Comp	GP	GPl	Mins	GA	GAA
Car	1995	OQ	1	0	0	0	0.00
Car	1996	WC	3	1	60	2	2.00
Car	1996	OQ	2	0	0	0	0.00
Car	1997	WC	6	2	120	8	4.00
Can	1998	WC	5	4	205	12	3.51
Car	1999	WC	7	5	300	12	2.40
Car	1999	WCQ	4	4	240	5	1.25
Car	2000	OQ	3	3	180	8	2.67
Car	2001	WC	5	5	270	8	1.78
Man	2002	WC	3	2	120	8	4.00
		Totals	39	26	1495	63	2.53

McCRONE John   b. 26-Feb-63

Club	Year	Comp	GP	GPl	Mins	GA	GAA
Ayr	1989	WC	2	1	30	0	0.00
Ayr	1991	WC	4	4	240	9	2.25
Ayr	1992	WC	3	3	122	4	1.97
Fif	1993	WC	7	5	280	13	2.79
Fif	1993	OQ	3	3	180	13	4.33
Fif	1994	WC	4	3	105	18	10.29
		Totals	23	19	957	57	3.57

McKAY Martin   b. 27-Apr-68

Club	Year	Comp	GP	GPl	Mins	GA	GAA
Mur	1990	WC	2	2	120	4	2.00
Mur	1992	WC	3	1	60	2	2.00
Mur	1993	WC	3	1	60	0	0.00
She	1993	OQ	3	1	60	8	8.00
She	1994	WC	4	3	118	14	7.12
		Totals	15	8	418	28	4.02

MORRISON Bill   b. 27-Oct-64

Club	Year	Comp	GP	GPl	Mins	GA	GAA
Bas	1995	WC	6	1	60	2	2.00
Bas	1995	OQ	3	3	180	4	1.33
Bas	1996	WC	6	3	180	10	3.33
K/R	1996	OQ	5	5	300	11	2.20
Rat	1997	WC	3	2	100	2	1.20
Pai	1998	WC	3	1	60	5	5.00
Rod	1999	WC	7	2	120	4	2.00
		Totals	33	17	1000	38	2.28

MURPHY Stephen   b. 11-Dec-81

Club	Year	Comp	GP	GPl	Mins	GA	GAA
Fif	2001	WC	5	1	30	1	2.00
Dun	2002	WC	3	1	60	2	2.00
		Totals	8	2	90	3	2.00

O'CONNOR Scott   b. 3-May-69

Club	Year	Comp	GP	GPl	Mins	GA	GAA
Pet	1992	WC	4	3	118	4	2.03
Pet	1993	WC	3	2	80	0	0.00
Mil	1993	OQ	2	0	0	0	0.00
		Totals	9	5	198	4	1.21

SMITH Jeff   b. 11-Jul-63

Club	Year	Comp	GP	GPl	Mins	GA	GAA
Car	1990	WC	3	1	60	2	2.00

WATKINS Joe   b. 27-Oct-79

Club	Year	Comp	GP	GPl	Mins	GA	GAA
Bas	1999	WCQ	1	0	0	0	0.00
Bas	2000	WC	6	4	240	10	2.50
Brk	2002	WC	4	2	120	6	6.00
		Totals	11	6	360	16	2.67

WORLD JUNIOR CHAMPIONSHIPS

U20 CHAMPIONSHIPS

Division II, Zagreb, Croatia, 30 December 2001-3 January 2002.

Age limit is under 20 years on 1 January 2002

The eight nations first competed in two groups, with each country playing the others in its group. The top team in group A played off against the top team in group B for promotion to Division I. The lower ranked teams similarly played off for the remaining division places.

GROUP STANDINGS

Group A	GP	W	L	D	GF	GA	Pts
Denmark	3	3	0	0	30	9	6
Latvia	3	2	1	0	22	6	4
Britain	3	1	2	0	7	19	2
Netherlands	3	0	3	0	3	28	0

BRITAIN'S POINTS SCORERS

	GP	G	A	Pts	Pim
Danny Meyers	4	3	3	6	6
Michael Wales	4	1	4	5	8
Jonathan Phillips	4	1	4	5	8
James Morgan	4	2	2	4	22
Russell Cowley	4	1	3	4	6
Neil Adams	4	0	4	4	2
Stephen Wallace	4	2	1	3	8
Ryan Lake	4	2	0	2	4
Paul Moran	4	1	1	2	10
Paul Sample	4	1	1	2	4
Shaun Yardley	4	1	0	1	2
Lewis Buckman	4	1	0	1	2
Michael Plenty	4	0	1	1	14

BRITAIN UNDER-20

Richard Ashton ALT, Andy Moffat HUL; Paddy Ward AYR, James Morgan BRK, Michael Plenty GUI, Andrew Munroe HUL, Adam Radmall NOT, Tyrone Miller ROM, Michael Wales SOL; Paul Sample CAR, Shaun Yardley COV, Ryan Lake, Stephen Wallace HUL, Danny Meyers, Jonathan Phillips MIL, Paul Moran NOT, Murray Johnston PAI, Lewis Buckman PET, Neil Adams SOL, Russell Cowley SWI. *Coach:* Kevin King. *Manager:* James Laing.

BRITAIN'S RESULTS

30 Dec Denmark-Britain   12-2 (4-1,5-1,3-0)
31 Dec Britain-Latvia   0-6 (0-4,0-1,0-1)
2 Jan N'lands-Britain   1-5 (0-2,1-3,0-0)
Fifth Place Playoff
3 Jan Britain-Hungary   9-4 (2-0,2-3,5-1)

FINAL RANKINGS

1 Japan *(promoted to Div I)*, 2 Denmark, 3 Latvia, 4 Croatia, **5 Britain**, 6 Hungary, 7 Netherlands, 8 Lithuania *(relegated to Div III)*.

BRITAIN'S NETMINDING

	GPI	Mins	SoG	GA	Sv%
Andy Moffat	4	210	134	18	86.57
Richard Ashton	1	30	22	5	77.27
GB TOTALS	4	240	156	23	85.26

GB'S BEST PLAYERS
DANNY MEYERS *selected by IIHF*
ANDY MOFFAT *selected by GBSC*

Danes make bacon of Brits

Despite icing several players with BNL and even Superleague experience, GB's top junior squad managed only two goals against the Danes and Latvians who ended ahead of Britain in the first round of games. Denmark, who finished fourth last year, could be the most improved hockey nation in Europe. They humbled the under-21s with a double-figure goal tally before their senior squad upset **Chris McSorley**'s GB in the opening game in World Division I.

U18 CHAMPIONSHIPS

Division II, Briancon, France, 22-29 March 2002.

Age limit is under 18 years on 1 January 2002

The eight nations first competed in two groups, with each country playing the others in its group.

BRITAIN'S FIRST ROUND GROUP

Group A	GP	W	L	D	GF	GA	Pts
France	3	3	0	0	47	1	6
Britain	3	2	1	0	16	11	4
Croatia	3	1	2	0	9	27	2
Romania	3	0	3	0	2	35	0

France and Britain then played in the second round against the winning teams in Group B, with the France-Britain result being carried forward.

FINAL ROUND

	GP	W	L	D	GF	GA	Pts
France	3	3	0	0	36	1	6
Poland	3	2	1	0	20	15	4
Britain	3	1	2	0	10	22	2
Estonia	3	0	3	0	3	31	0

FINAL RANKING

1 France, 2 Poland (promoted to Division I), 3 **Britain**, 4 Estonia, 5 Netherlands, 6 Hungary, 7 Croatia, 8 Romania.
As the Division was to be expanded to 12 teams, no nation was relegated, but the top two teams were promoted.

BRITAIN'S RESULTS

22 Mar	Britain-Croatia	8-1 (4-1,2-0,2-0)
24 Mar	Britain-Romania	8-0 (1-0,5-0,2-0)
26 Mar	France-Britain	10-0 (5-0,2-0,3-0)
28 Mar	Poland-Britain	10-2 (4-1,1-1,5-0)
29 Mar	Britain-Estonia	8-2 (3-0,4-0,1-2)

BRITAIN'S NETMINDING

	GPI	Mins	SoG	GA	Sv%
Allan Levers	3	180	93	13	86.02
Richard Ashton	2	120	63	10	84.13
GB TOTALS	5	300	156	23	85.26

Hat for Matt v Croats

Britain finished with a bronze medal for the second straight year, winning three of their five games. France and Poland, who won promotion, each inflicted double-digit defeats on the Brits.

Stephen Wallace of Hull and Milton Keynes' forward, **Matt Towalski**, dominated the scoring with both players scoring hat-tricks in the opening game against Croatia.

• Fascinating fact or is it those IIHF statistical gremlins again? The under-20s and under-18s each conceded 23 goals on 156 shots in their respective championships. What's the chances of that happening?

BRITAIN UNDER-18

Richard Ashton ALT, Allan Levers NOT; Paddy Ward AYR, David Thomas BIL, Rhodri Evans CAR, Leigh Jamieson MIL, Adam Radmall NOT, Danny Hughes SHE, James Hutchinson SUN; Tom Pope BAS, Joe Miller, Matthew Myers CAR, Stephen Wallace HUL, Matt Towalski MIL, Chris Colegate, Joe Wightman NOT, Terry Miles SLO, Dean Mills SWI, Adam Brittle TEL, Adam Carr, Tom Miller, Michael Timms (unatt.). *Coach*: Allan Anderson. *Manager*: Michael Evans.

BRITAIN'S POINT SCORERS

	GP	G	A	Pts	Pim
Stephen Wallace	5	6	3	9	12
Matt Towalski	5	7	1	8	0
Matthew Myers	5	2	3	5	8
Adam Radmall	5	1	3	4	0
Adam Brittle	5	1	3	4	2
Chris Colegate	5	3	0	3	2
Joe Wightman	5	0	3	3	0
Joe Miller	5	1	1	2	18
Adam Carr	5	1	1	2	4
Terry Miles	5	1	1	2	14
Tom Pope	5	0	2	2	0
James Hutchinson	5	0	2	2	2
Tom Miller	4	1	0	1	0
Leigh Jamieson	5	1	0	1	2
Michael Timms	5	1	0	1	4
Dean Mills	2	0	1	1	6
Paddy Ward	5	0	1	1	4
Rhodri Evans	5	0	1	1	4

CONTINENTAL CUP

The Continental Cup was established in 1997 as a replacement for the European Cup (inaugurated 1965). The name was changed to avoid confusion with the European League.

Costs are kept down by gathering clubs together geographically as far as possible and allowing games to be played by groups of teams in one venue, rather than home and away.

A record 49 clubs from 27 countries took part in the 2001 Continental Cup, including newcomers Turkey. But for the second year running, Russia and Sweden, two of the major hockey playing nations, declined to participate. Finland and the Czech Republic entered second division teams.

The competition was played over three qualifying rounds in September, October and November, with a four-team final round in January. In each round, the teams played a round-robin over three days.

Britain's representatives were Sheffield Steelers, the 2000-01 Grand Slam winners, and London Knights who won the Cup's silver medal in 2000. Steelers played in the Second Round but for the second successive year, Knights were granted a bye into the Third Round.

We give below details of both British teams' cup groups.

THIRD ROUND STANDINGS
Group P
Valerenga, Oslo, Norway

	GP	W	L	D	GF	GA	Pts
Jukurit Mikkeli FIN	3	2	0	1	12	5	5
Valerenga IF NOR	3	1	0	2	10	7	4
London Knights GB	3	1	1	2	11	12	3
Anglet Hormadi FRA	3	0	3	0	5	14	0

RESULTS
23 Nov	**Knights**-Jukurit	2-5 (1-3,1-2,0-0)
	Anglet-Valerenga	1-4 (1-0,0-3,0-1)
24 Nov	Anglet-**Knights**	3-5 (1-1,2-4,0-0)
	Valerenga-Jukurit	2-2 (0-1,1-1,1-0)
25 Nov	Jukurit-Anglet	5-1 (1-0,2-0,2-1)
	Valerenga-Knights	4-4 (3-0,1-2,0-2)

KNIGHTS' GAME SUMMARIES
23 November 2001

KNIGHTS-JUKURIT   2-5 (1-3,1-2,0-0)

Knights' scoring:

Bronilla (Mansi)	11.52	(1-2)
Mansi (Ahlroos, Leslie)	32.04	(2-4)

Penalty minutes: Knights 41 (Barrie 5+game - high-sticks), Jukurit 54 (Laakso & Kantelinen 5+game - high-sticks).
Knights' Man of Match: Ahlroos.
Knights' goalie: Robins (no shots available).
Referee: Reibee   *Attendance:* 554.

24 November 2001

ANGLET-KNIGHTS   3-5 (1-1,2-4,0-0)

Knights' scoring:

Kolesar (Blanchard)	5.46	(0-1)
Sacratini (Thornton, McIntyre)	28.19	(2-2)
Kolesar (Mansi, Blanchard)	33.47	(2-3)
Ahlroos (Rushforth, Mansi)	36.36pp	(2-4)
Sacratini (Mansi)	37.59	(2-5)

Penalty minutes: Anglet 10, Knights 31 (Barrie 5+match - spearing).
Knights' Man of Match: Kolesar.
Knights' goalie: Robins (no shots available).
Referee: Andersson NOR.   *Attendance:* 489.

25 November 2001

VALERENGA-KNIGHTS   4-4 (3-0,1-2,0-2)

Knights' scoring:

Blanchard	25.02	(3-1)
Ahlroos (Sacratini)	30.34	(3-2)
Sacratini (Ahlroos)	58.03sh	(4-3)
Rushforth	59.03	(4-4)

Penalty minutes: Valerenga 10, Knights 20.
Knights' Man of Match: Sacratini.
Knights' goalie: Trofimenkoff (no shots available).
Referee: Reibee.   *Attendance:* 1,781

LONDON KNIGHTS
Trevor Robins, Dave Trofimenkoff; Sean Blanchard, Maurizio Mansi, Ritchie Bronilla, Mike Ware, Rob Donovan; Kim Ahlroos, Dave Struch (capt), David Clarke, Nathan Leslie, Steve Thornton, Mark Kolesar, Mike Barrie, Ian McIntyre, Vezio Sacratini, Paul Rushforth.
Coach: Bob Leslie.   *Manager:* Martin Dodds.

SECOND ROUND STANDINGS

Group M, Anglet, France

	GP	W	L	D	GF	GA	Pts
Anglet Hormadi FRA	3	3	0	0	13	8	6
Sheffield Steelers GB	3	2	1	0	12	8	4
Herning IK DEN	3	1	2	0	13	13	2
Grenoble FRA	3	0	3	0	7	16	0

Anglet Hormadi *qualify for the Third Round.*

SECOND ROUND RESULTS

19 Oct	**Steelers**-Herning	5-3
	Grenoble-Anglet	2-5
20 Oct	Grenoble-**Steelers**	1-4
	Anglet-Herning	4-3
21 Oct	Herning-Grenoble	7-4
	Anglet-**Steelers**	4-3

STEELERS' GAME SUMMARIES

19 October 2001

STEELERS-HERNING   5-3 (0-0,4-0,1-3)

Steelers' scoring:

Allison (Miehm)	21.38	(1-0)
Benazic (Kruse)	27.46pp	(2-0)
Benazic	33.17	(3-0)
Brown (Maudie, Leboutillier)	39.45pp	(4-0)
Brebant (Brown, Mansoff)	50.19	(5-1)

Penalty minutes: Steelers: 32 (Laniel 10-misc), Herning 45 (Pander 5+game - check-behind).
Steelers' goalie: McInerney (no shots available).
Referee: Benoist FRA.   *Attendance:* 200.

20 October 2001

GRENOBLE-STEELERS   1-4 (1-0,0-0,0-4)

Steelers' scoring:

Lipsett (Lauer)	43.26	(0-1)
Allison (Sebastian, Benazic)	44.41sh	(1-2)
Brebant (Brown)	55.31pp	(1-3)
Miehm (Benazic)	58.44sh	(1-4)

Penalty minutes: Grenoble 29 (Elian 5+game - high-sticks), Steelers 16.
Steelers' goalie/Man of Match: Bach (no shots available).
Referee: Bertolotti ITA.   *Attendance:* n/a.

21 October 2001

ANGLET-STEELERS   4-3 (1-2,2-0,1-1)

Steelers' scoring:

Lipsett (Brebant)	1.09	(0-1)
Leboutillier (Mansoff, Laniel)	16.28pp	(1-2)
Miehm (Kruse, Allison)	45.12pp	(3-3)

Penalty minutes: Anglet 16, Steelers 20.
Steelers' goalie: Bach (no shots available).
Referee: Bertolotti ITA.   *Attendance:* 1,950

SHEFFIELD STEELERS

Ryan Bach, Eoin McInerney; Marc Laniel, Jeff Sebastian, Cal Benazic, Jason Mansoff, Jeff Brown, Steve Duncombe; Rick Brebant, Brad Lauer, Paul Kruse (capt), Kevin Miehm, Scott Allison, Keith Leyland, Brent Bobyck, Bob Maudie, Pete Leboutillier, Chris Lipsett.
Manager/Coach: Mike Blaisdell.

Hard act to follow

It was always going to be difficult for any British team to emulate London Knights' remarkable silver medal performance in the 2000 Continental Cup. And so it proved.

Bob Leslie's 2001 Knights were woefully under-strength and Sheffield Steelers came up against a hot goalie in their last game.

Two goals each from **Cal Benazic**, **Scott Allison** and **Rick Brebant** helped Steelers go into their third game as favourites against their hosts. Both teams were unbeaten.

But with former Manchester Storm goalie, **Eric Raymond**, playing what Steelers' coach **Mike Blaisdell** described as "the game of his life", Anglet came back from 2-1 down to beat Steelers on a goal from **Gregorie Dubois** less than four minutes from time.

Knights, drawn into the stronger Third Round, fared worse, losing their first game to the second tier Finnish side, Jukurit (not to be confused with Helsinki's elite side, Jokerit).

London seemed to be one of the worst sufferers from Superleague's reduced wage cap as they took only 15 fit skaters and two goalies to Oslo. In their second game, they beat Anglet, Steelers' nemesis, but lost **Rich Bronilla** and goalie **Trevor Robins** to injury, together with feisty forward **Mike Barrie**, who was ejected from his second straight game.

In the circumstances, their come-from-behind draw with the home team - who ran out of steam in trying to win by five to top the group - was a good result.

NORTH AMERICAN LEAGUES

NATIONAL HOCKEY LEAGUE

STANLEY CUP

Winners	DETROIT REDWINGS
Finalists	CAROLINA HURRICANES
Game scores	2-3h,3-1h,3-2a,3-0a,3-1h
	(*Redwings shown first*)

PRESIDENTS' TROPHY (*most league points*)
DETROIT REDWINGS (Western Conference)
Runners-up
BOSTON BRUINS (Eastern Conference)

FIRST ALL-STAR TEAM

Goal	**Patrick Roy**, Colorado
Defence	**Nicklas Lidstrom**, Detroit
	Chris Chelios, Detroit
Centre	**Joe Sakic**, Colorado
Right Wing	**Jarome Iginla**, Calgary
Left Wing	**Markus Naslund**, Vancouver

AWARD WINNERS

Art Ross Trophy (Most Points)
Jarome Iginla, Calgary Flames

Maurice 'Rocket' Richard Trophy (Most Goals)
Jarome Iginla, Calgary Flames

Hart Memorial Trophy (Most Valuable Player)
Jose Theodore, Montreal Canadiens

James Norris Mem'l Trophy (Best Defenceman)
Nicklas Lidstrom, Detroit Redwings

Vezina Trophy (Best Goaltender)
Jose Theodore, Montreal Canadiens

William Jennings Trophy (Fewest Goals Against)
Patrick Roy, Colorado

Lester B Pearson Trophy (Players' Player)
Jarome Iginla, Calgary Flames

Calder Memorial Trophy (Rookie of the Year)
Dany Heatley, Atlanta Thrashers

Lady Byng Mem'l Trophy (Most Sportsmanlike)
Ron Francis, Carolina Hurricanes

Jack Adams Award (Coach of the Year)
Bob Francis, Phoenix Coyotes

Conn Smythe Trophy (Playoff MVP)
Nicklas Lidstrom, Detroit Redwings

Frank J Selke Trophy (Defensive Forward)
Michael Peca, New York Islanders

Bill Masterton Memorial Trophy (Most Dedicated)
Saku Koivu, Montreal Canadiens

Two new stars and a pensioner

If Calgary Flames' sharpshooter, **Jarome Iginla**, and Montreal Canadiens' goalie, **Jose Theodore**, were the star players of the 2001-02 NHL season, then it was a coach who stole the limelight in the Stanley Cup playoffs.

Scotty Bowman, 68, couldn't wait to celebrate his record-breaking nine Cups. He was the first - after captain **Steve Yzerman** - to raise aloft Lord Stanley's ancient mug after his Detroit Redwings' fifth-game final victory over Carolina Hurricanes.

Bowman, who coached his first Cup winner with Montreal Canadiens in 1973, announced his retirement immediately after the win which took him past his Canadiens' predecessor, the legendary **Toe Blake**.

Unusually, the league's top scorer (goals and points) played for a team that failed to make the playoffs. Iginla, 24, matured during his sixth NHL season into a 52-goal man, 11 more than his nearest rival. He was the first player to win the Art Ross Trophy in 21 years who is not called **Mario Lemieux**, **Wayne Gretzky** or **Jaromir Jagr**. He also won the Lester B Pearson Trophy as the Players' Player.

That Montreal qualified for the playoffs for the first time since 1997-98 was due in large part to Theodore's spectacular goalminding. The Laval, Quebec native took over when the team's first choice netminder was injured and went on to compile a league-leading save percentage of 93.1, a figure bettered only by **Dominic Hasek.**

This won the 25-year-old the Vezina Trophy while his worth to his team was recognised by the league who awarded him the Hart Trophy as their most valuable player.

The goalie was the star of the NHL's annual awards ceremony, but he was shaken at winning the MVP trophy. "I knew I had only one chance in three of winning so I don't have a speech prepared," he said. "Now my legs are weak. I came here as a young player for the experience. Now I'm going home with two trophies."

In the way of sports, as one star rose, another went off into the sunset. Hasek, 37, perhaps the NHL's most unconventional goalie as well as one of its most successful, announced his retirement after winning a Stanley Cup to go with his Olympic gold medal with the Czech Republic, and almost every NHL honour.

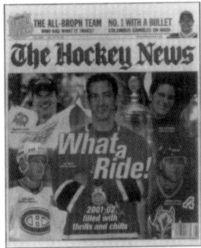

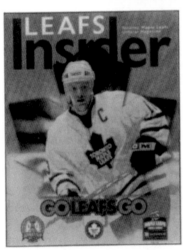

Tragedy in the NHL

The first death of a spectator due to a flying puck in the NHL's 85-year history prompted the league to introduce several safety measures.

They agreed to string netting behind the goals in all 30 of their arenas from the start of season 2002-03. In addition, the minimum height of the glass above the boards was to be raised by two feet to five feet. The moves came after **Britannie Cecil**, 13, died two days after she was struck in the forehead by the puck at a March 2002 game between the Columbus Blue Jackets and Calgary Flames.

According to the coroner, her death was due to a rare injury to an artery that was damaged when her head snapped back. The schoolgirl was sitting about 15 rows above the ice and behind the goal when the puck came flying into the stands from Columbus centreman **Espen Knutsen**'s slap shot. The puck appeared to be deflected and hit two other fans sitting nearby.

"Britannie was the league's first fatality in our history, and probably 800 million fans have attended games since then," commented league president, **Gary Bettman**, who announced the safety measures in June. "But we wanted to do the right thing."

Bettman added that he prefers black netting to white as tests showed that this is less distracting to viewers. "In less than three minutes," he said, "people won't even know it's there."

NHL's $10 million dollar men

A Czech, a Russian and a Canadian - all high scoring forwards - are the best paid players in pro hockey. Washington's Czech **Jaromir Jagr**, Anaheim's Canadian **Paul Kariya** and New York Rangers' Russian **Pavel Bure** all earn over US$10 million (about £7 million), according to figures released by the NHL Players' Association.

Bure was traded to the Rangers during the season with two years left on his five-year contract with Florida Panthers. The contract includes an option for $11 million in season 2004-05. A fourth NHLer, **Peter Forsberg** of Colorado Avalanche, was not on the list after being injured for the entire league season. Had he played, he was expected to be the highest paid player at $11 million.

Stanley Cup champs, Detroit Redwings, unsurprisingly had the biggest payroll at $64.4 million. Redwings are owned by **Mike and Marian Ilitch**, who have a pizza restaurant empire, *Little Caesar's*. Five other clubs shelled out over $50 million, including the perennially under-achieving New York Rangers who missed the playoffs for the fifth straight year.

MINOR LEAGUES
PLAYOFF WINNER*S*

American League (AHL) - Calder Cup
Chicago Wolves

East Coast League (ECHL) - Kelly Cup
Greenville Grrrowl

United League (UHL) - Colonial Cup
Muskegon Fury

Central League (CHL) - Bill Levins Trophy
Memphis RiverKings

West Coast League (WCHL) - Taylor Cup
Fresno Falcons

Canadian (Major Junior 'A') League (CHL) - Memorial Cup
Kootenay Ice (Western League)

Marty McSorley, brother of GB coach and Cardiff Devils' new owner, **Chris McSorley**, was hired as coach of the AHL's Springfield Falcons in June 2002. Falcons are a farm team of Phoenix Coyotes whose owner, **Wayne Gretzky**, was a team-mate of Marty's in Edmonton and Los Angeles.

Wolves carry off Calder Cup

Chicago Wolves won the **AMERICAN HOCKEY LEAGUE** playoff championship the hard way. They threw away a 3-0 lead over league winners, Bridgeport Sound Tigers, who forced the game into overtime before **Yuri Butsayev**'s goal 2.05 into the second extra period gave Wolves a 4-3 victory.

A crowd of 15,132 in the AllState Arena watched as Wolves clinched the best-of-seven series 4-1 and carried off the Calder Cup, North America's most prestigious pro hockey trophy after the Stanley Cup.

"It was the longest playoffs of my life," said Wolves' right winger, **Rob Brown**, a 15-year pro. Wolves were rank underdogs at the start of the playoffs, having finished seventh in the ten-team Western Conference.

The wonderfully named *Greenville Grrrowl* took the **EAST COAST HOCKEY LEAGUE**'s Kelly Cup, demolishing Dayton Bombers by a similar 4-1 series win.

Atlanta Thrashers' draft pick, **Simon Gamanche**, was credited with turning round the Grrrowl's season with 34 goals and 62 points in the 48 games after he joined the struggling club at Christmas-time. The ECHL is where Superleague find many of their players.

QUOTES OF THE YEAR

Perish the thought

"It wasn't just money. There were other things [in Ottawa] that I don't want to get into because this is such a nice day." *Ottawa Senators' Russian forward, Alexei Yashin, on signing a 10-year contract with New York Islanders which could pay him as much as $87.5 million, the longest, biggest contract in NHL history.*

Yashin sat out the entire 1999-2000 season in a contract dispute with the Senators. Islanders are owned by **Charles Wang**, the head of Computer Associates.

Skating wounded

'Blind-in-one-eye defenceman, head-traumatised no. 1 centre, 40-year-old captain and spiritual leader, goalie coming off reconstruction of both knees, incumbent leading scorer just out of substance rehab.' *Columnist Jay Greenburg summing up the chances of New York Rangers for the 2001-02 season in The Hockey News of Canada. [The players were Bryan Berard, Eric Lindros, Mark Messier, Mike Richter and Theo Fleury.]*

Scoring miracle

"The game is played behind the goal line now. If by some miracle you get through the neutral zone, you dump it in, you go on the forecheck and, if you get the puck, you cycle it behind the goal line." *Paul Kariya of Anaheim Mighty Ducks, on the lack of goal scoring in the NHL.*

Punch-up of the Year

"When you work for Disney, you must start to live in a fantasy world. Maybe he believes in Peter Pan." - *Calgary GM, Craig Button, in response to Anaheim coach Bryan Murray's claim that he put Ducks' tough guys, Kevin Sawyer and Denny Lambert. out on a late power play because he didn't want to run up the score against the Flames in a game on 8 December 2001.*

A series of brawls in the final 90 seconds of the game resulted in 15 players being penalised and produced a total of 309 penalty minutes. Calgary coach, **Greg Gilbert**, was suspended for two games for sending out three players with 1.24 left who started altercations the moment the puck was dropped. Flames were losing 4-0 at the time. The club was fined $25,000 and five players from both sides were suspended and fined.   Faceoff.com

Winning Stanley

"I'm not gay, but I love kissing these guys." *Steve Duchesne, Detroit Redwings' defenceman after his team won the Stanley Cup.*

"I haven't been out this late since I was 40." *Red Fisher, the 75-year-old Montreal Gazette reporter during the mammoth triple overtime in Game 3 of the Cup final that finished after 1 a.m.*

I'd invent hockey."
Sergei Fedorov of *Detroit Red Wings, when asked what he'd do if hockey didn't exist.*

STANLEY CUP FACTS

● Technically, players are not paid to compete in the Stanley Cup playoffs. Their contracts cover only the regular league season. But they don't play purely for the glory of having their name on the treasured trophy and wearing a championship ring. The league pays prize money to the teams to be divided as they see fit.

The Cup winning side receives US$2,142,500 (about £1.5 million) and the runner-up gets US$1,467,500.

The losing Conference finalists are on for US$902,500 per team and the losing Conference semi-finalists each win US$412,500.

Each of the first round losers has to squabble over US$237,500.

● Owing to the vagaries of the NHL's playoff qualifying system, the losing Cup finalists, Carolina Hurricanes, finished the league season with fewer wins, 35, than four teams that failed to make the playoffs.

They were Edmonton (38), Dallas (36), NY Rangers (36) and Washington (36). Buffalo had the same number of victories as the 'Canes.

MIKE BABCOCK

The former Whitley Warriors' forward was appointed head coach of the NHL's Anaheim Mighty Ducks in the summer of 2002.

Our correspondent, David Hall, writes - Mike Babcock played for the Warriors in the 1987-88 season, helping them to the runners-up spot in the Premier Division of the British League, their best ever placing.

Even though he wasn't coach - that was **Terry Matthews**, who picked up the Coach of the Year award - it was widely recognised that Babcock was the 'power behind the throne'.

OBITUARIES

CARL BREWER

Born 21 October 1938, died 25 August 2001.
Defenceman on three Stanley Cup winning Toronto Maple Leafs teams in the 1960s and with Canada in the 1967 World Championship.

In retirement, he was the driving force behind the successful attempt to reclaim $40 million Canadian in unpaid pensions for retired NHL players and helped to convict former NHL Players Association head, **Alan Eagleson**.

Played 604 NHL games, scoring 223 points. A speedy skater and stickhandler, he was voted to the All-Star team in 1962-63.

He also featured on the international scene. He helped Canada to win a bronze medal at the 1967 World Championships and was player-coach with Finnish champions, IFK Helsinki, in 1968-69.

WOODY DUMART

Former Boston Bruins left winger **Woody Dumart**, a member of the famed "Kraut Line" of the 1930s and '40s, died on 19 October 2001. He was 84.

"Woody was one of the truly great Bruins and one of the best players in the NHL in his time," said Bruins' president, **Harry Sinden**. Dumart played his entire professional career from 1935 to 1954 with the Bruins, interrupted only when he served in the Royal Canadian Air Force during World War II.

Dumart was a member of the "Kraut Line" with lifelong friends, **Milt Schmidt and Bobby Bauer**, all of whom grew up in Kitchener, Ontario. In the 1939-40 season, the trio became the first line in NHL history to finish 1-2-3 in league scoring. Dumart finished his career with 211 goals and 218 assists in 772 games.

He was a member of the Bruins' 1939 and 1941 Stanley Cup championship teams, a three-time All-Star and was inducted into the Hockey Hall of Fame in 1992, nearly 40 years after his last NHL game.

• *The Annual's resident hockey historian, **Martin C Harris**, told us about Dumart's playing career during World War II* - Woody spent three years during the war on this side of the Atlantic, dodging the timber posts located down the centre of the Durham ice pad. At that time, Durham was home to teams from the Canadian Bomber Group, based on nearby airfields such as Croft, Middleton, Leeming and Topcliffe.

The original Durham rink had opened in March 1940, when building materials had priority elsewhere. Hence seven wooden posts were procured to support a canvas roof to keep the sun and rain off the ice, two at each end and three down the middle.

Dumart first saw action in a team named after its Wing Commander - Carscallan, which won the ten-team Northern Services Championship in 1943. He then turned out for Topcliffe with whom it was said he played better hockey than as a high earning pro in the NHL!

Among others over from the big league during that time were **Howard (Howie) Meeker** (Toronto), **Roy Conacher** Boston) and **Lude Waering** (NY Rangers).

After three seasons on Durham ice, Flying Officer Woody Dumart, along with ex-Boston Bruins team-mate, Milt Schmidt, both now rival player-coaches, agreed that the timbers considerably revolutionised the mechanics of hockey. So the pair incorporated them into offensive and defensive tactics, making the rink hazardous in the extreme for the man who skated with his head down.

Dumart's career in Durham ended on New Year's Day 1945 when the Canadian authorities changed the rules regarding players posted abroad. He then served, along with several other ex NHLers such as **Syd Abel** (Detroit), **Johnny Quilty** (Montreal) and Conacher, as an official at the RCAF Overseas Championships in Ayr and Paisley. Woody rejoined Boston in time for the 1945-46 season.

BRYAN FOGARTY

Born 6 Nov 1969, died 6 March 2002
Defenceman chosen ninth overall in the 1987 NHL entry draft, died of apparent heart failure, aged 32

Fogarty fought a constant battle against alcoholism which prevented him from playing in more than 156 NHL games over six seasons.

He last played in the league for Montreal Canadiens in 1994-95 before coming to Europe where he played 69 games for Hanover Scorpions in the German DEL and had brief stops in Davos, Switzerland and Milan, Italy.

His last pro team was the Elmira Jackals of the United League in 2000-01.

As a junior with Niagara Falls Thunder, he broke the scoring records for defenders held by **Bobby Orr** and **Denis Potvin**. In his last junior season, 1988-89, he was voted the Major Junior League's Player and Defenceman of the Year.

ROLL OF HONOUR
Modern Era

Winners and runners-up in all major domestic club competitions since the start of the Modern Era.
Compiled exclusively for the Annual *by* **Gordon Wade** *with contributions from* **Martin Harris.**
The Roll of Honour for the years before season 1982-83 is in The Ice Hockey Annual 1998-99.

SEASON	COMPETITION	WINNER	RUNNER-UP	NOTES
2001-02	+ Superleague Playoff Ch'ship	Sheffield Steelers	Manchester Storm	Won 4-3 (ps) at Nottingham
	+*Sekonda* Superleague	Belfast Giants	Ayr Scottish Eagles	Giants' second season
	+ Challenge Cup	Ayr Scottish Eagles	Belfast Giants	Won 5-0 at Belfast
	Findus British Nat'l Lge Ch'ships	Dundee Stars	Coventry Blaze	Won 8-7 on agg. (7-4a, 1-3h)
	Findus British Nat'l Lge	Dundee Stars	Coventry Blaze	Stars' first season
	Findus Challenge Cup	Fife Flyers	Coventry Blaze	Won 6-3 at Nottingham
	Eng Nat'l Lge, Premier Div Ch'ship	Invicta Dynamos	Isle of Wight Raiders	Won 6-3 on agg. (2-1a, 4-2h)
	Eng Nat'l Lge, Premier Division	Invicta Dynamos	Solihull Barons	
	Eng Nat'l Lge, Premier Cup	Romford Raiders	Invicta Dynamos	Won 9-7 on agg. ((5-3h, 4-4a)
	Eng Nat'l Lge, Div. One Ch'ship	Whitley Warriors	Basingstoke Buffalo	Won on agg. 12-7 (6-6a, 6-1h)
	Eng Nat'l Lge, Div. One North	Whitley Warriors	Altrincham Aces	
	Eng Nat'l Lge, Div. One South	Basingstoke Buffalo	Flintshire Freeze	
	Eng Nat'l Lge, Cup	Whitley Warriors	Telford Wild Foxes	Won 10-8 on agg. (2-5a, 8-3h)
	Caledonia Cup	Dundee Stars	Fife Flyers	Won 8-4 on agg. (3-2a, 5-2h)
2000-01	+= Superleague Playoff Ch'ship	Sheffield Steelers	London Knights	Won 2-1 at Nottingham
	+ Sekonda Superleague	Sheffield Steelers	Cariddf Devils	Won by 19 points but censured for breaking wage cap.
	B&H Autumn Cup	Sheffield Steelers	Newcastle Jesters	Won 4-0 at Sheffield
	+Challenge Cup	Sheffield Steelers	Ayr Scottish Eagles	Won 4-2 at Belfast
	Findus British Nat'l Lge Ch'ships	Guildford Flames	Basingstoke Bison	Won 12-4 on agg. (7-2a, 5-2h)
	Findus British Nat'l Lge	Guildford Flames	Basingstoke Bison	
	Benson and Hedges Plate	Basingstoke Bison	Guildford Flames	Won 3-2 at Sheffield
	ntl Christmas Cup	Guildford Flames	Fife Flyers	Won 7-3 on agg. (4-1h,3-2a)
	Eng Nat'l Lge, Premier Div Ch'ship	Romford Raiders	Chelmsford Chieftains	Won 11-4 on agg. (7-2, 4-2)
	Eng Nat'l Lge, Premier Division	Swindon Phoenix	Chelmsford Chieftains	
	Eng Nat'l Lge, Premier Cup	Isle of Wight Raiders	Swindon Phoenix	Won 5-2 on agg. (3-2a, 2-0h)
	Eng Nat'l Lge, Div. One Ch'ship	Whitley Warriors	Billingham Eagles	Won 14-7 on agg. (4-6h,10-1a)
	Eng Nat'l Lge, Div. One North	Billingham Eagles	Whitley Warriors	
	Eng Nat'l Lge, Div. One South	Basingstoke Buffalo	Flintshire Freeze	
	Scottish Cup	Fife Flyers	Edinburgh Capitals	Won 7-4 at Kirkcaldy.
1999-00	+= Superleague Playoff Ch'ship	London Knights	Newcastle Riverkings	Won 7-3 at Manchester
	+ Sekonda Superleague	Bracknell Bees	Sheffield Steelers	
	B&H Autumn Cup	Manchester Storm	London Knights	Won 4-3 (ps) at Sheffield.
	+Challenge Cup	Sheffield Steelers	Nottingham Panthers	Won 2-1 at London Arena
	British National Lge Ch'ship	Fife Flyers	Basingstoke Bison	Won best-of-five series 3-0.
	British National Lge	Fife Flyers	Guildford Flames	
	Benson and Hedges Plate	Basingstoke Bison	Slough Jets	Won 5-1 at Sheffield
	ntl Christmas Cup	Fife Flyers	Basingstoke Bison	Won 6-5 on agg. (3-3,3-2)
	Eng. Lge, Premier Div. Ch'ship	Chelmsford Chieftains	Swindon Chill	Won 7-4 on agg. (5-2,2-2)
	English Lge, Premier Div.	Chelmsford Chieftains	Isle of Wight Raiders	
	Data Vision Millennium Cup	Chelmsford Chieftains	Swindon Chill	Won 10-7 at Swindon.
	English Lge, Div. One Ch'ship	Whitley Warriors	Billingham Eagles	Won 14-10 on agg. (7-4,7-6)
	English Lge, Div One North	Billingham Eagles	Whitley Warriors	
	English Lge, Div One South	Haringey Greyhounds	Basingstoke Buffalo	
	Scottish Cup	Fife Flyers	Paisley Pirates	Won 9-4 at Kirkcaldy

ROLL OF HONOUR

SEASON	COMPETITION	WINNERS	RUNNERS-UP	NOTES
1998-99	+=Superleague Playoff Ch'ship	Cardiff Devils	Nottingham Panthers	Won 2-1 at Manchester
	+*Sekonda* Superleague	Manchester Storm	Cardiff Devils	
	B&H (Autumn) Cup	Nottingham Panthers	Ayr Scottish Eagles	Won 2-1 at Sheffield
	+Challenge Cup	Sheffield Steelers	Nottingham Panthers	Won 4-0 at Sheffield
	British National Lge Playoffs	Fife Flyers	Slough Jets	Won 6-5 (ps) at Hull
	British National League	Slough Jets	Basingstoke Bison	
	Benson and Hedges Plate	Guildford Flames	Telford Tigers	Won 4-3 at Sheffield
	Vic Christmas Cup	Peterborough Pirates	Basingstoke Bison	Won 5-3 on agg. (2-1,3-2)
	Eng. Lge, Premier Div. Ch'ship	Solihull Blaze	Milton Keynes Kings	Won 5-3 on agg. (3-0,2-3)
	English Lge, Premier Div	Solihull Blaze	Milton Keynes Kings	
	English Cup	Milton Keynes Kings	Solihull Blaze	Won 13-9 on agg. (7-6,6-3)
	English Lge, Div. One Ch'ship	Whitley Warriors	Billingham Eagles	Won 14-10 on agg. (7-4,7-6)
	English Lge, Div One North	Billingham Eagles	Altrincham Aces	
	English Lge, Div One South	Cardiff Rage	Basingstoke Buffalo	
	Scottish Cup	Fife Flyers	Edinburgh Capitals	Won 6-4 at Kirkcaldy.
1997-98	+Superleague Playoff Ch'ship	Ayr Scottish Eagles	Cardiff Devils	Won 3-2ot at Manchester
	+Superleague	Ayr Scottish Eagles	Manchester Storm	
	B & H (Autumn) Cup	Ayr Scottish Eagles	Cardiff Devils	Won 2-1 at Sheffield
	+*The Express* Cup	Ayr Scottish Eagles	Bracknell Bees	Won 3-2 at Newcastle
	British National Lge Playoffs	Guildford Flames	Kingston Hawks	Won 5-1 at Hull
	British National League	Guildford Flames	Telford Tigers	
	Northern Premier League	Fife Flyers	Paisley Pirates	
	Southern Premier League	Guildford Flames	Slough Jets	
	Benson & Hedges Plate	Slough Jets	Telford Tigers	Won 4-3 at Sheffield
	Upper Deck Christmas Cup	Telford Tigers	Guildford Flames	Won 10-7 on agg. (5-5, 5-2)
	Eng. Lge, National Div Ch'ship.	Solihull Blaze	Chelmsford Chieftains	Won 18-6 on agg. (9-5,9-1)
	English Lge, National Div.	Solihull Blaze	Whitley Warriors	
	English Lge, Div One North	Solihull Blaze	Whitley Warriors	
	English Lge, Div One South	Invicta Dynamos	Chelmsford Chieftains	
	Scottish Cup	Fife Flyers	Paisley Pirates	Won 5-1 at Kirkcaldy
1996-97	+Superleague Playoff Ch'ship	Sheffield Steelers	Nottingham Panthers	Won 3-1 at Manchester
	+Superleague	Cardiff Devils	Sheffield Steelers	
	B & H (Autumn) Cup	Nottingham Panthers	Ayr Scottish Eagles	Won 5-3 at Sheffield
	Premier League Playoffs	Swindon IceLords	Fife Flyers	Won 5-0 at Manchester
	Northern Premier League	Fife Flyers	Paisley Pirates	
	(Southern) Premier League	Swindon IceLords	Solihull Blaze	
	English League Championship	*Wightlink* Raiders	Chelmsford Chieftains	Won 10-6 on agg. (5-2,5-4)
	English League, South	Romford Raiders	Chelmsford Chieatins	
	English League, North	Kingston Jets	Altrincham Aces	
	Scottish Cup	Paisley Pirates	Fife Flyers	Won 8-4 at Kirkcaldy
	British Jnr Championship	Sunderland Arrows	Fife Flames	Won 3-2 at Manchester
1995-96	British Championship	Sheffield Steelers	Nottingham Panthers	Won on 2-1 PS (3-3ot) at Wembley.
	British League, Premier Div.	Sheffield Steelers	Cardiff Devils	
	British League, Div One	Manchester Storm	Blackburn Hawks	
	Promotion Playoffs	Manchester Storm	Milton Keynes Kings	Two playoff group winners
	B & H (Autumn) Cup	Sheffield Steelers	Nottingham Panthers	Won 5-2 at Sheffield
	English League Championship	*Wightlink* Raiders	Durham City Wasps	Won 15-8 on agg. (8-0,7-8)
	English League, South	Oxford City Stars	*Wightlink* Raiders	
	English League, North	Humberside Jets	Altrincham Aces	
	Autumn Trophy	Dumfries Border Vikings	Chelmsford Chieftains	Won 23-0, second leg not played.
	British Jnr Championship	Guildford Firestars	Fife Flames	Won 3-2 at Wembley

ROLL OF HONOUR

SEASON	COMPETITION	WINNERS	RUNNERS-UP	NOTES
1994-95	British Championship	Sheffield Steelers	Edinburgh Racers	Won 7-2 at Wembley
	British League, Premier Div.	Sheffield Steelers	Cardiff Devils	
	British League, Div One	Slough Jets	Telford Tigers	
	Promotion Playoffs	Slough Jets	Whitley Warriors	Two playoff group winners
	B & H (Autumn) Cup	Nottingham Panthers	Cardiff Devils	Won 7-2 at Sheffield
	English League Championship	*Wightlink* Raiders	Sunderland Chiefs	Won 11-5 on agg. (7-2,4-3)
	English League, South	*Wightlink* Raiders	Peterborough Patriots	
	English League, North	Sunderland Chiefs	Nottingham Jaguars	
	Autumn Trophy	Solihull Barons	Swindon Wildcats	Won 19-16 on agg. (7-6,12-10)
	Scottish Cup	Fife Flyers	Paisley Pirates	Won 11-2 at Kirkcaldy
	British Jnr Championship	Fife Flames	Durham Mosquitoes	Won 5-1 at Wembley
1993-94	British Championship	Cardiff Devils	Sheffield Steelers	Won 12-1 at Wembley
	British League, Premier Div.	Cardiff Devils	Sheffield Steelers	Fife Flyers later placed 2nd
	British League, Div One	M Keynes Kings (N)	Slough Jets (S)	No playoff. Kings most points.
	Promotion Playoffs	Milton Keynes Kings	Peterborough Pirates	Two playoff group winners
	B & H (Autumn) Cup	Murrayfield Racers	Cardiff Devils	Won 6-2 at Sheffield
	English League Championship	*Wightlink* Raiders	Nottingham Jaguars	Won 17-7 on agg. (6-4,11-3)
	English League	*Wightlink* Raiders	Sunderland Chiefs	
	Autumn Trophy	Telford Tigers	Medway Bears	Won 11-7 on agg. (8-3,3-4)
	Scottish Cup	Fife Flyers	Murrayfield Racers	Won 6-5 at Kirkcaldy
	British Jnr Championship	Fife Flames	Swindon Leopards	1-1ot at Wembley. Trophy shared.
1992-93	*British Championship	Cardiff Devils	Humberside Seahawks	Won 7-4 at Wembley
	*British League, Premier Div	Cardiff Devils	Murrayfield Racers	
	*British League, Div One	Basingstoke Beavers	Sheffield Steelers	
	*Promotion Playoffs	Basingstoke Beavers	Sheffield Steelers	Two group winners
	B & H (Autumn) Cup	Cardiff Devils	Whitley Warriors	Won 10-4 atSheffield
	English League Championship	Solihull Barons	Guildford Flames	Won 16-13 on agg. (6-7,10-6)
	English League, Conference A	Solihull Barons	Bristol Bulldogs	
	English League, Conference B	Guildford Flames	Chelmsford Chieftains	
	BL Entry Playoffs	Trafford Metros	Chelmsford Chieftains	Also EL PO. Two group winners
	Autumn Trophy	Milton Keynes Kings	Solihull Barons	Won 11-4 at Sheffield
	Scottish Cup	Murrayfield Racers	Whitley Warriors	Won 8-7 at Murrayfield
	British Jnr Championship	Durham Mosquitoes	Fife Flames	Won 5-2 at Wembley
1991-92	*British Championship	Durham Wasps	Nottingham Panthers	Won 7-6 at Wembley
	*British League, Premier Div.	Durham Wasps	Nottingham Panthers	
	*British League, Div One	Fife Flyers	Slough Jets	
	*Promotion Playoffs	Bracknell Bees	Fife Flyers	Two group winners
	Autumn Cup	Nottingham Panthers	Humberside Seahawks	Won 7-5 at Sheffield
	English League	Medway Bears	Sheffield Steelers	No championship playoff.
	BL Entry Playoffs	Medway Bears	Sheffield Steelers	Also EL PO. Two group winners.
	Autumn Trophy	Swindon Wildcats	Milton Keynes Kings	Won 3-2 on PS (5-5ot) at Sheffield.
	Scottish Cup	Whitley Warriors	Ayr Raiders	Won 7-4 at Murrayfield
	British Jnr Championship	Fife Flames	Durham Mosquitoes	Won 3-2 at Wembley
1990-91	*British Championship	Durham Wasps	Peterborough Pirates	Won 7-4 at Wembley
	*British League, Premier Div.	Durham Wasps	Cardiff Devils	
	*British League, Div One	Humberside Seahawks	Slough Jets	
	*Promotion Playoffs	Humberside Seahawks	Bracknell Bees	Two group winners
	Norwich Union (Autumn) Cup	Durham Wasps	Murrayfield Racers	Won 12-6 at Whitley
	English League	Oxford Stars	Milton Keynes Kings	First Division
	BL Entry Playoffs	Lee Valley Lions	Milton Keynes Kings	Also EL PO. Two group winners.
	Autumn Trophy	Chelmsford Chieftains	Oxford City Stars	League format.
	Scottish Cup	Murrayfield Racers	Ayr Raiders	Won 9-4 at Murrayfield
	British Jnr Championship	Fife Flames	Romford Hornets	Won 5-0 at Wembley

ROLL OF HONOUR

SEASON	COMPETITION	WINNERS	RUNNERS-UP	NOTES
1989-90	*British Championship	Cardiff Devils	Murrayfield Racers	Won 6-5 PS (6-6 ot) at Wembley.
	*British League, Premier Div.	Cardiff Devils	Murrayfield Racers	
	*British League, Div One	Slough Jets	Cleveland Bombers	
	*Promotion Playoffs	Cleveland Bombers	Slough Jets	Div One top four
	Norwich Union (Autumn) Cup	Murrayfield Racers	Durham Wasps	Won 10-4 at Basingstoke
	English League	Bracknell Bees	Romford Raiders	First Division
	BL Entry Playoffs	Basingstoke Beavers	Romford Raiders	Also EL playoffs
	Autumn Trophy	Humberside Seahawks	Bracknell Bees	Won 23-17 on agg. (15-9,8-8)
	Scottish Cup	Murrayfield Racers	Cardiff Devils	Won 13-4 at Murrayfield
	British Jnr Championship	Nottingham Cougars	Fife Flames	Won 3-1 at Wembley
1988-89	*British Championship	Nottingham Panthers	Ayr Bruins	Won 6-3 at Wembley
	*British League, Premier Div.	Durham Wasps	Murrayfield Racers	
	*British League, Div One	Cardiff Devils	Medway Bears	
	*Promotion Playoffs	Cardiff Devils	Streatham Redskins	Premier winner v last in Div One.
	Norwich Union (Autumn) Cup	Durham Wasps	Tayside Tigers	Won 7-5 at NEC, Birmingham
	English League	Humberside Seahawks	Bracknell Bees	First Division
	Autumn Trophy	Cardiff Devils	Medway Bears	Won 15-8 on agg. (9-4,6-4)
	Scottish Cup	Murrayfield Racers	Ayr Bruins	Won 9-5 at Murrayfield
	British Jnr Championship	Durham Mosquitoes	Dundee Bengals	Won pen shots at Wembley (5-5)
1987-88	*British Championship	Durham Wasps	Fife Flyers	Won 8-5 at Wembley
	*British League, Premier Div.	Murrayfield Racers	Whitley Warriors	
	*British League, Div One	Telford Tigers (S)	Cleveland Bombers (N)	Won 21-14 on agg. (12-10, 9-4)
	Promotion Playoffs	Peterborough Pirates	Telford Tigers	Premier winner v last in Div One
	British League, Div Two	Romford Raiders	Chelmsford Chieftains	
	Norwich Union (Autumn) Cup	Durham Wasps	Murrayfield Racers	Won 11-5 at Kirkcaldy
	Autumn Trophy	Cardiff Devils	Trafford Metros	Won 11-10 on agg. (7-5,4-5)
	Scottish Cup	Murrayfield Racers	Fife Flyers	Won 9-6 at Murrayfield
	British Jnr Championship	Nottingham Cougars	Fife Flames	Won 4-2 at Wembley
1986-87	*British Championship	Durham Wasps	Murrayfield Racers	Won 9-5 at Wembley
	*British League, Premier Div.	Murrayfield Racers	Dundee Rockets	
	*British League, Div One	Peterborough Pirates	Medway Bears	
	British League, Div Two	Aviemore Blackhawks	Cardiff Devils	Won playoff 10-9 at Cardiff
	Norwich Union (Autumn) Cup	Nottingham Panthers	Fife Flyers	Won 5-4ot at NEC, Birmingham
	Scottish Cup	Murrayfield Racers	Dundee Rockets	Won 7-6 at Kirkcaldy
	British Jnr Championship	Durham Mosquitoes	Murrayfield Ravens	Won 11-1 at Wembley
1985-86	*British Championship	Murrayfield Racers	Dundee Rockets	Won 4-2 at Wembley
	*British League, Premier Div.	Durham Wasps	Murrayfield Racers	
	*British League, Div One	Solihull Barons	Lee Valley Lions	
	British League, Div Two	Medway Bears	Grimsby Buffaloes	Won playoff 26-4 at Medway
	Norwich Union (Autumn) Cup	Murrayfield Racers	Durham Wasps	Won 8-5 at Murrayfield
	Scottish Cup	Dundee Rockets	Murrayfield Racers	Won 7-3 at Dundee
	British Jnr Championship	Streatham Scorpions	Fife Flames	Won 7-0 at Wembley
1984-85	*British Championship	Fife Flyers	Murrayfield Racers	Won 9-4 at Wembley
	*British League, Premier Div.	Durham Wasps	Fife Flyers	
	*British League, Div One	Peterborough Pirates	Solihull Barons	
	British League, Div Two	Oxford Stars	Aviemore Blackhawks	Won playoff 6-1 at Oxford
	Bluecol Autumn Cup	Durham Wasps	Fife Flyers	Won 6-4 at Streatham
1983-84	*British Championship	Dundee Rockets	Murrayfield Racers	Won 5-4 at Wembley
	*British League, Premier Div.	Dundee Rockets	Durham Wasps	
	*British League, Div One	Southampton Vikings	Crowtree Chiefs	
	British League, Div Two	Whitley Braves	Streatham Bruins	Won playoff 14-9 on agg (6-7, 8-2)
	Autumn Cup	Dundee Rockets	Streatham Redskins	Won pen shots at Streatham (6-6)
1982-83	*British Championship	Dundee Rockets	Durham Wasps	Won 6-2 at Streatham
	British League Section A	Dundee Rockets	Murrayfield Racers	)
	Section B	Durham Wasps	Cleveland Bombers	)Div One - interlocking schedule
	Section C	Altrincham Aces	Blackpool Seagulls	)
	British League, Div Two	Solihull Barons	Grimsby Buffaloes	Won Play-off 8-5 at Solihull

= Sponsored by *Sekonda*   * Sponsored by *Heineken*   + All-professional competition

GOVERNING BODIES

ICE HOCKEY UK LTD

Chief Executive: Danny Carroll.
Administrator: Gill Short, 47 Westminster Buildings, Theatre Sq, Nottingham NG1 6LG.
Tel: 0115-924-1441. **Fax**: 0115-924-3443.
e-mail: hockey@icehockeyuk.co.uk
website: www.icehockeyuk.co.uk
The Board of Directors of the sport's national governing body are:
Jim Anderson (chairman), **Neville Moralee** (deputy), **Richard Stirling**, **Bob Zeller** (ISL), **Gary Stefan** (BNL), **Alan Moutrey** (EIHA), **Stuart Robertson** (SIHA), **David Longstaff** (GB captain - co-opted), **Fiona King** GB women's captain - co-opted).

ICE HOCKEY SUPERLEAGUE LTD

Chairman: Martin Weddell.
Chief Admin. Officer: Brian Storey, Grange Farm Business Park, Hugglescote, Leicester LE67 2BT
Tel No: 01530-838899. **Fax**: 01530-830055.
e-mail: isladmin@iceweb.co.uk
website: www.iceweb.co.uk

BRITISH NAT. ICE HOCKEY LGE LTD

Chairman: Tom Muir.
General Manager: Gary Stefan.
Secretary: Stan Wiltshire, Henleaze House, 13 Harbury Road, Henleaze, Bristol BS9 4PN.
Tel/Fax: 0117-907-8783.
e-mail: admin@britnatleague.co.uk
website: www.britnatleague.co.uk

ENGLISH ICE HOCKEY ASSOCIATION

Chairman: Ken Taggart.
Gen Secretary: Bill Britton, 7 Laughton Avenue, West Bridgford, Notts NG2 7GJ.
Tel/Fax: 0115-923-1461
website: www.eiha.co.uk

SCOTTISH ICE HOCKEY ASSN.

President: Frank Dempster.
Secretary: Mrs Pat Swiatek, 71 Prestwick Road, Ayr KA5 7LQ.
Tel/Fax: 01292-284053
website: www.siha.net

SCOTTISH NATIONAL LEAGUE
Secretary: Adeline Andrews, 3 Hollybank, Viewpark, Ayr KA7 3PN. **Tel**: 01292-265800.

ENGLAND WOMEN'S ICE HOCKEY ASSOCIATION

Chairman: Bill Britton.
Secretary: Jackie Mason, 17 Beckenham Drive, Maidstone, Kent ME16 0TG.
Tel/Fax: 01622-671065. **Fax**: 01622-754360.
e-mail: jackie@community-centre.demon.co.uk
website: www.eiha.co.uk

ICE HOCKEY PLAYERS ASSOCIATION (GB)

Executive Director: Joanne Collins, 25 Caxton Ave, Addlestone, Weybridge, Surrey KT15 1LJ.
Tel: 01932-843660. **Fax**: 01932-844401.
e-mail: ihpa@virgin.net
website: www.ihpa.co.uk

USEFUL ADDRESSES

BRITISH ICE HOCKEY WRITERS' ASSOCIATION

Chairman: Andy Costigan.
Secretary: Anthony Beer, 47 St Edwen Gardens, Heath, Cardiff CF4 4JZ.
Tel/fax: 02920-624348.
e-mail: secretary@bihwa.co.uk
website: www.bihwa.co.uk

GB SUPPORTERS CLUB

Secretary: Annette Petrie, 65 Leas Drive, Iver, Bucks SL0 9RB. **Tel/Fax**: 01753-710778.
e-mail: gbsc@vossnet.co.uk
website: www.gbsc.co.uk/

CLUB DIRECTORY 2002-03

ABERDEEN

Rink Address: Linx Ice Arena, Beach Leisure Centre, Beach Esplanade, Aberdeen AB2 1NR.
Tel: 01224-655406/7. **Fax**: 01224-648693.
Ice Size: 184 x 85 feet (56 x 26 metres).
Spectator Capacity: 1,200
Club Secretary: Carol Hogan, 326 Holburn Street, Aberdeen AB10 7GX.
Tel: 01224-594900.
Juniors only in 2002-03

ALTRINCHAM (MANCHESTER)

Rink Address: Devonshire Road, Altrincham, Cheshire WA14 4EZ.
Tel: 0161-926-8316. **Fax**: 0161-927-7632.
Ice Size: 190 x 85 feet (58 x 26 metres).
Spectator Capacity: 1,800.
Senior Team: Aces (English Nat Lge North).
Club Secretary: Paul Bayliss c/o the rink.
Tel: 0161-928-1360. **Fax**: 0161-489-8452
e-mail: paul@bayliss99.freeserve.co.uk
Colours: *Home*: White, Red & Black;
away: Black, Red & White.
website: www.alt-ice-rink.demon.co.uk/aces.htm

AYR/PRESTWICK

Rink closed at press-time.
Arena Address: Centrum Arena, Ayr Road, Prestwick KA9 1TR.
Tel: 01292-671600. **Fax**: 01292-678833.
Ice Size: 200 x 103 feet (61 x 31.5 metres).
Spectator Capacity: 2,745.

BASINGSTOKE

Rink Address: Planet Ice Basingstoke Arena, Basingstoke Leisure Park, Worting Road, Basingstoke, Hants RG22 6PG.
Tel: 01256-355266. **Fax**: 01256-357367.
Ice Size: 197 x 98 feet (60 x 30 metres)
Spectator Capacity: 1,600.
Senior Teams: Bison (British National League) and Buffalo (Eng Nat Lge South).
Bison's contact: Charlie Colon at the rink.
Tel: 01256-346159. **Fax**: 01256-357367
e-mail: charliecolon63@hotmail.com
Bison's Colours: *home*: White, Red & Silver;
away: Red & Silver.
website www.basingstokebison.co.uk

BELFAST

Arena Address: Odyssey Arena, Queen's Quay, Belfast BT3.
Tel: 02890-766000. **Fax**: 02890-766044.
Ice Size: 197 x 98 feet (60 x 30 metres).
Spectator Capacity (for ice hockey): 7,100.
Team: Giants (Superleague).
Club Secretary: Julie Orchard.
Club Address: Belfast Giants Ltd, Units 2 & 3, Ormeau Business Park, 8 Cromac Avenue, Belfast BT7 2JA.
Tel: 028-9059-1111. **Fax**: 028-9059-1212.
e-mail: bfsgiants@aol.com
Colours: *home*: White, Red & Teal; *away*: Teal, White & Red.
website: www.belfastgiants.com

DUNDONALD
Rink Address: Dundonald International Ice Bowl, 111 Old Dundonald Road, Dundonald, Co Down, N Ireland.
Tel: 02890-482611. **Fax**: 02890-489604.
Ice Size: 197 x 98 feet (60 x 30 metres).
Spectator Capacity: 1,500.
Senior Team: Goldwings (non-league).
Club Secretary: David Gibson, 43 Rossdale Heights, Cairns Hill Road, Belfast BT8 4XZ.
Tel/fax: 02890-403505.
Note: *Belfast Ice Warriors have applied to enter the British National League for 2003-04. Enquiries to John Lyttle, 16 Cabinhill Park, Belfast BT5 7AL.*
Tel: *02890-592284.* **Fax**: *02890-473081.*
e-mail: *info@belfasticewarriors.com.*
website: *www.belfasticewarriors.com*

BILLINGHAM

Rink Address: Billingham Forum Leisure Centre, Town Centre, Billingham, Cleveland TS23 2OJ. **Tel/Fax**: 01642-551381.
Ice Size: 180 x 80 feet (55 x 24 metres)
Spectator Capacity: 1,200.
Senior Team: Eagles (English Nat Lge North).
Club Secretary: Brian McCabe, 7 Cranstock Close, Billingham, Cleveland TS22 5RS.
Tel/Fax: 01642-534458.
e-mail: bmccabe_1@hotmail.com
Colours: *Home*: White/Red; *away*: Red/White.

CLUB DIRECTORY

BIRMINGHAM

Rink Address: Planet Ice Birmingham Arena, Pershore Street, Birmingham B5 4RW
Tel: 0121-693-2400. **Fax**: 0121-693-2401
Ice Size: 180 x 80 feet (55 x 24 metres)
Spectator Capacity: 300
Senior team: Barons (English Nat Lge South).
Club Secretary: Bob McWilliams, 15 Baddesley Road, Olton, Solihull B92 7LP.
Tel/Fax:.0121-684-1410.
e-mail: bobshe@blueyonder.co.uk
Colours: *Home*: White & Red;
away: Red & White.

BLACKBURN

Rink Address: Blackburn Arena, Lower Audley, Waterside, Blackburn, Lancs BB1 1BB.
Tel: 01254-668686. **Fax**: 01254-691516.
Ice Size: 197 x 98 feet (60 x 30 metres)
Spectator Capacity: 3,200.
Senior Team: Hawks (English Nat Lge North)
Club Secretary: Mark Halliwell c/o the arena.
e-mail: mark@blackburnicearena.co.uk
Colours: Pacific Teal, Grey, Black & White.

BRACKNELL

Rink Address: John Nike Leisuresport Complex, John Nike Way, Bracknell, Berks RG12 4TN.
Tel: 01344-789006, **Fax**: 01344-789201.
Ice Size: 197 x 98 feet (60 x 30 metres)
Spectator Capacity: 3,100.
Senior Teams: Bees (Superleague) and Hornets (English Nat Lge South).
Bees' Club Secretary: Jane McDougall c/o rink.
Tel: 01344-789209. **Fax**: 01344-789022
e-mail: bracknellbees@nikegroup.co.uk
Bees' colours: *home:* White, Gold & Black;
away: Black, Gold & White.
website: www.bees.nikegroup.co.uk

BRADFORD

Rink Address: Great Cause, Little Horton Lane, Bradford, Yorks BD5 0AE.
Tel: 01274-729091. **Fax**: 01274-778818.
Ice Size: 180 x 80 feet (55 x 24 metres)
Spectator Capacity: 700.
Senior Team: Bulldogs (English Nat Lge North).
Club Secretary: Phil Lewis, Glendair, Gawthorpe Drive, Bingley, W Yorks BD16 4DH.
Tel/fax: 01274-567735.
e-mail: phil_1@btopenworld.com
Colours: White, Green & Black.

BRAEHEAD (GLASGOW)

Arena Address: Braehead Arena, Kings Inch Road, Glasgow, G51 4BN
Tel: 0870 444 6062. **Fax**: no details.
Ice Size: 197 x 98 feet (60 x 30 metres).
Spectator Capacity (for ice hockey): 4,000.
Senior team: Scottish Eagles (Superleague)
Club Secretary: Lauren Lawson Pratt
Tel: 0776 990 0926 **Fax**: no details.
e-mail: laurenlp43@hotmail.com
website: www.eagleeye.co.uk
Colours: *Home*: White & Blue;
away: Blue & White.

BRISTOL

Rink Address: John Nike Leisuresport Bristol Ice Rink, Frogmore Street, Bristol BS1 5NA.
Tel: 0117-929-2148. **Fax**: 0117-925-9736.
Ice Size: 180 x 80 feet (55 x 24 metres).
Spectator Capacity: 650.
Club Secretary: Mary Faunt, c/o the rink.'
Juniors only 2002-03.

CAMBRIDGE UNIVERSITY

No home ice 2002-03.
Communications to: Marc Guilbert, CUIHC President, Sidney Sussex College, Cambridge CB2 3HU
e-mail: mg267@cam.ac.uk
Colours: Light Blue & White.
website: www.cam.ac.uk/societies/cuihc
Recreational.

CARDIFF

Rink Address: Wales National Ice Rink, Hayes Bridge Road, Cardiff CF1 2GH.
Tel: 02920-397198, **Fax**: 02920-397160.
Ice Size: 184 x 85 feet (56 x 26 metres).
Spectator Capacity: 2,700.
Senior Team: Devils (British National League).
Communications to: Paul Sullivan at the rink.
Tel: 02920-396669. **Fax**: 02920-396668
e-mail: paulsullivan@cardiff-devils.com
Colours: *home*: White, Red & Black; *away*: Red, Black & White.
website: www.cardiff-devils.com

CHELMSFORD

Rink Address: Riverside Ice & Leisure Centre, Victoria Road, Chelmsford, Essex CM1 1FG. **Tel:** 01245-615050. **Fax:** 01245-615056.
Ice Size: 184 x 85 feet (56 x 26 metres).
Spectator Capacity: 1,200.
Senior Team: Chieftains (Eng Premier Lge).
Club Secretary: Ollie Oliver, Kings Ridden, Chelmsford Road, High Ongar, Essex CM5 9NX. **Tel:** 01277-822688. **Fax:** 01277-364055
e-mail: ollie@highongar7.fsnet.co.uk
Colours: *home*: White, Blue & Red; *away*: Blue, White & Red.

COVENTRY

Rink Address: Planet Ice at Skydome Arena, Skydome Coventry, Croft Road, Coventry CV1 3AZ. **Tel:** 02476-630693. **Fax:** 02476-630674
Ice Size: 184 x 92 feet (56 x 28 metres)
Spectator Capacity (for ice hockey): 3,000.
Senior Team: Blaze (British National League).
Communications to: Michelle Wilson, Blaze Promotions Ltd, 1518a Stratford Road, Hall Green, Birmingham B28 9ET.
Tel: 0121-745-7222. **Fax:** 0121-733-3694.
e-mail: grantcharman@coventryblaze.co.uk
Colours: *Home*: White & Navy Blue; *away*: Navy Blue & White.
website: www.coventryblaze.co.uk

DEESIDE

Rink Address: Deeside Ice Rink, Leisure Centre, Chester Road West, Queensferry, Clwyd CH5 5HA.
Tel: 01244-814725. **Fax:** 01244-836287.
Ice Size: 197 x 98 feet (60 x 30 metres).
Spectator Capacity: 1,200.
Senior Team: Flintshire Freeze (English National League North).
Club Secretary Mike Welshe c/o the rink.
e-mail: mstokes@madasafish.com
Colours: *home*: White, Purple & Green; *away*: Green, Purple & White.

DUMFRIES

Rink Address: The Ice Bowl, King Street, Dumfries DG2 9AN.
Tel: 01387-251300, **Fax:** 01387-251686.
Ice Size: 184 x 95 feet (56 x 29 metres).
Spectator Capacity: 1,000.
Senior Team: Solway Sharks (Scot. Nat. Lge).
Communications to: Sandra Edgar, 5 St Anne's Road, Dumfries DG2 9HZ. **Tel:** 01387-264010.
e-mail: sedgar5701@aol.com
Colours: Blue, White & Green.

DUNDEE

Rink Address: Camperdown Leisure Park, Kingsway West, Dundee.
Tel: 01382-608060. **Fax:** 01382-608070
Ice Size: 197 x 98 feet (60 x 30 metres).
Spectator Capacity: 2,400.
Senior Teams: Dundee Stars (British National League) and Camperdown Stars (Scottish National League).
Club Secretary: Steve/Marie Ward, 223 Clepington Road, Dundee.
Tel: 01382-832244. **Fax:** 01382 884248
website: www.dundeestars.co.uk
Colours: *home*: White, Red & Blue; *away*: Blue, Red & White.
Senior Team: Dundee Tigers (Scot. Nat. Lge.).
Club Secretary: Joe Guilcher, 9 Merton Avenue, Clement Park, Dundee DD2 3NA.
Colours: *home*: White, Gold & Black; *away*: Black, Gold & White.

EDINBURGH

Rink Address: Murrayfield Ice Rink, Riversdale Crescent, Murrayfield, Edinburgh EH12 5XN.
Tel: 0131-337-6933, **Fax:** 0131-346-2951.
Ice Size: 200 x 97 feet (61 x 29.5 metres).
Spectator Capacity: 3,800.
Senior Team: Capitals (British National League and Scottish National League).
Communications to: Scott Neil at the rink.
Tel/fax: 0131-313-2977.
e-mail: edcapitals@aol.com
Colours: *Home*: White, Red & Blue; *away*: Red, White & Blue.
website: www.edinburgh-capitals.com

FIFE

Rink Address: Fife Ice Arena, Rosslyn Street, Kirkcaldy, Fife KY1 3HS.
Tel: 01592-595100. **Fax:** 01592-595200.
Ice Size: 193.5 x 98 feet (59 x 30 metres).
Spectator Capacity: 3,280.
Senior Teams: Flyers (British National League) and Kirkcaldy Kestrels (Scottish Nat. League).
Communications to: Tom Muir c/o the arena.
Tel: 01592-651076. **Fax:** 01592-651138.
e-mail: tom@britnatleague.co.uk
Colours: Flyers - *Home*: White, Gold & Blue; *away*: Blue, White & Gold.
Website: www.fifeflyers.co.uk

GILLI NGHAM

Rink Address: The Ice Bowl, Ambley Road, Gillingham Business Park, Gillingham, Kent ME8 0PP.
Tel: 01634-388477. **Fax:** 01634-374065.
Ice Size: 184 x 85 feet (56 x 26 metres).
Spectator Capacity: 1,500.
Senior Teams: Invicta Dynamos (Eng Prem Lge) and Invicta Mustangs (Eng Nat Lge South).
Club Secretary: Jackie Mason, 17 Beckenham Drive, Maidstone, Kent ME16 0TG.
Tel: 01622-671065. **Fax:** 01622-754360.
e-mail: jackie@community-centre.demon.co.uk
website: www.invictadynamos.co.uk
Dynamos' colours: *Home:* White, Red, Blue & Black; *Away:* Blue, White, Black & Red.

GOSPORT

Rink Address: Forest Way, Fareham Road, Gosport, Hants. PO13 0ZX.
Tel: 02392-511217. **Fax:** 02392-510445.
Ice Size: 145 x 73 feet (44 x 22 metres).
Spectator Capacity: 800.
Club Secretary: Peter Marshall, 15 Islands Close, Hayling Island, Hants PO11 0NA.
Tel: 02392-466809.
e-mail: peter.marshall@havant.gov.uk
Juniors only 2002-03

GRIMSBY

Rink Address: The Leisure Centre, Cromwell Road, Grimsby, South Humberside DN31 2BH.
Tel: 01472-323100. **Fax:** 01472-323102.
Ice Size: 120 x 60 feet (36.5 x 18 metres).
Spectator Capacity: 1,300.
Senior Team: Buffaloes (English Nat Lge North)
Club Secretary: Allan Woodhead, Weelsby Park Riding School, Weelsby Road, Grimsby, South Humberside DN32 8PL.
Tel/Fax: 01472-346127.
Colours: *Home:* Red & White, *away:* Black, White & Red.

GUILDFORD

Rink Address: Spectrum Ice Rink, Parkway, Guildford GU1 1UP.
Tel: 01483-444777. **Fax:** 01483-443311.
Ice Size: 197 x 98 feet (60 x 30 metres).
Spectator Capacity: 2,200.
Senior Team: Flames (British National League).
Communications to: Malcolm Norman at rink.
Tel: 01483-452244, **Fax:** 01483-443373.
e-mail: malcolm@guildfordflames.com
Colours: *Home:* Gold, Red & Black; *away:* Black, Red & Gold.
website: www.guildfordflames.com

HARINGEY (LONDON)

Rink Address: The Ice Rink, Alexandra Palace, Wood Green, London N22 4AY.
Tel: 0208-365-2121. **Fax:** 0208-444-3439.
Ice Size: 184 x 85 feet (56 x 26 metres).
Spectator Capacity: 1,250.
Senior Team: Racers (English Premier Lge).
Club Secretary: Roger Black, Haringey Racers Ice Hockey Club, 13 New North Street, London WC1N 3PJ.
Tel: 020 7420 5900. **Fax:** 020 7420 5911.
e-mail: roger@racershockey.com
website: www.racershockey.com
Colours: *Home:* Gold & Blue; *away:* Blue & Gold.

HULL

Rink Address: The Hull Arena, Kingston Park, Hull HU1 2DZ.
Tel: 01482-325252. **Fax:** 01482-216066.
Ice Size: 197 x 98 feet (60 x 30 metres).
Spectator Capacity: 2,000.
Senior Teams: Thunder (British National Lge) and Kingston Jets (English Nat Lge North).
Communications to: Mike Bishop at the rink.
Tel: 01709-527755. **Fax:** 017-9-527766.
e-mail: mikeandgaye@yahoo.com
Colours: Thunder - *Home:* White, Purple & Black, *away:* Purple, Black & Silver.
Website: www.hullthunder.co.uk

IRVINE

Rink Address: Magnum Leisure Centre, Harbour Street, Irvine, Strathclyde KA12 8PD.
Tel: 01294-278381. **Fax:** 01294-311228.
Ice Size: 150 x 95 feet (45.5 x 29 metres).
Spectator Capacity: 750.
Club Secretary: Jennifer Wilson, 18 Woodfield Road, Ayr KA8 8LZ. **Tel/Fax:** 01292-263739.
Junior and recreational teams only in 2002-03

ISLE OF WIGHT

Rink Address: Planet Ice Ryde Arena, Quay Road, Esplanade, Ryde, I of Wight PO33 2HH.
Tel: 01983-615155. **Fax:** 01983-567460.
Ice Size: 165 x 80 feet (50 x 24 metres)
Spectator Capacity: 1,000.
Senior Team: Raiders (English Premier Lge).
Club Secretary: Mavis Siddons, 6 Port Helens, Embankment Road, St Helens, Isle of Wight PO33 1XG.
Tel: 01983-873094. **e-mail:** twin2@lineone.net
Colours: *Home:* White, Red & Black; *away:* Red, Black & White.

CLUB DIRECTORY

KILMARNOCK

Rink Address: Galleon Leisure Centre, 99 Titchfield Street, Kilmarnock, Ayr KA1 1QY. **Tel**: 01563-524014. **Fax**: 01563-572395. **Ice Size**: 146 x 75 feet (44.6 x 23 metres) **Spectator Capacity**: 200 **Club Secretary**: Mrs Alison Crockatt, 58 Main Street, Ochiltree, Strathclyde KA18 2PB. **Tel/fax**: 01290-700550. **e-mail**: gcac@ntlworld.com **Team**: Avalanche (Scottish Nat. League).

LEE VALLEY

Rink Address: Lee Valley Ice Centre, Lea Bridge Road, Leyton, London E10 7QL. **Tel**: 0208-533-3156. **Fax No**: 0208-446-8068. **Ice Size**: 184 x 85 feet (56 x 26 metres). **Spectator Capacity**: 1,000. **Communications to**: Mike Smith at the rink. *Juniors only 2002-03.*

LONDON (DOCKLANDS)

Arena Address: London Arena, Limeharbour, London E14 9TH. **Tel**: 0207-538-1212. **Fax**: 0207-538-5572. **Ice Size**: 197 x 98 feet (60 x 30 metres). **Spectator Capacity** (for ice hockey): 10,000. **Senior Team**: Knights (Superleague). **Communications to**: Trish Green. **Tel**: 0207-536-2610. **Fax**: 0207-536-2603. **e-mail**: info@knightice.co.uk **Colours**: *home*: White, Blue, Red & Gold; *away*: Red, Blue, White & Gold. **website**: www.london-knights.co.uk

MANCHESTER

Arena Address: *Manchester Evening News* Arena, 21 Hunts Bank, Victoria Exchange, Manchester M3 1AR. **Tel**: 0161-950-8000. **Fax**: 0161-950-6000. **Ice Size**: 197 x 98 feet (60 x 30 metres). **Spectator Capacity** (for ice hockey): 17,250. **Senior Team**: Storm (Superleague). **Club Secretary**: Wendy James, PO Box 286, Salford M5 4NY. **Tel**: 0161-737-0444 **Fax**: 0161-736-1222. **e-mail**: info@manchesterstorm.co.uk **Colours**: *Home*: White, Purple & Black; *away*: Black, Purple & White. **Website**: www.manchesterstorm.com/

MILTON KEYNES

Rink Address: Planet Ice Milton Keynes Arena, The Leisure Plaza, 1 South Row, (off Childs Way H6), Central Milton Keynes, Bucks MK9 1BL. **Tel**: 01908-696696. **Fax**: 01908-690890. **Ice Size**: 197 x 98 feet (60 x 30 metres) **Spectator Capacity**: 2,200. **Senior Teams**: Lightning (English Premier Lge) and Thunder (Eng Nat Lge South). **Lightning's Club Secretary**: Harry Howton, Oldbrook House, Boycott Avenue, Oldbrook, Milton Keynes. **Tel**: 01908-696993. **Fax**: 01908-696995. **e-mail**: howtons.ltd@btinternet.com **Lightning's Colours**: *Home*: White, Gold & Black; *away*: Black, White & Gold. **website**: ww.mk-lightning.com **Thunder's Club Secretary**: Ken Burgin, 1 Four Acres Walk, Hemel Hempstead, Herts HP3 9LB. **Tel**: 01442-213640. **Fax**: 01582-671988.

NEWCASTLE

Arena Address: *Telewest* Arena, Arena Way, off Railway Street, Newcastle-on-Tyne NE4 7NA. **Tel**: 0191-260-5000. **Fax**: 0191-260-2200. **Ice Size**: 197 x 98 feet (60 x 30 metres). **Spectator Capacity** (for ice hockey): 7,500 **Senior Team**: Vipers (British National Lge) **Club Secretary**: Joanne Hutchinson c/o Arena. **Tel**: 0191-260-2327. **Fax**: 0191-260-2328 **e-mail**: johutchinson2000@yahoo.com **Colours**: *Home*: White, Gold & Black; *away*: Black, Gold & White. **website**: www.newcastlevipers.com

NOTTINGHAM

Rink Address: National Ice Centre, Lower Parliament Street, Nottingham NG1 1LA. **Tel**: 0115-853-3000. **Fax**: 0115-853-3034. **Ice Size**: 197 x 98 feet (60 x 30 metres). **Spectator Capacity** (for ice hockey): 7,500. **Senior Teams**: Panthers (Superleague), Lions (English Premier League). **Panthers' office**: Sarah Longden, 2 Broadway, The Lace Market, Nottingham NG1 1PS. **Tel**: 0115-941-3103. **Fax**: 0115-941-8754. . **e-mail**: office@panthers.demon.co.uk **Panthers' colours**: *Home*: White, Gold & Red; *away*: Black, Gold & Red. **Website**: www.panthers.co.uk **Lions' Secretary**: Allan Worthington, 76 Swains Ave, Bakersfield, Nottingham NG3 7AU. **Tel**: 0115-912-9849. **Lions' colours**: *home*: Gold & Black; *away*: Black & Gold.

CLUB DIRECTORY

OXFORD

Rink Address: The Ice Rink, Oxpens Road, Oxford OX1 1RX.
Tel: 01865-248076. **Fax**: 01865-243163.
Ice Size: 184 x 85 feet (56 x 26 metres).
Spectator Capacity: 1,025.
Senior Team: City Stars (Eng Nat Lge South)
Club Secretary: Gary Dent, 42 Westfield Way, Wantage, Oxon OX12 7EW.
Tel/fax: 01235-763264.
e-mail: rinkside.stars@ntlworld.com
Colours: Dark Blue & White.

OXFORD UNIVERSITY

Home Ice: The Ice Rink, Oxpens Road, Oxford OX1 1RX (details above).
Club Secretary: Joseph Place, Wadham College, Oxford OX1 3PN.
Tel: 07751 204 139
e-mail: joseph.place@wadham.oxford.ac.uk
Colours: Dark Blue and White.
website: users.ox.ac.uk/~crushtab/proto.html
Recreational.

PAISLEY

Rink Address: Lagoon Leisure Complex, Mill Street, Paisley PA1 1LZ.
Tel: 0141-889-4000. **Fax**: 0141-848-0078.
Ice Size: 184 x 85 feet (56 x 26 metres).
Spectator Capacity: 1,000.
Senior Team: Mohawks (Scottish Nat League).
Communications to: Tom Monson, 26 Cross Road, Paisley PA2 9QH.
Tel: 0141-581-9971.
e-mail: thomas.monson@ntlworld.com

PERTH

Rink Address: Dewars Ice Rink, Glover Street, Perth PH2 0TH.
Tel: 01738-624188. **Fax**: 01738-637812.
Ice Size: 151 x 118 feet (46 x 36 metres).
Spectator Capacity: 500.
Club Secretary: Gillian Latto, 14 Ruthven Street, Auchterarder, Perth PH3.
Tel: 01764-664480.
Perth Panthers are playing their Scottish National League games at Dundee in 2002-03.

PETERBOROUGH

Rink Address: Planet Ice Peterborough Arena, 1 Mallard Road, Bretton, Peterborough, Cambs PE3 8YN.
Tel: 01733-260222. **Fax**: 01733-261021.
Ice Size: 184 x 85 feet (56 x 26 metres).
Spectator Capacity: 1,500.
Senior Teams: Phantoms (English Premier League) and Islanders (Eng Nat Lge South).
Phantoms' contact: Phil Wing, Manor Farm, Great North Road, Stibbington, Peterborough.
Tel/fax: 01780-783963
e-mail: phil.wing@peterborough-phantoms.com
Phantoms' colours: *Information not available.*

ROMFORD

Rink Address: Rom Valley Way, Romford, Essex RM7 0AE.
Tel: 01708-724731. **Fax**: 01708-733609.
Ice Size: 184 x 85 feet (56 x 26 metres).
Spectator Capacity: 1,500.
Senior Team: Raiders (English Premier Lge).
Club Secretary: Joanne Cahill, 42 Greensted Road, Loughton, Essex IG10 3DL.
Tel: 0208-281-9266. **Fax**: 0208-925-9164.
e-mail: joanne.cahill@virgin.net
Colours: *Home*: White, Gold & Blue; *away*: Blue, Gold & White.
website: http://welcome.to/romfordraiders.

SHEFFIELD

Arena Address: Sheffield Arena, Broughton Lane, Sheffield S9 2DF.
Tel: 0114-256-5656. **Fax**: 0114-256-5520.
Ice Size: 197 x 98 feet (60 x 30 metres).
Spectator Capacity (for ice hockey): 10,000.
Senior Team: Steelers (Superleague).
Communications to: Betty Waring at Arena.
Tel: 0114-242-3535. **Fax**: 0114-242-3344.
e-mail: sheffsteel@freeuk.com
Colours: *Home*: White, Blue, Orange & Teal; *away*: Black, Blue, Orange & Teal.
website: www.sheffieldsteelers.co.uk.
NOTE **Sheffield Scimitars** *play in English Nat Lge North at the Sheffield Ice Sports Centre, Queens Road, Sheffield S2 4DF.*
Tel: 0114-272-3037.
Club Secretary: Dave Lawrence, 103 St Paul's Parade, Ardsley, Barnsley South Yorks S71 5BU.
Tel/fax: 01226-212754.

CLUB DIRECTORY

SLOUGH

Rink Address: The Ice Arena, Montem Lane, Slough, Berks SL1 2QG.
Tel: 01753-821555. **Fax**: 01753-824977.
Ice Size: 184 x 85 feet (56 x 26 metres).
Spectator Capacity: 1,500.
Senior Team: Jets (English Premier League).
Club Secretary: Pauline Rost, 37 Monks Avenue, East Molesey, Surrey KT8 0HD.
e-mail: pauline.postie@virgin.net or woz@sloughjets.co.uk
Colours: *Home*: White, Blue & Red; *away*: Blue, White & Red.
website: www.sloughjets.co.uk

SOLIHULL

Rink Address: Hobs Moat Road, Solihull, West Midlands B92 8JN.
Tel: 0121-742-5561. **Fax**: 0121-742-4315.
Ice Size: 185 x 90 feet (56 x 27 metres).
Spectator Capacity: 1,500.
Senior Team: MK Kings (British National Lge).
Communications to: Rick Strachan, Solihull MK Kings, PO Box 5412, Milton Keynes MK15 9XA.
Tel/fax: 01623-792860.
e-mail: info@smkkings.co.uk
Colours: Black, Dark Blue and Silver.
website: www.smkkings.co.uk

STREATHAM

Rink Address: 386 Streatham High Road, London SW16 6HT.
Tel: 0208-769-7771. **Fax**: 0208-769-9979.
Ice Size: 197 x 85 feet (60 x 26 metres).
Communications to: Hugh Carnegy, 13 Eynella Road, London SE22 8XF. **Tel**: 0208-693-7697.
Juniors only 2002-03.

SUNDERLAND

Rink Address: Crowtree Leisure Centre, Crowtree Road, Sunderland, Tyne & Wear SR1 3EL.
Tel: 0191-553-2600. **Fax**: 0191-553-2563.
Ice Size: 184 x 85 feet (56 x 26 metres).
Spectator Capacity: 1,200.
Senior Team: Chiefs (English Nat League North).
Communications to: Mike Hendry, 4 Floral Dene, South Hylton, Sunderland SR4 0NW.
Tel: 0191-534-7219. **Fax**: 0191-564-2695.
e-mail: tynetube@lineone.net
Colours: *Home*: White, Red & Blue; *away*: Blue, Red & White.

SWINDON

Rink Address: Link Centre, White Hill Way, Westlea, Swindon, Wilts SN5 7DL.
Tel: 01793-445566. **Fax**: 01793-445569.
Ice Size: 184 x 85 feet (56 x 26 metres).
Spectator Capacity: 1,650.
Senior Team: Lynx (English Premier Lge).
Club Secretary: Phil Jefferies, 9 Pennycress Close, Haydon Wick, Swindon SN25 1RT.
Tel: 01793-630733. **Fax**: 01793-630734.
e-mail: philjefferies@ntlworld.com.
Colours: *Home*: White, Blue, Silver & Gold; *away*: Blue, White, Silver & Gold.
website:www.swindonlynx.com

TELFORD

Rink Address: The Ice Rink, Town Centre, Telford, Salop TF3 4JQ.
Tel: 01952-291511. **Fax**: 01952-291543.
Ice Size: 184 x 85 metres (56 x 26 metres).
Spectator Capacity: 2,250.
Senior Team: Wild Foxes (Eng Premier Lge).
Club Secretary: Mrs Jen Roden, 12 Dee Close, Wellington, Telford TF1 3JH.
Tel/fax: 01952-405506.
e-mail: jenroden@blueyonder.co.uk
Colours: *Home*: White, Orange & Black; *away*: Orange, Black & White.

WHITLEY BAY

Rink Address: The Ice Rink, Hillheads Road, Whitley Bay, Tyne & Wear NE25 8HP.
Tel: 0191-291-1000. **Fax**: 0191-291-1001.
Ice Size: 186 x 81 feet (56.5 x 24.5 metres).
Spectator Capacity: 3,200.
Senior Team: Warriors (Eng Nat Lge North).
Club Secretary: Doreen Flynn c/o rink.
Tel/Fax: 0191-251-9554.
e-mail: icerink@ukonline.co.uk
Colours: *Home*: White, Gold & Maroon; *away*: Maroon, White & Gold.

LEGEND

The abbreviations used in the *Annual* are -

LEAGUES

ISL	Ice Hockey Superleague Ltd
BNL	British National Ice Hockey League
EPL	English Premier League

SCORERS

GP	-	Games Played
G	-	Goals
A	-	Assists
Pts	-	total Points
Pim(s)	-	Penalties in minutes
N	-	Netminder
Ave		Points per Games Played

NETMINDERS

GPI	-	Games Played In
Mins	-	Minutes played
SoG	-	Shots on Goal
GA		Goals Against
SO	-	Shutouts
Sv%	-	Save percentage

TEAMS

S	-	Seasons
W	-	Win
RW		Win in regulation time (60 Mins)
OW	-	Win in overtime
RL		Loss in regulation time
OL		Loss in overtime
D	-	Draw
GF	-	Goals For
GA	-	Goals Against
Pct	-	Points gained as a percentage of total games played.

PLAYERS

*	British born and trained (ISL only)
I	ITC holder (BNL & EL)
WP	Work Permit holder

TIE BREAKERS

The system for deciding league places varies between each league/competition (you know it makes sense). The various systems are -

Superleague
- total number of points
- total number of wins
- overall goal difference
- goals scored

British National League
English Premier League
as per IIHF Rule Book

ITC - INTERNATIONAL TRANSFER CARD
A signed International Transfer Card (ITC) is required by any player who has been a member of another national federation. There are two types of ITC - 'limited' for one season, and 'unlimited' for players who intend to remain in this country. Ice Hockey UK only keeps records for players needing 'limited' cards and these are the ones shown in the *Annual*.

SAVE PERCENTAGE - CALCULATION METHOD
Shots on goal less goals against, divided by shots on goal, multiplied by 100.
Example: 100 shots less 10 goals scored, equals 90, divided by 100, equals 90 per cent.